Conventional Deterrence

CORNELL STUDIES IN
SECURITY AFFAIRS

edited by Robert J. Art
and Robert Jervis

Conventional Deterrence
by John J. Mearsheimer

The Nuclear Future
by Michael Mandelbaum

Conventional Deterrence

John J. Mearsheimer

Cornell University Press

ITHACA AND LONDON

*This book was written under the auspices of the
Center for International Affairs, Harvard University.*

First published 1983 by Cornell University Press.
Published in the United Kingdom by Cornell University Press Ltd.,
London.

International Standard Book Number 0-8014-1569-1
Library of Congress Catalog Card Number 83-5317
Printed in the United States of America
*Librarians: Library of Congress cataloging information appears
on the last page of the book.*

*The paper in this book is acid-free and meets the guidelines for permanence
and durability of the Committee on Production Guidelines for
Book Longevity of the Council on Library Resources.*

Contents

[5]

Preface

This is a book about the origins of war. Why do nations faced with the prospect of a large-scale conventional war decide to attack in some cases but not in others? Why did the British and the French, for example, after declaring war against Germany on 3 September 1939, take no military action? Conversely, why did the Germans end the so-called Phoney War on 10 May 1940 by attacking the Allies in the West? Most important, when two large armies face each other in a crisis situation, under what conditions should we expect deterrence to fail?

The following chapters examine a number of crises that led to major conventional wars. By identifying certain common elements, I hope to generate propositions that will shed light on the success and failure of conventional deterrence. My purposes are two. First, I seek to explain why deterrence failed in some historically important cases. For example, I am concerned with the failure and success of deterrence at the start of World War II and in the Arab-Israeli wars. Second, I aim to illuminate some important issues in contemporary policy.

A study of past deterrence failures should shed light on the prospects for deterrence in Central Europe as well as elsewhere in the world. I am also concerned with relatively technical issues, such as precision-guided munitions and the debate between advocates of maneuver and attrition warfare. My book, in short, has much to say about the conduct of conventional warfare. I address questions of military strategy and tactics at length. Although such a discussion is obviously essential for an analysis of the more technical issues, an understanding of military strategy is also absolutely essential for an explanation of past deterrence failures and successes. As will become evident, conventional deterrence is largely a function of military strategy.

[7]

The topics of strategy and tactics suggest an important point about the book's scope. A variety of factors, many of them nonmilitary, act upon a nation contemplating war. I shall focus first on the military considerations that underlie the decision-making process—in other words, the military thinking that leads to or away from war. Second, I shall devote much attention to the interaction between those military factors and the broader political considerations that move a nation toward aggression.

Surprisingly little has been written on the subject of conventional deterrence. Two other subjects that fall under the rubric of military deterrence have received most of the scholarly attention. The first is nuclear targeting strategy—more specifically, how different strategies such as counterforce and countervalue affect deterrence between the superpowers. The second I term the *credibility-of-commitment* issue— the question of whether, given the great risks and costs associated with the use of military force, a nation will use it, especially outside national borders, to defend certain interests. I do not doubt the importance of these topics. I believe, however, that discussion of them has obscured a third important area, conventional deterrence, which equally merits analysis.

This book originated during the spring of 1976, when, as a first-year graduate student at Cornell University, I took Richard Rosecrance's seminar on strategy. Early in the course he suggested that I investigate any of several topics, one of which was conventional deterrence. I had never given any thought to the subject, and as I quickly discovered, very little had been published about it.

The theory outlined in my seminar paper in some respects resembles that presented in this book. There are, however, many important differences, and without a doubt this final product is a vast improvement over that initial effort. I did not find the task of writing easy. In the first place, theories are extremely difficult to develop. Second, because my predecessors had been few, there were not many signposts to guide me. I was more fortunate in finding help of other sorts: I owe a great debt of gratitude to numerous individuals and institutions.

George Quester and Richard Rosecrance, two leading experts on my chosen subject, helped me formulate and refine my basic argument and assisted me in countless other ways. Their support and encouragement were of tremendous importance, the more so inasmuch as the following pages directly challenge some of their principal ideas. Robert Art, Michael E. Brown, Jack L. Snyder, and William Tetreault each made very detailed and helpful comments on various drafts, significantly influencing the final version. Members of the Domestic Politics and Security Policy Working Group at Harvard University who also read large portions of the manuscript closely include Michael Mandelbaum, Steven E. Miller, Barry Posen, Jack L. Snyder, and Stephen Van Evera. The discussion at two meetings of the group was particularly useful in forcing me to clarify my arguments. I thank the following other individuals for their advice: Robert P. Berman, Richard K. Betts, Heinrich Buch, Eliot Cohen, Werner Dannhauser, Steven David, Mary Hughes Durfee, Joseph Grieco, Michael Handel, Lothar Höbelt, William Mako, Matthew Murphy, Williamson Murray, Stephen P. Rosen, William L. Schwartz, Janice Stein, Sidney Tarrow, Stephen Walt, and Dani Zamir.

I received financial support from various sources. Funds from the Cornell Peace Studies Program permitted me to do research in the Middle East, Europe, and the United States. I also received support from: the Arms Control and Disarmament Agency (Hubert H. Humphrey Fellowship), the Brookings Institution, the Walter S. Carpenter Chair at Cornell, Cornell University (Summer Research Fellowship), the Ford Foundation, Harvard University's Center for International Affairs, the Institute for the Study of World Politics, the Jewish Vocational Service of Cleveland (the Morris Abrams Award in International Relations), and the Smith Richardson Foundation. Without this generous assistance I could never have written the book.

During the summer of 1978, I held an internship at the Arms Control and Disarmament Agency. There I benefited greatly from the opportunity to talk with experts about various technical issues. I particularly thank Phillip Karber, who spent many hours that summer talking to me about armored warfare. From September 1979 to August 1980, I was a research fellow at the Brookings Institution, where I wrote the first major draft. From September 1980 to August 1982, I was a postdoctoral fellow at Harvard University's Center for International Affairs. There I rewrote the manuscript several times. I thank the many individuals at these two institutions, particularly Samuel P. Huntington (director of Harvard's CFIA) and John D. Steinbruner (director of the Brookings Foreign Policy Studies Program), who were so helpful to me. I also gratefully remember the many people in Europe and the Middle East as well as in the United States who spoke with me at length about the various aspects of my subject.

Chapter 6 of this work appeared in somewhat different form as an article in the summer 1982 issue of *International Security*, while Chap-

[9]

ter 7 appeared in altered form in the March–April 1979 issue of *Survival*. I thank both journals, and the M.I.T. Press, publisher of *International Security*, for granting me permission to include the two articles in the present volume. The Liddell Hart Centre for Military Archives at King's College, University of London, has also kindly given me permission to use various citations from the personal papers of B. H. Liddell Hart.

In *Supplying War: Logistics from Wallenstein to Patton*, Martin Van Creveld argues, "Logistics make up as much as nine tenths of the business of war" (*Supplying War* [Cambridge: Cambridge University Press, 1977], 231). His words apply equally to writing, as anyone knows who has completed a book. Especially important in this regard is typing, although there are numerous other areas in which an author needs assistance. For their work in the realm of logistics, I thank Gertrude Fitzpatrick, Janet Haouchine, Ronald Lively, Nancy Sokol, and Jean Twoomey. Finally, I gratefully acknowledge the editorial expertise of Marcia Brubeck of the Guilford Group and Kay Scheuer of Cornell University Press, who helped so much with the final version.

To my wife, Mary, the most significant influence, I dedicate this volume. She typed numerous drafts of each chapter, helped proofread the endless revisions, and carefully edited almost every one—not only ascertaining that the manuscript was readable but also making numerous substantive criticisms. Furthermore, she was a constant source of encouragement, especially important during those darker moments familiar to all writers. Without her, this book would have suffered appreciably. She bears much of the credit for the best of what follows.

JOHN J. MEARSHEIMER

Chicago, Illinois

Conventional Deterrence

Recognition of the reciprocal effects of tactics, strategy, political institutions, and politics throws light on the interconnections in universal history, and has illuminated much that until now lay in darkness or was misunderstood.

HANS DELBRÜCK
Geschichte der Kriegskunst im
Rahmen der politischen Geschichte

[1]

Introduction

Since the early 1960s the United States has increasingly relied on its conventional forces to deter Soviet aggression.[1] American policy makers have frequently stressed the need to keep the nuclear threshold as high as possible. Their concern has influenced the North Atlantic Treaty Organization (NATO), which is now giving serious consideration to fighting only conventional battles not unlike those of the Second World War. There is also evidence that since the early 1970s the Soviets have been preparing for possible nonnuclear conflict in Europe.[2]

Nuclear weapons of course continue to play a role in deterring war in Europe and will do so as long as they remain available. Nevertheless, growing acceptance of the disutility of nuclear weapons for purposes of defense has brought greater interest in the conventional balance in recent years. The subject of conventional deterrence therefore seems to warrant greater scholarly attention. Specifically, we must address a very important question: When two large armies face each other in a crisis, as Warsaw Pact and NATO forces do in Europe, what factors determine whether or not a potential aggressor opts for war? What military considerations might lead the Soviets to launch a conventional attack against NATO?

A rich history of deterrence failures and ensuing conventional wars could be tapped to answer such questions. Little effort has been made to use it, although there are certainly some individual case studies. In addition, as we shall see, two existing theories of conventional deterrence are discernible, neither of which has been tested against particular crises. Still, no published study develops general propositions based on close examination of a number of past cases involving conventional deterrence. No one has attempted, for example, to compare the German decision to strike against the Allies in 1940 with the 1967 Israeli decision to attack in the Sinai. Such a comparison would indicate whether lessons from these important incidents might be applied to the NATO–Warsaw Pact balance. A sound theory of conventional deterrence would, of course, do more than shed light on present policy issues. It would also provide a key for understanding the outbreak of war in a number of important historical cases.

Defining the Target

Deterrence, in its broadest sense, means persuading an opponent not to initiate a specific action because the perceived benefits do not justify the estimated costs and risks. Because the decision to fight is predicated on more than military considerations—on more than the calculation that a nation's forces are capable of achieving their objectives on the battlefield[3]—other, nonmilitary factors also affect deterrence. If we assume that there is a broadly defined political benefit to be gained from successful military action, we must recognize that a host of factors act upon decision makers.[4] More specifically, leaders must consider risks and costs of a nonmilitary nature. Decision makers might well assess the probable reaction of allies and adversaries, aspects of international law and possible reaction in a forum such as the United Nations, and the likely effect upon the economy. In short, deterrence broadly defined is ultimately a function of the relationship between the perceived political benefits resulting from military action and a number of nonmilitary as well as military costs and risks.

Given the difficulty, if not impossibility, of developing a theory that takes all of these elements into account, I must limit my study.[5] I have chosen to focus first on the military considerations that underlie deterrence and second on the relationship between them and the perceived political benefits, omitting risks and costs that are nonmilitary in nature. I try to answer two questions. First, how are decision makers who are contemplating military action affected by the projected outcome on the battlefield? Second, what are the dynamics between these military considerations and the broader political forces that are propelling a nation toward war? I should emphasize that I make no attempt to analyze these political forces in detail.

There is a well-known distinction between deterrence based on punishment, which involves threatening to destroy large portions of an opponent's civilian population and industry, and deterrence based on denial, which requires convincing an opponent that he will not attain his goals on the battlefield.[6] Dean Acheson expressed this distinction aptly: "We mean that the only deterrent to the imposition of Russian will in Western Europe is the belief that from the outset of any such attempt American power would be employed in *stopping* it, and if necessary, would *inflict* on the Soviet Union *injury* which the Moscow regime would not wish to suffer" (emphasis added).[7]

Deterrence based on punishment is associated usually with nuclear weapons but sometimes with conventional weapons.[8] Conversely, battlefield denial is usually linked with conventional forces, although one school of thought argues that nuclear weapons can and should be used on the battlefield.[9] Conventional deterrence, as defined in this study, is a function of the capability of denying an aggressor his battlefield objectives with conventional forces. Thus I focus on the question: When two large armies face each other in a crisis, what military considerations are likely to lead one side to conclude that it can launch a successful military operation?

Conventional deterrence is directly linked to battlefield outcomes, and the term *battlefield* has a broad connotation. This study examines deterrence failures related to a specific type of conventional battlefield, one on which two large armies directly face each other and, if war breaks out, directly engage each other in a relatively large amount of space. My theory therefore does not apply to guerrilla conflict, such as the Vietnam War, or to episodes dominated by naval and air warfare, such as Pearl Harbor.

Further delimitation is necessary, however. Although conventional wars of the sort I just defined can be found throughout the course of history, my theory applies only to the modern—that is, armor-dominated—battlefield. I do not purport to explain the failure of deterrence before the Franco-Prussian War or World War I. My reasons for so restricting my scope are the following. The decision to go or not to go to war is based in part on specific considerations regarding the conduct of war. Now, the passage of time has brought some fundamental changes in this area. The battlefield at Jena (1806), where Napoleon's forces soundly defeated the Prussian army, greatly differed from the battlefield at Sedan (1870), where the Prussians turned the tables and inflicted a decisive defeat on the French.[10] At Jena, railroads were nonexistent, general staff systems were in their infancy, and the muzzle-loading flintlock musket with bayonet was the principal infantry weapon. By 1870, railroads and general staff systems figured importantly in warfare, and the breech-loading rifle, a revolutionary development at the time, had become the standard

[15]

infantry weapon. Significant improvements had also been made in artillery. Strategy and tactics, as well as weaponry, had been greatly affected by the advances. In short, the conduct of war underwent a transformation in the sixty-four years between Jena and Sedan.

Such developments very much affect the detailed military calculations on which deterrence is based; the variables in the deterrence equation change with time. A policy maker considering war in 1939 faced problems very different from those confronting his counterparts in 1800. The point has been perhaps best articulated by Clausewitz, who wrote: "Every age had its own kind of war, its own limiting conditions, and its own peculiar preconceptions. Each period, therefore, would have held to its own theory of war, even if the urge had always and universally existed to work things out on scientific principles. It follows that the events of every age must be judged in the light of its own peculiarities."[11] This statement makes plain the difficulty of framing meaningful generalizations about conventional deterrence that apply to all periods of history. It is therefore necessary to determine what military calculations led to deterrence failures in a given era.[12]

I have chosen to concentrate on the period that extends from the end of World War I to the present. At the start of World War I, the tank did not exist, and none of the armies relied on motorized (wheeled) transport. European armies basically comprised foot-borne infantry and horse-drawn artillery. By the end of the conflict, both sides were deploying sizable numbers of mechanized (tracked) and motorized vehicles with their forces. That the introduction of new weapons, especially the tank, had fundamentally altered the conduct of war became clear only in the early stages of World War II, when the Germans overran France in six weeks. The tank's effect on the conventional battlefield will occupy us further in the next chapter.

Since World War II the nature of conventional war has remained essentially unchanged. Armaments (for example, tanks, artillery, attack aircraft), although more sophisticated today, remain basically the same; and today's armies are organized along the same lines as those of World War II. Furthermore, theoreticians debate the same doctrines today that they did before and during the Second World War (for example, the importance of the tank relative to infantry and artillery; the relationship between close air support and ground forces). In short, the lessons of the recent past have broad application to the present.

The relevance of World War II for contemporary problems is not widely appreciated in the United States, partly because most civilian defense analysts know very little about military history.[13] It is widely believed that nuclear weapons have disarmed the past for present purposes, removing the incentive to study it.[14] In addition, the American military has not been strongly disposed to draw on its experience in earlier times.[15] Such has not been the case, however, in other nations concerned with the prospect of fighting a conventional war. For example, the Israeli military places great stress on studying the campaigns of World War II,[16] and the Soviets constantly emphasize the lessons of the Great Patriotic War.[17] Strong threads bind the recent past with the present. This continuity permits us to generate propositions that are as relevant to the breakdown of deterrence in 1939 as they are to its failure in 1973 in the Middle East.

I am, of course, concerned not merely with the military considerations that underpin deterrence but also with the broader relationship between them and the perceived political gains. Generalizations about this relationship prove meaningful when applied to different periods of military history, making it worthwhile to examine the interaction between war and politics in connection with deterrence failures unrelated to the modern battlefield. Many of the problems associated with this more general level of warfare are not time bound, as are those that deal with the conduct of war.[18] Clausewitz's *On War*, which was written in the early 1800s, illustrates the point. The sections that deal with actual battlefield strategy and tactics are largely irrelevant today; *On War* offers few clues regarding battlefield denial. On the other hand, Clausewitz's words on the basic nature of war and on the relationship between war and politics remain insightful and account for his book's enduring greatness.

IMPLICATIONS FOR THEORY AND POLICY

Despite my self-imposed limitations, it will be evident to the reader that my scope encompasses a large number of very important historical cases: all the principal large-scale conventional wars of the past fifty years and a number of less important conflicts.

It may well be asked whether there is likely to be a fundamental shift in the nature of conventional war in the near future. We have no reason to expect one. This fact, coupled with the growing number of armies equipped with tanks and other mechanized vehicles, means that my theory of conventional deterrence will be relevant to future conflicts. It is also noteworthy that my theory can be used to evaluate present policy issues of two important sorts: the prospects for deterrence in regions where there is a possibility of a large-scale conventional war, and technical issues relating to military strategy and weaponry that affect deterrence. In short, my theory has broad application indeed.

The Deterrence Literature

Two subjects have received the lion's share of scholarly attention in the literature. The first is nuclear deterrence between the superpowers,[19] in particular that associated with specific targeting strategies. Analysts speak of concepts such as counterforce-damage limiting and mutual assured destruction. The nuclear deterrence literature, however, sheds little light on conventional deterrence.[20] The second topic is the matter of the credibility of a promised response, which I term the credibility-of-commitment issue.[21] The main reason for the great interest in this subject is that in the years since World War II the United States has sought to use its vast military power—both nuclear weapons and conventional forces—to deter conflicts in areas beyond its borders.[22] Regardless of the character of the promised threat, the United States has frequently had to assess the credibility of its commitments because of its role as a third party or outside guarantor. Appropriately, many writers have discussed subjects such as "the art of commitment" and "the manipulation of risk."[23] Two related questions have commanded attention. If an ally is attacked, should the United States respond or simply do nothing? And if some action is in order, on what level should the United States respond? In other words, what kinds of limits should be placed on the use of force?[24]

These questions are not directly relevant to my study for several reasons. First, my concern with situations in which two large armies directly face each other moots the question of whether or not the defender should respond when attacked. I assume that both forces immediately become entangled, and the defender's type or level of response seems plain: he will certainly—automatically, in a sense—employ all of his available resources (nonnuclear) to thwart the enemy.[25] It is therefore largely irrelevant for me to consider the defender's different levels of response or different options.

The issue of commitment is potentially relevant to conventional deterrence when a third party is involved. That is, given that the armies of Side A and Side B directly face each other, will Side C go to the aid of side B, as promised, when B is attacked by A? And how much assistance can Side C be expected to provide? I will not address these questions for two reasons. First, an extensive literature deals with the matter of third-party commitments.[26] Second, the issue is not significant in any of the cases considered in this book,[27] mainly because the third party usually integrates a portion of its forces into the forces of its allies. An example is the United States' commitment to NATO; thousands of American troops stationed in Europe ensure that their country will stand with its European allies against a Soviet attack.[28]

It should be evident that my concern lies with deterrence from the viewpoint of the nation that is contemplating war. I do not, however, exclude the defender's response from consideration, for conventional deterrence is a function of the capabilities of both sides. The attacker primarily wants to know, not whether there will be a response, but rather how effective it is likely to be. More specifically, will the defender's projected reply provide enough apprehension to deter an attack? I will therefore address the specifics of the expected response and the ways in which that response affects conventional deterrence. These questions are very different from those addressed in the existing body of literature.

METHOD AND PROCEDURE

To ground my theory historically, I have used the comparative case study method.[29] I selected a number of incidents involving deterrence failures and successes and examined them in as much detail as the available evidence would allow. I then compared the cases to determine whether there were similar patterns in the decision-making processes. I matched deterrence successes with deterrence failures to ascertain why wars broke out at some times but not at others. Finally I grouped successes and failures separately to see whether common elements emerged. In all I used twelve cases:

British-French decision making at Munich (1938)
British-French decision making in 1939–1940
The German decision to attack Poland (1939)
The German decision to attack France (1940)
The German decision to attack the Soviet Union (1941)
The Soviet decision to strike against Japan's Kwantung Army in
    Manchuria (1945)
The Israeli decision to attack in the Sinai (1956)

[19]

The Israeli decision to strike in the Sinai (1967)
The Egyptian decision to attack Israel (1973)
The North Korean invasion of South Korea (1950)
The Indian decision to attack Pakistan (1971)
The Vietnamese invasion of Cambodia (1979)

These cases include all of the principal deterrence failures and successes involving the modern battlefield, and available information about almost all of them is sufficient to permit considered judgments. Six other crises *might* be included in a study of conventional deterrence:

The Chinese decision to attack North Vietnam (1979)
The Iran-Iraq war (1980–present)
The North Vietnamese invasion of South Vietnam (1975)
The India-Pakistan war (1965)
The Japanese-Soviet conflict in the Far East (1939)
The Syrian decision to attack Israel (1973)[30]

Only two of my cases represent clear-cut deterrence successes (Allied decision making at Munich and Allied decision making in 1939–1940), and these two are closely linked. Although the list includes few examples of successful deterrence, their paucity poses no major problem. The decision to go to war is rarely simple and invariably involves considerable debate and controversy among the concerned policy makers. In a number of cases, even though the nation ultimately decided to go to war, there were periods in the decision-making process when deterrence actually held, as it did in the German decision to attack in the West in May 1940. Hitler told his generals in September 1939 that he intended to strike against the Allies. Deterrence subsequently held until February 1940 and broke down between February and May 1940. Other cases involving similarly distinct periods include: the 1956 and 1967 Israeli decisions to strike against Egypt; the 1973 Egyptian decision to strike against Israel; and Allied decision making in the months before May 1940.[31] I will examine all of these incidents in detail in subsequent chapters. It suffices to say here that deterrence obtained for some intervals in each instance. Thus the number of deterrence successes, however narrowly defined, is sufficiently large to permit us to generate propositions that explain why deterrence sometimes holds in a crisis.

The preceding discussion indicates that several of my examples include different subcases within the whole. I will therefore make comparisons *within* some of the twelve major cases and will, of

[20]

course, also compare the subcases with other major cases. My theory thus develops on the basis of combinations involving more than just twelve instances of deterrence failures and successes.

Although my reasoning draws on all twelve incidents, some of them figured more prominently in its development than others. I have necessarily had to concern myself with the details of the decision-making process that leads to or away from war; what actually happens on the battlefield once the war begins is, for my purposes, not directly relevant. But to explain why nations opted for or against war, the investigator needs to know how the actual decisions were made. Unfortunately, it is often very difficult to get the necessary information.

Lack of information was not a problem with the three cases of German aggression in World War II or with Allied decision making before and during the early stages of that same war. Accessible archival material exists in abundance. The situation was otherwise for the Middle East. On the Israeli side there is a great deal of information in the public domain for the 1967 decision, and a fair amount is also available for the 1956 decision. Unfortunately, however, the official records remain closed. On the Arab side, evidence is scarce—especially for the Syrian case in 1973.

When details about the making of a particular decision are not available, an investigator must extrapolate from events on the battlefield. Such a procedure is not ideal but is often unavoidable. My analyses of the North Korean (1950) and Vietnamese (1979) decisions were necessarily based on pure extrapolation because the needed information was almost totally lacking. I also found only limited data on the Soviet decision to invade Manchuria (1945) and the Indian decision to wage war against Pakistan (1971). As a consequence these cases have been much less influential in shaping my theory than the cases drawn from the Middle East and from World War II.

Chapter 2 describes my theory in detail. In the subsequent three chapters, I examine the specific cases from which it developed. Chapter 3 deals with the British-French decision not to attack Germany after declaring war in September 1939, Chapter 4 with the German decision to strike against the Allies in May 1940, and Chapter 5 with the 1956, 1967, and 1973 Arab-Israeli wars. Because these specific cases significantly shaped my theory, they cannot, of course, be used to test it. The reader should also bear in mind that I have made no attempt to write the definitive history of why war started or did not start in each case, nor have I sought to provide a comprehensive study of the origins of World War II in Europe. Instead, I examine each case in light of the specific questions that I have chosen to address. These questions represent a particular, but nevertheless very significant, aspect of many of the important incidents under scrutiny.

Chapter 6 uses the theory to examine the balance of conventional forces in Central Europe for the purpose of determining how well suited NATO's forces are to deter a conventional attack by the Soviets. My key point here is that Soviet decision makers contemplating war would be faced with basically the same military considerations that confronted, for example, the Allies in 1939 and the Israelis in 1967. Chapter 7 applies the theory to a relatively technical issue relating to weaponry. In the past few years, two such issues have received considerable attention: the impact of precision-guided munitions (PGMs) on conventional warfare and the debate between advocates of maneuver and attrition warfare. I consider the former issue directly, at length, and the latter only briefly, in Chapters 2 and 6.[32] Some analysts argue that PGMs are basically defensive weapons and are thus likely to enhance deterrence; others contend that they are offensive weapons and thus threaten deterrence. Since the core argument of this book is that deterrence is a function of specific military strategies, I gauge the impact of PGMs by asking whether (and how) they hinder or facilitate the implementation of various strategies. In addition, some observers view PGMs as threatening the existence of the tank and other armored vehicles, thereby heralding a revolutionary change in the conduct of war. Such an impact could call into question the continuing relevance of my theory, and accordingly I assess the long-range effect that PGMs can be expected to have.

Chapter 8 summarizes my principal findings and compares the twelve cases, describing their similarities and differences and showing how they fit into the theory. It is normally considered inappropriate to introduce new material in a concluding chapter. I have violated this rule for good reason. Not all of the cases from which the theory was developed warranted a chapter to themselves. I have therefore briefly discussed in the Conclusion the cases that were not treated in earlier chapters.

[2]

Conventional Deterrence

Let us first examine the military aspects of deterrence. I shall take as given the potential attacker's political objectives and shall focus on the risks and costs of employing the military instrument.

THE MILITARY ELEMENT

A potential attacker's fear of the consequences of military action lies at the heart of deterrence. Specifically, deterrence—a function of the costs and risks associated with military action—is most likely to obtain when an attacker believes that his probability of success is low and that the attendant costs will be high.

Cost on the conventional battlefield is a function of military casualties, equipment lost or damaged, civilian casualties that result from the fighting, and the expense of mobilizing, deploying, and maintaining the forces. Although cost is an important variable at the conventional level, it is not paramount, as it is at the nuclear level—simply because there is no possibility of annihilating an entire civilization in a matter of days or even hours. History clearly demonstrates that decision makers are willing, under the right circumstances, to accept the costs associated with conventional war. One reason is that in the military occupation, dying in defense of the national interest is an accepted risk. More important, costs in a conventional war accumulate in a gradual manner that is often difficult to anticipate. In World War I, the classic example, there was little appreciation beforehand of the losses that lay ahead.

At the nuclear level the threat exists that incalculable damage will be inflicted in a short period of time. Conventional war, on the other hand, is necessarily more protracted, thus allowing a nation to adjust to increasing losses. A nation might very well absorb losses in the end that it would have considered prohibitive at the outset of the conflict. For the purposes of securing deterrence, of course, a potential attacker should ideally be able to foresee that the costs of military action will be great. And in an age when wars are frequently characterized by the clashing of mass armies, the costs associated with conventional war can be exceedingly high.

Cost is directly linked with the second variable, probability of success. Actually the attacker's aim at the conventional level is not merely success but also rapid achievement of objectives on the battlefield. Short conventional wars are more desirable than lengthy ones because the former generally entail lower costs. Appropriately, war is most likely to start when the potential attacker envisions a quick victory. When the conflict promises to be more prolonged, but ultimate success is still considered probable, deterrence is nevertheless likely to obtain, largely because the protracted nature of the conflict will result in high costs.[1] This general statement formed the basis of Dean Acheson's deterrent formula for Europe in the early 1950s. He maintained that NATO needed, not to be able to defeat the Soviets in order to deter them, but only to make the Soviets pay an exorbitant price for victory.[2] Finally, a potential attacker who expects to lose a war is very unlikely to start it. Obviously, the costs of such an enterprise would be great.

It is clear that cost in a conventional war is largely a function of the speed with which the attacker can secure his objectives, since costs and time are directly related. Probability of success is not necessarily a more important variable than cost, however. On the contrary, both play a crucial role in a decision maker's calculations about war. Nevertheless, given that cost is largely dependent on the speed with which objectives are attained, we must concern ourselves with determining the conditions under which decision makers are likely to conclude that they can quickly achieve their objectives on the battlefield. It will, of course, also be necessary to determine when decision makers are likely to reach the opposite conclusion.

Competing Explanations

At a very general level, we might argue that war is most likely to occur when the offense has an advantage over the defense. This explanation, as it stands, is not very helpful and in fact comes close to being circular (when the offense has the advantage, war starts; war invariably breaks out because the offense is dominant). Nor does such a preliminary statement explain why the offense has an advantage over the defense. How can one recognize an offensive advantage? A theory of conventional deterrence must stipulate the conditions under which the offense has an advantage over the defense.

The paucity of literature on conventional deterrence notwithstanding, we can identify two theories of conventional deterrence. The first focuses on the type of weapons possessed by each side, while the second considers the balance of forces between the two. Both explanations, however, have serious shortcomings. I shall soon offer a third possibility that links deterrence to specific military strategies, but let us begin by examining the first two explanations.

The better-articulated theory assumes that specific weapons can be classified as either offensive or defensive in nature and that it is therefore possible to calculate a rough balance between offense and defense using our knowledge of the kinds of weapons that dominate the battlefield at a particular time.[3] Success in war depends largely on the weaponry available to the opposing sides. More important for our purposes, when offensive weaponry has the upper hand, deterrence is likely to fail, and when defensive weapons dominate, deterrence is likely to obtain. As George Quester noted in *Offense and Defense in the International System* (1977), "Likelihoods of war are thus clearly influenced by how effective the offensive weapon seems to be, as compared with the defensive."[4]

Deterrence is thus viewed as a function of existing weaponry.[5] Proponents argue, for example, that the machine gun is essentially a defensive weapon and therefore that from the latter part of the nineteenth century until the end of World War I, the defense was dominant. The tank, which developed in response to the deadly machine gun and artillery fire of the First World War, is considered an offensive weapon that has shifted the equation in favor of the offense.[6] Weapons that enhance mobility, such as the tank, are generally viewed as offensive and therefore as threatening deterrence.[7] This theory of deterrence held sway at the 1932 Disarmament Conference, where serious attempts were made to classify weapons as either offensive or defensive and then to limit those in the first category.[8]

Such an explanation is flawed. First, it is very difficult to distinguish between offensive and defensive weapons. For example, it is not clear that mobility favors the offense; in fact, we might well argue that mobility favors the defense. Consider the importance of mobility to both sides, first, in the initial breakthrough battles, and

[25]

second, in the exploitation phase of the conflict (we shall assume that the attacker has achieved a breakthrough). One important advantage held by the offense is the ability to choose the main point of attack for the initial battles, to move forces there surreptitiously, and to surprise the defender. It is not essential that the offense have highly mobile weapons to effect surprise—provided its movements can be concealed from the defense. Because the defense places a premium on rapid reaction to move its forces to meet the attacker in those initial battles, it requires highly mobile forces. Thus if any side benefits from mobility in the initial breakthrough battles, it is the defender. Now consider the exploitation phase. There is no doubt that after the breakthrough the attacker benefits greatly from having highly mobile forces. But so does the defender, who can move his forces rapidly to deal with the attacker's penetrating units.[9] Thus neither side derives a special advantage from mobility in the exploitation phase.[10] In sum, it appears that if anyone gains from increased mobility, it is the defender.

The fallacy of equating mobility with offensive capability is highlighted by an examination of World War II tank battles. Despite claims that the tank, because of its mobility, is an offensive weapon, in those battles where both the offense and the defense were skilled in the basics of mobile armored warfare, the offense often required a very significant force advantage to achieve success.[11] More specifically, the German army's conduct of a defensive war on the eastern front from 1943 to 1945 exemplifies the power of a tank-oriented defensive force.[12] The German army, although clearly outnumbered by the Soviets, was able to prolong the final defeat by taking advantage of the mobility built into its fighting forces.

In light of the difficulty of classifying weapons according to their offensive potential, we should not be surprised to discover from the cases examined in this study that there is no agreement among decision makers that the tank is an offensive weapon.[13] Certainly, before the Second World War few Allied officers, and few German officers for that matter, believed that the tank would confer an advantage on the offense. And the Egyptians, who have not suffered from a shortage of tanks, seem not to have viewed this weapon as providing them with an offensive capability.

The type of weapon available at a specific time is nevertheless important. After all, the introduction of the tank in the First World War led to a fundamental change in the nature of the battlefield, although the mere appearance of the new weapon did not revolutionize warfare. Large numbers of tanks were used in World War I,

[26]

and they did not change the character of the war in any significant way. Whether or not a tank is an offensive weapon depends on how it is employed—and the tank can be used in different ways. As I will explain, the tank became a revolutionary weapon only when it was used to support a specific and unconventional strategy. When it is employed otherwise, the tank has limited offensive potential. A tank force in the hands of the Israeli army thus differs from one in Arab hands. In short, it is much too simplistic to categorize weapons as either offensive or defensive in nature. We must concern ourselves not simply with weapons—and this distinction is crucial—but with their use and their probable effect on the course of the war. These questions are uppermost in the minds of decision makers.

Unlike the first explanation, which focuses on the nature of specific weapons, the second is concerned with the balance of forces. Analysts consider indicators such as the number of tanks, soldiers, artillery pieces, and aircraft on each side and then produce composite force ratios.[14] More sophisticated analyses take the quality of the weapons into account by weighing the relative value of different types as well as differences within a given type.[15] The principal tenet is that deterrence fails when the attacker has superiority in men and armor. Conversely, deterrence is expected to obtain when there is a rough equality in the size of the opposing forces.

Although it is very difficult to identify a study that explicitly describes deterrence as a function of the number of forces on each side, this theory is implicit in many works that discuss past deterrence failures as well as contemporary policy problems. For example, some studies of both the German attack in the West (1940) and the German invasion of the Soviet Union (1941) ascribe significant numerical superiority to the Germans, thus leaving the reader to infer that the Germans went to war in each case because they were in a position to overwhelm their opponent.[16] Very importantly, this theory of conventional deterrence is implicit in numerous studies that focus on the balance of forces between NATO and the Warsaw Pact. The key assumption is that, by simply comparing the number of forces on each side, it is possible to determine the prospects for conventional deterrence in Europe.

The extensive influence of macroscopic force ratios in the West is reflected in NATO's position in the ongoing Mutual and Balanced Force Reductions (MBFR) talks. The goal has been to reduce the number of troops and weapons in Central Europe, with the express purpose of creating a rough balance between the two sides.[17] Stability, according to the Western view, obtains when there is essential numerical parity between the opposing forces. This approach to conventional arms control stands in marked contrast to that of the 1932 Disarmament Conference, where the emphasis was on abolishing offensive weapons. Quantitative arms control has replaced qualitative arms control at the conventional level.

The major problem with this second explanation is that there are a number of important cases in which the attacker either was outnumbered by the defender or was roughly equivalent in size. In May 1940, for example, the German army had approximately the same number of tanks and soldiers as the Allies. Then, in June 1941, the Germans recognized that they would be outnumbered by the Soviets—although the Germans actually underestimated Soviet strength. The Israeli decision to attack in the Sinai in 1967 casts further doubt on the utility of force ratios as an explanation for deterrence failures. After all, the Israelis did not enjoy numerical superiority. There are cases, however, in which the imbalance of forces between the two sides does account, in large part, for the breakdown of deterrence. An example is certainly the point at which, in 1939, the Germans decided to invade Poland.

The force ratio explanation is thus not without some value. The same is true, of course, of the first explanation. The type of weapons available to the opposing forces does influence the conduct of war and thus deterrence. By themselves, however, both theories are unsatisfactory. Yet we must not simply discard them; rather it is necessary to go beyond them—to explain, for example, why deterrence failed when there was a balance of forces. In the following sections, which set forth an alternative theory, I shall argue that deterrence is a direct function of specific military strategies. There is no doubt, however, that strategy depends, in part, on an assessment of both the balance of forces and the type of weapons available to each side. In short, although the third theory is clearly an alternative, it includes rather than excludes the two competing explanations.

Strategy and Deterrence

Conventional deterrence is directly related to military strategy, or more specifically, to the matter of how a nation's armed forces are employed to achieve specific battlefield objectives. Decision makers are primarily concerned with determining how their forces are going to be used on the battlefield and with probable outcomes when the attacking forces meet the defending forces. In other words, decision makers attempt to foresee the nature of the war. Does the plan of attack—the proposed strategy—promise success at a reasonable cost? Such considerations lie at the heart of the decision-making process.

Although military strategy provides the key to understanding deterrence at the conventional level, it is necessary to provide more specific details about the relationship between strategy and deterrence. The crucial question is whether we can generalize about strategy in ways that explain deterrence failures and successes. As I have noted, a fundamental assumption of this study is that by limiting the scope of analysis to cases involving the modern battlefield, it is possible to develop powerful propositions about strategy and deterrence.

Basically, decision makers are faced with three distinct and narrowly defined strategies: the attrition, the blitzkrieg, and the limited aims strategies.[18] Each has different implications for deterrence. Before considering them, we must examine briefly the broad outlines of military strategy. At the most general level, an attacker can pursue either limited or unlimited military objectives. In more concrete terms, the pursuit of the latter is synonymous with total defeat of the opponent's military forces. It should be noted that *unlimited* war, as defined here, does not necessarily have to result in *total* war. The cornerstone of total war is unconditional surrender, which is another way of saying that the attacker is pursuing unlimited political objectives. It is possible for a nation, however, to disarm an opponent completely on the battlefield and not to seek unconditional surrender; in 1967 the Israelis decisively defeated the Egyptian military forces but were well aware that they would not be able to impose political terms on the Egyptians.[19]

In contrast to a disarming strike, pursuit of a limited objective requires the attacker to seize a portion of the opponent's territory. To effect the capture, of course, the attacker must defeat some of the enemy's forces. The principal aim, however, is to capture territory, not to defeat the opponent's army. This distinction between limited and unlimited objectives is clearly reflected in the writings of Clausewitz and other military strategists.[20]

Given a specific objective, how will the attacker employ his forces so as to achieve it? When the goal is to defeat the opponent decisively, an attacker can choose between the attrition and blitzkrieg strategies.[21] With the attrition strategy, the attacker seeks to defeat his opponent by engaging in numerous battles of annihilation, or set-piece battles. Ultimate success depends on wearing the defense down until resistance is no longer possible. The blitzkrieg, on the other hand, relies on the mobility and speed inherent in an armored force

[29]

to defeat an opponent decisively without a series of bloody battles. The remarkable victories achieved by Germany in the early years of World War II, and decades later by Israel in the Middle East, show that an opponent can be disarmed without numerous battles of annihilation. On the modern battlefield, the blitzkrieg is the ideal tool for achieving a quick victory at a low cost. Therefore deterrence is likely to fail when a potential attacker thinks he can launch a successful blitzkrieg. The attrition strategy, on the other hand, can promise at best a delayed success at a high cost and may very well fail to produce a decisive victory. Deterrence is greatly strengthened when a potential attacker envisions war as a series of set-piece battles.

Now consider the situation in which the military objective is limited. Here the attacker attempts to determine the best strategy for seizing a slice of the opponent's territory. Although it is possible to use the blitzkrieg or the attrition strategy for this purpose, the attacker is very unlikely to do so. Instead he will rely largely on surprise: the aim is to strike before the victim can mobilize his defenses. This "ideal" strategy, which is labeled the limited aims strategy, emphasizes minimizing contact with the defender. If the attacker *is* able to achieve surprise, this strategy is likely to be successful and also not very costly. The blitzkrieg and the attrition strategies are invariably riskier because they are almost always employed in pursuit of a more ambitious objective and because they both involve directly engaging the defender's forces. Still, several factors reduce the attractiveness of the limited aims strategy.

In sum, an attacker has three options.[22] The first two, the blitzkrieg and attrition strategies, are used when the objective is to inflict a decisive defeat on the enemy. With the limited aims strategy, on the other hand, the attacker seeks to capture some portion of the opponent's territory. Each strategy has different implications for deterrence. Thus the likelihood that deterrence will obtain in a specific instance largely depends on which strategy the potential attacker is considering. Let us now examine each of the three in detail and then explore the relationship between them and deterrence.

The Development of Armored Warfare

Prior to the mid-nineteenth century, armies were generally so small that large-scale maneuver was a very important element in warfare. To avoid costly frontal assaults, commanders attempted to encircle an opponent's army by striking at his exposed flanks. Maneuver, in the classical sense of the term, was directed toward envelopment of the enemy army—possible not only because armies were small enough to be moved about the battlefield with relative ease but also because they had exposed flanks.[23] With the advent of the mass army, not only was flexibility greatly reduced, but armies rarely had exposed flanks. It thus became pointless to speak of encircling, since the armies stretched across very broad fronts. As a result, commanders began searching for ways to pierce the opponent's extended front and to reach into his vulnerable rear. Penetration replaced maneuver as the alternative to the costly strategy of broad frontal attacks designed to overwhelm the defense.[24]

The new orientation was evident in World War I. In the latter stages of that conflict, when both sides were searching for a means to end the bloody stalemate, the Germans introduced *infiltration tactics*.[25] This new approach, which was used in the March 1918 German offensive, called for the attacking infantry to avoid Allied strong points and instead to concentrate on penetrating into the Allied rear, where the absence of enemy fighting forces would allow the German infantry to wreak havoc. After spectacular initial success, the German offensive failed, in large part because the Germans did not have the means to exploit their opening successes. Foot soldiers were not able to reach deep enough into the enemy's rear before the Allies shifted their forces and contained the penetration.

The Allies, on the other hand, took a different tack. They developed the tank, which was first used in September 1916 in the Somme offensive but without impressive results.[26] At Arras in April 1917, and at Amiens in August 1918, the tank first showed that it could markedly influence the course of battle. By 1918, plans were being prepared to employ tanks on a grand scale—to produce decisive results.[27] The war ended, however, before these plans were implemented. In the end, attrition determined the winner: the allies simply wore down the Germans. With the introduction of the tank, however, the stage was set for a fundamental shift in the nature of modern warfare. In retrospect, this point seems obvious. At the time, and in fact during the twenty year period between the world wars, most experts did not accept the claim that the tank had the potential to revolutionize warfare.

During the interwar period, there was intense debate in all the industrialized nations about the role of the tank in a future war. Virtually everyone agreed that the tank had a role to play, but there was significant disagreement as to what it should be. Three schools of thought emerged.[28] Proponents of the first argued that the primary

[31]

role of the tank, as exemplified in World War I, was to provide infantry support. Basically, tanks were envisioned as an integral part of a combined arms assault force that would roll back the opponent's front. There was no emphasis on using the tank's mobility and speed to penetrate deep into the defender's rear.

Representatives of the second school of thought argued that tanks should be used for the exploitation of battlefield victories earned by infantry and artillery. In other words, tanks should be employed in the traditional cavalry roles—either augmenting or substituting for horse cavalry. Even so, tanks were considered to be of only limited value in the exploitation role, since they were not capable of piercing strong, secondary defensive positions. Advocates of the mechanized cavalry role wanted to capitalize on the speed and mobility of the tank, not on its firepower or on the protection it afforded attacking infantry. This school of thought gained acceptance after World War I, as certain individuals came to believe that the tank was too vulnerable to be used in assaults on fixed positions.[29] In World War I, when there were few German tanks and few antitank guns, the tank's vulnerability did not cause as much concern as it did later. But the emphasis was still on battles of attrition, requiring the massive use of firepower. As infantry support, the tanks would actually participate in the firepower duel; when they served as mechanized cavalry, they were to be used after the firepower duel had been decided.

A third school of thought, unlike the other two, maintained that the tank, if properly employed, would have a revolutionary impact on the battlefield. Advocates of this view believed not that the tank should be considered a mere adjunct to infantry and artillery but rather that artillery and infantry should be used to support the tank, which was regarded as the chief weapon on the battlefield. Most important, proponents of this view believed that the tank provided the means for avoiding the battles of attrition that had dominated World War I. The revolutionaries agreed with the advocates of infantry support in maintaining that the firepower and protection offered by the tank could help puncture the opponent's forward defense. Advocates of this third school of thought, however, believed that the tank could also be used in a revolutionary way, to exploit the initial breakthrough and to achieve a deep strategic penetration before the defense had time to react. Victory promised to be swift.

In 1918, the German offensive was thwarted, in large part because the means to exploit the initial breakthrough and to effect a deep strategic penetration were not available. The tank offered a solution to the problem. The revolutionary strategy, which had staunch ad-

[32]

vocates in each industrial nation, was first employed by the Germans in the initial stages of World War II; it was appropriately labeled the blitzkrieg.[30]

It was clear by the late 1930s that the tank would play a more important role than that ascribed to it by the cavalry school. An attacker could employ his tanks in basically two different ways. He could use them to effect a blitzkrieg, or he could use them in close and constant coordination with infantry and artillery to pursue what we shall call an attrition strategy, which is essentially the same as the infantry support role previously described. Although the blitzkrieg and attrition strategies are employed in pursuit of the same objective (decisive defeat of the enemy on the battlefield), they are quite distinct and affect the prospects for deterrence very differently.

The Attrition Strategy

The essence of the attrition strategy[31] is best described by Clausewitz when he discusses war in its absolute form. According to Clausewitz, it is a fallacy to think that there is "some ingenious way to disarm or defeat an enemy without too much bloodshed."[32] He argues that "direct annihilation of the enemy's forces must always be the *dominant consideration.*"[33] He is unyielding in his disdain for "highly sophisticated theory . . . that claims to produce, by means of limited but skillfully applied blows, such paralysis of the enemy's forces and control of his will-power as to constitute a significant shortcut to victory."[34]

The attrition strategy is predicated upon the assumption that the modern battlefield is not fundamentally different from the battlefields of World War I—or from those of the second half of the nineteenth century, for that matter. Weapons may change, but basic strategy does not. In this regard, the attacker is primarily concerned with overwhelming a stubborn defense in a series of bloody set-piece battles. The continuity between the twentieth century and Clausewitz's day is reflected in Field Marshal Montgomery's comments to his senior officers before the Battle of El Alamein in 1942:

> Everyone must want to kill Germans. . . . I believe that the dog-fight battle will become a hard killing match and will last for 10 to 12 days; therefore our soldiers must be prepared not only to fight and kill, but to go on doing so over a prolonged period. . . . Determined leadership will be very vital in this battle. . . . nothing is ever hopeless so long as men have stout hearts.[35]

[33]

A successful offensive, like a steamroller, literally pushes the defender back along a broad front.[36] Rout and retreat alternate, eventually wearing down the defense.[37] Little emphasis is placed on achieving the battlefield equivalent of a knockout punch. Instead, victory follows a series of set-piece battles and is not expected to be quick. The process is protracted, and success ultimately comes when the defender can no longer continue to fight. It is of course assumed that the defender will weaken before the attacker does. Since there are no shortcuts to victory, an attacker does not shy away from striking at the defender's strong points. Strength is matched against strength.

It is generally agreed that in set-piece battles the offense suffers greater losses than the defense. Therefore the attacker must believe that he has enough soldiers and equipment to compensate for his heavier losses, a point suggesting that success in a war of attrition largely depends on the size of the opposing forces. Allowing for the asymmetry in losses between offense and defense, the side with greater manpower and a larger material base will ultimately prevail.[38]

The attrition strategy relies heavily on firepower to wear down the defense. Consequently, an attrition strategy is characterized by widespread use of artillery. The underlying assumption is that the attacking force can save precious manpower and can still inflict heavy casualties on the defense by substituting, as much as possible, firepower for manpower. "Firepower saves lives." The defense follows the same logic, and both sides inflict tremendous casualties on each other. The tank plays an important role on the battlefield because it has a main gun that acts as another artillery tube and because it affords some protection to attacking infantrymen. The tank is important because of the emphasis on firepower.

An attrition strategy makes it difficult to take advantage of the tank's mobility and speed because the tank must cooperate closely with infantry and artillery. Nevertheless, the tank can be used to exploit holes that are ripped in the defender's front. Still, and this point is crucial, the attacker attempts to penetrate only shallowly— *not* deeply—into the defender's rear, so as to maintain the integrity of the effort to push the defender back along a broad front.

The attrition strategy, even when it proves ultimately successful, entails high costs. The attacker assumes that he can simply outlast the defender. Inherent in this strategy is the recognition that success will demand considerable casualties and significant losses of equipment. Again, as Clausewitz emphasized, there are no shortcuts to victory. Even an attacker who enjoys an advantage in numbers can

[34]

never feel very confident about the final outcome, however, since success depends on the ability to outlast the opponent. It is difficult to predict the distribution of costs or the point beyond which offense and defense will find the costs unacceptable. Moreover, it is not easy to anticipate political developments, both nationally and internationally, in the course of a lengthy war. Because the cost of an attrition strategy is always high and because success is relatively uncertain, deterrence is very likely to obtain when an attacker has this strategy as his only option.

The Blitzkrieg Strategy

Despite the widespread use of the term *blitzkrieg*, it has never been defined with precision. The books written on the subject have major shortcomings.[39] B. H. Liddell Hart, the intellectual father of the blitzkrieg and one of its champions, only once attempted to describe it—and the result was a very short memorandum.[40] J. F. C. Fuller, who, together with Liddell Hart, argued during the interwar period that the tank would revolutionize the conduct of war, did collect his views in a single comprehensive work.[41] There are, however, a number of important differences between the blitzkrieg and Fuller's concept of armored war.[42] Although practitioners of the blitzkrieg such as Heinz Guderian and Erich von Manstein have written about their wartime experiences, they have not directly tackled the problem of defining the strategy.[43]

Since there is no agreed-upon definition of a blitzkrieg, we should not be surprised to find the term loosely applied. It is frequently used to describe a quick victory on the battlefield. For example, Hans Rothfels, in his widely cited essay on Clausewitz, speaks of the "ascendancy of the Napoleonic blitzkrieg."[44] Although we might certainly use *blitzkrieg* to mean simply any lightning war or rapid victory, such a definition so broadens the meaning of the term that it loses all significance.

In fact, the blitzkrieg is concerned with the way in which tanks are used with other combat arms to achieve a specific objective. This strategy is therefore peculiar to the modern battlefield, and its emergence as a viable option in fact led to the very concept of a modern battlefield. If tanks are employed merely to support the attrition strategy (as advocated by proponents of the infantry support and mechanized cavalry schools of thought), there would be little reason to distinguish between the battlefields of the two world wars. As should be clear from the previous section, the attrition strategy is older than the modern battlefield. The use of the tank to effect a deep penetration, however, which is the heart of the blitzkrieg, introduced to the battlefield a revolutionary strategy that has no parallel in the immediate past. Furthermore, it clearly applies only to a specific universe of cases. In light of this limitation, we must define its essential characteristics very carefully.

The concept of the blitzkrieg stands in marked contrast to the view of war as a series of "bloody and destructive" battles that grant victory to the side with the greatest "physical and moral strength."[45] The German victories in the early part of World War II and the Israeli successes against the Arabs show that an enemy's military forces can be defeated decisively without relying on bloody set-piece battles to wear down the enemy. Furthermore these conflicts demonstrate that an attacker can succeed even when he does not have superiority of numbers.

The blitzkrieg is predicated upon the assumption that the opponent's army is a large and complex machine that is geared to fighting along a well-established defensive line. In the machine's rear lies a vulnerable network, which comprises numerous lines of communication, along which supplies as well as information move, and key nodal points at which the various lines intersect. Destruction of this central nervous system is tantamount to destruction of the army.[46] The principal aim of a blitzkrieg is therefore to effect a strategic penetration. The attacker attempts to pierce the defender's front and then to drive *deep* into the defender's rear, severing his lines of communication and destroying key junctures in the network.[47]

Appropriately, the attacker aims to concentrate his forces at a specific location or two along the front line so that he can achieve a significant superiority in numbers at those point(s) of main attack. It is important to repeat that, because only a few points of attack are involved, the offense need not have an overall advantage in forces;[48] he can choose the location of his main attack and can move forces there before the defender can react.[49] The attacker uses his force advantage at that point to open a hole in the front; then he penetrates deep into the enemy's rear.[50] The aim is to avoid a broad frontal attack and instead to drive one or two armored columns into the depths of the defense. Although it may be necessary to engage in a set-piece battle to accomplish the initial breakthrough, a high premium is placed on avoiding further battles of this sort. Instead the attacker follows the path of least resistance to the enemy's rear.[51] The tank with its inherent flexibility is of course the ideal weapon for implementing such a strategy.

[36]

The defender seeks to contain the penetrating armored forces either by establishing new defensive positions in front of the attacking forces or by driving into the flanks of the attacker's expanding salient.[52] Still, significant problems face the unprepared defender. Unless his forces are properly deployed and trained, it will be very difficult to shift them quickly so as to contain the penetrations—which are expanding rapidly as a consequence of the tank's speed. Here we see the crucial difference between the tank-dominated blitzkrieg and the 1918 German offensive, where the speed of the penetrating forces was governed by the speed of foot-borne infantrymen. Furthermore, the attacking forces make it difficult to develop new defensive positions by disrupting the defender's vulnerable lines of communication. While the defense is attempting to contain the armored thrusts, the attacking forces are striving to advance with the greatest possible speed. The offense literally outruns the defense. The attack succeeds because the defense is incapable of containing what Liddell Hart aptly called "the expanding torrent."[53]

Given the importance of maintaining the rate of advance that prevents the defender from concentrating his forces for a second engagement, it naturally follows that pitched battles, which can only serve to slow the attack, are antithetical to the blitzkrieg. Consequently, the armored forces that spearhead the attack bypass enemy strong points and leave them for the second echelon, whose infantry and artillery units can deal with them. During World War II, the Germans had basically two armies in one: the armored units that drove deep into the opponent's rear and the infantry forces that followed the armor and concentrated on eliminating the remaining strong points and on consolidating the attacker's position.[54] The contrast between these two parts was starkest in the Russian campaign, where the attacking armored forces often operated a hundred miles or more in front of the infantry divisions. The distinction would not be as great today because of the mechanization of infantry divisions. Nevertheless, this second echelon of forces, whether mechanized or not, would not be able to keep pace with the armored spearheads— simply because they would have to spend considerable time eliminating enemy strong points, consolidating the gains made by the armored spearheads, and protecting the vulnerable flanks of the expanding salient.

The blitzkrieg's ultimate success results from the paralysis of the defense. Large elements of the defender's forces may still be intact at the conflict's end, but the defender is no longer able to coordinate them and thus to combat the attacker.[55] As large-scale fighting units are separated from one another, the offender's forces profit from their isolation, attacking them one by one. Parts of the defense are unable to receive supplies or reinforcements. Logistical support, so essential on the modern battlefield, becomes difficult for the defending forces.

As the attacking armored columns push deeper into the defender's rear, the defense, aware of its predicament, must retreat—turn itself around—and establish a new line of defense. Even under the best circumstances, that is, when the attacking forces are only in front of the defense, strategic retreat is a difficult task. When large concentrations of the attacking forces are in the defender's rear and when the offense is also continuing to exert pressure along the entire front, the chances that the defender can conduct a successful retreat and can reestablish a viable defensive front are remote.

The blitzkrieg, however, is successful not only because it places an opponent at a physical disadvantage but also because it involves psychological dislocation and demoralization, which are difficult to describe in detail because they are forces in the mind of the military commander. Psychological dislocation of course results directly from the initial stages of the attack, when the armored forces catch the defense off balance. When the attacker keeps the defense off balance by disrupting the enemy's lines of communication, a feeling of helplessness spreads among the defender's military commanders. They soon realize that they are facing an attack for which they have no antidote. The ensuing psychological dislocation and demoralization contribute to the overall paralysis of the defense.[56]

A controversial point is whether or not battles of encirclement are consistent with the blitzkrieg. If, after making the initial penetration into the defender's rear, the attacker engages in battles of encirclement, it necessarily follows that he is not heeding the maxim that the attacker should seek to effect a deep strategic penetration as quickly as possible. This issue was the focus of considerable controversy during the German invasion of the Soviet Union in 1941.[57] After reaching the Dnieper River, Guderian and a number of other German generals argued that the armored forces should concentrate on driving straight for Moscow, which was the hub of the Soviet defense. They maintained that if Moscow were captured, the Soviet defense would be paralyzed and would consequently collapse.[58] Hitler and others argued that it was necessary first to eliminate the numerous Soviet forces that stood between the German army and Moscow so that the Soviets could not threaten the flanks of the armored thrusts converging on the city. Hitler prevailed, and although enormous numbers of Soviet prisoners were captured in the ensuing battles of encirclement, the Germans never succeeded in delivering the paralyzing blow that is the centerpiece of the blitzkrieg.[59]

As the discussion thus far suggests, advocates of the blitzkrieg acknowledge that the flanks of the attacking armored columns will be somewhat vulnerable. Certainly the attacker will use second-echelon forces to line the walls of the expanding salient. Nevertheless, there are limits as to how quickly second-echelon forces can be brought forward to cover lengthy flanks that are constantly expanding. It is assumed, however, that the constant forward movement of the attacking forces will so unbalance the defender that he will be unable to strike at the attacker's vulnerable flanks. As one German general noted, "The safety of an armoured formation in the enemy's rear depends on its continued movement."[60] In a sense, the attacker is betting that he can deliver the decisive blow before the defense can move against those exposed flanks. It is impossible to prove that the Germans would have defeated the Soviets had they pushed straight for Moscow, but it is clear that, in this case, the battles of encirclement, which were all great German victories, did not produce a decisive result.[61]

Napoleon wrote that "the strength of an army, like power in mechanics, is estimated by multiplying the mass by the velocity."[62] The blitzkrieg, as we have seen, places a premium on the second variable. The key to success in the great armored victories of the past has been the armor columns racing at breakneck speeds to capture critical objectives in the enemy's rear. Liddell Hart's description of the German drive across France in May 1940 captures this point perfectly:

> It is clear that Guderian and his tankmen pulled the German Army along after them, and thereby produced the most sweeping victory in modern history.
> The issue turned on the time-factor at stage after stage. French counter-movements were repeatedly thrown out of gear because their timing was too slow to catch up with changing situations, and that was due to the fact that the German van kept on moving faster than the German high command had contemplated.[63]

The blitzkrieg seeks to limit mass because, after a certain point, increases in mass are purchased at the expense of velocity. In contrast, a military force that employs the attrition strategy, which emphasizes overwhelming the enemy with superior numbers, places a premium on mass and largely ignores velocity. An offense that depends on mass to wear down the defense will almost always rely heavily on land-based artillery. Not surprisingly, a popular aphorism among French officers in World War I was: "Artillery conquers, infantry occupies." Appropriately, set-piece battles are dominated by artillery exchanges, whereas the blitzkrieg emphasizes mobility at the expense of firepower, as is apparent from the ancillary role assigned artillery in the German successes of World War II and in the Israeli victories of recent years, as well as in the writings of Liddell Hart and J. F. C. Fuller.[64] We should not conclude, however, that firepower is of no consequence. Actually, both the Germans and the Israelis relied instead on excellent close air support—in essence, "flying artillery"—to support their attacking tanks.

Dependence on land-based artillery presents two major problems. First, artillery exchanges waste valuable time, although the amount of time expended depends on whether the offense uses towed or self-propelled artillery. Second, extensive use of artillery requires large increases in the logistical support to sustain an attack. As the mass of the attacking force increases in size, the velocity naturally decreases.[65] Given the critical importance of timing for a blitzkrieg, reductions in speed imperil its very existence. Close air support, on the other hand, presents none of these problems. Because it is inherently flexible, the airplane functions as the perfect complement to fast-moving armored forces.

Problems similar to those associated with artillery arise when the attacker relies heavily on infantry support. It is simply not acceptable to restrict the speed of the attacking armored columns to the pace of foot soldiers battling with the defense. Although there will be a need for close coordination between infantry, artillery, and armor at certain points in the course of the attack—most certainly for the breakthrough battle—the blitzkrieg seeks to avoid situations that make combined arms operations necessary. For this reason I emphasized earlier that the attacker must follow the path of least resistance deep into the enemy rear. The blitzkrieg is most likely to succeed when the armored forces are allowed to lead the attack, unencumbered by the need to coordinate with supporting infantry and artillery. This rule applies to an army at two general levels. First, it is essential that the armored divisions not be hindered in their advance by being compelled to coordinate with infantry divisions that are not highly mechanized.[66] As I have noted, the German army in World War II operated according to this principle. It became two armies in one: the armored divisions, pacing the attack, and the infantry divisions, which followed in their wake. Second, the same situation applies to armored divisions themselves and again was reflected in the organization of the German army. Recognizing that their armored divisions would have to engage in some combined arms operations, the Germans included in them an armored brigade, an infantry brigade, and a number of supporting elements (artillery batteries, engineer battalion, and so forth).[67] German armored divisions were clearly not all-tank units. In the German successes of the early war period, however, the armored brigades invariably raced ahead of the other elements in the division, establishing the pace of the attack[68] and ultimately determining the final outcome of the battle. Thus the objective was—and properly is—to allow the largest all-tank unit within the division as much freedom as possible to operate independently.

We have reached a very important point. A fundamental issue associated with the blitzkrieg is the level at which artillery, infantry, and armored forces are first mixed within an armored division. In other words, in a unit of what size does a commander start combining different arms? If the armored force is designed to effect a blitzkrieg, it is important to have as large an all-tank unit as possible within the division. After all, the larger it is, the more effective it will be on the battlefield.[69]

Finally, the blitzkrieg demands a flexible command structure peopled from top to bottom with soldiers capable of exercising initiative in combat situations. A blitzkrieg is not based on a rigid plan that commanders must follow closely. In fact, the exact opposite is true. Before launching the attack, an overall objective is established, and detailed plans for the breakthrough battle are prepared. Still, there are no rigid guidelines for the commanders to follow as they conduct the deep strategic penetration. German doctrine, for example, sets great store by the concept of *Auftragstaktik*, which dictates that commanders be given a battlefield objective but not lengthy orders that tell them how to attain it.[70] The assumption is that no one can predict with any degree of certainty how the battle will develop. "A plan is merely a basis for changes."[71] In what Clausewitz called "the fog of war," commanders will often be required to make decisions with only a modicum of information at hand. Uncertainty will be commonplace, and therefore risks will have to be taken.[72] A high premium is placed on commanders' ability to make rapid-fire decisions that will enable the armored columns to maintain a high speed of attack.[73] Boldness is essential, even when information is incomplete, so that the offensive can maintain the initiative. Both the German army and the Israeli army place great emphasis on battlefield initiative and on flexible command structures.[74]

The British and American approach to armored warfare in World War II was quite different; neither employed a blitzkrieg. In the immediate aftermath of the French collapse, both the British and the American armies began to organize their armored forces along the lines of the German panzer forces, and their doctrine as well began to reflect the basic precepts of the blitzkrieg. Yet as the tide began to turn against the Germans and the Germans started diluting the strength of their armored forces, the Allies quickly reversed themselves and began placing greater emphasis on infantry and artillery, at the expense of the tank.[75]

The Allies' best opportunity for employing a blitzkrieg arose in the late summer of 1944, when the German defenses were disintegrating.[76] Montgomery, whose forces were north of the Ardennes and who had been as cautious since landing on the Continent as he had been in North Africa, argued that his army group, supported by the First American Army, should be given the green light to drive to the Ruhr and then on to Berlin.[77] Patton, whose forces were located south of the Ardennes, argued that *he* should be allowed to drive through the Saar and into the heart of Germany.[78] Both proposals stood in marked contrast to the original preinvasion plan, which envisioned the Allies pushing a stubborn German army back across a broad front.[79] In the end, Eisenhower insisted on continuing the attack along a broad front, thus forfeiting any chance of ending the war before 1945.

A number of studies dealing with the Allied drive across Europe argue that logistical considerations precluded a rapidly delivered, knifelike thrust into the German heartland.[80] Although it is very difficult to determine with any degree of confidence whether such a drive was logistically possible, the more important point is that the Allies never envisioned employing a blitzkrieg. When the original projections of the battle's development proved wrong[81] and the opportunity for effecting a blitzkrieg presented itself, the Allies "were not prepared, mentally or materially, to exploit it by a rapid long-range thrust."[82]

Although the discussion of the blitzkrieg in this section has been comprehensive, this strategy can be defined simply. First, its central ingredient is the deep strategic penetration. The attacker defeats the defender by concentrating his forces at one or more points along the front, piercing that front and then driving deep into the defender's rear. Second, the attacker relies on large-scale armored formations, operating independently of large infantry formations, to effect deep strategic penetration(s).

The Defense and the Terrain

The preceding discussion has focused almost exclusively on the offense, on the essential characteristics of the blitzkrieg. Success, however, depends on more than just the attacker's proficiency. Two factors over which the attacker has no control must be taken into account and greatly influence the blitzkrieg's chances of success: terrain and the capabilities of the defense.[83] If the Soviets were considering an attack in Europe, they would be concerned with accurately assessing not only their own capabilities but also NATO's capabilities and the character of the terrain on which the war would be fought. Although I consider terrain and the capabilities of the defense separately for analytical purposes, these two factors are closely related.

A blitzkrieg can only operate in terrain that is conducive to mobile armored warfare. In other words, the attacker requires terrain that will facilitate his penetration of the defender's front and will then allow his columns to race forward with a minimum of interference. Therefore, the fewer the obstacles with which the attacker has to deal—be they natural or man-made—the better. Not only is it difficult for tanks and other vehicles to negotiate rivers and woods, but such obstacles also afford the defense excellent cover. After landing at Normandy in June 1944, for example, the Allies spent several weeks fighting among the hedgerows of the Cotentin Peninsula. In this area of France, tanks could not be used for anything other than infantry support.[84] Once the Allies reached the rolling plains of central France, where there were few natural obstacles, it was feasible to consider employing a blitzkrieg.

Surprisingly, the area of northeastern France, where the Germans launched the May 1940 blitzkrieg, was not particularly well suited for mobile armored operations. The Franco-German border was covered by the Maginot Line, which the Germans recognized as a formidable barrier. Southern Belgium was covered by the Ardennes Forest, and in northern Belgium a network of natural and man-made obstacles could be used to thwart a blitzkrieg. The Allies' demise was a result of their decision to place a small number of ill-equipped forces behind the Ardennes Forest, where the Germans concentrated the majority of their armored divisions. Thus despite the obstacle-ridden terrain in southern Belgium, the Germans were able to pierce the Allied front without much difficulty and quickly reached the rolling plains of central France, which were ideally suited for the rapid movement of large armored forces. The German experience suggests that we must consider the terrain not only along the front but also throughout the depths of the battlefield.

The length of the battle front is another terrain-related factor that influences the blitzkrieg's chances of success. If the attacker is faced with a defender who is protecting a narrow front, the probability that the blitzkrieg will succeed is much less than if the attacker can strike at a defender deployed across a broad front. Not only does a narrow front limit the number of axes of advance from which the attacker can choose, but since the number of forces needed to hold a narrow front is not very great, the defender can place a greater number of troops in reserve, where they can be employed against the attacker's main armored thrusts, should they pierce the defender's front line.

The preceding discussion suggests a very important concept. There is an optimum number of troops required to hold a specific length of territory, an optimum *force-to-space ratio*.[85] In other words, if a defender has to hold a 300-kilometer front—and it is generally agreed that one division can hold 10 kilometers for an extended period— then he must place thirty divisions on the front line. If the defender actually has fifty divisions, he can place the "extra" twenty in his rear area, where they can be used to deal with problems that arise in the course of the battle. He may try to squeeze a few more divisions into the front line, but past a certain point it is inadvisable, if not impossible, to increase the density of the defense. If, on the other hand, the defender has only ten divisions to protect that same 300-kilometer front, the defense will be very weak and will present the offense with numerous opportunities for a breakthrough.[86] Thus a crucial consideration is the size of the front that the defender must cover and the size of the defender's forces. The two affect not only the attacker's prospects of breaking through the defender's forward positions but also the defender's ability to deal with breakthroughs that do occur.[87]

Depth of the battlefield also affects the blitzkrieg's chances of success. If a defender does not have large expanses of territory behind his front-line forces—and a large-scale retreat is therefore not feasible—then an attack that penetrates deep into the defender's rear is certain to be decisive. If the defender has space to trade for time, however, and is able to extricate a substantial number of his forces after the initial blow, then he may be able to establish a second line of defense. In essence, the attacker's first blitzkrieg fails, requiring a second.

A number of new factors complicate the attacker's prospects for success with the second blitzkrieg. First, an attacking force can advance only so far before it must be halted and refurbished. Thus there will undoubtedly be a lengthy pause before the attacker can strike for a second time. Such a pause provides the defender with needed time to regroup his forces. Second, the attacking forces will not be able to rely on surprise to gain an advantage, since the defense will be alerted. Third, the defender's forces will have benefited from the experience of combating the initial blitzkrieg, especially if the defender has not previously engaged one. Finally, the lines of communication of the attacking forces will be lengthened, while those of the defense will be shortened.

The German invasion of the Soviet Union in June 1941 (Operation Barbarossa) is an excellent example of a case in which an attacker was forced to launch successive blitzkriegs—both of which failed. The initial German plan called for inflicting a decisive defeat on the Soviet army west of the Dnieper River. The Germans understood the dangers of allowing the Soviets to retreat into the depths of the Soviet Union.[88] Interestingly, Stalin played into German hands by insisting that his armies stand and fight against the Germans.[89] Although the Germans were able to destroy the majority of the Soviet army located west of the Dnieper, the Soviets were able to withdraw a portion of their forces behind the Dnieper and to bring forward sufficient reserves to form a new defensive front.[90] Launching of the second German blitzkrieg was delayed for several weeks because the attacking forces had to be replenished and because agreement could not be reached on the military objective.[91] When they finally struck, the Germans initially met with great success.[92] The Soviets, however, were able once again to extricate forces and to bring forward more reserves. At the same time, the German lines of communication were being stretched and the Soviets were learning how to combat the blitzkrieg.[93] As winter set in, the Germans had not delivered the decisive blow, and the Soviets still maintained a solid defensive front. The blitzkrieg failed because the Soviets were able to trade space for time and to establish successive defensive lines that slowed the German offensive and prevented the decisive blow from being delivered.

The depth of the terrain in the Soviet Union contrasts sharply with the circumstances in northern France in 1940. The Allies had the coast of France directly to their rear. The Germans split the Allied forces and pinned the Allies' northern armies against the English Channel. For these armies, there was no question of retreating into the depths of France and forcing the Germans to launch a second blitzkrieg.[94]

The capabilities of the defense are also of paramount importance. A defender's ability to stymie a blitzkrieg depends on three factors. First, the defender must recognize the threat, must understand how the blitzkrieg operates, and must know how to combat it. Second, a defender must have the organizational capacity for fighting against the blitzkrieg: he must concentrate his tanks in large armored units. Finally, those units must have the actual capability to fight a mobile armored war. In other words, the defense must be peopled with soldiers who are capable of engaging the attacking armored forces. A defense may be properly organized and may know what measures are necessary to stop a blitzkrieg but may still not have commanders and soldiers trained to fight a mobile armored war. In sum, the defender must understand the nature of the threat and how to deal with it, must have the organizational capacity for doing so, and must have the soldiers capable of implementing the solution. Past experience shows that if the defender fails to satisfy all of these requirements, he is not likely to stop a blitzkrieg.

Prior to World War II, Allied military leaders had little, if any, appreciation of the blitzkrieg's potential. The German attack in the West in May 1940 completely surprised the Allies.[95] The Soviets, who as late as 1939 were describing the blitzkrieg as a misguided "bourgeois" strategy, recognized their error after the fall of France.[96] They then tried to reorganize their forces into large-scale armored units. The Germans struck before the reorganization had been completed, however, and the Soviet army suffered a series of tremendous defeats, none of which proved decisive.[97] As the war progressed, the Soviets, as well as the British and the Americans, developed the appropriate organizational structure for arresting the blitzkrieg. Because the Allied armies also had soldiers capable of fighting a mobile armored war, the blitzkrieg was checked. After the 1956 Middle East war, Egypt and Syria were aware of Israel's capability to launch a blitzkrieg. Furthermore, the Arab armies, which were structured on the Soviet model, were properly organized for engaging in mobile armored warfare. As Arab leaders themselves recognize, however, their armies are simply not capable of engaging the Israelis on an open battlefield, where a high premium is placed on mobility.[98] This point was clearly demonstrated in 1967 and again in 1973. In specific

[46]

terms, what does it mean to be capable of fighting a mobile armored war? What demands are placed on the defender?

Since the attacker's success depends, above all else, on his ability to effect a deep strategic penetration, the defender must prevent the attacking armored spearheads from reaching into his rear. Let us consider in greater detail the defender's chances of stopping the attacker from making the initial breakthrough. It is necessary to re-introduce the concept of force-to-space ratios.[99] As I have noted, it is probable that an attacker can achieve numerical superiority over the defender at specific points along the front. As a rule of thumb, it is widely agreed that if the attacker achieves more than a 3:1 advantage in forces at those points of attack, he is likely to overrun the defender.[100] He would not necessarily do so, however; the ratio of forces at the point of main attack alone does not indicate reliably whether or not the attack will succeed. We must also consider the defender's force-to-space ratio. If the defender has the optimum number of forces needed to hold a specific front for an extended period of time, then it matters little whether the attacker enjoys a 5:1 or even an 8:1 advantage at the points of main attack. The attacker might of course seek to wear down the defender in a series of long and costly battles. (In such an eventuality, the defender would have ample time to transfer forces from other locations in the theater of battle.) This tactic, however, would certainly lead to a Pyrrhic victory. Moreover, it is evident that if the overall force ratio is close to parity, or at least substantially smaller than 3:1, then the attacker is not likely to win even a Pyrrhic victory.

A related phenomenon compounds the attacker's problem in piercing the defender's front. Although the attacker may have a significant advantage in the number of forces available for the crucial breakthrough battles, the attacker will undoubtedly not be able to line up all of his forces along the front; there will simply not be enough room for all of them. A portion will have to be placed in rear echelons, behind the forces that directly engage the defender. Located behind the front they will have little direct impact on the battle, so that the defender will be in the enviable position of being able to combat the attacker's forces piecemeal. This bonus is analogous to the crossing-the-T phenomenon known in naval warfare.[101]

Now, if the attacker pierces the defender's front, the defender will next want to halt the penetration. This task is generally more difficult for the defender to execute than is preventing the initial breakthrough. The defender must be able to move his forces (whether they are reserves or units from other points along the front) quickly so that they can contain the expanding salient. The defensive forces might attack the flanks of the salient, or they might be placed directly in the path of the attacking forces. Whichever course of action the defense pursues, it will require excellent coordination among the defender's units and a speedy response—all in the face of a continually changing military situation. Whereas the breakthrough battle is, in essence, a set-piece battle, once the penetration has occurred, the defender needs great mobility and flexibility. A defender not skilled in fighting mobile armored battles has little hope of surviving if he cannot prevent a breakthrough.

Our discussion of the defender's prospects against a blitzkrieg has not thus far considered specific defensive strategies. It is necessary to examine briefly a few of the specific possibilities, focusing on how the configuration of the defense affects its success. To a large extent the choice of a defensive strategy and its utility are functions of the size of the forces on each side and of the basic shape of the theater of battle. Although we might imagine an endless variety of defensive strategies, it is most useful to distinguish between four ideal sorts.[102]

The first two defenses are linear in nature; that is, the forces are predominantly stationed in forward positions, and the number of reserves is limited. The *static defense* is a linear defense employing forces that have little tactical mobility.[103] In other words, the mission of the units that are deployed along the front is to defend preestablished positions rather than to maneuver in response to attacks in or near their sectors. Defensive units are basically consigned to fighting from the positions they occupy when the attack begins. The Allied defense of Belgium and France in 1940 was essentially a static defense. Certainly, the opposing sides in World War I employed static defenses. It is widely accepted that such a defense is the ideal target for a blitzkrieg, because the defender does not have the capability to shift forces to deal with potential trouble spots. The likelihood that the defender can maintain the integrity of his fixed position is largely a function of force-to-space considerations, which would have to be very favorable before the defender could succeed. Should the attacker break through the front line, the defense would be helpless, since it has few reserves and little ability to shift forces to deal with the penetration.

The second possibility is the *forward defense*, which is a linear arrangement of forward-deployed forces that have significant tactical mobility. More specifically, commanders of large-scale units along the front have the capability to shift forces rapidly within their sector and to move forces to an adjacent area to help contain an armored penetration. In other words, the defender can shift forces up or down the front line. If the appropriate means of transportation is available and time permits, it might be possible to transfer forces from one sector to a distant region. Still, a forward defense cannot depend on such a contingency. It must be emphasized that tactical mobility is useful only in containing shallow penetrations. Once the attacking forces have reached deep into the defender's rear, the outcome has been determined. As I shall note in detail in Chapter 6, NATO employs a forward defense.

The underlying assumption for both the static defense and the forward defense is that the defender is going to contain the blitzkrieg at or near the front line. The forward defense, however, because of tactical mobility, is much more likely than the static defense to prevent a dangerous penetration. Furthermore, should a penetration occur, the forward defense is more likely to deal with it successfully. Nevertheless, if the attacker is able to effect a large-scale penetration of the front line and to begin moving into the defender's rear, neither of these defenses is well suited to counter the attacking forces.[104]

Unlike the static and forward defenses, the other two defenses do not require the majority of the defender's forces to be placed along the front line. The *defense in depth* is basically a series of prepared defensive positions arrayed in great depth and designed to wear the attacker down as he fights his way past each position. A defense in depth can be either a sequence of defensive lines or a widely dispersed pattern of individual strong points, which F. O. Miksche calls "islands of resistance."[105] The latter configuration is sometimes designated a *checkerboard defense*.[106] Although every effort is made to stop the attack at the forward positions, the defender assumes that the offense will pierce them, and he therefore distributes his resources somewhat evenly among his various strong points or lines of defense.[107] The defender could rely on retreating forces to augment his secondary and tertiary defensive positions, although some argue that defensive positions bypassed by the attacking armored columns should remain in place, where they would pose a threat to the attacker's lines of communication.[108]

Although an attacker can obviously pierce the forward positions of a defense in depth more easily than those of a static defense or a forward defense, which clearly emphasize winning the first battle and preventing the loss of territory,[109] the defense in depth is excellent for thwarting a blitzkrieg. The attacker cannot prevent the establishment of secondary defensive positions; there is no possibility of outrunning the defense. The attacker must fight a series of set-piece battles as he

[49]

attempts to punch through the defender's various positions. The defense in depth does not place a high premium on mobility, since the emphasis is on fighting from established defensive positions. Its effectiveness, however, is enhanced if forces with tactical mobility are employed. Mobility allows the defender to reinforce threatened points as well as to retreat, when forced, to secondary positions.

The major drawback of the defense in depth is that it usually requires an enormous amount of manpower. All of the various defensive positions must be well defended. Therefore this strategy is practical only when the front is relatively narrow. Since it rarely is, a defender is more likely to employ a defense in depth to protect a particularly important section of his front. The Soviets did just that in 1943 with the Kursk salient.[110]

Although the defense in depth differs from the forward defense and the static defense in that it accepts the loss of some territory (which, of course, can be recovered by launching a counterattack), all three defenses start from the assumption that the best way to counter a blitzkrieg is to contest the attacking forces vigorously at the forward edge of the battlefield, making every effort to prevent a deep strategic penetration. The same is not true of the final defense.

The *mobile defense* is a bold strategy: the defender actually allows the attacking forces to penetrate well into his rear and then, at the appropriate time, drives into the flanks of the penetration and cuts the attacking forces off from their base.[111] The attacking forces are thus encircled, allowing the defender to deal with an isolated and vulnerable target. Such a defensive strategy assumes that the flanks or shoulders of the penetration will be weak enough to cut through and that the defender will be able to isolate the armored penetrations before the attacking forces paralyze him.

A mobile defense uses a small portion of forces in forward positions and keeps the majority of them in one or more strategic reserves. The defender uses the forward-deployed forces as a screen to determine the location of the attacker's main strength and to help channel—and obstruct—the attacking forces. Once the defender has ascertained the locations of the main axes of advance, he can move his main forces to meet the attack. A mobile defense affords the defender, who relies on strategic mobility, considerable flexibility in the movement of his main forces about the battlefield. The aim is not to wear down the attacker but instead to discover and to strike at the Achilles' heel of the advancing forces, causing their collapse.[112] Doing so essentially involves delivering a counterstroke against the exposed flanks of the attacking armored spearheads. The defender employs a small fraction of his forces (sometimes called the *fixing force*) to contain and slow the attacker and then at the most propitious moment strikes at the attacker's flanks with overwhelming force. If properly executed, this counterstroke will not only inflict a decisive defeat but will also restore the territorial status quo ante.

There is widespread belief that a mobile defense is the best strategy for thwarting a blitzkrieg.[113] Reference is often made to the Germans' success with a mobile defense against the Soviets in World War II. The Germans, however, did not employ a mobile defense on the eastern front; such a defense would have been wholly inconsistent with Hitler's mandate that the German army not concede any territory to the Soviets.[114] Furthermore, there are few historical examples of a defender's employing a mobile defense and no cases of a mobile defense being used against a blitzkrieg.[115] Why? Two features of a mobile defense help account for its neglect and cast doubts on its utility. First, the task of containing or slowing the attacker's armored columns with a small portion of the defensive force and then delivering a devastating counterstroke against the attacker's vulnerable points requires excellent intelligence and considerable skill—to say the least. It is a high-risk strategy, especially as compared with one that aims simply to wear down the attacker by forcing him to fight his way through well-fortified defensive positions. Should the defender fail to find the attacker's weak points, or should he be slow in finding or exploiting them, then the blitzkrieg will succeed.

Second, it is generally accepted that when two forces clash in a battle, the defense enjoys approximately a 3:1 advantage over the offense.[116] This advantage basically results from the fact that the defender can fight from prepared positions, while the attacking forces must expose themselves as they move forward. Once the defender launches a counterstroke, which is the key ingredient in a mobile defense, he is actually assuming the offensive and is thereby forfeiting the advantages that accrue to the defender. Soviet military literature frequently refers to *encounter battles*, or to *meeting engagements*, which are battles that occur when the defender's mobile forces, while moving forward, clash directly with the attacking forces.[117] In a sense, two offensive forces meet head-on. Under such circumstances, the defender will not enjoy the natural advantages that he would have fighting from prepared positions. It is even possible, if the attacker is able to organize a coherent defense along his flanks, that that advantage will shift against the side employing a mobile defense.[118] The defender of course assumes that he will be able to identify the vulnerable points in the offensive forces and will therefore not have to combat a coherent defense. This is a risky assumption.

In sum, it is not possible to say that there is any single best strategy for stopping a blitzkrieg—simply because the utility of each depends on the circumstances. If, for example, a defender does not have enough forces to protect his forward positions, then he may be forced to adopt a mobile defense. Although this strategy is risk laden, a first-rate army should be able to employ it. The static defense is undoubtedly the least desirable strategy, although there are circumstances in which it could be used with great effect. After all, if the Allies in May 1940 had not pushed deep into Belgium and had placed a handful of first-rate divisions behind the Ardennes, the German offensive would very likely have failed.

A defense in depth is clearly an excellent strategy for meeting a blitzkrieg, although the manpower requirements make it the least likely to be selected. Finally, a forward defense is well suited for stopping an armored offensive, especially when there is a favorable force-to-space ratio along the front line and when reserve forces are available to augment those that are forward deployed.[119]

The Reemergence of the Attrition Strategy

If a blitzkrieg fails to achieve decisive results, it will evolve into an attrition strategy, as it did on the eastern front in World War II. After 1942 the Germans were clearly no longer capable of effecting a blitzkrieg against the Soviets. At the same time, the Soviets, who then had the initiative and who respected German military prowess, did not attempt to employ a blitzkrieg. As a consequence, the war on the eastern front was settled by sheer attrition. The Soviets, employing what Manstein aptly labels a steamroller strategy, simply wore down the Germans, slowly pushing them from Moscow to Berlin.[120] After the war, Guderian succinctly summarized the course of events in the European theater: "Our adversaries, so far as they were accessible to our first onslaught, were beaten by our new methods. They did not hesitate to learn from their defeats and, supported by their recurring numerical and material superiority, they then turned our own combat methods against us with the same result as in World War I."[121]

It is apparent that whether or not a blitzkrieg succeeds depends on more than the capabilities of the attacker. Simply having the organizational structure and the trained forces for a blitzkrieg is a necessary, but not sufficient, condition for success. The defender's skills as well as the terrain significantly affect the final outcome. A skillful defender can thwart a blitzkrieg; this strategy is not a foolproof means for achieving a rapid and decisive victory on the battlefield. Certainly the Soviets would have to consider the matter should they contemplate an attack against NATO. Although the Soviets might believe that their forces are organized and trained to implement a blitzkrieg, they would be fighting against NATO forces trained for an armored battlefield, and it might simply not be possible for such a Soviet strategy to succeed. The question both parties face is: will a Soviet attack resemble the German blitzkrieg of May 1940 or the fighting on the eastern front? The answer to that question will depend as much upon NATO as upon the Soviets.

The Limited Aims Strategy

To this point, our attention has focused on the attrition and blitzkrieg strategies, in which the aim is to inflict a decisive defeat on the enemy army. Now let us consider the limited aims strategy, in which the goal is to capture a segment of enemy territory. Although it is inevitable that territory will be captured when the blitzkrieg and attrition strategies are employed, the acquisition of territory is merely a by-product of the principal mission: to destroy the opponent's army.

The limited aims strategy, on the other hand, is directly concerned with seizing a specific piece of territory; at the same time, the attacker seeks to limit contact with the main body of the opposition's forces. The key to success for the attacker is the achievement of strategic surprise, which means catching the defender unprepared. The attacker seeks to gain his territorial objectives when the defense is weakest, so that it is necessary to defeat only a limited portion of the defender's forces. Given this emphasis on "the quick land grab," which places a premium on avoiding bloody engagements with the main body of the defender's forces, the choice of battlefield tactics is not as significant a concern as it is with the first two strategies. Instead, success is predicated on the ability of the attacker both to achieve surprise and to overwhelm the defender's forces that are at hand before the defender can mobilize his main forces.

After securing his objectives, the attacker shifts from an offensive to a defensive posture and prepares for a possible counterattack. The attacker-turned-defender not only enjoys the natural advantages that accrue to the defense but also ought to be well prepared to meet a counterattack. The victim, should he choose to strike back, would have to attack an alerted and prepared defense. In essence, the attacker-turned-defender is saying to the victim: you can reestablish the status quo ante only by starting a war of attrition.

[53]

Obviously the attacker will encounter some resistance during the initial offensive. Thus it will be necessary to destroy some portion, albeit a small one, of the enemy's force. The attacker deals with this resistance by relying on the overall superiority of his forces (which is a consequence of achieving strategic surprise) to crush those of the defender. It should be emphasized, however, that a limited aims strategy is *not* concerned with punishing an opponent by inflicting great damage on his army. Such damage would require the attacker to engage the defender's main body of forces in a series of bloody battles. In such a circumstance the attacking forces are hardly likely to inflict more punishment on the defender than the defender would inflict on the attacker.[122] More important, however, once the two forces are so engaged, the attacker would find it extremely difficult to stop the war at his convenience.[123]

An attacker who seeks to punish an opponent by inflicting heavy casualties on him is, for all practical purposes, pursuing an attrition strategy, which fundamentally differs from a limited aims strategy. As I have noted, with a limited aims strategy, the attacker seeks to gain his objectives before the main forces of each side become entangled; then the attacker shifts quickly to the defense. At that point, the burden of starting a war of attrition is transferred to the defender. The assumption is that the defender would not start such a war and that therefore the conflict will remain limited.

If the attacker plainly cannot achieve strategic surprise of the sort that I have described and must instead rely on tactical surprise, then he must undoubtedly reduce his territorial objectives.[124] An offender who cannot effect strategic surprise has fewer opportunities to secure his objectives before the defender can respond with *his* main body of forces. From the attacker's point of view, it is essential to avoid large-scale battles with the defender's alerted forces. Without strategic surprise, however, this is a difficult task—especially against a defender who has the capability of reacting quickly to unexpected threats. Thus we see the desirability of achieving strategic surprise.

As with the blitzkrieg, we must consider the limited aims strategy in light of specific defensive strategies. Success depends, to a large extent, on the configuration of the defense, although the defender's capabilities cannot be ignored. With the static and forward defenses, the majority of the defender's forces are deployed in forward positions. If the forces are maintained in these positions during peacetime and are kept at a reasonable rate of readiness, then even if the attacker achieves strategic surprise, he is likely to meet stiff resistance. On the other hand, if the defender does not normally maintain his forces in their forward positions (which is the case with NATO), then the attacker should have little trouble gaining his objectives if he achieves strategic surprise. When strategic surprise is impossible, tactical surprise is necessary. This alternative is not desirable, especially if the defense has the requisite mobility (forward defense) for countering the advantages that accrue to the offense as a consequence of tactical surprise. Obviously, a defense designed to stop an attack at its starting points is best for thwarting a limited aims strategy—assuming, of course, that the defender's forces are in their forward positions when the attack begins.

The defense in depth is a somewhat more attractive target than either of the linear defenses, because here the defender has some forces placed in secondary and tertiary positions. In this case the defender accepts penetration of the forward units. Therefore the danger is that the attacker, taking advantage of tactical surprise, will pierce the forward positions, will capture a piece of territory, and will stop—refusing to wear himself out by striking further. If the defender's forces are not normally located in their fighting positions, of course, and if the attacker believes he can gain strategic surprise, then there is good reason to pursue a limited aims strategy.

The ideal defense when the attacker is pursuing limited objectives is the mobile defense. In this case the defender actually encourages deep penetration by the offense. In effect, the attacker is guaranteed the benefits of strategic surprise, since the defense is willing to concede territory. The defender accepts the loss of territory because he believes that his counterstroke will inflict on the attacking forces a defeat that will enable him to regain any territory initially lost. Against such a defense, an attacker pursuing limited objectives will succeed if he is not greedy. More specifically, the attacker must be sure to halt his forces before the defense launches its counterstroke, thus forcing the defender to strike against a well-prepared offense-turned-defense. In sum, the configuration of the defense and the level of readiness of the defender significantly affect the attacker's chances of effecting a limited aims strategy.

When strategic surprise is possible, the limited aims strategy has a high probability of success; it is simply not as ambitious a strategy as one that aims at decisive defeat of the enemy. Furthermore, given strategic surprise, the specific capabilities of the defense, which are so important for an attacker contemplating the employment of a blitzkrieg or an attrition strategy, are really not very important—since the attacker is betting that he can achieve his goals before the defender can respond with all of his forces. Simply stated, the limited aims strategy, relative to the two other options, is low risk. Equally important, the costs associated with this strategy are low, obviously because of the assailant's interest in avoiding costly engagements with the defender's main forces.

Given such a deterrence matrix, we might expect a potential attacker with the capability of implementing the limited aims strategy to do so in a crisis. It seems reasonable to conclude that, viewed in terms of military costs and likelihood of success, the limited aims strategy would be more attractive than the blitzkrieg and certainly more attractive than the attrition strategy. Two important factors, however, diminish its appeal. First, as I will argue, modern nation-states display a strong tendency to favor the pursuit of decisive victories, and decision makers invariably first seek a way to score one. Only if they cannot find a suitable strategy do they consider the limited alternative. Second, the limited aims strategy is predicated on the assumption that, once the attacker's military objectives have been achieved, the victim will either do nothing militarily or will launch a large-scale counterattack eventually so costly that he will abandon further military action. Thus there will be an explicit and rapid conclusion to the military phase of the conflict. If the victim chooses to continue fighting, however, the result will be a lengthy war of attrition, which is hardly desirable. Such an outcome is very likely because the defender's key decision makers will undoubtedly be under great pressure to recapture the lost territory and to punish the aggressor. If such a scenario seems very probable, the attacker is most likely to conclude that he would do well to defeat the opponent decisively—thus erasing any chance of a lengthy and costly war. At that point, only one consideration remains: Does the attacker have the capability to inflict a rapid and decisive defeat on the victim? More specifically, does he have the capability to effect a blitzkreig?

Employing the Blitzkrieg and Attrition Strategies for Limited Objectives

Although a blitzkrieg might be employed to capture a piece of an opponent's territory, for a number of reasons it is unlikely to be used for such a purpose. First, the strategy is, by its very nature, concerned with the destruction of the opponent's forces. Success results from the deep strategic penetration, which paralyzes the defender's army. To halt the attacking forces after they had occupied some territory would be to vitiate the blitzkrieg, since the defender would be allowed to regroup and to establish new defensive positions. More important, the vulnerable flanks of the attacking armored columns would be exposed to a counterattack by a defense allowed to regain its balance.[125] Once a blitzkrieg has been launched, it must be allowed to pursue its objective of bringing about the collapse of the opponent's military forces.

Second, if a potential attacker has the capability of implementing a successful blitzkrieg, he is highly unlikely to undertake one for limited purposes, given that the same strategy can be used to achieve a decisive victory—which, as I have noted, modern nation-states invariably prefer to limited victories. Furthermore, the attacker must consider the disturbing possibility that a limited victory will evolve into a protracted conflict.

Under one circumstance, however, a blitzkrieg might be used to gain limited objectives. When the defender has a number of separate armies that are deployed across a vast land mass, then the attacker could launch a blitzkrieg to destroy one of the defender's armies and could occupy the territory that the vanquished army was holding. Certainly the Germans could have followed such a course of action when they invaded the Soviet Union in 1941. They could have destroyed the Soviet forces west of the Dnieper River and could then have halted their forces to establish a strong defensive position.[126] In the end, however, the Germans tried to defeat the Soviet military machine decisively.[127]

Unlike the blitzkrieg, the attrition strategy could easily be employed in pursuit of limited objectives. An attacker would be unlikely, however, to use a truncated version of the attrition strategy for such a purpose. If we accept the supposition that the objective of a limited strategy is to capture territory, then the limited aims strategy is much more desirable than an abridged version of the attrition strategy. The cost of the former strategy is much lower, and the probability of success is greater. In sum, an attacker would hardly ever employ either the blitzkrieg or the attrition strategy for limited purposes.

We must consider one final aspect of battlefield strategies. As I have noted, success with the limited aims strategy depends largely on achieving strategic surprise. Ideally the attacker would present the defender with a fait accompli. We may well ask whether the same strategy could be used on a grander scale to defeat the enemy decisively. Although it might be theoretically, realistically such use would be impractical. For such a strategy to succeed, the defender would have to be caught completely unaware, and then the attacker would have to be able to destroy the defender's army before the defender had a chance to mobilize his forces and to offer serious resistance. In an area of potential conflict, neither condition is likely to obtain. During the period between the world wars, the French were deeply concerned that the Germans would inflict just such a defeat on them, by means of what the French termed an *attaque brusquée*.[128] These fears proved to be unfounded. The fear of such an attack by the Warsaw Pact is also mentioned from time to time in the West.[129]

In sum, policy makers are likely to be faced with at least one of three different options: The attrition, blitzkrieg, and limited aims strategies. Each has different implications for deterrence. Although I shall discuss this matter in greater detail shortly, a brief word is in order at this point. The blitzkrieg, because it promises a quick victory at a relatively low cost, is very likely to lead to deterrence failures. The attrition strategy, because of its very high costs, is likely to lead to deterrence successes—even if the attacker believes that he will ultimately prevail. The implications of the limited aims strategy for deterrence are more difficult to assess. This strategy is attractive because the task facing the attacker is not particularly difficult. It is the least ambitious of the three strategies. It has, however, two important drawbacks. There is the possibility that the victim will not accept the change in the status quo and will continue fighting, turning the conflict into a war of attrition. Moreover, as I shall explain, modern nation-states view limited wars with considerable skepticism.

Finally, I should emphasize that no strategy is risk free. The amount of risk depends on the defender's capabilities and on the terrain as well as on the attacker's capabilities. This point brings us to a very important subject: the overall balance of forces as it affects deterrence.

Strategy and Numbers

Implicit in the foregoing discussion is the assumption that the forces available to both sides show no great disparity.[130] For this reason an attrition strategy necessarily involves a long war. Although an attacker might have the requisite advantage to win a protracted war, he does not have an advantage so great that he could win a quick victory by simply overwhelming the defender. My discussion of the blitzkrieg also assumed that both sides were somewhat evenly matched in terms of force levels. Appropriately, a failed blitzkrieg would lead to a war of attrition.

Now consider the case where the potential attacker's force is significantly larger than the defender's. By *significantly larger* I mean a clear-cut superiority on one side that does not preclude all possibility that the outnumbered defender could thwart the attack. In other words, our numerically superior attacker must consider the possibility that he might not achieve his aims on the battlefield. This situation contrasts with the case in which the asymmetry is so great that the attacker does not have the slightest doubt that he will succeed on the battlefield. After all, if the attacker is certain of the outcome, the concept of deterrence does not really apply, since military considerations could not possibly act as a brake. Therefore, I focus here on cases that show only a marked asymmetry and admit of some uncertainty regarding ultimate victory.

Even with a marked force advantage, the attacker will still have to employ one of the three principal strategies. Given such a balance of forces, the attacker is highly unlikely to pursue a limited aims strategy. Nevertheless, should he choose to do so, he is almost certain to succeed. It *is* possible that an attacker would launch a blitzkrieg, in which case an imbalance of forces would certainly enhance the prospects for success.[131] A marked imbalance of forces has the most profound impact on the attrition strategy. As I previously noted, an attrition strategy involves a long war in which the side with greater resources is likely to emerge victorious. The war is protracted simply because there is no great disparity between the resources available to both sides. If there is a marked disparity, however, and the potential attacker believes that his forces will have to be employed in accordance with the dictates of the attrition strategy, he will strike across a broad front, using the advantage in numbers to overwhelm the defender. In this case the conflict can be expected to be short, since the attacker is clearly superior to the defender. Thus, in a strict definitional sense, this is not an attrition strategy. When an attacker is faced with the prospect of employing such a modified attrition strategy, deterrence is likely to fail.

As an example, consider the summer of 1939, when the Germans contemplated an attack on Poland.[132] The Germans believed that their army was far superior to the Polish army in terms of both quality and quantity. They were confident that they could overpower the Poles in a short campaign. At the time, the Germans had not adopted a blitzkrieg, as we shall see in Chapter 4. When they struck on 1 September 1939, they employed an attrition strategy that (very importantly) promised a rapid success.[133]

Generally when one side has an overwhelming advantage in forces, deterrence is very likely to fail—regardless of the chosen strategy.

This finding is hardly surprising when the attacker is considering either a blitzkrieg or a limited aims strategy. Deterrence is also very likely to fail, however, when the attacker plans to employ his forces in accordance with an attrition strategy, because the attacker can expect to overwhelm the defender quickly and thus to avoid a long, costly conflict.

THE POLITICAL-MILITARY CONTEXT

To this point, I have focused on the military considerations that underlie the decision to go to war. Conventional deterrence, however, is ultimately based on a broader relationship. In the final analysis, the military factors must be viewed in conjunction with the expected political gains.[134] In other words, we assume that, in a crisis, decision makers weigh the value of the desired political objective against the risks and costs of a military campaign to achieve them.

The Dynamics of the Decision-Making Process

When nations resort to war, they do so because they have political objectives worth fighting for, not simply because they have the military capability to defeat the opponent. There must be an underlying political purpose, however broadly defined, for using military force. As Clausewitz noted, war may have its own language but not its own logic.[135] Although political considerations provide the impetus, the actual decision to go to war results from the complex interplay of political and military considerations. We must examine this dynamic process in some detail.

During a crisis, tremendous pressure is placed on the military to devise a strategy that minimizes the costs and risks of military action yet promises attainment of the desired political aims. It is certainly possible that the military might have a well-regarded strategy at an early point in the crisis, thus removing this tension in the decision-making process. Such is *often* not the case, however, as will be evident from my case studies. Until an unexceptionable plan is produced, pressure on the military continues, stemming both from the political leadership and from within the military itself. All participants have a vested interest in reducing the risks and costs of military action.

However much stress is placed on the military, the final plan may be one that barely satisfies a small number of the key decision makers. It is also possible that no feasible military strategy will be found. There are limits as to how far any military can be pushed. For this reason wars are ultimately shaped not only by the chosen political objectives but also by the military means available to achieve them: military capabilities inevitably affect political calculations. More generally, in a crisis, military and political considerations constantly interact in a dialectical fashion. Although nations wage war for political reasons, the reciprocal relationship between military and political considerations determines whether or not they decide to go to war.

Another aspect of the relationship between political and military factors merits attention. Given that war is an instrument of policy, we might assume that civilian policy makers determine the specific political objectives and then oversee the military's conduct of war, ensuring that military objectives are commensurate with political goals. This view is not inconsistent with the fact that military capabilities influence the choice of strategy. I am assuming, of course, that the political element has considerable flexibility in selecting (specifically, in limiting) political objectives, as well as the appropriate influence over the selection of military objectives.

In practice, however, civilian decision makers exert much less control over the direction of policy than they do in theory. The principal reason for this lack of firm control is, as noted above, that the modern nation-state shows a strong tendency to favor pursuit of decisive victories. Conversely, there is a strong prejudice against strategies based on limited objectives. The bias toward decisive victories results from a number of factors that I shall mention only briefly. They include the natural preference of military officers,[136] the rise of the mass army, the effect of industrialization on warfare, the increasing democratization of societies, and the impact of nationalism.[137]

Which considerations, then, are decisive? First, although political considerations drive a nation toward war, policy makers are likely to be constrained by the limitations of their military instrument as well as by pressure to aim for a decisive victory. In certain circumstances, undeniably, the key policy makers themselves may favor a decisive victory and, moreover, may have a military fully capable of achieving that end. Second, I have emphasized that significant pressure is always placed on the military to devise a strategy that minimizes both risks and costs while also leading to a decisive victory. Finally, given the bias toward decisive victories, the most effective countervailing forces are two: an uncharacteristically strong political leader and a military known to be incapable of achieving a decisive victory.

The Final Decision

Although decision makers constantly analyze the balance between the perceived political benefits and the potential costs and risks of military action, the final judgment in this dynamic process determines whether or not deterrence fails.[138] I have emphasized throughout this chapter that deterrence is most likely to obtain when a potential attacker believes his probability of success on the battlefield to be low and the attendant costs to be high. Although raising both the costs and risks of military action significantly reduces the likelihood of war, however, it does not guarantee that deterrence will obtain, simply because the political consequences of continued peace may be so unacceptable that a nation is tempted to pursue an unattractive course of action. That is, decision makers must weigh the political risks of not striking in the balance with the military risks of striking.[139] Let us examine this matter in greater detail.

Suppose that the political costs of not going to war are not great, that although there are compelling reasons to consider war, the decision makers may yet decide either for or against it. In such a case, if the costs and risks of military action are thought to be high, deterrence is almost certain to obtain. War is likely to break out only if the decision makers believe that military action will be relatively risk free and that the attendant costs will be quite low.

Actually, however, the political considerations that move a nation toward war are likely to be much more unyielding in nature, hence the great pressure brought to bear on the military to find a military solution. Naturally, if a satisfactory plan is found, deterrence will almost surely fail. The more interesting question is: What happens if such a solution is not found? In this case, the risks of both military action and continued peace are great.

The political consequences of continued peace might be so unacceptable as to tempt a nation to launch a war it did not expect to win. Such a course of action is most unlikely, for two reasons. First, how could a nation improve its position by starting a war it expected to lose? As Bismarck once noted, the nation would be "committing suicide from fear of death."[140] Second, the future is unlikely to seem so hopeless that suicide is warranted. In short, if a nation is certain that failure awaits it on the battlefield, deterrence is very likely to obtain. The whole matter becomes much more problematic when decision makers generally disagree about the probable outcome on the battlefield but agree that the operative military strategy is risky and potentially costly. In such a case the degree of military risk that

[62]

a potential attacker is willing to accept will vary directly with the political costs that result from continued peace. In other words, intense political pressures may force decision makers to take risk-laden military actions.

The theory developed in this book starts with the assumption that deterrence is a function of the particular military strategy available to the potential attacker. Policy makers are concerned with determining the deployment of their forces on the battlefield and the course of events when the attacker engages the defender. In other words, a potential attacker must consider not only his own capabilities but also those of the defender and the nature of the terrain on which the battle will be fought.

Each of the three strategies that an attacker may employ on the battlefield has different implications for deterrence. The limited aims strategy, in terms of execution, is the least risky and also the least costly of the three because it is the least ambitious strategy and because the attacking forces seek to minimize contact with the defender's forces. Nevertheless, the limited aims strategy is not nearly as commonplace as we might expect. Two factors detract from its appeal. First, modern nation-states show a pronounced preference for decisive victories. As the threat of war grows, pressure builds to find a way "to win the war." Second, there is a real danger that a successful limited attack will evolve into a protracted war—simply because the defender, who has not been decisively defeated, will continue fighting. The same powerful forces that make it so difficult for an attacker to pursue limited objectives serve to increase the likelihood that the defender will not accept a limited defeat. This possibility of a protracted war, when it exists, makes the limited aims strategy a risky course of action. For these reasons, nations prefer to find a way to defeat an opponent quickly and decisively.

The blitzkrieg provides a means to score a rapid and decisive victory. For this reason, there will be great pressure moving a nation's military planners toward a blitzkrieg. Those planners will of course not necessarily always reach the conclusion that they can effect a blitzkrieg. There are limits as to how far a nation's military can be pushed. Nevertheless, if a potential attacker believes that he can launch a successful blitzkrieg, deterrence is very likely to fail.

[63]

The blitzkrieg is clearly the most desirable of the three strategies and therefore the one most likely to lead to a deterrence failure.

If a potential attacker believes that he can secure a decisive victory only by means of an attrition strategy, deterrence is very likely to obtain. Because of the very high costs and the difficulty of projecting the final outcome in a long war, the attrition strategy is the least desirable of the three—and the one most likely to be associated with deterrence success. Liddell Hart, whose views were profoundly influenced by his experience in the Great War, once remarked, "Of what use is decisive victory in battle if we bleed to death as a result of it?"[141] His rhetorical question lays bare the foundation of conventional deterrence.

If a potential attacker cannot effect a blitzkrieg, he will undoubtedly consider employing a limited aims strategy. Despite the lack of real enthusiasm for this strategy, it is an attractive alternative to the attrition strategy. Once the limited aims strategy is deemed worthy of consideration, the key question is: Will a limited victory lead to a war of attrition? If the answer is yes, deterrence is likely to obtain; if the answer is no, deterrence is likely to fail. As I noted above, deterrence is best served when the attacker believes that his only alternative is a protracted war: the threat of a war of attrition is the bedrock of conventional deterrence.

We must also recall that the course of events on the battlefield depends on the defender's actions as well as on the offender's. A war of attrition, in other words, might be the deliberate choice at the outset *or* the result of a failed blitzkrieg or limited aims strategy.

Risk and Deterrence

Once policy makers have decided to employ either a blitzkrieg or limited aims strategy, the possibility still remains that the chosen strategy will fail. Although decision makers, on balance, may be confident that they can successfully implement the chosen plan, there will always be attendant risks. The key question is: Just how risky is the chosen strategy? Obviously, the riskier it is, the less likely that it will be employed. There will certainly be great pressure to reduce the risks, but at best it is possible only to lessen their degree, not to eliminate them completely. But we must bear in mind two other important points about risk.

First, as I have emphasized, risk is a function of the capabilities of both the attacker and the defender. My discussion to this point has assumed that the size of the opposing forces is roughly equal. Thus capability is largely a function of such factors as strategy and fighting skills. Now let us assume marked disparity in the size of the opposing forces such that the attacker has a clear-cut numerical advantage.[142] In such cases, the attacker's risks are likely to diminish significantly. Although this point may seem obvious, it merits some elaboration.

Military planners generally tend to be conservative when estimating enemy capabilities.[143] They are more likely than not to overestimate enemy strength. This bias, coupled with the general desire to find the optimum way to defeat the enemy, means that even when the attacker enjoys a significant force advantage, he will still feel considerable pressure to find an alternative to the attrition strategy—pressure, more specifically, to opt for a blitzkrieg.[144] If a potential attacker greatly outnumbers his opponent and also believes that he can effect a blitzkrieg, deterrence is almost certain to fail—regardless of the risks—because, even if the blitzkrieg fails, the attacker will still have the important advantage of numbers. We should recall that when a definite asymmetry in the size of the opposing forces favors the attacker, he can employ his forces in accordance with the dictates of an attrition strategy and can still win a relatively quick and decisive victory.[145]

Thus we may reasonably conclude that when a potential attacker enjoys an overwhelming force advantage, the importance of discovering and successfully implementing the optimum military strategy is not as great as when the forces are essentially balanced. In the former case, if problems arise in executing the strategy, the attacker can still rely on his numerical strength to overwhelm the defender quickly. He cannot do so in the latter case. Thus risk is likely to figure more importantly when there is little disparity in the size of the opposing forces. And in such cases risk is directly linked with the fighting skills and chosen strategies of both sides.

The second point about risk concerns the relationship between military considerations and the broader political forces that move a nation toward war. As I have noted, decision makers must consider the political consequences of continued peace as well as the purely military aspects of war.[146] In other words, planners must weigh the political risks of *not* striking together with the military risks of striking. In a crisis, therefore, a nation might well be forced to employ a risk-laden military strategy simply because the political consequences of not going to war would be so ominous. Increases in military risks do not guarantee that deterrence will hold in a crisis, although they certainly increase the likelihood that it will. Because in the final analysis the degree of risk that an attacker is willing to assume is determined by political considerations, the possibility of conventional deterrence is ultimately a function of the relationship between military calculations and the political considerations that drive a nation to consider war.

[3]

The Allied Decision Not to Attack
Germany, March 1939–May 1940

The German army invaded Poland on 1 September 1939. Two days later, Britain and France, having given Poland a security guarantee some five months earlier, declared war against Germany. The Allies, however, took no military action against Germany while Hitler's forces were fighting in Poland.[1] After the fall of Poland the Allies remained on the defensive. Soon the situation on the western front was being referred to as the *Phoney War*, or *Sitzkrieg*. The period of inactivity, which lasted eight months, ended on 10 May 1940, when the Germans struck in the West. The Allies, who were awaiting the German onslaught, had had no concrete plans themselves for ending the Phoney War. In essence, they had simply been deterred from attacking Germany.

Allied inaction is usually not described in these terms because, de jure, a state of war existed between Germany and the Allies. And since we know that a real war broke out in May 1940, it seems inappropriate to talk about deterrence. Moreover, Allied grand strategy called for assuming the offensive in the distant future, regardless of whether or not the Germans attacked in the West. Thus it can be argued that the Phoney War was only a temporary delay before the Allies launched their offensive. Yet even if we accept this argument, the fact remains that the Allies were deterred from taking military action against Germany in the short run which, according to Allied calculations, would have been a period of at least two to three years. The Allies believed that if they had attacked Germany before 1942, they would not have been successful and would have paid a high price for their failure. Both the French and the British felt that it was to their advantage to remain on the defensive. In short, deterrence operated. Although the Allies hoped that the situation would change significantly in the long run so that they could launch an attack and crush Germany, we might cogently argue that if the Germans had not attacked in the West, the Allies would have never assumed the offensive. The same reasoning that led the Allies to eschew the offensive in the early period of the war would undoubtedly have prevailed in the distant future as well. Although any discussion about probable events after May 1940 had the Germans not attacked must remain somewhat speculative, such is not the case for the period from September 1939 to May 1940. The record clearly indicates that the Allies were deterred from striking Germany. In this chapter I shall show why.

Allied decision makers believed that a war with Germany would be, for the most part, a repetition of World War I; an attrition strategy would again be necessary to defeat Germany. Allied leaders saw no alternative to this strategy, which had produced a narrow victory two decades earlier at a staggering cost. Although the Allies were willing to declare war, they were not willing to launch an offensive predicated on an attrition strategy. They preferred to remain on the defensive. Although there was talk of eventually taking the offensive, we have little reason to believe that the Allies would ever have left their defensive positions along the western front to strike Germany. The prospect of employing an attrition strategy against a strong Germany was a powerful deterrent to offensive action.

The Allied decisions made in the months before the fall of Poland, as well as those that followed in the wake of Poland's defeat, cannot be viewed in isolation from the evolution of British and French military thought during the interwar period. The roots of Allied behavior are deeply embedded in the events of those twenty years. Allied decisions in the 1939–1940 period were wholly consistent with the military doctrine and plans that the French and British had developed in the 1920s and 1930s; the conduct of the Allies in the early stages of World War II was merely the final chapter in a long story. To understand this conduct it is therefore necessary to explore in some detail the development of military thought in Britain and France[2] during the interwar period.

FRENCH MILITARY THOUGHT

The Threat

Throughout the period between the World Wars, French leaders, whether military or civilian, left wing or right wing, were fully aware

[68]

of the German threat on their eastern frontier.[3] They had no illusions about the long-term viability of the agreement reached at Versailles. Appropriately, they committed much time and considerable resources to preparing for a possible conflict with Germany.[4] For them, the security problem was of paramount importance.

Generally, the French felt that they had been matched against an aggressive neighbor whose military potential far outstripped their own. A number of factors lay at the heart of the French security problem. First, the French manpower base did not compare favorably with the German. In the early 1920s the German population totaled 60 million, the French population 40 million.[5] By the late 1930s, the German population had grown by approximately 10 million, while the French figure had increased by only 2.7 million.[6] The French problem was compounded by anticipation of the "hollow years" (1935–1939), when the low birth rates of the World War I period would be reflected in a diminished pool of conscripts.[7]

The second element of the problem was that the French industrial base was smaller than the German industrial base. In fact, Germany's industrial strength was approximately three times as great as France's.[8] Moreover, the 1930s were a period of serious economic decline for France, while at the same time Germany experienced sustained economic growth.[9] As will become apparent, for the French military, comparative industrial strength and manpower levels were key indicators of battlefield prospects. Relative to Germany, France was in a precarious position.

The third problem facing France was that her eastern border from Switzerland to Dunkirk had few natural obstacles that would help stop an invader.[10] To make matters worse, a significant portion of the French industrial base was located close to the German border.[11] The French felt that the loss of a large portion of northeastern France, which occurred in World War I, would make it impossible to continue the war. The French had to prevent the Germans from capturing any French territory.

The final element of the French predicament was the absence of powerful allies. In light of the existing French and German manpower levels and industrial strength, the French needed allies to balance the scales, if not to tip them in France's favor. In short, France needed Britain. Thus the French declared in April 1939: "Even today we could only defeat Germany in a war if we were assured, in every possible respect, of total British assistance."[12] Still, Anglo-French relations between the wars were characterized by bitter conflict and mutual distrust.[13] Throughout the 1920s and 1930s, the French had little reason to believe that Britain would commit itself to a land war on the Continent. In fact, it was not until the early months of 1939 that the British finally decided that they would fight alongside the French against Germany.

Given the dimensions of their security problem, the French naturally focused their attention on protecting themselves. Defense became the overriding concern of French policy makers.[14] Such a frame of reference was hardly conducive to thinking in terms of offensive action against Germany. In addition, however, the views of the French military on the nature of modern warfare helped shape the French preference for a defensive posture. It is therefore appropriate for us to turn from the specifics of the French predicament to the more abstract matter of French military thinking on the probable nature of the post–World War I battlefield.

The French Concept of Modern Warfare

On the eve of World War I, French military doctrine emphasized that success on the battlefield resulted when the attacking forces manifested the proper offensive spirit.[15] Moral force was considered the key to victory. Employing this philosophy in the first years of the war, the French suffered overwhelming losses. Clearly they had underestimated the importance of firepower on the battlefield. In response to this costly misjudgment, the French completely reversed their position. By 1918 they were firmly convinced that firepower and material superiority were the keys to victory. After the war this view continued to prevail among French military leaders. For the vast majority of French officers, the battlefields of the future would hardly differ from those of the Great War.[16] War was viewed primarily as a series of firepower exchanges in which the defender enjoyed a decided advantage.

The introduction of the tank did not alter the view of the French. A handful of officers, however, believed that the tank could revolutionize warfare. In the 1920s, the most vocal proponent of this notion was Gen. Jean-Baptiste Estienne, who had little success in promoting his ideas.[17] A lively debate centered on the role of the tank and on the content of army doctrine when in the 1930s DeGaulle became the principal advocate of using tanks to effect a blitzkrieg.[18] DeGaulle had a powerful ally in Paul Reynaud, who championed the general's views before parliament.[19] Still, DeGaulle's views never posed a real threat to the official French concept of war.[20] Looking back on the interwar period, we must be impressed by the continuity of thought between the last years of World War I and the fall of France in May 1940.[21]

The specific features of the French concept of war that evolved between the world wars are not difficult to discern. The core assumption was that war is a veritable slugging match; the opposing sides attempt to wear each other down with greater and greater increments of firepower. French military literature of the period repeated the same message: "La défense est le feu qui arrête; l'attaque est le feu qui marche; la manoeuvre est le feu qui se déplace."[22] For the French, victory on the battlefield resulted from successful employment of an attrition strategy. Consequently, the French placed great emphasis on artillery, which they officially christened the "arm of fire *par excellence*."[23] The artillery, of course, was to be used in coordination with advancing infantry. Concentrated artillery fire, however, made it possible for the infantry to move forward.

The central premise that attrition resulting from firepower exchanges determines battlefield success had a corollary: material superiority is essential for victory. If both sides were going to try to wear each other down to the point of capitulation, then obviously the side with material superiority would prevail. But the matter was not quite so straightforward, because there was an important asymmetry between the offense and the defense. Specifically, the defending forces suffered fewer losses than the attacking forces. Therefore, if a nation planned to assume the offensive, it needed to have a significant advantage in material and in numbers of soldiers. Conversely, a defender who had neither material nor numerical superiority might conduct a successful defense. Not surprisingly, the French envisioned themselves in the latter position.

Nevertheless, French military leaders clearly envisioned their offensive, maintaining that it should employ frontal attacks like those of World War I. The *Instruction sur l'emploi tactique des grandes unités* (1936), which outlined basic French doctrine, advocated the "use of large numbers of tanks, spread out over a wide area, and echeloned in depth" to "aid the progression of infantry and disperse enemy anti-tank and artillery fire."[24] Furthermore, the French offensive would be methodical, emphasizing careful planning and preparation and taking time to unfold. Describing a possible Allied offensive, General Gamelin said in 1939: "The advance of the Allied forces will be very methodical, and governed by the speed of infantry elements, from one battlefield to another, and care will be taken on each of these to establish anti-tank defences."[25] The speed of the infantry, however, depended on the speed of the supporting artillery. In light of the

[71]

importance that the French attached to massing artillery along a broad front, there were very significant limits on the speed with which a French attack could proceed: it would be like a slow-moving steamroller.

French military leaders considered the tank to be an essential component of their army, and they did in fact deploy it in large numbers. Tanks were, however, to be used, in accordance with the dictates of an attrition strategy,[26] as infantry support and like traditional cavalry, following the precedent set by the Allies in the Great War. Thus not until after the start of the Second World War did the French organize their first armored divisions.[27] Significantly, the French did not believe in the possibility of penetrating the opponent's front and then using the tank's mobility to strike deep into his rear.[28] The defender, they reasoned, would be able to seal off any penetrations quickly, reestablishing the continuous front.

The French also placed a high premium on fortifications, a tradition with deep roots in French history.[29] Of course, the recent French experience at Verdun had demonstrated the value of fortifications in a firepower-oriented battle. In addition to affording protective cover for combatants and guns, fortifications allowed the manpower-hungry French army to make the most economical use of its forces. Although fortifications were primarily defensive in nature, they also facilitated offensive operations by serving as points of departure for the attacking forces.

One peculiar aspect of French military thinking merits our attention. In light of French views on the proper conduct of an offensive, we might expect to discover that France expected Germany to launch a similar sort of attack. After all, the French believed that war is a series of firepower duels between two cumbersome armies engaged on a broad front. Interestingly, during the interwar period, the French constantly worried that the Germans would launch what was commonly termed an attaque brusquée,[30] "a sudden attack of extreme intensity by a German striking force of small but powerful units."[31] The attaque brusquée would succeed primarily because the Germans would strike when the French were unprepared to fend off an attack. That is, the Germans would catch the French off guard and would deliver a knockout blow before the French army could fully mobilize.

At first glance, such an offensive would seem to produce a type of war very different from that for which the French were readying themselves. Yet such was not the case. The French felt that if they were properly prepared, they could thwart an attaque brusquée, and a war of attrition would ensue. If the attaque brusquée succeeded, it would do so not because the Germans defeated the French on the battlefield but instead because the Germans caught the French unprepared. In sum, the French believed that if the Germans were forced to fight against them, the French notion of attrition warfare would prevail.[32]

The French Plan for Meeting a German Attack

Given the dimensions of the French security problem and the prevailing French view regarding the nature of warfare in the post–World War I era, how did the French plan to deal with the German threat? Anticipating a war similar to the Great War, the French mapped out a coherent plan that enjoyed widespread acceptance in military as well as political circles.[33] Its first component was the belief that the conflict with Germany would be long. There would be no quick victories, no lightning knockout blow. Furthermore, to defeat Germany, it would be necessary to mobilize the entire French nation.[34] The French economy would have to be organized so as to maximize its war potential,[35] and the army would have to expand to absorb all available manpower. In a protracted war of attrition, the side with superior manpower and firepower would emerge victorious.

The third component of the French plan was the assumption that the projected long war would have a defensive and an offensive stage. It would be necessary to stop the Germans first and to wear them down with a defensive strategy while France and her allies built up their strength for an offensive. Only after a lengthy period in a defensive posture would the French consider taking the offensive. This sequence of events guaranteed that French military planners would be preoccupied with devising a successful defensive posture, not an offensive strategy.

The lengthy defensive stage would serve two important functions. First, it would provide time for France and her allies to mobilize and to develop the superiority in material and manpower required for an offensive. The underlying supposition was that France and its allies would prove stronger than Germany in the long run. Given the necessary time, an allied force could be built that would overwhelm the German army. Second, because the attacker usually suffers greater casualties than the defender, the attacking Germans would suffer more casualties in the initial period of the war. German losses would help shift the balance of forces in France's favor, which would make the offensive stage much easier.

Finally, the French plan called for establishing a continuous front along the eastern border, behind which the entire nation would mobilize for total war.[36] It was imperative not to surrender territory to the Germans. The French therefore required a tight, unyielding line of defense. Because of their belief in fortifications, the French had built the famed Maginot Line along the Franco-German border (see figure 3.1). Ironically, however, this barrier, which was formidable, greatly increased the likelihood that a German attack would come through Belgium—a point not lost on the French.[37] For a variety of reasons, the French did not seriously consider extending their fortification to the Channel coast. Instead they preferred to move their forces into Belgium and to fight from fortified positions in that country. If it were necessary to retreat, they could move back to the Franco-Belgian border, thus ensuring that no French territory would be lost. After Belgium declared its neutrality in 1936, however, the problem of defending the Franco-Belgian border became more complex.

In short, the French plan for fighting the Germans was clearly oriented toward maintaining the defensive in a long war of attrition. The French were primarily concerned with protecting themselves against a German onslaught. Once they had done so, then it might be possible to consider an offensive. Marshal Pétain, who greatly influenced French military thinking during the interwar years, succinctly summarized the French objectives in a war: "first, not to be beaten; then, to beat the enemy."[38]

The Diplomatic Front

Diplomacy was also a crucial element in the French design. It was widely recognized in both military and political circles that diplomatic initiatives and military considerations were inextricably linked.[39] If a nation plans to fight a protracted war in which numbers of men and industrial strength ultimately decide the outcome, then allies can significantly increase that nation's prospects for success. Since France did not compare favorably with Germany in either of these categories, allies were essential—especially if there was to be any hope of assuming the offensive.

As I have previously noted, the French were committed to enlisting British support in a war with Germany. They were particularly

Figure 3.1. The Maginot Line

interested in having the British fight side by side with them on the Continent. The French were also concerned about finding allies in Eastern Europe. Here, the aim was to force Germany to fight a two-front war, a situation that would work to France's advantage in a number of ways. First, a two-front war would force Germany to divert resources to her eastern front, thus limiting the strength of the forces she could deploy in the west. Moreover, the French would have assistance in bleeding the Germans white, which in turn, would hasten the day of reckoning when France and her allies had the numerical and material superiority necessary for assuming the offensive. Finally, a second front would deny Germany access to the raw materials and trading partners otherwise available in Eastern Europe. This consideration was crucial, since the French, envisioning

British assistance, planned to rely on a naval blockade to strangle Germany economically.[40]

Without an eastern front, the French position in a war with Germany would be seriously impaired. Germany could then concentrate all her forces against France. Furthermore, Germany's military machine would then have access to the economic resources of Eastern Europe. As General Weygand noted, "The Eastern front was so important [because] the East possessed the raw materials which would enable Germany to prosecute a war of long duration."[41] Without a second front, the French task in a war with Germany would be awesome.

Although the French sought to build a cohesive alliance structure that could sustain a second front, their overall plan contained a fundamental contradiction. Since the French army was designed to defend France and did not have the capability to take rapid offensive action, Germany might possibly eliminate France's eastern allies while the French remained on the defensive, putting little, if any, pressure on Germany.[42] In other words, there was a basic conflict between the military and the diplomatic aspects of the French scheme. This problem prompted DeGaulle to advocate developing an offensive capability. He argued:

> What happens, for instance, to Central and Eastern Europe, to Denmark, to Belgium, to the Saar or to Switzerland affects us substantially.
>
> In the present state of the world the very trend of our destiny leads us to make use of an ever-ready instrument of intervention for purposes of active assistance. *Then only shall we have the army of our policy.* [Emphasis added][43]

DeGaulle's proposal was not accepted; the French (and the British, too) maintained that the eastern allies' salvation rested in the war's final outcome.[44] The chances of a favorable outcome would of course be seriously damaged once the French (and the British) were without allies in the East. The French were not oblivious to this problem.[45] French military leaders, however, could not find a way to escape from this predicament. They believed that they could deal with the Germans only by assuming a defensive posture for what was expected to be a long war of attrition. Their views on the nature of modern warfare, coupled with the realities of their geopolitical position, led the French to adopt a comprehensive plan that was very inflexible. The French army was prepared to fight a total war and nothing less.

BRITISH MILITARY THOUGHT

Introduction

Although the French were deeply interested in securing a firm British commitment to fight on the Continent, the British were wary of involvement in another European land war. Whether or not Britain should accept a Continental commitment was one of the most controversial issues confronting British planners during the interwar period. The debate over a Continental commitment indicates a key geopolitical difference between France and Britain that had important ramifications for military thought in each country. For the French, the grand strategic issues were well defined: France was a Continental power with a powerful and potentially aggressive Germany on its eastern border. The overriding concern of French diplomats and military planners was how to deal with Germany. Thus French military thought focused on finding the appropriate military strategy for protecting France against a German attack.

For the British, on the other hand, there was constant debate throughout the interwar period regarding grand strategic issues. Physically removed from the Continent and possessing a sprawling empire, the British had to weigh the German threat against other threats and had then to decide whether circumstances justified a Continental commitment.[46] This decision had profound importance because it determined how much attention could be given to questions of military strategy in a European land war. The evolution of Britain's position with regard to a Continental commitment greatly influenced British thinking as to how to fight a land war in Europe, which in turn shaped British input into Allied decisions about how to deal militarily with Germany. For that reason, we must briefly consider the grand strategic debate that took place in Britain between the world wars.

The Grand Strategic Debate

By the end of the nineteenth century, the British empire extended over expanses of the globe so vast that, under the best of circumstances, it would have been difficult to provide for its defense. In addition, two developments were complicating Britain's task. First, new industrial powers such as Germany and Japan, not to mention the United States, Russia, and Italy, were emerging as potential threats to Britain's far-flung empire. To add to British woes, the importance of naval power, which had traditionally been Britain's most effective instrument for policing the empire, was declining in relation to that of land-based military power.[47]

By 1900 the British clearly recognized that they did not have the economic strength required to outfit a military capable of meeting all possible threats. The British obviated this problem in the years before World War I by diplomatic means.[48] World War I did not alleviate their difficulty; in fact, the predicament was more acute than ever at the war's conclusion. With the victory, the territorial size of the British empire reached its zenith, while Britain's position in the world economy continued to decline.[49] Thus, the General Staff reported in 1921 that "our liabilities are so vast, and at the same time so indeterminate, that to assess them must be largely a matter of conjecture."[50] Fortunately for the British, there were no real threats to the empire or to the existing European balance of power during the 1920s. Consequently, they did not have to confront their strategic dilemma.

The situation changed in the 1930s, first with the appearance of an aggressive Japan in the Far East and then with the rise of Nazi Germany. It became increasingly clear that the British would not be able to deal with these threats diplomatically and would have to respond with a military solution. Great Britain would have to assess the relative importance of the different threats and would have to allocate limited resources among the air force, the army, and the navy—two difficult tasks. To help accomplish them, the British established the Defense Requirements Committee (DRC) in November 1933.[51] The DRC Report, which envisioned Germany as "the ultimate potential enemy," recommended a balanced rearmament program that assumed a Continental commitment. The ruling government, however, felt that it would not be possible to allocate significant resources to all three services.[52] Some hard decisions would be needed. For approximately four years, while rearmament lagged, the British debated the matter; finally a decision was reached in December 1937. The British cabinet agreed that the nation's commitments could be categorized under four general headings: (1) protecting the homeland; (2) protecting sea lanes; (3) protecting the empire; and (4) the Continental commitment.[53] British ranking of these commitments would significantly influence the composition of the British armed forces.

The resolution of the matter proved to be quite simple. There was never any doubt that the first commitment would be defense of the homeland. Thus the cabinet mandated on 22 December 1937 that "our first and main effort should be directed to two principal objectives—namely, to protecting this country against attack, and to preserving the trade routes."[54] To support these two commitments, the British would need a powerful air force and navy. Given the limitations of the British defense budget, the two services were to receive the majority of rearmament monies while the army was largely neglected. The British would not, in other words, prepare for another land war in Europe. Appropriately, the Continental commitment went to the bottom of the list of British priorities. The cabinet dictated that the army should concern itself with imperial defense and with providing antiaircraft protection of the homeland.[55] Furthermore, eschewing a Continental commitment meant that the air force did not need to concern itself with providing close air support for the army.[56]

The British Army before World War II

Having made their decision, British leaders now felt that they could cease to hold the army budget constant and could actually reduce the army's size.[57] Not surprisingly, therefore, from December 1937 to March 1939, while the navy and air force rearmed, the army was consciously neglected, with devastating effects.[58] So crippled did it become that it was possibly not even capable of policing the empire,[59] particularly since a significant proportion of the army's meager appropriations had been designated for antiaircraft defense.[60] Recalling much discussion during the early 1930s about the need to develop "a highly-equipped small and professional army," the *Official History* comments: "Small it indeed was. . . . But highly equipped it certainly was not."[61] The situation did not change through that decade. In March 1938, for example, during the Czechoslovakian crisis, the British were capable of sending only two divisions to the Continent, both of them "seriously deficient of equipment."[62] As late as August 1939, the army had 60 infantry tanks "against a total requirement of 1,646."[63] The situation with regard to artillery and infantry weapons was equally grim.[64]

In these circumstances, the army could hardly pay serious attention to the question of the role that armored forces would play on the modern battlefield. Since the British had only a few tanks, which were not intended for use in a European land war in any event, it was unrealistic to expect the army to formulate a position on the proper organization and deployment of armored forces for a Continental war. As the *Official History* notes, "What hesitation, doubt, and then the decision against a continental commitment did was to inhibit that thinking and innovation which any army needs when it faces a new war."[65] The matter of incentive aside, the army was so deficient in material that it was virtually impossible to train forces to fight on a modern battlefield. General Ironside relates an interesting story that highlights the problem. In April 1938, General Gort, who was then chief of the Imperial General Staff, gave a "small dissertation upon the *attaque brusquée*." Commenting on Gort's talk, Ironside wrote, "He delivered it well, but it did not seem to fit in with anything we were doing or were likely to be doing. Training for war was missed out."[66] In this environment the military could not even prepare to fight World War I all over again, much less develop new ideas on armored warfare.

After Munich, the British began to reconsider their policy regarding a Continental commitment; finally, in late March 1939, they decided to reverse their position with respect to a land war against Germany.[67] Naturally, preparations had to be made for raising, equipping, and training a British expeditionary force. Given the pathetic state of the army, the task was enormous. The army leadership began working feverishly to build a force capable of standing with the French against a German onslaught. The British quickly encountered a host of problems. British industry, for example, could not provide enough equipment to satisfy training requirements or to arm the expanding ground forces.[68] Consequently the army had great difficulty absorbing all the manpower being supplied by conscription, which had been instituted on 26 April 1939.[69] Furthermore, there were not enough trained officers and noncommissioned officers to fill all the positions of responsibility in the expanding army.[70] Then, too, no plans existed for mobilizing the British army and for transporting it to the Continent. Numerous other problems of an organizational nature compounded the difficulty of the task.

When war broke out in September 1939, only five months after the British had begun laying the groundwork for a Continental army, the same organizational problems were still plaguing army leaders. Because of the extraordinary time and effort required to find solutions, British planners were unable to devote sufficient attention to doctrinal issues. They were too busy forming an army to worry about abstract questions relating to the nature of modern warfare. A lengthy entry from Ironside's diary provides an excellent example of the preoccupation with organizational problems as it stultified thinking about strategic issues. Commenting on a meeting of the Army Council held on 23 October 1939, he notes:

I went into the tank situation. We found that we had 50 "I" [infantry] tanks, that is, the tanks that we use to break the line. For 12 to 15

[80]

divisions we need 450 tanks in first line and have only 100 in all in sight by June [1940]. One can hardly believe that all we can do between now and June—eight months—is 50 tanks. Where is all our boasted power of manufacture?

We had the most ridiculous Army Council taking two hours to discuss the most trivial matters. My report on the strategical aspect was never even reached. Belisha [Leslie Hore-Belisha, Secretary of State for War] knows nothing and cares nothing of what is happening strategically. The wretched Army Council never has a chance to understand the war it is running.[71]

As a consequence of the decisions made at the grand strategic level during the interwar period, British military planners never seriously addressed the question of whether the tank would revolutionize warfare. Certainly the issue was debated at an intellectual level in British service journals, books, and newspapers. After all, Liddell Hart and J. F. C. Fuller were British. Furthermore, there were a number of small-scale exercises involving armored forces in the 1920s and early 1930s. Still, the army was never forced to come to grips with the hard questions surrounding the issue of military strategy in a major land war. In the latter half of the 1930s, when the Continental powers were beginning to address these difficult issues, the British army had been told not to prepare for another European war. When the British finally reversed themselves, the organizational problems at hand were so overwhelming that they reached a position on military strategy more by default than by choice. Under such circumstances, it was inevitable that the British would look to World War I for a frame of reference. Consequently, the army began preparing to fight World War I all over again.[72]

The frame of reference was reflected in the subsequent training that the army underwent and in the formal doctrine with which it entered the war.[73] In the months before the war, while the British raised forces to fight on the Continent, few officers in key leadership positions indicated any interest in the revolutionary ideas about armored warfare articulated by Liddell Hart and J. F. C. Fuller. Certainly Generals Ironside, Gort, and Pownall, three of the most influential military leaders of the period, believed that the battlefields of World War II would hardly differ from those of the Great War.

As we have seen, then, the British, like their French counterparts, saw no alternative to employing an attrition strategy against Germany. Given the state of Britain's army and the need for material and numerical superiority in a war of attrition, the British naturally envisioned themselves on the defensive for the first part of a long war.[74] They also were prepared for comprehensive economic planning that would allow them to harness all their resources to defeat Germany.[75] At the same time they planned to rely on a naval blockade to help strangle the German economy.[76] Obviously there would be little, if any, disagreement between the French and British regarding questions of military strategy.

Although the two allies did not discuss issues of military strategy prior to late March 1939, and although the French carefully analyzed questions of military strategy while the British largely neglected these matters, they both reached the same conclusions as to how to deal with Germany. Gen. Henry Pownall, the chief of staff of the British Expeditionary Force, noted in his diary more than two months after the war had begun: "It's very interesting to note how French Staff officers in discussing these problems of strategy, tactics, and staff duties talk and think on exactly the same lines as we do. There is an 'Esperanto' between us in these sort of things."[77]

ALLIED PLANNING FOR MILITARY OPERATIONS AGAINST GERMANY, MARCH 1939–MAY 1940

The Question of Aiding Poland, March 1939–September 1939

The compartmentalization that characterized Franco-British relations during the interwar period began to erode after Munich, and on 8 February 1939 the British cabinet decided to initiate staff talks with France. Before the talks opened on 29 March 1939, the Germans occupied the remainder of Czechoslovakia (15 March) and then Memel (23 March). In response to these developments, Neville Chamberlain told the House of Commons: "In the event of any action which clearly threatened Polish independence, and which the Polish Government accordingly considered it vital to resist with their national forces, His Majesty's Government would feel themselves bound at once to lend the Polish Government all support in their power."[78] This guarantee to Poland, which was issued on 31 March 1939 (two days after the staff talks began), represented a sudden and radical shift in British policy. As General Pownall remarked in his diary: "A continental commitment with a vengeance!"[79] Chamberlain also announced that the French had authorized him "to make it plain that they stand in the same position in this matter as do His Majesty's Government." The French, in fact, followed the British lead with reluctance.[80]

In the aftermath of the Polish guarantee, the British sought to determine what course of action the Allies would follow if Germany attacked Poland. Specifically, Britain wanted to determine what action the Allied armies were going to take against Germany while the Germans were attacking Poland. The British were interested in directly addressing this issue for a number of reasons. First, the British knew that because the French would carry the burden in a land war with Germany, France would determine the nature of the Allied response.[81] The British wanted to know where the French were going to lead them. Moreover, since the British had devoted so little attention to such questions in the past, they were looking to the French as experts on the matter. Second, the British felt that it would be "extremely difficult to undertake staff conversations with the Poles in the absence of any agreement with the French" about the military action that the Allies were planning.[82] Finally, the British were understandably anxious to find a way to keep Poland in the war and to preserve the eastern front.[83]

The French, on the other hand, were reluctant to respond to British questions about aiding Poland. Although the French had no intention of responding militarily to an attack on Poland, from the French perspective, no useful purpose could be served by telling the Poles that the Allies could not help them. There was no point in discouraging Polish resistance; and furthermore, the French hoped that if Germany struck first in the West (see note 45), Poland would aid France. Like their British counterparts, the French recognized the importance of forcing Germany to fight a two-front war.[84] The French, however, had a long-standing conviction that they could not prevent Germany from winning a war in the East. This fundamental contradiction had been a central ingredient in the resolution of the Czechoslovakian crisis in 1938.[85]

Despite their concern, the British were quite reluctant to bring up the issue of military action with the French because the British contribution to any effort would be so paltry.[86] They broached the issue for the first time, however, on 3 May 1939 at the Franco-British staff talks. General Lelong, the head of the French delegation, answered for the French: "A very thorny problem would be presented to the French and British [if Poland were attacked]. The Maginot Line and Siegfried Line faced [*sic*] each other, and *France could not seriously attack Germany on land without long preparation. . . . There could be no question of a hurried attack on the Siegfried Line*" (emphasis added).[87] The British were uneasy about the French reply.[88] On 18 May, the British received further indication of French intentions. Colonel Petibon, who was General Gamelin's chief of staff, told the British military attaché in Paris that "the main [Allied] offensive must be initially in the Mediterranean area and not against Germany."[89] He did indicate, however, that the French were prepared to take "ground action [that] would include offensives well prepared and with limited objectives." The French provided a third glimpse of their intentions on 26 May when the French delegation at the staff talks provided the British with a sketchy memorandum. The French maintained that "the form, the extent and the date of these operations cannot be determined *a priori*."[90]

While the British were raising the issue in the staff talks, General Gort, who was then the chief of the Imperial General Staff (CIGS), was directed to pursue the matter directly with General Gamelin.[91] Gort learned that the French had no intention of launching an offensive to support Poland.[92] When the British chiefs of staff met on June 1 to discuss the various French responses, it was widely recognized that despite the rhetoric about limited offensives and about waiting until the actual attack to decide on the course of action to pursue, the French had no intention of aiding Poland.[93] The British were clearly frustrated by the French position; they recognized the implications of allowing Germany "to deal with her enemies in turn, and in detail."[94] Gen. Ronald Adam, the deputy CIGS, exclaimed at the meeting, "We *must* do something to assist Poland."

British vexation aside, it is very important to emphasize that the British did not disagree with the French position. They accepted the logic of the policy, although they found its implications distasteful. Gen. John Slessor, one of Britain's three principal representatives at the staff talks, recalled:

> On the probable initial moves in the coming war and on the general lines of strategy to be adopted by the Allies, we soon found ourselves in pretty close agreement. The French were as uncomfortably aware as we of the dilemma with which we might be faced if Germany concentrated on Poland and stood on the defensive in the West. . . .
> The French staff . . . entirely agreed with us that in fact there was nothing that either of us could do to save Poland.[95]

Their dissatisfaction with French thinking notwithstanding, the British could offer no alternative to remaining on the defensive in the West. The British view of how to deal with Germany accorded with the French view.[96] Actually, before Britain had assumed a Continental commitment, the chiefs of staff had stated that "if war broke out in Eastern Europe, neither France nor ourselves could render direct assistance to a victim of German aggression."[97] The chiefs reasoned that "the German Siegfried line . . . now forms a formidable barrier.

Any idea of a rapid break through is, therefore, out of the question."[98] Not surprisingly, the British accepted the French position, although they were justifiably disturbed by the prospect that Germany would have a free hand in the East.

The Allies were deterred from taking military action to support Poland in September 1939 because they believed that they would have to employ a terribly costly attrition strategy that would ultimately result in failure. Their conclusion reflected the belief that the defense enjoyed a great advantage over the offense and that the only way for the attacker to offset its disadvantage was to acquire overwhelming material and numerical superiority. Then the attacker, employing his forces in accordance with the dictates of the attrition strategy, could use his superior numbers to crush the defender in a quick campaign.[99] Such a favorable balance of forces, however, could be realized only in some distant future. Until then, the Allies would remain on the defensive and would let the Germans, if they wanted, bleed themselves white while attacking Allied defenses.[100]

Such a position was perfectly consistent with French military thinking during the interwar years; and in fact the same logic had prevailed during the 1938 Munich crisis. The majority of French military officers felt that France did not have the necessary forces to score a decisive victory in the West while the Germans were engaged in Czechoslovakia.[101] This pessimistic assessment existed despite the French estimate that France would be able to commit 56 of its 100 divisions to an offensive against the 8 German divisions that would defend Germany's western front. The British, who were not in a position to contribute ground forces to a French offensive, did not encourage the French to act in support of Czechoslovakia. They, too, felt that the French would fail to score a decisive victory. Thus the British chiefs of staff concluded in March 1938: "In short, we can do nothing to prevent the dog [from] getting the bone, and we have no means of making him give it up, except by killing him by a slow process of attrition and starvation."[102] Since the strength of the German army increased significantly between September 1938 and September 1939, the French were unlikely to consider military action in support of Poland.[103]

Appropriately, the British and the French formally adopted a four-stage plan for defeating Germany.[104] First, the Allies would concentrate on establishing a successful defense. In the second phase, the Allies would begin gathering resources while bringing economic pressure to bear on Germany. In the third phase, the Allies would deal with Italy. Then, according to General Slessor, they "hope[d] to be in a

[85]

position to turn to the offensive and the defeat of Germany [although they] . . . did not attempt to crystal-gaze into how that would be done."[105] It was clear that neither the French nor the British saw any alternative to allowing Germany a free hand in Poland. "The fate of Poland [would] depend upon the ultimate outcome of the war, and this, in turn [would] . . . depend upon [the Allies'] . . . ability to bring about the eventual defeat of Germany."[106]

Concerning the Allied decision not to aid Poland, we must consider one further point: the Allies' failure to give serious consideration to a limited aims strategy. It is not difficult to understand why the Allies overlooked the blitzkrieg, given its revolutionary nature. It is much more difficult, however, to comprehend their failure to pursue a limited aims strategy. Aside from the fact that this strategy is not particularly ambitious, there were two prominent targets in Western Germany: the Ruhr and the Saar. Capturing the Ruhr, which was the industrial heartland of Germany, would have dealt Germany a crippling blow.[107] The Saar, with its vast coal deposits, was also of crucial economic importance.[108] These should have been particularly attractive targets for the French and British, who ascribed such great importance to achieving material superiority, which of course was largely a function of relative economic strength. Actually, the probability that either of these areas could have been captured must have been quite high in early September—simply because a large contingent of Germany's best troops were engaged in Poland. Yet the Allies never gave serious consideration to employing a limited aims strategy.[109]

The explanation for this peculiarity is quite straightforward. The Allies, especially the French, believed that modern defenses were so formidable that the Allies, should they attempt even a limited offensive, would suffer excessive losses and at the same time would fail to attain their objective. The Allies' prospects for success were clouded by the fact that they refused to attack Germany by passing through neutral Belgium.[110] Consequently they were limited to striking Germany at points along the Franco-German border, where the German's Siegfried Line was located. Since the Ruhr was opposite Belgium, the Allies were not able to take the most direct route to reach this lucrative target. The Allies were also paralyzed by the fear of repeating the abortive French offensive of 1914, which was also launched at points along the Franco-German border. (I shall return to this matter shortly.) Finally, a limited offensive would force the Allies to abandon their carefully prepared defensive positions along the Maginot Line, thus forfeiting the advantages that

[86]

went with fighting from such well-prepared positions. For the Allies, a successful offensive could come only after a lengthy period of preparation, at the end of which the Allies had achieved the overwhelming superiority that they sought.

When the war broke out on 1 September 1939, the Allies remained inactive while the Germans and the Soviets dismembered Poland. On 12 September, the first meeting of the Supreme War Council convened at Abbeville in France. In the following lengthy extract from the minutes of that meeting, the comments of the French and British leaders succinctly summarize the key elements in the Franco-British plan and also indicate the extent to which the decisions taken in the first days of the war were merely the culmination of a policy whose roots reached deep into the past.

Mr Chamberlain felt sure that the lessons of the last war had not been lost. In many ways a start was now being made where the last war had left off. He said that Mr Winston Churchill, on joining the War Cabinet, had remarked on the great improvement in the preparatory arrangements to-day as compared with those which had existed in 1914.

M Daladier said that ["the general military situation"] had developed exactly as had been anticipated, and hoped for, by the French General Staff. . . .

Mr Chamberlain thought the decision not to undertake large-scale operations as yet in France had been wise. In his view there was no hurry as time was on our side. Moreover, the Allies required time to build up their full resources, and in the meantime it might well be that the morale of Germany would crumble. M Daladier was quite certain that large-scale offensive operations at the beginning would be an error. . . .

It was clear that nothing the Allies could do would save Poland from being overrun.[111]

Planning for an Offensive against Germany,
September 1939–May 1940

After the fall of Poland, the Allies concentrated on refining their plan for meeting a German attack in the West. They also began applying pressure to the German economy while marshaling their economic resources for the protracted conflict ahead. Since any offensive against Germany would take place in the distant future, planning for such an eventuality was not a matter of urgent concern. Moreover, since the Allies expected the Germans to strike first in the West, an Allied offensive would be shaped, in part, by the outcome of that attack. Therefore, it was difficult to prepare precise plans. Nevertheless, the Allies had to consider the possibility that the Germans would remain behind the Siegfried Line. Appropriately, the Allies began making preliminary preparations for an offensive.

The Allies never established a formal mechanism with responsibility for developing plans for an offensive in the West. French and British thinking on this subject was outlined in an exchange of letters and memoranda between the military leaders of each country.[112] The discussion focused on two specific issues: the nature of the offensive and the projected date of attack. The British recognized that the French, who would provide the majority of the ground forces, would be largely responsible for determining the shape and timing of the offensive.

In December 1939, the French, responding to British prodding, forwarded the British a detailed "Appreciation" outlining French thoughts regarding an Allied attack in the West.[113] For the first and only time, the French elaborated on their plans for the projected offensive. Not surprisingly, the "Appreciation" makes clear the French belief that the Allies would have to employ an attrition strategy. The "Appreciation" is noteworthy not only because it demonstrates the continuity of French thinking but also because it provides support for the claim that the Allies would never have assumed the offensive in the West.

The French emphasized that "the [Allied] attack would . . . take the form of brute force" and would be, in effect, "a modernized Verdun or Somme."[114] The key assumption was that material superiority would enable the Allies to wear down the Germans: success would result from "the incontestable superiority of [Allied] resources compared to those of the enemy."[115] Since the French believed that modern war was fundamentally a series of firepower exchanges, artillery was of course the resource on which they placed the highest premium.[116] The tank also had an important role to play in the projected Allied offensive, although its primary mission was to be infantry support. Thus the French concluded that the offensive would require the "employment of material and munitions of great destructive power [artillery] and of powerful tanks."

The French also stipulated in their "Appreciation" that the Allies would have to employ frontal attacks against the German defenses.[117] Appropriately, when detailing the "Requirement in tanks," the French argued that the Allies would require "one battalion of light tanks to the km." and "one battalion of powerful heavy tanks per 2 kms." The projected Allied offensive would also be very methodical and would move at a slow pace. Basically, French strategy called for a series of offensives designed "to seize the successive positions which constitute the Siegfried Line." For each offensive, "the preparations . . . [would] be exceedingly complicated and . . . [would have to] be worked out in great detail." Little importance was attached to achieving surprise, except in the narrowest tactical sense.[118] Once the offensive was launched, the French hoped for "methodical progress strongly supported by artillery and tanks." There was no hope of exploitation or quick victories, which was hardly surprising in light of the tremendous amounts of material required for an Allied offensive.[119] It was unrealistic to expect anything more than "methodical progress" during a conflict in which the attacking forces expected to match strength against strength and to prevail by virtue of their material superiority.

The French also addressed the question of when to assume the offensive. There had been some discussion in Allied circles about the possibility of attacking Germany in spring 1940. The French concluded, however, that "if the very considerable requirements of every kind necessary for the breaching of the Siegfried Line are compared with all the resources on which we can count, it does not seem as if it will be possible to undertake the contemplated breach with prospects of success in the spring of 1940." An Allied offensive might be possible in spring 1941, but only if "we begin straight away to produce the war material estimated to be necessary." Another section of the "Appreciation," however, emphasized that in light of "the present strategic and war material situation no date can therefore be fixed for beginning such an offensive." General Ironside, after reading the document, remarked that "the French have no intention of carrying out an offensive for years, if at all. There is none of that fire which animated them in 1914."[120] Ironside's comments aside, the British themselves felt that an offensive probably would not be possible until spring 1942.[121]

Moreover, as was the case throughout the entire period of close Allied cooperation (March 1939–May 1940), the British did not contest the French position regarding the shape of an Allied offensive. A British study responding to the French "Appreciation" noted, however, that it was "questionable whether these methods would every [sic] succeed in breaking the Siegfried Line."[122] In response to this pessimistic estimate, the British sought to discover a special technical device that would allow the Allies to defeat Germany without having to engage in a war of attrition.[123] The French placed a correspondingly great emphasis on the search for such a revolutionary development.

[89]

In their "Appreciation" they commented: "It is to be hoped that science will place at the disposal of our armies new methods which will permit of a more rapid breaching of the fortified positions."

There was also discussion in Britain during this period of employing what Liddell Hart called the indirect approach to defeat Germany.[124] This strategy started from the assumption that Germany had an Achilles' heel which, if found and targeted, could bring the Allies victory with a minimum of bloodshed.[125] An indirect approach was especially attractive to those who believed that Hitler's position was precarious; apply some pressure at a critical point, and the Third Reich would collapse.[126] The French were sympathetic to the indirect approach, not because they saw it as an alternative way of defeating Germany, but because they thought it might shift attention away from the western front.[127]

The attention given to finding a means other than the attrition strategy for defeating Germany invites our consideration of an important question: Would the Allies ever have taken the offensive in the West if the Germans had remained entrenched behind the Siegfried Line? Clearly the Allies were deterred from striking in the West at the height of the Czechoslovakian crisis, and then between September 1939 and May 1940, because they felt that given the existing balance of forces, employing an attrition strategy against Germany would be suicidal.[128] It is difficult to imagine the Allies employing this strategy at a future date when, they said, it would result in "a modernized Verdun or Somme." Actually, some British military leaders wondered whether the French would ever be willing to assume the offensive in the West. As I noted earlier, Ironside, after viewing the French "Appreciation," expressed his doubts. At the height of the Czechoslovakian crisis, Gen. C. L. N. Newall, the chief of the Air Staff, traveled to France to discuss military strategy. Afterward, Newall wrote that he was "particularly impressed by the account of General Gamelin's strategical ideas."[129] Then, however, he commented: "But further, it seems to me an occasion for some disquiet to read of General Gamelin's 'conviction' that, in spite of the great superiority of the defensive in land warfare, and the inferiority of the French air force to that of the Germans, he can still 'wear down' the Germans by a system of carefully executed offensives." The assumption fundamentally underpinning Allied thinking was, of course, that in the long run, an offensive would be possible because the balance of forces would shift decisively in their favor. Allied strength rested in a long war, in which they would attain the "incontestable superiority of resources" that would allow them to defeat Germany. Despite the widespread acceptance of this assumption, there is no evidence that the Allies ever examined it in any detail. General Slessor, referring to an eventual offensive against Germany, noted that the Allies "did not attempt to crystal-gaze into how that was done."[130] Then, too, as I just noted and as my discussion will shortly make plain, the Allies actually had serious doubts about their capability to achieve superiority over Germany.[131] Allied claims that the balance of forces would shift dramatically in their favor were clearly based more on wishful thinking than on careful analysis. Simply stated, the British and the French did not have the resources necessary to shift the balance of forces in their favor.

First consider the number of divisions that each side was capable of raising. The French entertained no illusions about Germany's ability to raise a large number of divisions. They estimated that Germany would have 170–175 divisions by spring 1940, 200 by the end of 1940, and 240 by early 1941.[132] Actually, Germany was able to raise approximately 300 divisions during the Second World War.[133] Without the threat of a two-front war, the Germans would have been able to concentrate almost all of their divisions along the Franco-German border. France, with its smaller population, would not have been able to match the Germans if both sides had mobilized all available manpower. When the Germans struck in May 1940, the French had 126 divisions, 101 of which were stationed on the German front.[134] The French mobilization had tapped almost all the available manpower; it would have been very difficult for the French to have significantly increased the size of the army, although it could probably have been expanded to 150 divisions.[135] The British were expected to tip the balance of divisions in favor of the Allies. In the First World War, Britain and its empire had raised 95 divisions, 74 of which were British.[136] Still, with "the expansion of the R.A.F., the need for large Anti-Aircraft and Civil Defences at home, and the complicated modern weapons which required many men to make and maintain them,"[137] the British were not able to match their effort in the Great War. Britain's goal was to raise 55 divisions, 32 of which would be British.[138] In fact, Britain and its empire were able to form only 49 divisions, and that total was reached only in the last year of the war.[139] By January 1943, the British empire had raised only 19 divisions and one year later, the figure was 23 2/3 divisions.[140] Moreover, given the needs of the empire, it was not possible to deploy all these divisions in Western Europe.

In early 1940, the British estimated that they would need to place 40 divisions on the western front before the Allies could assume the offensive.[141] Let us make the most optimistic assumptions: that the British could have achieved this objective in three or four years; and that, concomitantly, the French army expanded to 150 divisions, 130 of which would be located on the western front. The Allies would have then had 170 divisions for an offensive. This total would not have been nearly enough to match the German army, much less to achieve any meaningful superiority of forces. The Allies simply did not have the capacity to outdistance the Germans in a race to raise divisions for the western front.[142]

The Allies should have clearly understood this point from their experiences during World War I. After eliminating the Russians from the war in 1917, the Germans had been able to concentrate 192 divisions on the western front for their March 1918 offensive. They were opposed by 160 Allied divisions.[143] The balance was eventually tipped in the Allies' favor by the addition of 42 U.S. divisions and the German losses resulting from the March offensive.[144] By 1939, the disparity between the French and German populations had increased. Moreover, the British empire was capable of raising only half as many divisions as it had in the Great War despite the fact that its population had grown during the interwar period. If anything, the Germans, not the French and British, could look forward to numerical superiority in a long war.[145]

Now consider the assumption that the Allies would have superior economic strength in a long war. In Britain in April 1939, a representative from the Treasury told the Strategic Appreciation Subcommittee, "If we were under the impression that we were as well able as in 1914 to conduct a long war, we were burying our heads in the sand."[146] His assessment was proven correct. The British economy was not capable of raising and supporting a fifty-five division army. The *Official History* notes that "by the end of 1942," when the British had raised nineteen divisions, "the limit of British mobilisation was near."[147] By the fall of 1943, after Britain had just passed the twenty-division mark, the *Official History* notes: "It . . . [was] clear that, left to her own production, Britain would be compelled to make drastic reductions in her combatant forces."[148] There was simply no way that the British empire would have been able to raise the forty divisions necessary for an Allied offensive. In short, the British war effort was bankrupting the British economy. It was clear that at some point in the near future, the British economy would collapse. As the *Official History* bluntly concludes, "the Government's economic, financial and strategic pre-suppositions . . . [were] wrong and the earlier reliance on them extremely dangerous."[149] The British were rescued from this desperate situation by the entry of the United States into the war.[150]

It seems reasonable to assume that the French would not have encountered problems of this magnitude. They had spent significant amounts of money equipping and training their army prior to the outbreak of war. Furthermore, the French air force and navy were much smaller than the Royal Air Force and the Royal Navy.[151] Nevertheless, the French economy, which had felt the full impact of the depression only in the late 1930s, was ill suited for a long war.[152] There is no doubt that the French, unlike the Americans, would not have been able to provide Britain with needed economic and material assistance. Leaving aside for the moment the dimensions of German economic strength, the Allies would have faced severe economic problems in a lengthy war of attrition.

As noted earlier, before the start of World War II, Germany's industrial strength was approximately three times as great as France's. When the figures for Britain are added to those of France, the Allies and the Germans are closely matched.[153] The Allies believed that they could shift this balance in their favor by making adjustments in their own economies while simultaneously hurting the Germany economy.[154] It is clear that the Allies could not rely on their own economies to alter the balance of war materials significantly. The French and British economies were simply not strong enough. Thus great emphasis was placed on weakening the German economy by blockade and by air attacks.

When the war started in September 1939, the Allies refused to launch air strikes against the Ruhr or any other industrial targets in Germany simply because they feared German retaliation against Allied cities (see note 96). Assuming that Germany had remained on the defensive in the West, it is hard to imagine that the French and British would have initiated a massive air war.[155] Even if they had, the effect on the German economy would have been negligible, as was demonstrated from June 1940 to August 1942, when Bomber Command struck Germany without U.S. assistance. The air offensive against economic targets had so little impact on the German economy that the British abandoned this policy in mid-1941 and adopted area bombing instead. The new objective was to hurt German morale. Here, too, the British failed.[156]

The French and the British did implement a blockade against Germany. Its effectiveness on the German war effort was negligible.[157] It was extremely difficult, if not impossible, to strangle a nation that had access to the resources of Eastern and Southern Europe and could also trade openly with Italy and the Soviet Union. Even when the United States entered the war and the scope of the blockade increased significantly (and of course, by this time, Germany was fighting with the Soviet Union), the blockade's effectiveness was limited.[158] The German war economy, faced with an aggressive American-British blockade as well as a massive American-British air offensive, expanded in the face of this pressure and actually reached its peak in July 1944.[159] It is inconceivable to think that France and Britain, had they been willing to combine an air offensive with their blockade, could have severely damaged the German war economy. As was demonstrated from 1939 to 1945, Germany had the economic strength to engage in a long war of attrition. It was the Allies (specifically the British), not the Germans, who were incapable of refighting World War I.

These macrolevel comparisons aside, other factors further reinforce the argument that the Allies would not have launched an offensive in the West had the Germans remained behind the Siegfried Line. The Allies refused to launch an offensive through neutral Belgium. Consequently, they were forced to strike Germany from points along the Franco-German border. Since this border was only 225 miles long and was covered on the German side by the Siegfried Line, the Germans would be able to defend it with a relatively small portion of their forces. Thus the French "Appreciation" notes:

> Covered in front by the fortifications of the Siegfried Line, on the flanks by the neutral Netherlands, Belgium and Switzerland, the German Higher Command will not need more than 70–80 divisions in the West in order to resist eventual powerful Allied attacks which will have to be frontal. They would therefore still have left some 80–90 divisions.

The French recognized that Germany, with such a favorable force-to-space ratio, would be capable of thwarting any Allied offensive.

> Germany . . . is only effectively threatened on one front. The excellence of her material resources (aviation, motorization), the transport facilities of her railways, the existing organization of her front, *will always allow her to bring up against us the forces necessary to check our attack*. The very most we can hope for is that our tanks and aircraft will make it possible for us to achieve a local advantage. [Emphasis added]

The problem of attacking across the Franco-German border was further compounded by the fact that, for geographical reasons, an Allied offensive had to be confined to the area between the Rhine and the Moselle rivers.[160] Furthermore, the Allies had to face the prospect of attacking the Siegfried Line, which the Germans would undoubtedly have strengthened in the period between the start of the war and the Allied offensive. The French believed that a German attack against the Maginot Line would turn into "a formidable Verdun." Thus the French concluded that the Germans would probably attack through Belgium. Not surprisingly, the French described an Allied attack on the Siegfried Line as a "modernized Verdun or Somme." It is hard to imagine the Allies' precipitating such a bloodbath, especially when both the French and the British thought that it would ultimately result in failure.

Another important factor weighed against an attack on the Siegfried Line. At the start of World War I, the French launched a large-scale offensive across the Franco-German border (Plan XVII). Simultaneously, the Germans launched their offensive through Belgium (Schlieffen Plan). The majority of the French forces were thus poorly positioned to meet the attacking German forces that swept into northeastern France and came very close to knocking France out of the war (see figure 3.2). The French were particularly sensitive to the danger of repeating this error. Thus, they note in their "Appreciation":

> The strategic problem of a French attack in the direction of Mainz is not new. . . . The classic counter to this is for the Germans to take the offensive in Belgium, with the object of trying to envelop the French troops engaged in Lorraine. . . .
> We must therefore always be in a position to ward off an enveloping attack through Belgium.[161]

The French maintained that they would require approximately 40 to 50 divisions to protect the Franco-Belgium border, an estimate that suggests the question: How many divisions would the Allies then have had available for an offensive against the Siegfried Line? The French calculated that they would also have to station about 10 divisions in the Alps and 6 to 10 divisions in North Africa and to hold 10 to 20 divisions for "quiet sectors and to continue the battle." They would then have "40 to 50 divisions earmarked for the offensive between the Rhine and the Moselle." The attacking force would be facing a German army able to place most of its 150–160 divisions (the figure used by the French) behind the Siegfried Line. In light of the emphasis the French placed on achieving an "incontestable superiority of resources," it is no wonder that the French "Appreciation" concluded: "In the present strategic and war materials situation no date can therefore be fixed for beginning such an offensive."

It is virtually impossible to conceive of circumstances in which the Allies would have had the superiority of forces necessary for taking the offensive. The assumption that the Allies had the capability to build up their forces until they could launch an offensive was wrong; in fact, in the long run, their situation became increasingly desperate. The decision to employ an attrition strategy against the Siegfried Line in 1942 or 1943 would have been suicidal; and it is hard to imagine the British, and especially the French, committing suicide over Poland.

CONCLUSION

As it happened, the Germans were not content to remain behind the Siegfried Line, and their offensive in spring 1940 removed from the Allies the burden of attacking. The German blitzkrieg completely surprised the Allies, who had expected the Germans to use large numbers of tanks supported by tactical aircraft but who had no idea that the Germans would employ these weapons to support such a revolutionary strategy. For the Allies the result was shock and paralysis. Winston Churchill, the British prime minister when the Germans attacked, describes a telephone conversation that he had with French President Reynaud.

Reynaud, the only Allied leader who appreciated the blitzkrieg's potential before May 1940, telephoned Churchill on 15 May (only five days after the German offensive had begun) and told him, "We have been defeated. . . . We are beaten; we have lost the battle."[162] Since the Germans had only crossed the Meuse one day earlier, Churchill was taken aback. "Surely it can't have happened so soon?" he responded. Reynaud told him that the Germans had broken through at Sedan and armored forces were "pushing through in great numbers." Churchill retorted: "All experience shows that the offensive will come to an end after a while. I remember the 21st of March 1918. After five or six days they have to halt for supplies, and the opportunity for counter-attack is presented. I learned all this at the time from the lips of Marshall Foch himself." Reynaud, who knew better, merely repeated his earlier statement: "We are defeated; we have lost the battle."

Churchill then flew to Paris for an emergency meeting of the Supreme War Council. At the end of this frustrating meeting, during

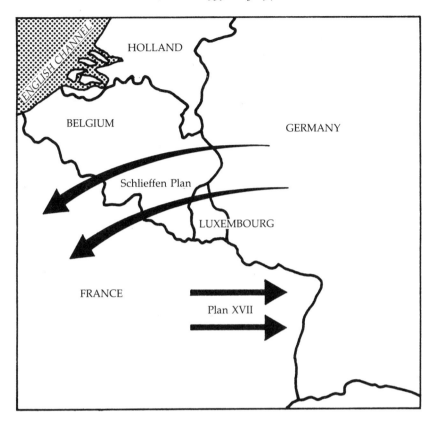

Figure 3.2. 1914 offensives

which it became clear that the Germans were about to inflict a decisive defeat on the Allies, Churchill remarked, "It had seemed not in the least possible that great Armies in fortified positions could be pierced and thrust aside."[163] Much to his credit, Churchill later admitted, "I did not comprehend the violence of the revolution effected since the last war by the incursion of a mass of fast-moving heavy armor. I knew about it, but it had not altered my inward convictions as it should have done."[164] The candid Churchill is not an exception in this regard; the overwhelming majority of military and political leaders in both France and Britain shared his views on the nature of modern warfare.

Ironically, the German victory, which eliminated France from the war and pushed the British army off the Continent, spared the Allies from the long war of attrition that they had so dreaded. The war in

[97]

the West was quick and produced relatively low casualty levels on both sides. If the Allies had stopped the German blitzkrieg, they would have found themselves in a situation not unlike that on the western front in 1914 when the French stopped the Germans on the Marne. In the Second World War, the Germans were finally stopped on the eastern front by the Soviets.[165] Like the French and the British in World War I, however, the Soviets paid a tremendous price to defeat Germany. The Allies were correct in their assessment that only an immense effort involving appalling costs would be sufficient to defeat Germany in a war of attrition. They had learned their lesson well in World War I.

As this chapter has clearly shown, when a potential attacker has no alternative to an attrition strategy, deterrence is very likely to obtain. Accordingly, the Allies discounted the possibility of striking against Germany at the time of Munich (1938) and then one year later when the Germans invaded Poland. There was of course much talk of taking the offensive in the distant future, when the Allies had acquired an "incontestable superiority of resources." The British and the French alone, however, did not have the capability to effect such a shift in the balance of forces. Since many Allied leaders, at the very least, suspected as much, there was considerable skepticism as to whether the Allies would ever take the offensive against Germany. The prospect of engaging in a war of attrition is a powerful deterrent to military action.

Although the Allies' aim of achieving overwhelming superiority was not realizable, it indicates an important point: a potential attacker who is faced with no alternative but to employ an attrition strategy will only strike if he has an "incontestable superiority of resources." The reason is that the attacker can expect to use that superiority to crush the defender and to win a quick and relatively cheap victory. When there is a rough balance of forces, however, an attrition strategy affords no cheap victories. Thus deterrence can be expected to hold.

Finally, it is important to emphasize that those broader political forces that move a nation to consider war were extremely powerful in the Allies' case. After all, they declared war against Germany with no real idea of how they were going to achieve victory. Although there was certainly incentive at that point, if not beforehand, to devise an acceptable military strategy for striking against Germany, the Allies simply could not do so. Consequently, the Allies were deterred from striking in the West.

[4]

The German Decision to Attack
in the West, 1939–1940

The so-called Phoney War ended on 10 May 1940 when the German army struck in the West. Unlike Britain and France, Germany was not deterred from attacking, and we may well ask why not.

The subsequent German victory in France, which clearly stands as one of the most remarkable in military history, has been the subject of many studies. Almost all of them focus on two broad aspects of the campaign: the faulty French and British strategy for meeting the German attack and the mechanics of the German victory.[1] Little attention has been paid to the German decision-making process that led to the attack.[2] This chapter will concern itself directly with that planning process.

There are three schools of thought regarding the failure of deterrence in the case of Germany, although I should emphasize that these schools are not well defined, and some authors actually combine explanations. The first theory is that the Germans attacked because they enjoyed overwhelming military superiority; the Germans possessed a powerful war machine that stood in marked contrast to the ill-equipped, outnumbered Allied forces.[3] This view squares nicely with the belief that the democracies remained passive in the late 1930s while the German economy turned out stupendous quantities of military equipment.[4]

The roots of this explanation can be traced to the prewar period when Hitler and his cohorts went to great lengths to create the impression that the Wehrmacht was a mighty war machine. The wooing of Charles Lindbergh is one of the best-known examples of this ploy.[5] During the war the notion of an overpowering German war machine was not seriously challenged. Marshal Pétain's claim that "when battle was joined, all we had to set against this superiority were words of encouragement and hope" represented the conventional wartime wisdom.[6]

When the war ended and scholars had the opportunity to examine German records, it became apparent that the conventional wisdom was wrong. German military strength in early 1940 was approximately equal to the combined strength of Britain and France;[7] and the German economy, which everyone assumed to have been fully mobilized for war since the late 1930s, was not so until 1942.[8] In short, there was little difference in the material strength of the opposing sides at the outbreak of World War II.[9] Significantly, the Germans recognized this fact at the time.[10]

The second school of thought, like the first, starts with the assumption that the critical consideration was the balance of forces but recognizes that the opposing forces were of roughly equal size. Accordingly, proponents conclude that the decision to attack was not rational; it was a leap into the dark.[11] This explanation casts Hitler as the principal actor, with firm control over the military, which he drags, kicking and screaming, into a war in the West.[12] When proponents of this view are forced to account for the overwhelming military victory that followed, they maintain that Hitler was lucky. Neither he nor his generals could possibly have foreseen a decisive victory. A. J. P. Taylor writes: "He [Hitler] had no idea that he would knock France out of the war when he invaded Belgium and Holland on 10 May 1940. This was a defensive move: to secure the Ruhr from Allied invasion. The conquest of France was an unforeseen bonus."[13]

None of the accounts of the actual planning process by the German generals supports this view.[14] Still, the postwar efforts of the German generals to distance themselves as much as possible from Hitler, as well as their efforts to describe Hitler as a madman with little understanding of military matters, indirectly contributed to this view of an irrational decision.[15] The generals sought to create a picture of a reasonless but powerful Hitler matched against a military with limited influence that was doing everything in its power to control him. All for naught, of course, since one cannot reason with a madman. The problem with this explanation is that a close examination of the decision-making process reveals that the decision was not irrational. The claim that Hitler dragged an unwilling military to war on 10 May 1940 and that everyone, including Hitler, was surprised by the outcome is not true.

The third school of thought focuses on the blitzkrieg, which is widely acknowledged as the key to the Germans' stunning success.

The basic argument in this case is that the Germans, unlike the French and the British, learned the proper lessons from World War I and developed the blitzkrieg during the interwar period.[16] The blitzkrieg, according to some accounts, was designed to accommodate the economic policy of the Third Reich, which, as I emphasized earlier, did not call for a wartime economy.[17] This explanation is consistent with the view that Hitler had a well-defined plan, or grand strategy, when he went to war in 1939.[18] Given the development of the blitzkrieg during the interwar years, it is easy to account for the German attack on Poland as well as for subsequent aggression against the West and the Soviet Union.

My position is congruent with the third school's explanation at a very general level (that is, the German attack was predicated on the assumption that a blitzkrieg would result in a decisive victory); but there are important differences between my argument and that of the third school. There were two distinct periods in the German decision-making process, and they were characterized by two fundamentally different strategies for striking the Allies. From the end of September 1939, when Hitler alerted the military that he planned to launch an offensive in the West, until mid-February 1940, the Germans intended to pursue a limited aims strategy. The objective was limited because the key decision makers did not envision a blitzkrieg as a viable alternative, and an attrition strategy was simply out of the question. Even so, there was a great deal of opposition to the limited aims strategy. For this reason, as well as others, Hitler did not strike in the fall and early winter of 1939–1940. In mid-February 1940, with the emergence of the blitzkrieg as a viable option, opinion shifted dramatically on the question of whether the German military could decisively defeat the Allies. Appropriately, the key decision makers supported Hitler's decision to attack in the West.

THE ORIGINAL STRATEGY AND THE PRINCIPAL ACTORS

The Original Strategy

On 27 September, before the formal conclusion of the Polish campaign, Hitler informed his military leaders that he planned to strike in the West in the immediate future.[19] At the time, no plans existed for such an operation, and in fact, the military was preparing to assume a defensive posture in the West.[20] There was widespread agreement among the top military leaders that the Allies would not move into Belgium and Holland, much less strike against Germany.

[101]

In the words of Gen. Alfred Jodl, the chief of the Operations Staff at the High Command of the Armed Forces (OKW), "There was, particularly in the Army, a widespread opinion that the war would die a natural death if we only kept quiet in the West."[21]

Hitler's view of the situation was very different and more complex. Basically, there were two motives behind Hitler's insistence that Germany strike against the Allies. First, unlike his generals, he believed that the Allies were preparing to move into the Low Countries, where they would be in an excellent position to attack the Ruhr.[22] Hitler was determined to beat the Allies to the punch and to occupy the Low Countries before they did. But he had a second and ultimately more important reason for taking the offensive. He intended to establish German hegemony on the Continent, and to do this he realized that he had to conquer France and to drive the British from the Continent.[23] Hitler saw no possibility of peace with the Allies.[24] His political goals, however, had to be weighed against the capabilities of the German military. As will become evident, this weighing process led to much controversy.

In the wake of Hitler's announcement that he would strike in the West, pessimism prevailed among his top military advisers, who believed that it would not be possible to duplicate the victory in Poland and to score a decisive victory in the West. In his diary for 29 September, the army chief of staff, Gen. Franz Halder, wrote: "Techniques of Polish campaign no recipe for the West. No good against a well-knit Army."[25] Here is the first challenge to the notion that the Germans had developed a carefully formulated blitzkrieg strategy during the interwar period that they tested in the Spanish civil war and then used for the first time in Poland. The German plan in Poland was not a blitzkrieg but an attrition strategy. The Germans struck at both ends of the Polish defensive line, pushed the Polish army back, and enveloped it.[26] In effect, the Germans attacked across a broad front and simply overwhelmed the outnumbered and poorly equipped Poles. Although the Germans' panzer divisions and motorized divisions played an important role in the victory, they were tied to the attacking infantry divisions and were not allowed to effect deep strategic penetrations.

German military leaders recognized that a similar strategy used against the French and the British, who were expected to provide much more formidable opposition than the Poles, would undoubtedly lead to a war of attrition. These fears were reinforced by the lackluster performance of the German infantry in Poland and the recognition that the German economy was not geared to support a long war.[27] Matters were further compounded by the loss of significant amounts of equipment in Poland.[28] Clearly, an alternative strategy was needed. Since the possibility of employing a blitzkrieg was not considered in the early days of the planning process, Hitler and his generals lowered their sights and opted for a limited aims strategy. This is reflected in Directive No. 6, the first official directive concerning the conduct of the war in the West; it was issued at Hitler's insistence by OKW on 9 October 1939. The directive states:

> The purpose of this attacking operation will be, to defeat as strong [a] contingent of the French operational army, as possible, as well as the allies fighting by its side, and at the same time to gain as large an area as possible in Holland, Belgium, and Northern France as a base for conducting a promising air and naval war against England and as a broad area on the immediate front of the vital Ruhr area.[29]

As I emphasized in Chapter 2, a limited aims strategy is concerned with capturing a segment of the opponent's territory as quickly as possible so as to minimize casualties. Directive No. 6 clearly stipulated that the objective was to capture territory ("to gain as large an area as possible") and not to defeat the Allies decisively. It is not so clear from this directive that the Germans were interested in striking quickly so as to minimize casualties. After all, the directive does stipulate that the German military should strive to defeat "as strong [a] contingent of the [Allied forces] . . . as possible." The wording suggests considerable fighting.

At this juncture a number of points are noteworthy. First, the military leaders recognized that a limited strategy that involved so much combat would surely lead to a lengthy war of attrition. Therefore they were very firmly opposed. It was Hitler who wanted to engage as large a portion of the Allies' forces as possible. He desperately sought a decisive victory, and he recognized that only a very "ambitious" limited aims strategy promised any chance of achieving that end. Accordingly, throughout fall 1939, Hitler sought to enlarge the scope of the offensive.[30] In these months he talked often about scoring a decisive victory, although he was not able to devise a satisfactory plan.[31]

In an important sense, Hitler sought to avoid a slugging match with the Allies. He believed very strongly that with the passage of time, the Allies would become significantly stronger, while German military strength would remain constant.[32] Also he recognized that the British contribution to the Allied effort, which was only a meager four divisions in mid-October 1939, would increase greatly in time.

Hitler had great respect for the fighting capabilities of the British, and he wanted very much to strike before the British presence became more substantial.[33] In short, he was motivated to strike by the unfavorable shift he envisioned in the balance of forces. Thus Directive No. 6 mandates that the "attack must be carried out . . . at as early a date as possible."[34] The goal was to avoid engaging a powerful Allied force and instead to capture territory before Allied strength increased significantly. Given a relatively weak Allied contingent and the fact that Hitler wanted to employ a formidable German strike force ("This attack must be carried out with as much strength . . . as possible"),[35] he could realistically talk about defeating "as strong [a] contingent of the French . . . [and] the allies . . . as possible" without having to worry about bleeding his own forces white. He believed, however, that he would not be able to do so for long.

The German forces facing the Allies were divided into three army groups: A, B, and C. Army Group C, which was the southernmost of the three, was located along the Franco-German border, opposite the Maginot Line (see figure 4.1). Its role was basically defensive; the Germans did not intend to attack the Maginot Line. Opposite the border between Germany and the Low Countries, where there was no Maginot Line, were Army Groups A and B. They were the offensive arm of the German army.

On 19 October, OKH (the Army High Command) issued the first operational order for the attack, which translated the general guidelines of OKW's Directive No. 6 into a concrete military plan. Basically, the first plan called for Army Group B (the northernmost army group) to make the main attack across northern Belgium and southern Holland.[36] This provision was not surprising, since the territory that the Germans sought to capture was along the coastline—from which vantage they could prosecute an air and naval offensive against Britain. Army Group A, located to the south of Army Group B, was to protect Army Group B's southern flank. Naturally, Army Group A was smaller than Army Group B. This first plan is frequently but incorrectly described as a mere replica of the 1914 Schlieffen Plan.[37] Although the main weight of the attack was located on the right wing in both plans, the Schlieffen Plan was designed to swing forces through Belgium on into France and to produce a decisive victory. In October 1939, the German aim was to occupy the Channel coast, not to score a decisive victory.

In subsequent months, a number of changes were made in the original OKH plan. Despite these alterations, the Germans continued to pursue a limited aims strategy until mid-February 1940. Perhaps

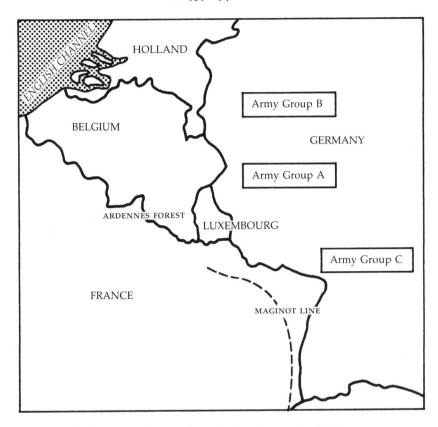

Figure 4.1. Deployment of German forces for the attack in the West

there is no better summary of this basic strategy than an abstract from the OKW War Diary written in late September 1939, before Directive No. 6 had been issued. It reads:

> *Decision of the Fuehrer* to attack *in the West* and this as soon as possible since the French/British Army is not yet ready. Intention of attacking through Belgium and Holland . . . is certain from the start. From the very beginning it is the Fuehrer's idea not to repeat the Schlieffen-plan but to attack in approximately a west-north western direction through Belgium and Luxembourg under strong protection of the Southern flank, and to gain the Channel coast.[38]

The Principal Actors

In fall 1939, Hitler was virtually the only individual in favor of implementing OKH's limited plan. Arrayed in direct opposition to

Hitler were all of the military leaders (see figure 4.2).[39] There were, however, two coalitions within the military, each of which opposed the limited aims strategy for different reasons.[40] One coalition saw no alternative to the limited aims strategy and thought that such a strategy would result in another World War I. This contingent was largely responsible for drafting the first OKH plan. The second group, which formed only after that original plan had been released to the field commanders in mid-October, maintained that it was possible to inflict a decisive defeat on the Allies. Its members were sharply critical of the first coalition for arguing that it was possible to achieve only a limited victory. Despite this difference with regard to objectives, both coalitions adamantly opposed Hitler's decision to attack in fall 1939. We may thus identify three main actors: Hitler and two groups within the military. The complex interplay among the three not only stymied Hitler's efforts to launch the German military in pursuit of the limited aims strategy but also led to the adoption of the blitzkrieg used in May 1940.

The first coalition comprised three generals who felt that a decisive victory in the West was not possible and that the only feasible alternative was a limited aims strategy. They were hardly enthusiastic about this strategy, however, since they thought it would lead to a war of attrition. At the heart of their belief was a deep-seated respect for both French and British military prowess.[41] They felt that the Germans would be matched against skillful and tenacious opponents who would not accept a limited defeat, thus transforming the war into a virtual replay of the Great War. Like their contemporaries on the other side of the hill, the German generals wanted desperately to avoid repeating that earlier experience. Gen. Ritter von Leeb (the commander of Army Group C), one of the three key figures in this coalition, summarized the coalition's viewpoint in a memorandum dated 11 October 1939. He wrote:

> The decision to attack *must* be preceded by the question, what can such an attack achieve for us? As explained above, it leads to a war of attrition either before the French fortifications or already on Belgian territory. If it is *a priori* given a limited objective—say, the capture or extension of our bases for aerial and submarine warfare—this limitation will not prevent the war of attrition, and a secure basis for final victory is not won by it, either.[42]

General Brauchitsch (the commander in chief of the army) and General Halder (the army chief of staff) were the other leading figures in this coalition. As the two most powerful army leaders, they

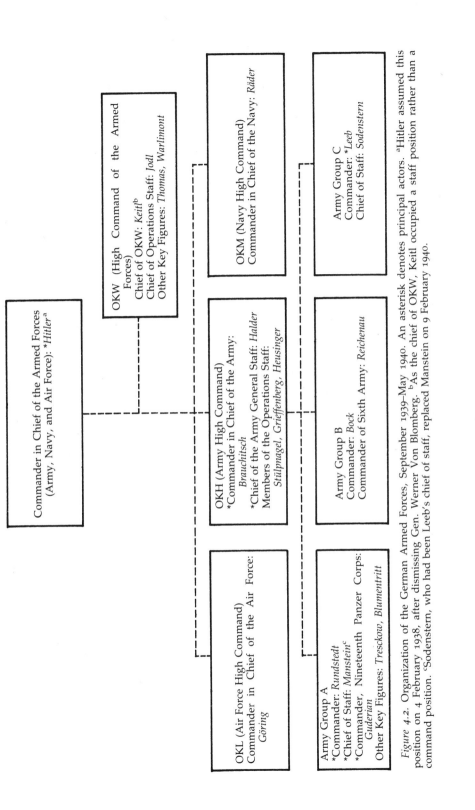

Figure 4.2. Organization of the German Armed Forces, September 1939–May 1940. An asterisk denotes principal actors. [a]Hitler assumed this position on 4 February 1938, after dismissing Gen. Werner Von Blomberg. [b]As the chief of OKW, Keitl occupied a staff position rather than a command position. [c]Sodenstern, who had been Leeb's chief of staff, replaced Manstein on 9 February 1940.

were responsible for the OKH plan that operationalized the limited aims strategy. They were, nevertheless, dissatisfied with their own plan, which they thought would lead to a war of attrition. They preferred to stay on the defensive and to let the Allies, if they chose, wear themselves out by attacking the well-entrenched Germans.[43] As will become evident, Brauchitsch, Halder, and Leeb made a concerted effort to thwart Hitler's efforts to implement the OKH plan.

These three officers were basically conservative army generals who were not sympathetic to Nazism. Their attitude, of course, was the cause of much friction with Hitler, who was well aware of the formidable political power of the German military. Their political views aside, Brauchitsch, Halder, and Leeb were not innovative thinkers in the military realm; there, too, they were basically conservative. They placed themselves in the tradition of the elder Moltke, Schlieffen, and Seeckt.[44] But while Brauchitsch and his colleagues were conservative in military matters they were not rigid thinkers.

Because of Germany's central location in Europe and the consequent threat of a two-front war, the German military had traditionally placed a high premium on winning quick victories. Speed would allow them to defeat one opponent and then to deal with the other. Appropriately, German officers were always searching for opportunities to inflict such defeats. The German military had, not surprisingly, always placed great emphasis on maneuver and mobility, and Brauchitsch, Halder, and Leeb certainly recognized that the tank facilitated increased mobility.[45] Any reservations they may have felt in this area were undoubtedly erased in the Polish campaign. Thus the three generals did not oppose the use of panzer divisions in a German offensive.[46] The three did not believe, however, that the tank offered a means of revolutionizing warfare and thus provided Germany with the capability to win a quick and decisive victory against a formidable opponent such as the Allies.[47] Leeb articulated the following view:

> One could counter the above [the argument that a war in the West in 1939 would inevitably turn into a war of attrition] with the success of our mobile forces, especially the armored troops, in Poland. Such a comparison is dangerous. . . . the high value of the French Army and its leadership must not be underrated and the equipment with armored units and antitank weapons of the French and the English Armies must not be forgotten. It can hardly be expected that the proven courage of the armored forces will enable them to display once more against the Western Powers the nerve which in the East carried them from success to success.[48]

Although the members of this coalition were not advocates of the blitzkrieg in the fall of 1939, we must recall that they stressed the need for mobility and accordingly were favorably disposed toward the tank. Thus the gap between their beliefs and those of the blitzkrieg's advocates was not unbridgeable. It therefore became possible for the proponents of the blitzkrieg to win converts from the ranks of the more conservative army officers.

The members of the second coalition, like their counterparts in the first coalition, believed that the OKH plan would lead to another World War I.[49] This second group, however, maintained that it was possible to defeat the Allies decisively without resorting to an attrition strategy. The moving force in this group was Gen. Erich von Manstein, who was the chief of staff of Army Group A. His two principal allies were Gen. Gerd von Rundstedt (the commander of Army Group A), and Gen. Heinz Guderian (the commander of the Nineteenth Panzer Corps, which was assigned to Army Group A). The members of this coalition, all members of the army group that had been assigned a secondary role in the original OKH plan, believed that the Allies could be dealt a knockout blow if the main weight of the attack was shifted from Army Group B to Army Group A, and if Army Group A was then allowed to effect a deep strategic penetration. The maneuver would, of course, require a complete revamping of the OKH plan. These men were the exponents of the blitzkrieg that was eventually adopted.[50]

During the interwar period, Guderian had been the leading advocate of the blitzkrieg in Germany. He believed that panzer divisions operating independently of traditional infantry divisions could pierce a defensive front and could then cause the defender's collapse by driving deep into his rear.[51] He had written and lectured extensively on the subject,[52] and he had worked assiduously for the creation of an armored force that could translate his ideas into practice.[53] Guderian's views, however, were not widely accepted during the interwar period.[54] Significant opposition came from the more conservative senior officers, who believed that the tank was a very important development but did not accept Guderian's claim that large armored forces should be allowed to operate independently. They preferred to use the panzer divisions the way they used infantry divisions.

Manstein, who was the driving force within the coalition, was widely recognized as a general staff officer of great talent.[55] There is no evidence, however, that in the years prior to World War II he was an advocate of the blitzkrieg. Like the majority of his contemporaries, Manstein placed a high premium on mobility. Appropriately, he felt that the tank had an important role to play on the battlefield. Yet we have no evidence that he counseled using panzer forces to spearhead penetrations into the depths of the enemy rear. Manstein changed his viewpoint in fall 1939, and he and Guderian became staunch allies.

The third member of this coalition was Rundstedt who, as the commander of Army Group A, was both Guderian's and Manstein's boss. He was a very senior general who actually had much in common with the three generals in the first coalition. Not surprisingly, his view of the role of armor in early fall 1939 was essentially the same as Manstein's initial position. Unlike Manstein, he never completely accepted Guderian's claim that large-scale armored units acting independently of infantry divisions should be allowed to effect a deep strategic penetration. Rundstedt favored much closer coordination between armored and infantry divisions. He was important to the coalition primarily because he used his influence as a highly respected senior officer and as the commander of Army Group A to lobby vigorously for Manstein's proposals.[56] Although Manstein was the principal architect of plans espoused by Army Group A, he alone could not have hoped to influence the key decision makers at OKH.[57]

Although Manstein's plan eventually prevailed, this fact should not obscure the disadvantage under which the members of the second coalition operated. They were not strongly positioned to win acceptance of their ideas. First of all, since they were latecomers to the debate, they were forced to argue against a plan that had already been formally adopted. Furthermore, throughout the fall and early winter of 1939–1940, Hitler was constantly threatening to launch the offensive, so that the German military was in a continual state of alert. Under such conditions, it was very difficult to expect OKH seriously to consider a proposal that called for radical changes in the existing plan. Perhaps most important, however, members of the second coalition did not have direct access to Hitler, who was dissatisfied with the original OKH plan and was searching for an alternative.[58] Halder and Brauchitsch, who simply refused to accept Manstein's arguments, blocked the path to Hitler.

Finally we must consider Adolf Hitler himself. He was very knowledgeable about military matters, which held great fascination for him.[59] Specifically, he was a forceful advocate of heavy reliance on armored forces.[60] During the 1930s, when Guderian was having difficulty establishing a panzer force, Hitler promised Guderian his assistance.[61] Hitler's interest in creating a panzer force aside, what were his views on the blitzkrieg? In his "Memorandum and Directives for Conduct of the War in the West," dated 9 October 1939, Hitler provides a rare glimpse of his thinking about armored forces.[62] His views are certainly not very different from those of Guderian. Nevertheless, when we examine the entire memorandum, and when we carefully study Hitler's thinking during the months between October 1939 and February 1940, it becomes clear that Hitler had not yet fully grasped the revolutionary potential of the tank. Specifically, no evidence indicates a belief on his part during this period that the panzer divisions could be employed so as to produce the decisive victory in the west that he wanted so badly. Before February 1940, Hitler saw no alternative to a limited aims strategy in the West.

Hitler eventually became a proponent of the blitzkrieg. As will become evident, it is difficult to determine to what extent he changed his mind on his own.[63] At any rate, given his views on armored forces, he certainly did not have to make a great shift to endorse the blitzkrieg. In this regard, he was like the conservative generals in the first coalition.[64] Actually, between October 1939 and February 1940, Hitler's views on a war in the West showed a number of similarities with those of Brauchitsch, Halder, and Leeb. As noted, neither Hitler nor these three generals fully appreciated the revolutionary potential of the tank. Second, none of them was able to devise a plan that promised a decisive victory. They all agreed, Hitler included, to accept a military plan that called for a limited victory. Third, Hitler did not take issue with the conclusion of Brauchitsch and associates that a limited aims strategy was very likely to evolve into a long war.[65] Finally, like his generals, Hitler had fought in the First World War and clearly understood the necessity of avoiding a protracted war.[66] Given these similar views on such important matters, why did Hitler and his generals clash to such an extent?

The answer is directly linked to the previously described differences between Hitler and his generals with respect to questions of grand strategy. Hitler believed that the Allies were preparing to move into the Low Countries, while his generals did not. They believed that the war in the West would remain "phoney." Furthermore, Hitler, who was determined to establish German dominance on the continent as soon as possible, believed that he had to defeat France decisively in a war. The generals, in fall 1939, did not share Hitler's enthusiasm for such a policy.

Hitler believed that there was a real chance that the German offensive, although calling for a limited victory, would produce a decisive victory and would thus fulfill his goal of knocking France out of the war and of driving Britain from the Continent. He was willing to take this gamble and sought to maximize his chances of succeeding. Accordingly, he tried to enlarge the scope of the offensive and to launch the attack immediately, when the British contribution to the Allied effort was still small. With the passage of time, the size of the British contingent would increase substantially. For Hitler, as long as the tenacious British were not physically committed to the Continent in large numbers, the Germans stood a reasonable chance of winning a decisive victory.[67] This "window" of opportunity, however, would not remain open for long.

There is no doubt that it was terribly risky to pursue a strategy for attack on the assumption that a decisive victory *might* result. Hitler clearly recognized this fact. In a speech to his generals on 23 November 1939, he said:

> It [the decision to attack in the West] is a difficult decision for me. None has ever achieved what I have achieved. . . . I have led the German people to a great height, even if the world does hate us now. I am setting this work on a gamble. I have to choose between victory or destruction. I choose victory. . . . The question as to whether the attack will be successful no one can answer. Everything depends upon the favorable incident.[68]

The generals in the first coalition considered such a risk categorically unacceptable. For them, no political rationale could justify pursuing a risk-laden strategy that, if it failed, might very well lead to catastrophe. For Hitler, who was driven by the desire to make Germany a world power, such risks were necessary to achieve his aim.[69]

There was a second reason why Hitler was willing to pursue such a perilous course of action. He believed that the Allies planned to move into the Low Countries, and even if his attack failed to produce a decisive victory, he would have placed Germany, at worst, in a good position to wage what promised to be a long war.[70] The generals, of course, had made a different assessment of Allied intentions. For these reasons, Hitler pushed hard for an immediate offensive while his generals vigorously contested him.[71]

THE DECISION-MAKING PROCESS:
OCTOBER 1939–MAY 1940

*The Movement to Dissuade Hitler
from Attacking in the West*

Three days after Hitler announced his plan to strike in the West, Brauchitsch and Halder met with him and submitted a memorandum calling for a defensive posture in the West.[72] On 4 October General Jodl, the chief of the Operations Staff at OKW, told Halder that Hitler was very upset with his commanders for dragging their feet.[73] Jodl's warning had little impact. On 7 October, Brauchitsch and Halder met with Hitler and again attempted to dissuade him from assuming the offensive in the West.[74] They were not successful. Hitler made it clear at this meeting that he was willing to attack even if he could achieve only limited objectives. He told Brauchitsch and Halder that they must take the offensive, "even if we fall short of the original objectives and attain only a line which would afford better protection for the Ruhr."[75]

During the next few days, Hitler prepared a lengthy description (the aforementioned 9 October memorandum) of his rationale for attacking and the benefits to be gained. He then called a meeting for 10 October with his military chiefs. At this meeting, Hitler read his memorandum and tried to persuade the generals of the merits of his scheme.[76] Neither side altered its position. That same day, OKW issued Directive No. 6, which provided the first formal guidance on the shape of the projected offensive. At this point, the army leaders realized that in light of Hitler's unbending position it would be necessary to devise a concrete plan to implement the limited aims strategy outlined in Directive No. 6. Thus, serious planning commenced at OKH. Nevertheless, Brauchitsch and Halder continued their efforts to dissuade Hitler from his plans for an offensive.

The officers' fears that an offensive in the West would prove disastrous were reinforced on 12 October by a detailed memorandum from Leeb (the commander of Army Group C), which presented the arguments against attacking in the West. In his cover letter Leeb wrote of his "grave anxiety for our future" and "the serious situation in which we find ourselves which might decide our people's future for several decades to come."[77] He concluded by noting: "I am sure that my views are shared by many others."[78] The "many others" certainly included Brauchitsch and Halder.

On 17 October, Brauchitsch met with Hitler and tried again to persuade him not to strike in the West. Afterward Brauchitsch described the situation as "hopeless."[79] Two days later, on the nineteenth, the army forwarded its first plan of attack to OKW.[80] As noted, the plan called for Army Group B to make the main attack. The main force of Army Group B was two armies that were located north and south of Liége.[81] The two armies were to launch a pincer attack that would close to the west of Liége but east of Brussels (see figure 4.3). The objective was to encircle the Allied forces on the northern wing of the Allied front. The northern army was the stronger of the two pincers. After closing the pincers, the forces of Army Group B were expected to push westward through Bruges and Ghent to the Channel coast. The objective was limited. In fact, the plan did not even address the question of occupying French territory. "The order dealt only with operations against Holland, Belgium, and Luxembourg."[82]

There was widespread dissatisfaction with the plan from the start. On 25 October, Hitler met with Brauchitsch and Halder to discuss the matter. Hitler told the generals that he wanted to place the main axis of advance south of Liége and to strike toward Amiens and Reims.[83] Hitler's proposal to place the weight of the attack south of Liége and to strike in a southwesterly direction contrasted sharply with the army's plan to locate the weight of the attack north of Liége and to strike in a northwesterly direction. Significantly, Hitler's proposal would force the German army to defeat a larger portion of the Allied forces than would the army plan, as was consistent with his view that the strategy, even if proffered as a limited one, should maximize the chances of achieving a decisive victory. Hitler and the OKH leaders could not agree on how to alter the plan, although

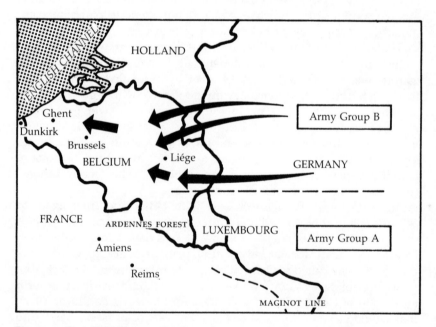

Figure 4.3. First OKH Plan, 19 October 1939

Halder noted in his diary that the "offensive will be broadened later on."[84]

While this meeting on the twenty-fifth was in progress, General Bock and his subordinates, Generals Reichenau and Kluge, joined the discussion. Bock was the commander of Army Group B, which would make the main attack in the forthcoming offensive. Reichenau was the commander of the forces that composed the powerful northern pincer in the OKH plan, while Kluge commanded the southern pincer. Bock, Kluge, and Reichenau, who realized that Hitler was intent on launching the attack in fall 1939 joined with Brauchitsch and Halder to discourage Hitler from attacking.[85] At this point, Hitler must have realized how widespread the opposition was to his scheme. Although Brauchitsch and Halder had never demonstrated any sympathy to Nazism, Reichenau had; and now Reichenau was the main spokesman for the dissenting triumvirate from Army Group B.[86] Hitler certainly had not expected resistance from him.[87] General Keitl, the chief of OKW, aptly summarized the situation when he noted that two points of view in October 1939 "stood diametrically opposed to each other."[88]

Brauchitsch and Halder met again with Hitler two days later, on 27 October, and Hitler told them that the attack would commence on 12 November. Brauchitsch said that the army would not be prepared for action before 26 November. Hitler responded that this date was "much too late."[89] Time was growing short for Halder and Brauchitsch. The two army leaders met again the following day with Hitler, who outlined the changes he wanted made in the first OKH plan.[90] There would still be armies from Army Group B located north and south of Liége,[91] but the main weight of the attack was to shift to the south of Liége, and the envelopment west of Liége was to be abandoned. Instead the Germans would launch an essentially frontal attack with the aim of driving the Allies straight across central and northern Belgium to the Channel coast (see figure 4.4). Army Group A was to move across the southern part of Belgium and to protect Army Group B's southern flank. Although the new plan was somewhat more ambitious in scope than the original, the two were very similar. Both relied on Army Group B to make the main attack and to capture the northern portion of Belgium. Although the original plan relied on an envelopment west of Liége, it was, like the second version, basically a frontal attack designed to push the Allies back along a broad front. This point was not lost on German military leaders, who recognized that such a strategy would lead to a repeat of World War I.[92]

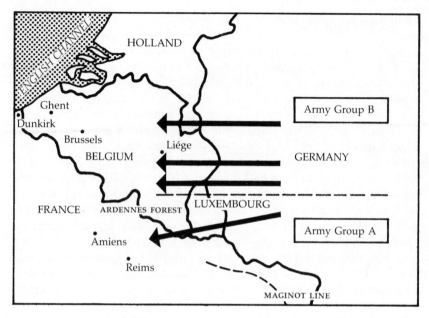

Figure 4.4. Second OKH Plan, 29 October 1939

The mood of Brauchitsch and Halder remained pessimistic. Then, on 31 October, they received another memorandum from Leeb spelling out the grave dangers associated with an attack in the West. The intensity of Leeb's concern is reflected in his concluding sentence: "I am prepared to stand behind you personally to the fullest extent in the days to come and to bear the consequences desirable or necessary."[93] That same day they received a memorandum from Army Group A arguing that the existing plan would lead to catastrophe.[94] Brauchitsch and Halder were scheduled to visit the headquarters of the army groups on 2 and 3 November. On the eve of their departure, Ulrich von Hassell, one of the main actors in the conspiracy that was developing against Hitler, visited Brauchitsch and his wife. After the meeting, Hassell wrote in his diary: "I did my best to show them the tremendous responsibility the general now bears."[95] The subsequent visit to the army group headquarters confirmed their worst suspicions. Halder wrote in his diary for 3 November: "None of the higher headquarters thinks that the offensive . . . has any prospect of success. No decisive success can be expected from ground operations."[96]

On his return from the front, Halder met with Gen. Georg Thomas, the head of the War Economy and Armaments Office at OKW. Thomas told Halder that significant economic problems would result from an offensive in the West.[97] Previously, in September, Thomas had given Halder and Gen. Walter Warlimont of OKW information about the state of the German economy that provided ammunition for those who opposed Hitler's plan to attack in the West.[98] If the German military could not deliver a rapid knockout blow and was thus forced to fight a protracted war (which Brauchitsch, Halder, and Leeb saw as the logical outcome of a limited aims strategy), then a strong German war economy would be essential. Thomas, who was an active member in the group conspiring to depose Hitler, provided Halder with evidence that the German economy was not prepared to sustain the protracted war that now seemed inevitable.

After returning from the meetings with the commanders at the front, Brauchitsch asked to meet with Hitler. He felt that he should make one more effort to change Hitler's mind. The meeting took place on 5 November, and the results were disastrous. Brauchitsch took a memorandum with him that had been written in direct response to Hitler's 9 October Memorandum; it "attempted to prove that any offensive was ruled out at the moment."[99] After failing to make any headway with the standard litany of arguments, Brauchitsch tried to convince Hitler that the German troops might not be prepared to assume the offensive. He told Hitler that the troops had not been aggressive in Poland and that there had been discipline problems in that first campaign.[100] For Hitler, who was not familiar with these claims, this was the last straw. He launched into a tirade that left Brauchitsch stunned and badly shaken. As a consequence of this key meeting, Brauchitsch's influence with Hitler plummeted.[101] Moreover, after the 5 November meeting, it was manifest that Hitler could not be dissuaded from an offensive against the Allies.[102]

The opposition to an offensive nevertheless continued. In the wake of the 5 November meeting, the three army group commanders (Bock, Leeb, and Rundstedt) held a secret meeting to discuss how to prevent Hitler from striking in the West.[103] The commanders voiced some differences. For example, Leeb was against an offensive altogether, while Rundstedt wanted to adopt a different strategy and then to attack. Such differences were not crucial in fall 1939 because there was an overriding concern: stopping Hitler from opening an offensive in the West. The three army commanders agreed to do everything possible to achieve that end.[104]

The Emergence of the Blitzkrieg

While the generals were doing their best to keep Hitler from striking, the blitzkrieg began to emerge as a viable option. It took approximately four months before this strategy was formally adopted, and the decision-making process was complex. Army Group A was the main driving force behind the blitzkrieg, although it is clear that Hitler's influence was of crucial importance. Moreover, a number of events in the early part of 1940, principally an airplane crash and two sand table exercises, facilitated the adoption of the blitzkrieg.

The leaders of Army Group A were particularly dissatisfied with the first two OKH plans. They believed that it would be suicidal to launch an offensive that did not promise a decisive victory.[105] They also believed that a plan of their own would allow the German army to defeat the Allies decisively. On 31 October, Rundstedt, the commander of Army Group A, forwarded a letter and a memorandum outlining Army Group A's views to OKH. During the next three months, Rundstedt and Manstein, Army Group A's chief of staff, sent seven more memorandums to OKH.[106] Furthermore, they talked directly with Halder and Brauchitsch on a number of occasions, trying always to convince the OKH chiefs of the merits of their plan.[107] More often than not, OKH refused to respond to Army Group A's memorandums. When there was a response, Rundstedt and Manstein were told that the existing plan could not be altered.[108] By late January 1940, when the weather had finally forced postponement of the operation until spring, there was no evidence that Army Group A had made any headway in winning acceptance of its proposal. The limited aims strategy was still in place.

Army Group A's initial proposal differed in a number of important respects from the final plan that operationalized the blitzkrieg. Nevertheless, the general outline of the final plan is present in the first proposal that Rundstedt sent to OKH.[109] Most important, he called for shifting the main weight of the attack from Army Group B in the north to Army Group A in the south. Actually, Rundstedt envisioned Army Group A's forces working closely with the southernmost elements of Army Group B. Their objective was not to push the Allies back along a broad front, as was the case with the existing plan, but instead to pierce the Allies' front somewhere between Liége and Namur and then to drive deep into the Allies' rear. It is clear that Army Group A was concerned to effect a deep strategic penetration, the central element in the blitzkrieg.

As we know, a blitzkrieg provides that large armored units operating independently should conduct the deep attacks. It is evident from Rundstedt's first memorandum that the panzer forces were expected to play an important role in Army Group A's proposed plan.[110] This emphasis is hardly surprising, since panzer forces had contributed significantly to the recent German victory in Poland. Nevertheless, no details are provided regarding the precise role that the panzer divisions were expected to play. At that point, all of them were assigned to Army Group B. Although Rundstedt's memorandum suggests that at least some of those divisions would be transferred to Army Group A, no mention is made of the need to transfer the main body of armored forces from Army Group B to Army Group A. The chief consideration at this early moment, of course, was switching the main point of attack rather than determining how much armor Army Group A would need and how to employ that armor. The question of the role to be played by the armored forces in the offensive, however, was of crucial importance. Not surprisingly, Army Group A began to address this issue in subsequent memorandums. In the final stages of the decision-making process, it became the source of considerable controversy. Army Group A's failure to provide details on the employment of armor notwithstanding, the plan laid out in the first memorandum was very close to being a blitzkrieg.

During this same period, Hitler began to focus attention on Army Group A. His new interest was a consequence of his general dissatisfaction with the existing plan as well as of his specific desire to broaden its scope so as to maximize the chances of achieving a decisive victory. At the aforementioned 25 October meeting, where Hitler had discussed the first OKH plan with his generals, he actually asked about the possibility of placing the main weight of the attack opposite the Ardennes, the principal topographical feature in southern Belgium.[111] He quickly dismissed his own idea, however, and none of the assembled generals saw fit to defend it. But on 30 October, one day after the second OKH plan was issued, Jodl noted in his diary: "Führer comes with new idea about having an armored and a motorized division attack Sedan via Arlon."[112] In effect, this meant giving Army Group A a *small* armored force that would attack through the Ardennes. There is no evidence that at this point Hitler was aware of Army Group A's idea for shifting the main weight of the offensive. Brauchitsch was made aware of Hitler's "new idea," and on 12 November the Nineteenth Panzer Corps, which was commanded by Guderian, was assigned to Army Group A.[113]

This change was significant for a number of reasons. First, Army

Group A had hitherto comprised only infantry divisions. The new assignment also meant, however, that the panzer divisions would not be concentrated with one army group but would instead be spread out across a broad front. Third, and very important, Guderian, the foremost proponent of the blitzkrieg in Germany, was now united with Manstein and Rundstedt, who had by this time already given OKH two memorandums outlining their plan.[114]

Although Hitler was responsible for assigning the Nineteenth Panzer Corps to Army Group A, he was not shifting the main weight of the attack away from Army Group B. The attack through Sedan was of secondary importance. Equally important, Hitler still did not see any alternative to a limited aims strategy. Thus, Hitler's position at this point stands in marked contrast to that of Army Group A, which called for shifting the weight of the attack as a way to deal the Allies a knockout blow.

Soon after Nineteenth Panzer Corps had become part of Army Group A, Hitler asked his military advisers whether it would be possible to reinforce Guderian if he achieved initial success. On 20 November, OKW issued Directive No. 8, which stipulated that OKH should be capable of switching the main point of effort from Army Group B to Army Group A should the opportunity present itself *during* the campaign.[115] Accordingly, the Fourteenth Motorized Corps was moved up behind Army Group A from east of the Rhine. Nevertheless, it was not formally assigned to Army Group A but remained a part of the OKH reserve.[116] Despite these developments, the existing plan remained intact, although there now existed the possibility of shifting the weight of the attack *after* the campaign had started. This strategy of hedging bets of course meant that there would be strong pressure to spread the panzer forces between Army Groups A and B.

Shortly after Nineteenth Panzer Corps joined Army Group A, Guderian and Manstein met to discuss the upcoming offensive.[117] Guderian told Manstein of his displeasure with the distribution of the panzer divisions across a wide front. Manstein then described his plan to Guderian, who reacted enthusiastically, although he warned Manstein that it was imperative to employ a large number of armored divisions at the main point of attack.[118] Specifically, this caution meant that Army Group A should rely on panzer divisions to make the initial breakthrough and then to effect the deep strategic penetration. Manstein did not disagree. It is clear that, from this point forward, Manstein and Guderian completely agreed on the shape of the proposed offensive.[119]

Their agreement is apparent in the first memorandum that Manstein forwarded to OKH after the Nineteenth Panzer Corps had been assigned to Army Group A:

> For the A Gp it is, however, important, after dashing through Luxembourg making maximum use of the element of surprise, to break through the fortified Belgian positions before the French are able to form up their defence forces and to entirely defeat in *Belgium* those French elements initially to be expected for encounter. This is the prerequisite both for the continuation of the operation over the Meuse and for the formation of a defensive front toward the south. Therefore the A Gp has placed the XIX Corps with 3 div in the front line *forward of the front* and has allocated to it alone four trunk roads to try to break through the fortified Belgian positions.[120]

Now, Army Group A's proposal contained all the ingredients of the blitzkrieg, although it was clear that Army Group A would need more armored forces.[121] The Nineteenth Panzer Corps alone was not enough to effect a breakthrough and to conduct a deep strategic penetration. As I noted earlier, OKH placed the Fourteenth Motorized Corps *behind* Army Group A in late November. Shortly thereafter, Manstein and Rundstedt asked OKH to assign the Fourteenth Motorized Corps to Army Group A so that it could be employed with the Nineteenth Panzer Corps in the front of the army group.[122] OKH refused the request.[123]

As 1939 came to a close, OKH remained tied to its own limited plan. Although Army Group A continued sending memorandums to OKH, no more important changes were made in the disposition of forces until the blitzkrieg was adopted in mid-February 1940. On 27 December 1939, OKW announced that the date for the beginning of the offensive would be decided by 9 January.[124] On 10 January, the weather forecast was favorable, and Hitler decided that the attack would start on 17 January.[125] Also on 10 January, a German airplane carrying a copy of the OKH plan crashed in Belgium. Jodl's subsequent entry in his diary sums up the German reaction to this development: "If enemy is in possession of all the files, situation catastrophic."[126] The attack was canceled for the last time on 13 January.[127] In light of the plane crash and the onset of winter, it was decided to postpone the attack until spring 1940.

With this decision, the military leaders, as well as Hitler, had time to consider the options in front of them carefully. Then, too, the divulgence of the existing plan had certainly made it imperative to consider alternatives.[128] Army Group A continued to plead its case. The final two of its eight memorandums were forwarded to OKH after the plane crash.[129] At a key conference on 25 January, Rundstedt and Manstein tried to persuade the OKH chiefs of the merits of their plan.[130] Again they were unsuccessful. As the month ended, the limited plan devised in October and slightly modified in November remained intact.

In February, that plan was finally abandoned, and the blitzkrieg championed by Army Group A was adopted. It appears that the change came about largely because of two very important sand table exercises and the intervention of Hitler. Ironically, Manstein was informed on 27 January that he was being transferred to command a reserve infantry corps, effective on 9 February.[131] Before the transfer took place, Manstein helped run a sand table exercise at Army Group A headquarters in Coblenz (7 February). At this exercise, which was attended by the OKH chiefs, a large-scale simulation of the existing plan was conducted for the first time. Here it became evident that the Nineteenth Panzer Corps would have to be reinforced immediately.[132] Perception of this need was due in part to new intelligence indicating that the French were increasing the strength of their forces opposite the Ardennes.[133] In any case, however, Army Group A had always recognized that one armored corps would not be sufficient to pierce the Allied front and then to effect a deep strategic penetration. It was also apparent that Guderian would reach the Meuse within four days. Guderian and Halder engaged in a heated debate as to whether Army Group A should attack across the Meuse immediately (Guderian) or whether it should wait until the "ninth or tenth day of the offensive" (Halder).[134] In effect, Halder wanted to wait for the infantry to catch up with the armor before he crossed the Meuse. Guderian maintained that the panzer divisions could cross the river alone. Nevertheless, Manstein believed that Halder was finally beginning to see the merits of Army Group A's proposal.[135]

Another sand table exercise was held one week later on 14 February. Again it was clear that the Nineteenth Panzer Corps would reach the Meuse very quickly and that, moreover, if Army Group A had any hope of driving into the depths of the Allied rear, reinforcements would be needed before the attack was launched. Guderian and Halder continued their argument about the proper time to cross the Meuse and the proper kind of formations to use. Halder, who still favored using infantry divisions and armored divisions together, remarked in his diary for that day: "*Guderian and Witersheim* [commander of the Fourteenth Motorized Corps] plainly show lack of confidence in success. Guderian: Has lost confidence—The whole tank operation is planned wrong!"[136] Unfortunately for Guderian, Manstein was not present at this second war game.[137] He had departed for his new assignment five days earlier. Although Halder had not formally acknowledged acceptance of the Army Group A plan and disagreed with Guderian's ideas concerning the Meuse crossing, he did recognize the need to increase the weight of Army Group A.

As this perceptible shift in Halder's view was taking place, Hitler was reviewing the existing plan. On 13 February, he was given the detailed breakdown of the disposition of German forces that he had requested. After examining the report, Hitler remarked to Jodl:

> Most of the gun-armed tanks have been expended on places which are not decisive. The armoured divisions with the Fourth Army [which formed part of Army Group B's attacking force] can do little in areas where there are obstructions and fortifications. They will come to a standstill at the Meuse, if not before. . . . They should be concentrated in the direction of Sedan where the enemy does not expect our main thrust. The documents carried by the aircraft which made the landing have still further confirmed their opinion that our only concern is to occupy the Channel coastline of Holland and Belgium.[138]

Jodl warned Hitler that "the thrust against Sedan is a tactical gamble, where one can be surprised by the God of War."[139] Hitler was not impressed. That same afternoon, Colonels Grieffenberg and Heusinger, both from the Operations Staff at OKH, were summoned to Jodl's office. Jodl told them about Hilter's ideas and then directed them to provide a detailed study of the matter.[140] Four days later, on 17 February, Hitler called Manstein aside after a routine meeting of recently appointed corps commanders.[141] He asked Manstein to outline his views on the offensive in the West. When Manstein had finished detailing his plan, Hitler "indicated his agreement with the ideas put forward."[142] The next day (18 February) Halder met with Hitler to present the results of the study that OKH had conducted in response to Jodl's 13 February meeting with Grieffenberg and Heusinger. OKH recommended shifting the main weight of the attack to Army Group A, as Hitler had prescribed.[143] OKH's position was now of course consistent with Army Group A's views on the reshaping of the offensive. Shortly thereafter, the new plan was formally adopted. To see exactly how it came to the fore, however, we must examine the events of February more closely to determine the real lines of influence.

The 17 February conversation between Hitler and Manstein did not effect a major change in Hitler's thinking on the shape of the offensive. Hitler had already indicated on 13 February that he intended to alter the plan radically; the meeting with Manstein merely confirmed Hitler's earlier decision. The key question is: Why did Hitler change his mind on 13 February and decide to shift the weight of the attack to Army Group A? As always, it is difficult to determine the underlying reasons for Hitler's actions, but well-grounded speculation is nevertheless possible.

First, Hitler was familiar with Manstein's proposal before 13 February. In late December, Col. Rudolf Schmundt, who was Hitler's adjutant, visited Army Group A.[144] Col. Guenther Blumentritt, one of Manstein's chief lieutenants and a staunch advocate of his boss's plan, was detailed to escort Schmundt. Blumentritt took this opportunity to show Schmundt Manstein's proposal. Schmundt then requested a copy so that he could show it to Hitler. After securing Manstein's permission, Blumentritt forwarded the proposal to Schmundt in Berlin. The following day, Schmundt telephoned Blumentritt and told him that Hitler "had read the plan with great interest . . . and liked [it] for its audacity." Obviously Hitler was not so impressed that he moved to adopt the plan immediately. After all, the strategy was very bold and therefore not without risk.[145]

Nevertheless, Hitler remained dissatisfied with the existing OKH proposal. When the plane carrying a copy crashed in January, he proceeded to reevaluate the entire strategy. His subsequent movement toward the Manstein plan might have been influenced by the results of the 7 February sand table exercise, although there is no evidence that he was informed of the results. There is evidence, however, that Colonel Schmundt continued to serve as a conduit to Hitler for Army Group A's ideas.[146]

The new plan itself undoubtedly held a certain attraction for Hitler. Although it was audacious, it would, if successful, produce the decisive victory that he wanted so badly. Furthermore, Hitler had always been favorably disposed toward upgrading Army Group A's role in the offensive. OKW Directive No. 8, which mandated that the capability be developed to shift the main weight of the attack to Army Group A, highlights this point. Furthermore, as I noted earlier, Hitler at a meeting in October 1939 had actually mentioned the possibility of placing the main axis of advance through Sedan. Not surprisingly, once Hitler was convinced that the idea of attacking through Sedan was sound, he claimed credit for having devised the scheme.[147] Given that the OKH plan was in extreme disarray by late January, it is hardly surprising that Hitler, who was aware of Manstein's proposal and had always favored strengthening Army Group A, opted to shift. Manstein personally briefed Hitler on 17 February, and Halder added the OKH stamp of approval on the following day. Thereafter the decision to adopt the blitzkrieg strategy was final. Only the details remained to be determined.

Let us briefly consider Halder's change of heart. As noted, the two sand table exercises (7 and 14 February) forced Halder to reconsider his opposition to strengthening Army Group A. Although Halder still did not accept Manstein's claims about the location of the main point of attack, Halder was forced to admit that Army Group A needed to be strengthened before an offensive could be launched. After returning to OKH headquarters from the second sand table exercise, Halder was told about the 13 February meeting of Grieffenberg and Heusinger, from his staff, with Jodl. Halder, who had never been enamored of the original OKH plan and who had just seen that plan's weaknesses displayed in two sand table exercises, was now facing pressure from Hitler to move in the direction that Manstein and his supporters had been advocating for months. It is hardly surprising, then, that Halder presented Hitler with a plan calling for a knockout blow to be delivered by Army Group A through Sedan.

The New Plan

On 24 February, Halder reviewed the proposed plan with his commanders at OKH headquarters and issued the final operations order.[148] Despite the OKH leadership's hostility to the Manstein proposal before February, they staunchly supported it once they had been won over. In fact, as Telford Taylor notes, OKH's version of the Army Group A plan was actually "far more drastic than anything Manstein had ever proposed."[149] The key assumption was that once the fighting in the West began, the Allies would push forward into northern and central Belgium, placing the majority of the Allied forces opposite Army Group B, which was now the weaker of the two principal German army groups. In southern Belgium in the area of the Ardennes, the Allies would have a relatively weak force matched against the main weight of the German army. While the Allies were engaged with Army Group B in northern and central Belgium, Army Group A would drive through the Ardennes, would cross the Meuse, and would then head straight for the French coast. In effect, this group would pin the bulk of the Allied forces against the North Sea (see figure 4.5). By moving their main forces forward into Belgium, the Allies would make it much easier for the Germans, once they had penetrated the Allied line opposite the Ardennes, to effect a deep strategic penetration. If the Allies remained along the

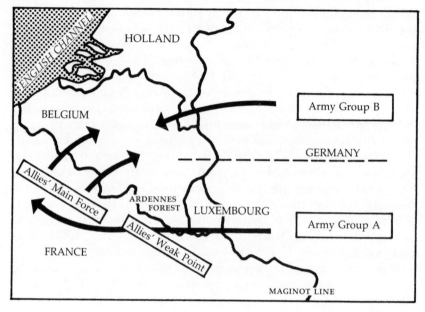

Figure 4.5. The Manstein Plan .

Franco-Belgian border, they would be in a much better position to retreat and to prevent the Germans from penetrating into their rear. As a result of information gleaned through intelligence channels, the Germans were confident that the Allies would play into their hands by moving into Belgium.[150]

It is noteworthy that the majority of panzer divisions were transferred from Army Group B to Army Group A. To make the breakthrough and effect the deep strategic penetration, the Germans created an "armored wedge" within Army Group A. Two armored corps and a motorized infantry corps were placed under a special command. A third armored corps was also assigned to Army Group A. The armored forces, operating independently of the standard infantry divisions, were to be the main striking arm of the German army. This was to be a classic blitzkrieg.

Opposition to the Blitzkrieg

A small number of senior officers were not pleased with the role assigned to the panzer divisions. Specifically, they questioned whether armored forces *alone* were capable of piercing the Allied front and then effecting a deep strategic penetration. They felt that the infantry

[126]

divisions should fight the breakthrough battles, with the armored forces held in the rear, waiting to exploit any breakthroughs that might occur. Furthermore, once the panzer divisions were employed, there should be greater emphasis on having them work in tandem with standard infantry divisions. These ideas, of course, threatened the very essence of the blitzkrieg.

The principal proponent of reducing the role of the panzer divisions was Gen. Georg von Sodenstern, who replaced Manstein as chief of staff of Army Group A. The other two officers who were skeptical of the idea of assigning the armored forces an independent role were Rundstedt and Blumentritt, who were also from Army Group A. Ironically, Rundstedt, who played such an important role in the fight to win acceptance of Army Group A's plan, began doubting the capabilities of the armored forces before the first sand table exercise on 7 February.[151] Rundstedt's doubts, as well as Blumentritt's, were based, in large part, on the fear that armored forces alone would not be capable of handling the Allied forces opposite the Ardennes, which, according to new intelligence, had increased in size.[152] They believed that Guderian's ideas on the employment of armor made sense in late fall 1939, when the balance of forces was more favorable for Army Group A. Of course, both Rundstedt and Blumentritt supported Manstein's and Guderian's position on the employment of armor during this period.

At the second sand table exercise on 14 February, when the question of how to employ the panzer divisions was raised, Rundstedt sided with Halder against Guderian.[153] Then, at the 24 February meeting, where the new plan was discussed, Rundstedt expressed his doubts about the planned employment of the "armored wedge."[154] Although Rundstedt entertained reservations, the record shows that he did not feel very strongly about them. He did not vigorously contest the issue, as he had done earlier when he and Manstein sought to win acceptance of their plan. In fact, once Halder mandated that the new plan would not be changed, Rundstedt accepted the decision.

Manstein's replacement, Sodenstern, was the most forceful opponent of assigning panzer divisions the key role in the forthcoming offensive. He secured Rundstedt's permission to send a memorandum to OKH expressing his own concern. In this memorandum, which Rundstedt significantly did not sign, Sodenstern argued:

> I have grave misgivings with regard to the commitment of strong panzer and motorized forces moving ahead of the front line of the attacking armies.

[127]

These mobile formations . . . should be held back as an operational reserve to be employed in seeking the decision only *after* a successful breakthrough of the enemy front has been achieved. I fear that they will not be able to fulfill the tasks assigned to them within the scope of the forthcoming offensive.

I am . . . convinced that we cannot force the crossing of the Meuse with motorized forces, but that we must fight our way across with infantry.[155]

Sodenstern's doubts went even further. He also questioned whether it was wise to rely so heavily on armored forces to conduct the deep strategic penetration. He favored closely coordinated efforts between infantry and panzer divisions.

This memorandum, however, had little effect at OKH because Halder, who was the most powerful individual in the German army at this point, had completely broken with his earlier position and had accepted the arguments of Guderian and Manstein. The extent of Halder's conversion is reflected in the new plan, for which he bore full responsibility. Halder, who had consistently rejected Army Group A's proposals and who had challenged Guderian on the issue of how to use panzer divisions at both of the sand table exercises, had now become one of the principal defenders of the blitzkrieg. This transformation is perhaps best reflected in his reply to Sodenstern's memorandum, which is worth quoting at length.

The mission assigned to the German Army is a very difficult one. Given the terrain (Meuse) and the ratio of forces on both sides—especially with regard to artillery—this mission cannot be fulfilled if we employ those means which were relevant in the last war. We will have to use exceptional means and take the resulting risk.

Whether the panzer divisions of the forward wave appear on the Meuse in full combat power is less important to me than the necessity of demonstrating resolute daring in pursuit of the retreating enemy and in making the initial crossing to the western Meuse bank decisive. . . .

I am absolutely aware of the fact that these units, when dashing forward, will have hours of severe crisis on the western Meuse bank. The Luftwaffe will relieve them by fully bringing to bear its superior combat power. Without taking this risk we might never be able to reach the left Meuse bank. But I am convinced that, in this operation, too, our panzer leaders will have an advantage, due to their energy and flexibility, combined with the effect of setting personal examples. Against an enemy proceeding methodically and less trained in commanding panzers, they will be able to exploit the severe psychological burden imposed by the appearance of German panzers on a unit which lacks battle testing.

Assuming that all the possibilities for an adequate allocation and a carefully considered disposition of our forces have been exploited, I cannot accept the argument that our mobile forces, organized and armed as they are, do not meet the necessary requirements for such a task.[156]

Halder's reply to Sodenstern ended debate on this issue. Army Group A did not raise the question again. When the principal commanders of Army Group A met with Hitler and Halder to discuss the new strategy on 15 March, they addressed the question of how the Nineteenth Panzer Corps would be employed in the upcoming offensive.[157] Guderian, that staunch advocate of the blitzkrieg, told the assembled leaders that armored units would operate independently of the infantry units. Here was the perfect opportunity for Rundstedt to contest Guderian. Yet he remained silent. Guderian, not Sodenstern, had triumphed.[158]

DETERRENCE AND THE BLITZKRIEG

With the adoption of the blitzkrieg, deterrence no longer obtained, simply because there was widespread agreement among the key German decision makers that the Allies would be defeated rapidly and decisively. Gen. Friedrich Fromm, the commander of the Home Army and a conservative military thinker, told Hassell on 25 April: "We will push through Holland and Belgium at one blow, and then finish off France in fourteen days."[159] Although Fromm's prescience was unique, the fact that a conservative military leader would make such a claim reflects the confidence that prevailed on the German side during the months prior to the May attack.

Although Rundstedt was never fully comfortable with Guderian's ideas about the use of armor, there is no evidence that Rundstedt's long-standing confidence in Army Group A's plan ever wavered. It is not possible to determine whether Halder convinced Sodenstern of the merit of the new plan, although he certainly silenced Sodenstern.[160] Still, Sodenstern's views did not reflect the dominant opinion within Army Group A. The influential Guderian, who was the most vocal proponent of using armored forces to effect a deep strategic penetration, remained in command of the Nineteenth Panzer Corps. He had a number of key allies within Army Group A. Colonels Blumentritt and Tresckow, two of Manstein's most loyal supporters throughout the battle to win acceptance of his proposal, remained in their influential positions in Army Group A.[161] Furthermore, the various commanders of the armored and motorized units that would deliver the decisive blow were convinced that they would accomplish their goal.[162]

The only other person, aside from Sodenstern, who expressed serious reservations about the plan was General Bock, whose Army Group B had been greatly weakened to strengthen Army Group A. Not surprisingly, Bock complained to Halder that his main force (Reichenau's Sixth Army) was "too weak to take advantage of its opportunities" and required "more Armd. Divs."[163] Giving it more would of course mean dispersing the armor that had been concentrated with Army Group A. Halder's response to Bock provides further evidence of the degree to which Halder had come to accept the blitzkrieg. He records his reply to Bock in his diary: "Cannot be done. Giving R. [Reichenau] the Armor would break up the concentration of the Armd. Echelon, as now planned; *Armor would then have to be committed teamed up with Infantry*" (emphasis added).[164] At one point, Bock told Halder that he was "gambling with Germany's fate"; he predicted that the Ardennes would become "the grave-digger of the Panzer arm."[165] Bock's arguments fell on deaf ears, however, because the key decision makers were convinced that the plan would produce a decisive victory. The principal commanders of Army Group A met with Hitler and Halder on 15 March to discuss the new plan. Then, on the following day, the key commanders in Bock's Army Group B met with Hitler and Halder. The lead entry in Halder's diary for 17 March summarized the impact of the criticism from both Sodenstern and Bock. It reads: "Fuehrer conference on 16 as well as that on 15 March produced no new viewpoints."[166]

Hitler, who had never been satisfied with the various versions of the original OKH plan, was firmly convinced that the new plan would succeed. Halder remarks in his diary for 17 March, "The Fuehrer now approves the preparations made and is manifestly confident of success."[167] At OKH, which had long been the center of resistance to the Manstein plan, a radical change of heart took place. The most important convert was Halder, whose influence at OKH had grown after Brauchitsch's fall from grace in early November 1939. Halder became the leading proponent of the new plan. Despite Brauchitsch's decreased influence, he too supported the blitzkrieg. Thus we find him telling Hitler in April that it is imperative not to postpone the attack because "long waiting would not improve the situation."[168] Furthermore, two of the principal staff officers at OKH, Colonels Heusinger and Grieffenberg, had been favorably disposed toward Army Group A's plan even before it was formally adopted.[169]

Even Leeb, the commander of Army Group C and a vociferous opponent of the original plan, raised no arguments against the final version.[170] Bock simply could not marshall any support for his position. Even Reichenau, the commander of Bock's main army, was satisfied.[171] The majority of military leaders had accepted the new plan and expected to score a decisive victory. Gen. Walter Warlimont, one of the most respected officers at OKW, aptly characterized the general outlook of the German military in the spring of 1940 when he wrote: "The criticism was often made that senior officers, including Hitler himself, were prisoners of their memories of the first World War and therefore did not reckon on such a resounding success of the offense in the West. This may have been true in the autumn of 1939 but it clearly was not early in 1940."[172]

It should be evident by this point that the evidence contradicts the claim that the Germans were leaping into the dark in May 1940 and that an irrational Hitler was dragging a reluctant military into another world war. Furthermore, A. J. P. Taylor's claim that the Germans merely hoped to occupy the Channel coast in May 1940 and that their overwhelming success caught them by surprise is not accurate. The Germans had abandoned the limited aims strategy by mid-February 1940 and had replaced it with a blitzkrieg. When one side thinks that it has the capability to launch a successful blitzkrieg, deterrence is very likely to fail, as it did in spring 1940. On the other hand, when a potential attacker sees either an attrition strategy or a limited aims strategy as the only possibility, deterrence is much more likely to obtain, as it did in fall 1939.

CONCLUSION

Although the Germans did not attack in fall 1939, Hitler wanted to do so very badly. He was thwarted in part by the weather but mainly by the determined opposition of his generals, all of whom firmly believed that to attack with the existing plan would lead to disaster.[173] In essence, deterrence obtained. Nevertheless, it is important to emphasize that Hitler was willing to attack with the plan that his generals found so unsatisfactory and about which even he had reservations. He believed that if the offensive was launched while the British forces were still few in number, the Germans stood a good chance of winning a decisive victory. Still, he recognized that this was an extremely risky endeavor. He was willing to take such a gamble, however, because of an overriding political consideration:

his desire to establish German hegemony on the European continent. He also believed, of course, that the Allies were preparing to launch an offensive into the Low Countries, and he wanted to strike before they did. His generals, however, did not accept his reasoning, and without their support, Hitler was unable to strike in the West.

In the early months of 1940, the Germans radically altered the existing plan and adopted the blitzkrieg. From that point forward, there was no doubt that the German military would strike as soon as the weather permitted. Some further words about the emergence of the blitzkrieg are in order. It clearly cannot be argued that the Germans developed and adopted the blitzkrieg during the interwar period and then applied it for the first time in Poland. When the German military finally adopted the blitzkrieg in February 1940, it won acceptance outside a small circle of advocates for the first time. Plainly neither Hitler nor the majority of the German generals grasped the potential of the blitzkrieg before February 1940. It is noteworthy, however, that those generals, and especially Hitler, were favorably disposed toward panzer divisions. In this respect, the importance of the Polish campaign cannot be underestimated. Although the Germans did not employ a blitzkrieg in Poland, the operation demonstrated that, regardless of the strategy, panzer divisions were a valuable asset on the battlefield. The Polish campaign was an important first step in erasing the more conservative officers' doubts about the general utility of panzer divisions. The growing respect for the armored forces, coupled with the German military's traditional emphasis on winning quick victories, meant that the senior German generals did not have to alter their views greatly to endorse the blitzkrieg. These German generals were not like their counterparts in France, who were irrevocably tied to an obsolete image of war.

Although Germany's military leaders were more likely to accept Guderian's ideas on the employment of armor than were the French military leaders, it is clear that the blitzkrieg would not have emerged had Hitler not maintained relentless pressure on all of the decision makers, including himself, to devise a plan for defeating the Allies decisively. Hitler, who was determined to make Germany the dominant power on the Continent, drove his military advisers, as well as himself, toward the blitzkrieg. If the German generals had been left to their own devices, the blitzkrieg would not have emerged.

Hitler, of course, did more than simply pressure the military to find an acceptable strategy. He also directly intervened in the planning process—and, as I have noted, he played a key role in the evolution of the various plans. In fact, without his direct interference, it is hard to imagine how Army Group A's strategy would have been adopted. I do not deny the importance of efforts by Rundstedt, Manstein, and Guderian to win acceptance of their scheme, nor do I deny the importance of the proposal itself—which not only influenced Hitler but also formed the basis of OKH's final plan. Army Group A, however, working through the normal chain of command, was unable to persuade the top leaders of the wisdom of its plan. OKH was a formidable roadblock. Hitler's intervention, coupled with three key events in the first months of 1940 (the airplane crash and the two sand table exercises), was needed to break down OKH's resistance.

After the overwhelming victory in spring 1940, Hitler turned to the East and invaded the Soviet Union. The German military, fresh from its victory in the West, enthusiastically supported Hitler's decision, believing that it could employ the blitzkrieg against the Soviets and could gain a quick and decisive victory.[174] The Germans were wrong this time. The Soviets stopped the German offensive, and after 1942, the Germans were on the defensive on all fronts. In the end, World War II, like World War I, was won through attrition. The Allies on both the eastern and western fronts simply wore down the Germans.

[5]

Conventional Deterrence and the Arab-Israeli Conflict

Since the British left Palestine in May 1948, there have been seven major conflicts involving Israel and its Arab neighbors: the 1948, 1956, 1967, and 1973 wars; the 1969–1970 war of attrition; and the 1978 and 1982 Israeli invasions of Lebanon. Only three of these conflicts (the 1956, 1967, and 1973 wars), however, were fought on a modern battlefield. The 1948 war was basically a series of isolated, medium-sized engagements between infantry units. There was very little armor in the Middle East during this period. The war of attrition was basically a series of air attacks, artillery exchanges, and commando raids. There were no major engagements between large ground units. The same is true with the two Israeli invasions of Lebanon. The powerful Israeli military was matched against a Palestinian military organization that simply cannot be called a modern army. Conventional deterrence, as defined in this book, does not apply to such conflicts. This chapter is therefore concerned with determining why deterrence failed in October 1956,[1] June 1967, and October 1973.

THE 1956 WAR

After the 1948 war, the Israelis began building an army that would serve their needs in a future conflict. Although the specifics of Israeli military doctrine were not firmly established for a number of years, there was widespread agreement from the start about the broad outlines.[2] Given the small size of Israel, its lengthy borders, and the fact that it shared borders with three potential enemies (Egypt, Jordan, and Syria), Israeli decision makers recognized that it would not be possible to absorb an Arab attack and then to assume the offensive at a later date. The side that strikes first in a war, because it can take advantage of surprise and because it can mass its forces at points of its own choosing, is very likely to achieve some success in the conflict's initial stages. In light of Israel's geographic position, any Arab success threatened to be decisive and was therefore unacceptable. Appropriately, the Israelis decided in favor of an offensive doctrine. If war seemed likely in a crisis, they would preempt. In the words of a former Israeli chief of staff, Israel had opted for a "defensive strategy, executed offensively."[3]

Second, Israel could not afford to become involved in a war of attrition with the Arabs. Aside from the fact that no state wants to sacrifice any more men than necessary in a war, other factors contributed to the Israeli desire to avoid a slugging match. Israel's population is significantly smaller than the combined populations of its Arab opponents.[4] Also, the Israelis are especially sensitive to high casualty levels, for important historical reasons. Therefore, it was axiomatic that Israeli doctrine would place a high premium on winning quickly and decisively. There were, however, other reasons for favoring rapid victories. The Israelis feared that the superpowers would intervene when the Israeli Defense Forces (IDF) were in the process of inflicting a decisive defeat on the Arabs. A quick victory precluded this eventuality. Furthermore, since there was a strong possibility that Israel would be involved in a two-front or even a three-front war, it was imperative to be able to win quickly on each front.[5]

Although there was widespread agreement about these general precepts, it was still necessary to find an offensive military strategy that would satisfy the requirements of this broad doctrine. Specifically, it was essential to determine how to employ Israel's burgeoning army on the battlefield so as to produce quick, decisive victories. Yigal Yadin was appointed chief of staff of the IDF after the 1948 war. During his tenure (1949–1952), he concentrated on organizational matters, working to build a strong IDF.[6] A specific strategy for fighting a large-scale conventional war was not developed during his tenure.[7] His successor, Mordechai Makleff, whose term of service was only one year, also focused on organizational matters.

In December 1953, Moshe Dayan replaced Makleff. During the next four years, Dayan developed and institutionalized a military strategy that provided the IDF with a potent offensive capability.[8] In essence, Dayan prepared the IDF to implement a blitzkrieg strategy. Israel would rely on highly mobile forces to effect deep strategic penetrations that would cause the opposing forces to collapse. Besides developing a strategy for fighting a major war against the Arabs, Dayan was also a central character in both the 1956 and 1967 decisions. Furthermore, he was one of the principal actors in October 1973, when the Egyptians and Syrians struck against Israel.

The Emerging Crisis and the Principal Actors

Late in the summer of 1955, a series of developments greatly disturbed Israeli leaders.[9] On 25 August 1955, fedayeen raids started. They were directed by the Egyptian army and were launched from the Gaza Strip. Then, in early September, the Egyptians, who were already blockading the Gulf of Aqaba, declared that Israeli commercial aircraft would be prohibited from flying over the southern Sinai to reach Africa. Finally, in late September, the Egyptians announced that they had concluded a comprehensive arms deal with the Soviets, a development that promised to upset the delicate balance of forces in the Middle East.[10]

On 22 October 1955, David Ben-Gurion, who had returned from retirement nine months earlier to become minister of defense and who expected to assume the prime ministership shortly, asked Moshe Dayan to meet with him.[11] The following day, Ben-Gurion told Dayan, who was then chief of staff, that war was possible and that the IDF should "be prepared to capture the Straits of Tiran—Sharm e-Sheikh, Ras Natsrani and the islands of Tiran and Sanapir."[12] Less than two weeks later, Ben-Gurion returned as prime minister. Shortly thereafter, he queried his cabinet about taking military action against Egypt. The cabinet was opposed, and Ben-Gurion did not press the issue. Dayan, who felt that the time for military action was at hand, was deeply disappointed with the decision.[13] He was not, however, able to persuade Ben-Gurion to resurrect the proposal.

More than six months later on 26 July 1956, the Egyptians, who had been feuding with the British and the French, nationalized the Suez Canal. Soon thereafter, the French contacted the Israelis to see whether Israel would join with France and Britain in a military operation against Egypt.[14] During the next three months, Israeli decision makers wrestled with the question of whether or not to launch an offensive against Egyptian forces in the Sinai.

The decision to strike was made by a very small number of individuals, largely because of Ben-Gurion's suzerainty (he was defense minister as well as prime minister) in the realm of national security. Moreover, Moshe Sharett, Ben-Gurion's dovish and influential for-

[136]

eign minister, resigned in June 1956.[15] He was replaced by Golda Meir, who was then a less influential force than Sharett and who knew very little about military matters.[16] Actually, the question of whether or not to take military action was not debated in the Israeli cabinet. After the cabinet's December 1955 decision against military action, Ben-Gurion did not raise the issue in that body again until after he had decided to attack in the Sinai.[17] Then he effectively presented the cabinet with a fait accompli, which it quickly ratified. The war began on the following day. In short, the decision-making process was restricted to a small, ad hoc group that was dominated by Ben-Gurion.

Aside from those officers on the General Staff involved in planning the operation, only ten other persons were privy to the debate over military action.[18] All evidence indicates that the three cabinet ministers who knew about the debate (Moshe Carmel, transportation; Levi Eshkol, finance; and Golda Meir, foreign affairs) did not have much influence in this case. Only three individuals played central roles in the decision: Ben-Gurion, Dayan, and Shimon Peres, who was the director-general in the Ministry of Defense.

As prime minister, Ben-Gurion bore ultimate responsibility for the decision to launch an offensive—although he certainly had to have his cabinet's approval. Although he was also minister of defense, Ben-Gurion was not an expert on military strategy. This was clearly Dayan's bailiwick. As the head of the IDF, as well as the individual responsible for developing a strategy for decisively defeating the Arab armies, Dayan was in an excellent position to evaluate the prospects for victory in a major conflict in the Sinai. Moreover, he was hardly reluctant to voice his views on matters relating to Israeli security. Despite Dayan's expertise and outspokenness, it should be emphasized that Ben-Gurion maintained tight control over the decision-making process. There was never any doubt that the ultimate decision rested in Ben-Gurion's hands.

Peres, the third person involved in the decision, was Ben-Gurion's right-hand man in the Defense Ministry. Like his boss, Peres was not an expert on military strategy and thus was not in a position to judge the capabilities of the IDF relative to the Egyptian army.[19] Peres's primary responsibility during this period was diplomatic in nature. He was largely responsible for negotiating with the French to secure arms for Israel; he also served as the main conduit of French proposals for increased cooperation between Israel and France.[20] As will become evident, Peres was influential in convincing Ben-Gurion to strike. Peres was not, however, concerned with the purely military aspects of the proposed operation. These considerations fell squarely within Dayan's purview, and Peres, like Ben-Gurion, relied heavily on Dayan's judgment.

Throughout the decision-making process leading to the 29 October attack, Dayan never displayed any doubts about the IDF's capability to defeat the Egyptian army. Dayan was supremely confident because he believed that the Israelis had the capability to launch a blitzkrieg. This confidence is clearly reflected in his *Diary of the Sinai Campaign*, where he describes the Israeli plan in considerable detail. The objective was "to bring about as quickly as possible the collapse of the enemy forces" by rapidly driving deep into the rear of the Egyptian defenses.[21] Dayan writes, "From the operational point of view, rapidity in advance is of supreme importance to us."[22] Furthermore, he emphasized that Israeli "infantry and armoured forces should advance, wherever they can, by going round the enemy emplacements, leaving them in the rear and pressing on."[23] He argued that "there is no need to fear that Egyptian units who will be by-passed will launch a counterattack or cut our supply lines."[24]

Dayan emphasized that it was imperative to avoid "a frontal attack and gradual advance."[25] The IDF had "no interest in killing a maximum number of . . . [Egyptian] troops."[26] Instead, success would ultimately be a consequence of the Egyptians' inability to deal with the Israeli penetrations. Dayan believed that the Egyptian army was very inflexible. He writes:

> The Egyptians are what I would call schematic in their operations, and their command headquarters are in the rear, far from the front. Any change in the disposition of their units, such as forming a new defence line, switching targets of attack, moving forces not in accordance with the original plan, takes them time—time to think, time to receive reports through all the channels of command, time to secure a decision after due consideration from supreme headquarters, time for the orders then to filter down from the rear to the fighting fronts.[27]

In contrast, Dayan saw the IDF as a very flexible instrument: "We on the other hand are used to acting with greater flexibility and less military routine. We can base our operations on units which are not interdependent, and whose commanders, receiving reports and giving the necessary orders, are right on the spot, together with their fighting men."[28] Dayan went on to explain that "This advantage, if we can exploit it, will enable us, after the initial breakthrough, to press on before the Egyptians can manage to adjust to the changes in their front. I am confident that we can run the campaign in such a way that the enemy will be given no time to reorganize after the assault and that there will be no pause in the fighting. This is the basis for our plans."[29] Significantly, Dayan was confident that the IDF's battlefield commanders were capable of making the quick decisions necessary to ensure that the advancing spearheads were not slowed down.[30] He recognized that "the plan . . . is based on a huge measure of independence to commanders in the field. It is they who will be taking vital decisions on the spot in the midst of battle. Their action and their powers of leadership will determine the success or failure of the campaign."[31] Dayan's view of the blitzkrieg included one important qualification. As I have emphasized throughout this book, an attacker employing a blitzkrieg uses armored forces to effect the deep strategic penetrations. Dayan, however, was initially opposed to relying on Israel's armored units for this purpose and instead preferred to use mechanized infantry units.[32] Although this preference might appear to be inconsistent with the precepts of the blitzkrieg, such is not the case.

Unlike so many of the opponents of the blitzkrieg in Europe during the interwar period, Dayan did not want to rely on foot-borne infantry to engage in slugging matches with the defender. He believed in employing mechanized infantry as tanks would be used in a blitzkrieg. He envisioned infantry in half-tracks and command cars racing into the depths of the Egyptian defense.[33] Dayan did not want to rely on tanks because he believed that they were mechanically unreliable and would break down, thus slowing the advancing spearheads.[34] There was considerable controversy at the time as to whether tanks were capable of maintaining the high rate of advance that a blitzkrieg requires.[35] Very interestingly, it appears that some armor advocates like Chaim Laskov did not believe that using tanks to effect deep strategic penetrations would lead to the collapse of the Egyptian army. Instead, they argued that IDF armor units would have to engage in "prolonged tank battles over every locality."[36] This view was based on the assumption that the IDF simply could not afford to bypass Egyptian strong points as a blitzkrieg would require. The ensuing campaign, as well as the 1967 war, proved Dayan correct on this matter.

Although Dayan was initially skeptical about tanks, he switched his position shortly before the war.[37] The operational plan was then altered. The shift meant merely changing the assignments of the armored units.

Dayan never wavered from his position that the IDF could decisively defeat the Egyptian army. His steadfastness was due, in large part, to his confidence in the plan of operations. This confidence, however, was undoubtedly reinforced by the knowledge that the Israelis had a decided advantage in terms of the balance of forces. The IDF had twelve brigades "assigned to—or available to—the Southern Command," while the Egyptians had six "poorly trained and lightly armed" brigades stationed in Sinai.[38] Furthermore, once Israel had agreed to launch a joint operation with Britain and France, the IDF would not need to concern itself with Egyptian reinforcements moving into the Sinai. In fact, the Franco-British operations would force the Egyptians to withdraw forces from the Sinai to the west side of the Canal.

Ben-Gurion considered it essential for basically two reasons that Israel have a European ally before starting a war against Egypt. First, he did not think that the Israeli air force had the capability to defend Israeli cities against Egyptian bombers. He believed that only a European power could provide this service.[39] Second, Ben-Gurion maintained that should war come, Israel must not be isolated diplomatically.[40] Dayan ascribed much less importance to these concerns of Ben-Gurion.[41] For Dayan, the fact that the IDF could rout the Egyptian army provided sufficient grounds for launching an attack. Ben-Gurion, however, had to be convinced not only that the Egyptian army would be defeated rapidly and decisively but that Israel would have a European partner in the war. In the hectic months before the operation was launched, Peres worked to hammer out an agreement between Israel and the Europeans that Ben-Gurion would find acceptable, while Dayan concentrated on reassuring the prime minister that the IDF could easily defeat the Egyptian army.

Although Dayan maintained that the IDF was capable of acting independently, cooperation with the French and British certainly enhanced the IDF's prospects for success. First, it assured that Israeli cities would not be attacked from the air. Second, it guaranteed that the IDF would be supplied with badly needed equipment. Commenting on the arrival of 200 French trucks two days before the war began, Dayan, who had earlier minimized the importance of French cooperation, noted: "I do not know what we would have done if these French trucks had not arrived."[42] Finally, as Dayan recognized, an Anglo-French attack on the Egyptian coast would force Egypt to move troops from the Sinai to the western side of the Canal, thus facilitating the Israeli advance across the desert.[43] Thus it was clear that European participation in a war against Egypt would considerably ease the IDF's task in the Sinai.

The Decision to Attack

On 1 September 1956, the Israelis received word that the British and the French had a plan to seize the Suez Canal.[44] Shortly thereafter, Dayan "ordered the branches of the General Staff to examine the various operational plans on the Egyptian front."[45] Until this point, there had been no serious discussion between Israel and France about a joint operation. The situation began to change on 20 September, when Ben-Gurion agreed to initiate formal cooperation between France and Israel on military and political matters. His decision, however, did not commit Israel to military action. After the Israeli cabinet approved Ben-Gurion's decision on 26 September, the French requested that Israel immediately send a high-level delegation to Paris. Ben-Gurion chose Dayan, Peres, Golda Meir, and Moshe Carmel to represent Israel. The talks, which took place on 30 September and 1 October, did not result in a decision to launch a joint attack. Dayan "ordered the branches of the General Staff to examine the war, the IDF would defeat the Egyptian army and "capture the Sinai Peninsula within a fortnight."[46]

After returning from France, Dayan called a meeting of the General Staff and alerted the assembled officers that although no formal decision had been made, war with Egypt was likely. Dayan notes: "My news that we had to prepare for battle electrified the meeting. . . . one could sense the tension in the room. It was as if, for them, the campaign had already begun."[47] Nevertheless, when Dayan met the following day with "the inner General Staff" doubts were expressed about the planned operation. Dayan explains in his *Diary*:

> Those at the meeting who had reservations about my presentation said that the problem was not the conception of the plan but the ability to implement it, and we had to examine its feasibility, particularly its logistics. They thought the plan was very ambitious and did not take into account the chance of anything going wrong. The discussion ended with the feeling that our plans are not yet ripe enough to be transmitted to the units.[48]

This journal entry stands alone in the public record as an expression of doubt about the IDF's capability to inflict a decisive defeat on the Egyptians.[49] The skepticism of the officers was short-lived. In meetings the following week (8 and 9 October) when the plan was discussed in detail, no one questioned the IDF's capability to implement it.[50] Moreover, all evidence indicates that in the weeks before the campaign started, the IDF commanders were very confident that they would accomplish the assigned task.[51]

The British and the French, who had not been able to agree on the issue of joint military action with Israel, finally did so between 15 and 16 October. The French then invited Ben-Gurion to come to France to discuss a possible military operation. Ben-Gurion accepted the invitation and left for France with Dayan, Peres, and his military secretary, Nehemia Argov. In the subsequent meetings that took place between 22 and 24 October in France, the British, the French, and the Israelis devised a joint plan that was acceptable to all parties.[52] France would provide the air cover necessary to protect Israeli cities, and with the joint action, Israel would not have to worry about diplomatic isolation. Ben-Gurion, however, still had to make the final decision as to whether Israel should participate in the operation.

On the morning of the twenty-fourth, while he was still in France, Ben-Gurion summoned Dayan and Peres to his temporary residence. It was clear to all that Ben-Gurion was about to make his final decision. With the air threat to Israeli cities removed and the threat of diplomatic isolation nullified, Ben-Gurion turned his attention to the operational plan. Appropriately, he started the meeting by asking "Dayan to sketch once again the operational plan he had suggested."[53] Dayan then explained the plan to Ben-Gurion. Although no record of the conversation is available, Dayan remarks in his *Diary* for the following day:

> On this question of the defeat of Egypt's forces I have had *several* talks with Ben Gurion [while in Paris]. It is clear that we have no interest in "destroying the enemy's forces" . . . and it is better that as little blood as possible should be shed. I therefore used the formula "to confound the organization of the Egyptian forces and bring about their collapse." [Emphasis added][54]

The available evidence indicates that Ben-Gurion always believed that the IDF could win a decisive victory. As early as 15 October 1956, when addressing the Knesset, he "cited with approval Dayan's words a few weeks earlier about the strength of Israel's army."[55] He went on to say, "I am as confident as every one of our commanders that any conflict with the Egyptians or the rest of the Arab armies will end in our victory."[56] On 23 October, one day before the meeting with Dayan and Peres at Ben-Gurion's temporary residence, Ben-Gurion told the French leaders: "If the war is conducted with full co-operation, we can start it even tomorrow. We would be ready to take upon ourselves the main land burden. . . . We will do the work on the ground. . . . It is possible to finish the action in a number of hours. . . . and you will be able to send your divisions home."[57]

Ben-Gurion was concerned less with the question of ultimate success than with casualties, a subject about which he was particularly sensitive.[58] He feared that the IDF would have to pay a high price to defeat the Egyptians.[59] Thus Dayan sought to convince him that the operational plan would enable the IDF to win a decisive victory while suffering few losses. This emphasis is clearly reflected in Dayan's account of his discussions with Ben-Gurion in France. At the conclusion of the 24 October meeting, Ben-Gurion turned to Dayan and Peres and simply said, "Moshe's plan is good. It saves lives."[60] Nothing more was said on the subject.

Sometime after that meeting and before the Israeli delegation left France on the following day (25 October), Ben-Gurion decided to go to war.[61] Dayan had convinced Ben-Gurion that an Israeli blitzkrieg would result in a decisive victory at an acceptable cost. In the following days, Ben-Gurion secured his cabinet's approval. On 29 October, war began.

THE 1967 WAR

After Israel's victory in the 1956 war, Dayan and his lieutenants decided that henceforth the IDF would rely heavily on its armored forces. Appropriately, the Armor Corps became the dominant element in the army. In a future conflict, armored units working closely with the air force would effect the deep strategic penetrations that would lead to the enemy's collapse. In the period between the 1956 and 1967 wars, Israeli military leaders tailored their forces to implement a blitzkrieg.[62] Given the doctrine of the IDF after the 1956 war and the fact that it scored such a stunning victory in June 1967 we might expect to find that during the crisis preceding the war, the military chiefs simply told the responsible political leaders that the IDF was fully prepared to inflict a decisive defeat on the Egyptian army. Then, at the appropriate moment, the prime minister turned to the chief of staff and gave him the green light. Yet this is not what happened.

The crisis that led to the 1967 war came as a complete surprise to the Israelis. The first signs appeared on 14 May, when Israeli intelligence detected Egyptian forces moving into the Sinai. Three days later Nasser ordered the United Nations forces out of the Sinai; then on 22 May he declared that he would blockade the Straits of Tiran. It was clear by the following day, when the Straits were actually closed, that the new status quo was unacceptable to the Israelis, and something would have to be done to reverse these Egyptian moves. The critical question at hand was whether to pursue a military course of action or a political one.

During the period from 23 May to 1 June, the Israelis debated this question. At two key meetings, one on 23 May and the other on 27–28 May, the Israeli leadership opted for the diplomatic route. By 1 June, it was apparent that diplomacy was not going to solve the problem. Thus in the period between 1 and 5 June, the decision was made to employ the military instrument. Two questions emerge from these developments. First, why did the Israelis decide *not* to take military action between 23 May and 1 June? Second, what considerations led the Israelis to decide for war? Regarding the decision-making process strictly from the diplomatic perspective, we could argue that the Israelis chose the diplomatic route in the 23 May–1 June period because there was evidence that outside powers might solve the problem. Moreover, to avoid repeating the 1956 experience, it was necessary to secure American acquiescence for a military strike. When the Israelis recognized that the diplomatic course of action would not bear fruit and that they would have to solve the problem themselves, they opted for war.

Although this explanation of events in the weeks before 5 June 1967 is accurate, it is incomplete. Military considerations were also crucial in shaping Israeli decisions. The Israelis were reluctant to take military action before 1 June because they did not have a satisfactory plan for defeating the Egyptian army. The absence of an attractive military option contributed significantly to the decision to seek a diplomatic solution. Contrary to some accounts of the 1967 war, in this case a highly confident military was not held back by weak-kneed civilians looking for any alternative to military action.[63] Confusion in military circles contributed to the decision to postpone military action. Moreover, the failure of diplomacy was not alone in prompting the Israelis to go to war. On 1 June, Moshe Dayan, who was then outside the government, was appointed minister of defense. The military option immediately became much more attractive because of Dayan's optimistic view of IDF capabilities.

Principal Actors

The structure of the decision-making process in 1967 differed greatly from that in 1956. Many more individuals were involved in the 1967 decision than had participated in that of 1956, when essentially three persons decided Israeli policy. In 1967 the cabinet decided what Israel would do at each point in the decision-making process; Prime Minister Levi Eshkol did not see fit to exclude the cabinet from deliberations as Ben-Gurion had some eleven years earlier. Also, Yitzhak Rabin, the chief of staff, was not the dominating influence that Dayan had been when he filled the same position. Although Rabin was the military's principal spokesman, other officers were allowed to voice their opinions at the highest levels of government.

Like Ben-Gurion, Prime Minister Eshkol also occupied the post of defense minister. Given this dual responsibility, Eshkol could have dominated the decision-making process. He did not, nor did any other individual, although Abba Eban was a particularly influential force. Eban, the foreign minister, argued forcefully in favor of a diplomatic solution. It is very important to note that no individual in the cabinet could speak with authority about military issues. Despite his position as defense minister, Eshkol knew little about military matters. Yigal Allon, Moshe Carmel, and Israel Galili had all been prominent generals at one time, but it had been years since they had been immersed in the details of defense policy. The lack of military expertise within the cabinet was due, in large part, to the fact that Ben-Gurion, Dayan, and Peres, the triumvirate that had led Israel to war in 1956, were now outside the government in consequence of a split within the ruling Mapai party in 1965.[64]

Given the lack of military expertise at the cabinet level, it was inevitable that the advice of the military leadership would be accorded greater weight. As I previously noted, although Rabin was the main spokesman for the military, the views of his key subordinates were also considered. Besides Rabin, the key actors in uniform were: Ezer Weizman, the head of the General Staff Branch (the director of operations) and, in effect, Rabin's deputy; Aharon Yariv, the head of intelligence; Chaim Bar-Lev, who was recalled from France on 23 May and was appointed deputy chief of staff, effective on 1 June, ostensibly to replace Weizman as Rabin's deputy; and Yeshayahu Gavish, the chief of the Southern Command.

Before examining what happened between 23 May and 5 June, we must consider one final matter: the balance of forces. In 1956, the IDF was numerically stronger than the Egyptian forces located in the Sinai. Moreover, Israel was allied with Britain and France, which further tipped the balance of forces in Israel's favor.[65] The situation was quite different in late spring 1967: the opposing forces were approximately equal in size; Israel would be fighting alone; and there was the strong possibility of a three-front war.[66] In light of the subsequent victory, it is easy to dismiss these factors as unimportant. In the period before the war, however, when few people were predicting such a stunning success, these factors weighed heavily on key Israeli decision makers and contributed greatly to the air of pessimism that was so prevalent at all levels of Israeli society.[67]

23 May–1 June 1967: Opting for Diplomacy

In the wake of Nasser's closing of the Straits of Tiran, Eshkol convened a meeting (23 May) of the Ministerial Defense Committee. The military was represented at the meeting by Rabin, Weizman, and Yariv.[68] When discussing the shape of a possible military response, Rabin spoke in terms of a limited offensive with the objective of occupying the Gaza Strip. Then the Israelis would have something to use as a bargaining chip with the Egyptians. Rabin emphasized that Israel would be faced with a difficult campaign. "I cannot promise a walkover. This will not be similar to Sinai, it will not be easy. There will be sacrifices."[69] Significantly, there was no pressure from the military to initiate war. It was agreed that Israel would try to solve the problem through diplomatic channels.[70] Immediately thereafter, the Ministerial Defense Committee met again, although this time leaders of the opposition were included. Israel's options were once again discussed. This larger forum voiced no disagreement with the decision to pursue the diplomatic route.[71]

Later that day, Rabin met with the General Staff and discussed alternative military plans. It is clear from Rabin's memoirs that he was committed to a limited aims strategy that called for capturing the Gaza Strip. He emphasized at the meeting that "our immediate objective was not the occupation of the Sinai," which, of course, would have required the Israelis to defeat the Egyptian army decisively.[72]

Dayan, who held no government position at this point, had started a tour of the Southern Command on 23 May. On the evening of the twenty-third, he met with General Gavish, the head of the Southern Command, at Gavish's headquarters.[73] Gavish had just returned from the General Staff meeting during which Rabin had articulated his views on a limited offensive. Gavish informed Dayan that "authorization had been given [in the case of war] for the aerial bombing of Egyptian airfields and for the capture of the Gaza Strip."[74] Gavish, who spoke about "the difficulty of breaking into the heavily fortified Egyptian strongpoints," supported the official strategy. Dayan told Gavish that he disagreed with the limited nature of the projected campaign. Reflecting on the meeting, Dayan thought that he "detected a certain doubt on the part of some of the officers as to whether we had the strength to rout the Egyptian forces."

Since the start of the crisis, Rabin had felt increasingly burdened by the responsibilities of his position. On 22 May, he arranged to meet with Ben-Gurion and Dayan to discuss Israel's predicament. Ben-Gurion gave Rabin a blistering "dressing down," arguing that Israel was in desperate straits and that Rabin bore much of the responsibility for the situation. According to Rabin, Ben-Gurion's words struck him "like hammer blows."[75] Rabin later remarked, "Never have I experienced such a profound sense of disappointment and dismay." He left the meeting "feeling doubly despondent." On the following day (23 May), after the two Ministerial Defense Committee meetings previously described, Rabin met privately with Interior Minister Moshe Chaim Shapira.[76] Repeating many of Ben-Gurion's arguments, Shapira lambasted Rabin, who was beginning to wilt under the weight of these arguments. In his memoirs, Rabin writes, "The heavy sense of guilt that had been dogging me of late became unbearably strong on May 23."[77] Then, at the previously described General Staff meeting in the afternoon of 23 May, he felt faint and was taken home. By his own admission, he "returned home in a state of mental and physical exhaustion."[78] Rabin telephoned Weizman that night and asked Weizman to come to his home. Although there is some disagreement between the two as to exactly what was said at this meeting, it is beyond dispute that Rabin was consumed with self-doubt.[79] Clearly, this man was not confident that the IDF could decisively defeat the Egyptians in a showdown.[80]

It is important to emphasize that cabinet members looked to Rabin as the final authority on military matters, which, of course, was why he was subjected to so much pressure.[81] When he was ill, news of his condition "spread quickly in the inner circle."[82] Without a doubt, this development contributed significantly to the atmosphere of foreboding in Israel at the time.[83] Rabin remained at home under a doctor's care until the twenty-fifth. Weizman, still the number two man in the IDF, temporarily assumed the reins of power.

The following day (24 May) Weizman called a meeting of the General Staff to review the operational plan. Once again, the IDF leadership opted for a limited aims strategy, although the territorial objective was somewhat more ambitious in the revised plan.[84] In Rabin's original version, the aim had been to capture the Gaza Strip. Now the IDF was to attack into the Sinai along the northernmost axis in the direction of El-Arish.[85] A strip of the northern Sinai would be captured. The finalized plan, which remained *the* operational plan until 2 June, was then reviewed in Eshkol's presence. Weizman reports that Eshkol "asked everyone for his opinion about the prospects for the southern-front plan. No one opposed it."[86] Despite the absence of vocal opposition at this meeting, there was considerable dissatisfaction with the operational plan. Weizman himself "supported a different plan," which placed greater reliance on airpower.[87] Weizman admits, however, that within the air force there were "considerable doubts and uncertainties about our ability to face the Arabs' growing strength and their powerful anti-aircraft systems."[88] Rabin reports that there were different opinions within the IDF as to the course of military action that Israel should pursue.[89] Among the field commanders in the Southern Command, for example, "there was a growing sense of dissatisfaction . . . with the top army command and its operational approach."[90] Also, and very important, Dayan continued to complain about the plan's limited scope. He argued that the IDF was "capable of putting the Egyptians to rout" and should do so.[91]

From 24 May to 27 May, Israeli leaders waited while Foreign Minister Eban traveled to France, Britain, and the United States to gain support for a diplomatic solution. Finally, Eban returned empty-handed. For two days (27–28 May), the cabinet debated whether to pursue military action or to continue searching for a diplomatic solution. The final vote on the issue was 9–9, which translated into a victory for Eban and the proponents of a diplomatic solution. After this meeting Rabin asked Eshkol to explain the decision to the military leaders.[92] The ensuing discussion was heated, with Yariv and a number of other senior officers arguing for immediate military action. Actually, the pressure for military action from within the military had begun to build on the twenty-fifth. When Rabin returned to work on that day, he found Yariv and Weizman anxious to commence military operations.[93] On that same day, Eshkol visited the Southern Command and found that the commanders of the major combat units were sharply critical of the decision to work through diplomatic channels.[94] Thus there was already strong pressure within the IDF for military action when the Israeli cabinet again decided to rely on diplomatic initiatives.

Although by 28 May there were very strong feelings about the need for military action among certain elements of the IDF, there was hardly unanimous sentiment among military leaders on this matter. It would be a mistake to think in terms of an enthusiastic military opposed by recalcitrant political leaders. Surely, Weizman,

Yariv, and the senior officers in the Southern Command were in favor of launching an attack. Yet neither Rabin nor Bar-Lev, who was the de facto and then the de jure deputy chief of staff, advocated military action. The chief of staff did not share the enthusiasm of his subordinates for military action. As one cabinet member recalled after the war: "the Chief of Staff never called expressly for war. He pointed out all the possibilities to us, the comparative strength of the forces, and he did say that we could win—but he never put pressure on us to open hostilities."[95] Throughout the period from 25 to 28 May, Rabin functioned basically as a broker, arranging meetings and passing information between Eshkol and the more hawkish generals.[96] Rabin did not try to persuade Eshkol of the merits of military action. Furthermore, the influential Bar-Lev was noncommittal on the question of military action.[97] Invariably there were four officers in attendance at the most important meetings during the crisis: Rabin, Bar-Lev, Weizman, and Yariv. Only the latter two, who were the least influential of the four, advocated immediate military action.[98] Moshe Carmel, a member of the cabinet (transport minister) and an avowed hawk, describes the attitudes of the military leaders during the myriad meetings that took place during the crisis: "When I recreate before my eyes those fateful days of May-June 1967 . . . [I remember] the long meetings and many discussions of the Government—in some of which members of the General Staff participated with all their forebodings, hesitations, and soul-searching."[99]

It is not difficult to understand why there was uncertainty among the IDF's leaders. The prevailing opinion within the IDF was that a war with Egypt would be costly and that the IDF could not count on winning a decisive victory.[100] It had been eleven years since the 1956 war, and during that time the Israelis had watched the Soviets train and equip the Egyptian army. Certainly, the balance of forces in 1967 was far less favorable for the Israelis than it had been in 1956.[101] Rabin noted after the crisis that "many believed, and I among them, that the gap between Israeli and Arab might [was] . . . narrowing."[102] Basically because the Egyptians were regarded as a formidable foe, the Israeli plan called for implementing a limited aims strategy.[103] And to add further to the uncertainty, there was considerable dissatisfaction with that plan.

Actually, hawks like Yariv and Gavish accepted the fact that a war with Egypt was likely to be costly, and they also did not dispute the belief that Israel might not win a decisive victory. They favored military action for basically two reasons.[104] First, they felt that the longer Israel waited, the more costly it became to attack. Second, they believed that if Israel did not strike soon, the Egyptians might strike first, gaining the attendant benefits of delivering the first blow. Although Yariv and his fellow hawks were not particularly optimistic about Israel's prospects on the battlefield, they felt that a limited aims strategy was better than no action. Nevertheless, the cabinet decided on 28 May to continue working through diplomatic channels.

1 June–6 June 1967: Opting for War

In spite of the 28 May decision, events were rapidly pushing Israel toward military action. On 30 May, Egypt and Jordan signed a bilateral military pact, which was a facsimile of the existing treaty between Egypt and Syria. Two days later, on 1 June, Israel received the first clear indication that the United States was not going to resolve the crisis.[105] Also, by this point the Israeli economy was beginning to feel the acute strain of mobilization, which had been in effect in various degrees for more than two weeks.[106] In the midst of these developments, dissatisfaction with Eshkol's handling of the crisis reached the boiling point, and he was forced to relinquish his post as defense minister. Dayan was selected as his replacement.

Dayan's return to goverment had a marked impact on the course of events. First, it helped end the bickering about Eshkol's management of the crisis.[107] Israel could now devote all of its attention to the Egyptian threat. Dayan's inclusion in the government also had important military ramifications. For weeks he had been arguing that Israel should seek a decisive victory in the Sinai. Dayan consistently maintained that the IDF's operational plan was not ambitious enough. He could take such a position because he believed that the IDF could rout the Egyptians. Rabin relates that when he met with Dayan on 22 May (the same day when Rabin had talked with Ben-Gurion), Dayan told him that "he had been profoundly impressed by the IDF's prowess. He had been more or less aware of the progress made by the air force, but the expansion and qualitative advance of our armored forces [which Dayan had set in motion after the 1956 war] had surprised and impressed him. He spoke of the IDF with admiration."[108] With the appointment of Dayan as defense minister, the high-level decision makers finally included a proponent of military action who was confident that the IDF could decisively defeat the Egyptians. Moreover Dayan's opinions on military matters carried great weight. As chief of staff from 1953 to 1957, he had borne much responsibility for building the IDF. He had also led the IDF to victory in the 1956 war. His extensive experience and thorough knowledge of military affairs aside, Dayan was a forceful personality who would seek to dominate the decision-making process as much as possible.[109]

In light of Eshkol's lack of knowledge about military affairs and Rabin's personal problems as well as his noncommittal position on the use of force, it was inevitable that Dayan would become the dominant figure in the government as the pressure to go to war increased.[110] Dayan admits in his memoirs that his respect for Eshkol by June 1967 was so low that he felt that for "the first time I would be acting without being subject to higher authority."[111] A senior officer succinctly summarized Rabin's relationship with Dayan: "Rabin was Dayan's Chief of Staff—Dayan was Commander-in-Chief."[112] In short, there was now an authoritative voice in the higher councils who believed that the IDF had the capability to win a decisive military victory. Dayan exuded confidence, something that had been lacking not only among the principal decision makers but throughout the country at large. Dayan helped alter this attitude. Ezer Weizman writes: "He brought with him to General Headquarters a distinct flavour of leadership. There was something about his appearance, his speech and his confidence that dispelled gloom and replaced it with smiles, that drove away uncertainty and, in its place, created a sharp awareness that our path had been shortened."[113]

Dayan's appointment was confirmed by the cabinet late in the evening of 1 June. The following morning Dayan met with the General Staff and the Ministerial Defense Committee. There was a lengthy discussion of the military situation and the operational plan. Not surprisingly, Dayan was dissatisfied with the existing plan, although he did not propose an alternative.[114] Later that morning, Dayan met with Eshkol, Eban, Allon, and Rabin. Eshkol called on Dayan to open the meeting, and Dayan argued: "We should launch a military attack without delay. . . . The aim of our action should be to destroy the Egyptian forces concentrated in central Sinai. We should have no geographical aim whatsoever and we should not include the Gaza Strip in our fighting plans."[115] Despite some minor disagreements among those present, it was clear by the end of the meeting that military action was fast becoming inevitable and that opposition to Dayan's proposal was not significant.[116]

That evening (2 June) the General Staff met with Dayan to review the operational plan, which still called for a limited attack in the northern portion of the Sinai. The day before this key meeting, Rabin had discussed the plan with Gavish, who told Rabin that the limited plan should be abandoned in favor of one that aimed to score a decisive victory.[117] Rabin did not agree but told Gavish to bring the two plans (the limited one and his new proposal) with him to head-quarters on the following day (2 June). Immediately before the 2 June evening meeting with Dayan, Rabin instructed Gavish to present Dayan with the plan that called for a decisive victory. It is clear that Rabin had changed his mind after the morning meetings with Dayan and the other key decision makers.[118]

The new plan, which was given formal approval by Dayan, was a classic blitzkrieg. "It called for penetrations along four axes. . . . There would be no conquest of the Gaza Strip, no reaching the Suez Canal."[119] The objective was to use Israeli armor to inflict a decisive defeat on the Egyptians. There was no opposition; no one argued that the IDF lacked the necessary capability. In fact, there was wide-spread enthusiasm among the military leaders for this more ambitious proposal.[120]

It is clear from the various accounts of events in Israel between 15 May and 2 June that almost all the leaders, both military and civilian, had temporarily lost sight of the extent to which the IDF was a formidable military instrument. Plainly no one expected the IDF to suffer a defeat on the battlefield. Real doubts, however, were expressed by people who might have been assumed to bristle with self-confidence. It was Dayan who provided a badly needed injection of confidence at the highest levels of government. As Weizman notes, he "gave people heart and dispelled their doubts."[121]

Between the 1956 and 1967 wars, the IDF was built and trained to implement a blitzkrieg: the Armor Corps was greatly strengthened and was designated the decisive combat arm; a special logistical system was devised to supply the fast-moving armored columns; close coordination between armored forces and the air force ("the flying artillery") was emphasized; and Arab defensive tactics were carefully studied so that the IDF could exploit the weaknesses of the opposition.[122] In the weeks before the 1967 war, the IDF was a finely tuned instrument fully capable of defeating the Egyptian forces in the Sinai with a blitzkrieg. Dayan's important contribution was that he recognized this capability. Again, Weizman's comments on the subject are worth quoting.

After the victorious conclusion of the war, when political accounts were being settled, those angered by Dayan's success used to say: "Can you imagine that Dayan altered things completely in the few days between his appointment and the outbreak of war? Did he make new plans? Did he supply the armed forces with equipment they lacked?" Of course, the answer is no; he didn't change things around completely, and that wasn't his great contribution. But he gave a tremendous push to the will to fight. He gave tremendous impetus to the demand not to restrict ourselves to some limited, incomplete operation instead of the total annihilation of the Egyptian army.[123]

By 3 June, Eshkol's political problems at home had been solved and a well-regarded military plan had been adopted. The remaining obstacle to military action was the United States. On 3 June, Eshkol received word from his special emissary to the United States (Meir Amit) that the Americans were not going to resolve the crisis and that they would not stand in the way if Israel used force.[124] Eshkol recognized that military action was now inevitable. He met with his key advisers that same evening; it was agreed to recommend military action to the cabinet.[125] The following day (4 June) the Ministerial Defense Committee and the cabinet met. Dayan told the assembled leaders: "Our best chance of victory [is] to strike the first blow. The course of the campaign would then follow our dictates. If we opened the attack and effected an armored breakthrough into Sinai, the enemy would be forced to fight according to the moves we made."[126] The cabinet voted unanimously to go to war on the following day.

Conclusion

Two hypothetical questions emerge from this analysis. First, if Dayan had been defense minister when the crisis first began, would Israel have decided before 4 June to launch an offensive? It seems certain that Dayan's presence in the cabinet would not have affected the decision reached at the 23 May meeting. At this point there was overwhelming agreement that diplomacy should be given a chance.[127] At the next decision point, the 27–28 May cabinet meeting, however, many members believed that diplomacy would not solve the problem and that the time for military action was at hand. The vote on whether to abandon the diplomatic approach was 9–9, with even Eshkol voting for military action. It seems very likely that Dayan, with a viable, if not attractive, military strategy and a united military behind him, would have been able to win approval for launching an offensive.[128] Certainly there were compelling reasons for continuing to seek a diplomatic solution; however, the proponents of this approach were greatly aided by the absence of an attractive military option.[129]

Second, what would have happened after 1 June had Dayan not entered the cabinet? There are those, including Golda Meir, who maintain that Dayan's presence made no real difference.[130] There is no doubt that by 3 June (when Eshkol received Meir Amit's report) there was wide recognition that the crisis would not be solved diplomatically.[131] Thus we might argue that with or without Dayan, military action was inevitable. Three points are in order concerning the possible course of events if Dayan had not become defense minister. First, it is possible, although not likely, that Israel might have decided to make a fresh attempt to solve the problem diplomatically. Having decided to go to war, the Israeli decision makers would have been forced to confront the question of military strategy directly. A lengthy debate over the existing plan (limited aims strategy) might have provided enough time for some diplomatic channels to open. We must remember that, by 3 June, Dayan had an attractive plan that enjoyed widespread support in the military. Undoubtedly, such would not have been the case had the limited plan still been in effect. Furthermore, it should be noted that although Israel felt besieged in those weeks before the 1967 war, there is evidence that some of the key decision makers did not believe that the Egyptians intended to attack Israel, so that there was no need to strike quickly.[132] Still, it is unlikely that Israel would have eschewed military action in that first week of June—which brings us to the second point.

Although there are drawbacks to employing a limited aims strategy, it is in many respects attractive. There is no doubt that the IDF could have captured some portion of the northern Sinai and in the process could have inflicted enough damage on the Egyptian army to have precluded an effective counteroffensive by the Egyptians. Moreover, given the extent to which the superpowers were committed to the area, it was unlikely that a limited offensive would have turned into a lengthy war of attrition, one of the principal drawbacks of a limited aims strategy. Still, there was never great enthusiasm for this strategy, which did not promise a decisive victory. Regardless, by June it was clear that the value of continued peace had diminished to the point where going to war with a limited aims strategy was preferable to the status quo.

The matter of lingering uncertainty about such a strategy brings us to the third point. It is probable that even without Dayan the Israelis would have employed a blitzkrieg. As I have noted, the IDF was organized during the years between 1956 and 1967 to conduct a blitzkrieg. There is also evidence that Gavish, the head of the Southern Command and a proponent of the limited aims strategy, had decided just before Dayan ordered the plan changed that the IDF was fully capable of launching a blitzkrieg—and should do so.[133] Gavish's change of view, as well as the tremendous pressure that forced Eshkol to appoint Dayan to the post of defense minister, highlights the very important point that in a crisis there is great pressure to find a way to defeat the enemy decisively and rapidly. Thus Dayan was brought into the government largely because he was an expert on military matters who was confident that the military could successfully extricate Israel from the crisis.[134] In short, there was significant pressure moving the IDF toward the blitzkrieg.

THE 1973 WAR

During the crisis that preceded the 1967 war, Egypt's leaders were confident that if the IDF attacked, the Egyptian army would be able to parry the attack.[135] Anwar Sadat relates that, when he was told that the Israeli offensive had begun, he thought: "Well, they'll be taught a lesson they won't forget."[136] The subsequent defeat shook the Arab world. Mohamed Heikal writes: "That defeat had been a complete surprise to everybody. It may be that Egypt had not expected victory, but nobody had been prepared for defeat on such a shattering scale. Everybody was shocked, including the Russians."[137] Aside from the shock there was the humiliation generated by the defeat. Sadat maintains that "the period from June 1967 to September 1970 was one of intense suffering, unprecedented, I believe, in the entire stretch of Egyptian history."[138]

After June 1967, it was unmistakably clear that the Egyptian army would not be capable of decisively defeating the IDF in the foreseeable future.[139] Since the Sinai would be the battlefield, a war to achieve such an end would have to be a large-scale armored war. Given Israeli air superiority and Israeli prowess in armored battles, both of which were beyond dispute, the Egyptians had to avoid this type of warfare. The Egyptians, however, believed that further armed conflict with Israel was inevitable, and therefore, the deficiencies that had led to the 1967 debacle had to be corrected. Accordingly, President Nasser established a commission headed by Gen. Hassan el Badri to study the defeat and to offer recommendations for rebuilding the army.[140] In the six years between the 1967 and 1973 wars, the Egyptian army was completely overhauled.[141]

During this period, the Egyptians kept military pressure on Israel; this was accomplished mainly through the war of attrition that lasted from March 1969 to August 1970.[142] Despite this pressure, Israel remained firmly entrenched on the east bank of the Canal and showed no willingness to return any of the territory captured in 1967. Nor was there any reason to believe that the superpowers, particularly the United States, were going to pressure Israel to change the status quo.[143] Sadat concluded that "it was impossible . . . for the United States (or, indeed, any other power) to make a move if we ourselves didn't take military action to break the deadlock."[144] Thus Sadat decided in November 1972 to resort to force.[145]

But what kind of military action should Egypt take? As Badri notes in his study of the 1973 war, "There were two courses of action open to the Egyptian Military Command: either return to the War of Attrition or launch a limited war."[146] The former option was ruled out: "the War of Attrition had exhausted its usefulness."[147] The Egyptians would instead employ a limited aims strategy. Badri describes the proposed strategy: "Egypt was to deliver a carefully planned assault across the Suez Canal, capture the Bar Lev Line, and establish five bridgeheads of ten to fifteen kilometers depth each on the eastern bank of the canal. The attacking troops were to inflict the heaviest possible losses upon the enemy and to repel and destroy the enemy's counterblows."[148] In essence, the Egyptian army would capture a narrow band of territory running along the Canal's east side and would quickly turn it into a formidable defensive position. It should be emphasized that the Egyptians considered the military operation the first step in a comprehensive political strategy. They felt that in light of superpower involvement in the area and the potential for economic warfare, a limited military victory was likely to lead to sharp changes in the political situation.[149] Also they believed that the political landscape would be significantly altered if they could just demonstrate that the IDF was not infallible.[150] Appropriately, the military operation was called "Operation Spark."

The Egyptians recognized that they were not capable of launching a blitzkrieg. "There was never any question of a Patton—or Rommel-like penetration."[151] Egyptian planners assumed that the IDF would be at a decisive advantage in tank versus tank battles.[152] They ascribed even greater importance to Israeli air superiority, which they viewed as Israel's most important asset.[153] After the war, some analysts questioned Egypt's decision not to exploit her initial victory and at least to capture the Giddi, Khatmia, and Mitla passes.[154] Both Badri and Gen. Saad el Shazly, the army chief of staff prior to and during the 1973 war, maintain that there never was any intention to move beyond the narrow bridgehead captured at the outset of the war.[155] In light of their experience in the 1967 war, the Egyptians did not want to risk venturing beyond their surface-to-air missile (SAM) umbrella, which extended ten to fifteen kilometers east of the Canal, or to risk engaging the IDF in large-scale armored battles.[156] Sadat argued, "I don't want to make the mistake of pushing forward too fast just for the sake of occupying more territory."[157] His minister of war and commander of the army, Gen. Ahmed Ismail, one of the chief architects of the plan, emphasized that the army "must at all costs avoid being dangerously extended."[158]

The Egyptians could also not hope to defeat the IDF by employing an attrition strategy, unattractive as that strategy might be. First, the Israelis would stop such an offensive and would exact an extremely high price from the Egyptian army. This likelihood was clearly demonstrated on 14 October 1973 when the Egyptians, under great pressure from the Syrians and against the better judgment of the Egyptian commanders, launched a massive frontal attack in the Sinai.[159] As both sides expected, the second Egyptian offensive proved to be a clear-cut Israeli victory.

Second, even though the Israelis would suffer far fewer losses than the Egyptians in a slugging match, the Israelis would never allow themselves to become engaged in a war of attrition. Instead, they would use their advantage in fighting armored wars to effect a blitzkrieg. In essence, the Israelis were in a position where they could determine the shape and outcome of the war—as long as the Egyptians attempted to defeat the IDF decisively. Such was not the case, however, with a limited aims strategy.

The Egyptian operational plan called for crossing the Canal, capturing a narrow slice of territory in the Sinai, and then organizing a formidable defense that the Israelis could not penetrate. The Egyptians expected the Israelis to suffer heavy casualties as they attempted to pierce the Egyptian positions. The Egyptians, however, did not think that the conflict would turn into a lengthy war of attrition for basically two reasons. First, it was expected that the superpowers would intervene at some point after the initial Egyptian success. Second, the Israelis would not engage in such a conflict.

Our discussion has reached an important aspect of the Egyptian plan. The Egyptians expected and welcomed Israeli attacks on their defensive positions.[160] The Egyptians believed that the Israelis would suffer very heavy casualties because they would be taking the offensive against troops fighting from fixed defensive positions. The Egyptians recognized that the Israelis were extremely sensitive to casualties[161] and believed that if the Israelis suffered high losses, "this would have a great divisive and direct effect upon Israeli thought, behavior, and morale."[162] The Egyptians, on the other hand, were prepared to accept high casualty levels.[163] They expected the Israeli attacks to cease once the costs became apparent. The Egyptians would be forcing the Israelis into pursuing an attrition strategy, which they would then abandon.[164]

The Egyptians were confident that they could effect a limited aims strategy. First, they believed that they had the appropriate weapons for dealing with Israeli armor and with the Israeli air force (IAF). Their greatest fear was the IAF. As a result of the war of attrition, however, the Soviets had provided Egypt with an elaborate air defense system (SAM and air defense guns) that not only extended to the Canal but also covered the skies over a portion of the Canal's east bank.[165] To deal with Israeli tanks, the Egyptians would rely on infantrymen equipped with antitank guided missiles (ATGMs).[166] Egyptian military leaders had much faith in "the staunchness of the Arab infantry soldier in defense [*sic*] combat."[167] Before the deployment of ATGMs, however, infantrymen did not have the means to engage enemy tanks. A defender had to rely primarily on his own tanks to stop those of the attacker. ATGMs significantly altered the relationship between infantry and armor, providing infantrymen with the wherewithal to counter tanks.[168] Armed with numerous ATGM, the Egyptians would be able to avoid the armor versus armor battles that the Israelis invariably won and instead to adopt a plan "based mainly on infantry operations with armor acting as support."[169] Egyptian military leaders believed that the widespread use of ATGMs and SAMs would help make it possible to overrun the Bar-Lev Line and then to stymie the expected Israeli counterattacks.

Second, the Egyptians had a carefully prepared and detailed plan for the operation.[170] In devising the plan, they considered the IDF's strengths and weaknesses, something they had neglected to do before the 1967 war.[171] Equally important, they trained extensively for the operation. Heikal writes, "They had trained as few armies had trained by performing the same operations scores of times, month after month, year after year."[172] Third, the plan placed a high premium on achieving surprise, which would enable the Egyptians to establish their defensive positions in the Sinai before Israel mobilized its forces. This move would minimize the amount of actual battlefield conflict during the most difficult stage of the operation. Thus an elaborate deception scheme was designed to maximize the chances of achieving surprise.[173] Finally, the Egyptians persuaded the Syrians to join with them in the attack on Israel.[174] As a result, the Israelis would not be able to concentrate all of their forces in the Sinai. Egyptian decision makers were confident that they and the Syrians could achieve surprise and could successfully implement the operational plan.

Badri summarized Egyptian thinking on the prospects for success: "The bold political decision was not taken haphazardly or as a result of psychological pressures, but was based on a realistic knowledge that the time was right and that most, if not all, factual dimensions of the situation appeared to be suitable to achieve the desired goal."[175]

Although the Egyptians were confident that they could achieve their aims, they were clearly aware that the operation involved real risks. There were even some individuals in the Egyptian decision-making elite who doubted whether Egypt could execute the plan. Sadat relates in his memoirs that, after he made the decision to go to war in November 1972, a number of senior commanders balked when they were told to begin preparations.[176] They did not believe that the Egyptian army was ready for war—even for a limited one. Sadat fired them.[177] Even Badri notes, "It almost seemed that success would be impossible."[178] These doubts can be explained in part by the lingering effects of the humiliating loss the Egyptian army suffered in 1967. Two other important considerations, however, worked to temper Egyptian expectations of success. First, the Suez Canal was a formidable barrier that would not be easy to negotiate.[179] Compounding that problem was the fact that the Israelis maintained a forward defense along the Canal (the Bar-Lev Line), so that the Israelis would be able to contest the Egyptian army as it moved to cross the Canal.[180] Executing the operational plan would have been a demanding task for the best of armies. Badri writes: "When the Egyptian command determined to undertake the offensive, it realized the magnitude of the problem. The action would involve crossing the Suez Canal with massive forces—as much as two armies fully equipped and armed crossing simultaneously—and in the face of violent resistance from Israeli troops, full prepared [to] meet them on the eastern bank."[181] Certainly, the operation would be risky. The available evidence indicates, however, that the Egyptians were confident of their ability to accomplish the objectives laid out in the plan. It was, in the words of the Egyptian army chief of staff, "a calculated risk rather than a quixotic gamble."[182]

After the war some analysts argued that the Egyptians and the Syrians had started a war that they had expected to lose. Former IDF chief of staff, Chaim Bar-Lev writes: "Today, after the experience of the Yom Kippur War, it is clear to us that willingness to start even a lost war for the sake of restoration of Arab honor is consistent with the Arab mentality. Before the Yom Kippur War, many of us did doubt this."[183] In essence, Bar-Lev is arguing that the Arabs acted irrationally. To quote an American intelligence expert's immediate reaction to the Arab attack, "The Arabs do what they think they have to do even if it's suicidal."[184] If this statement were true, of course, it would help explain why the Israelis were surprised in 1973. Accepting the premise that the Arabs expected to lose the war, a more charitable interpretation is that the value of continued peace was so low that even a lost war was preferable to maintenance of the status quo.[185] These explanations are wrong simply because the assumption that the Arabs expected to suffer another crushing defeat is fallacious. It is important, nevertheless, to consider why Bar-Lev and many others believe that the Egyptians were willing "to start even a lost war." The misconception involved is in part responsible for the fact that the Israelis were caught almost completely by surprise in October 1973.[186]

As a consequence of the Holocaust and the proclaimed Arab goal of eliminating the Jewish state, Israelis tend to think that any war, by definition, is a war for survival.[187] Zeev Schiff, the influential Israeli journalist and author, aptly expresses this view:

> Unlike other nations, Israel does not face an enemy whose sole aim is to defeat her army or to conquer a specified area of land. The overall Arab plan has been and continues to be the total destruction of the Jewish state. The fact is that the Mideast conflict is nothing less than a war for Israel's very existence. . . . Israel assumes in advance that defeat in war means an end to the Jewish nation and she wages war accordingly.[188]

Israelis, by and large, find it quite difficult to conceive of the Arabs launching a war with limited objectives. An Israeli author maintains, for example, that just prior to the start of the 1973 war, Sadat told Kissinger that his aims were limited. When Kissinger relayed this information to Prime Minister Golda Meir, she refused to believe it.[189] Sharon maintains that in the wake of the Egyptian crossing of the Canal, Bar-Lev assumed that "the Egyptians wanted to go all the way to Tel Aviv, or at least to the middle of the Sinai."[190] Bar-Lev, who was well aware of the IDF's capabilities in armored battles, was anxious for the Egyptians to make such a move. The Egyptians, though, had no such intentions. Prior to the 1973 war, the Israelis believed that it would have been suicidal for the Arabs to attempt to defeat the IDF decisively. The Egyptians agreed and lowered their sights accordingly. Yet the Israelis, for the most part, were not able to envision the Arabs employing a limited aims strategy.[191] This factor contributed significantly to Israel's failure to recognize that the Arabs were preparing to strike.

[160]

The Israelis not only misread Arab intentions but also underestimated Arab capabilities. As a result of the IDF's overwhelming victory in the 1967 war, their self-confidence soared while they viewed the Arab armies with barely disguised contempt.[192] The Egyptians were particularly sensitive to what they described as "wanton Israeli conceit."[193] Nevertheless, the Israelis had long recognized that the Egyptians "fought well during the static phase of their combat."[194] At the same time, the Israelis held that any war in the Sinai would be a mobile armored war, thus rendering the Egyptians' strong suit moot. Dayan wrote in his *Diary of the Sinai Campaign*: "In desert terrain like Sinai there is no alternative to armour, aircraft, paratroopers and motorized infantry. The defending forces must be able to meet such attacking units with its [*sic*] own counterpart mobile units."[195] The Egyptians, however, had no intention of engaging in large-scale tank battles in the Sinai. They chose to employ a limited aims strategy instead because it would enable them to exploit the strengths of the Egyptian soldier while not exposing his weaknesses. The Israeli view of Egyptian intentions plainly defined the nature of the battlefield, which in turn influenced the Israeli view of Egypt as an opponent.

What made a limited aims strategy feasible in October 1973 was the widespread use of SAMs and ATGMs. These weapons greatly enhanced the Egyptian army's chances of maintaining defensive positions in the face of Israeli efforts to turn the battlefield into a mobile armored conflict. The Israelis seriously underestimated the utility of SAMs and ATGMs. Although they had fought against Soviet-built SAMs in the war of attrition, they failed to appreciate the effectiveness of the air defense system that had been constructed on the west bank of the Canal.[196] They were even more surprised by the potency of the Egyptians' ATGMs. At a more general level, they failed to see that these weapons, when employed in support of a limited aims strategy, could be used to complement the strengths of the Egyptian soldier. It is hardly surprising that Israeli General Matti Peled remarked after the war that "this time the war developed not the way we expected."[197] Not only were the Israelis surprised by the way the war developed, they were also surprised that the war even started.

The Israelis were not the only observers to underestimate Egyptian capabilities and intentions. U.S. decision makers were also convinced that, in light of the existing military balance, the Arabs would not dare attack.[198] Not surprisingly, once the war began, U.S. leaders expected a very quick Israeli victory.[199] Since the conclusion of the 1967 debacle, the Soviets had been telling the Egyptians that "resumption of the war is out of the question"; some form of political solution would be necessary.[200] Heikal reports that "the Soviets were as much astonished as delighted by the results of the first days' fighting."[201] Even Libya's Colonel Qaddafi, when told of the projected operation by Sadat, argued that it would lead to disaster.[202] Despite the widespread belief outside of Egypt that an Egyptian offensive stood hardly any chance of succeeding, the Egyptians believed that they were capable of accomplishing a limited military victory. That they ultimately failed on the battlefield does not detract from this fact.[203]

Conclusion

To appreciate more fully the fate of deterrence in the Middle East, it is necessary to place the 1973 Egyptian attack in a broader context. Specifically, we must examine Egyptian policy before the 1967 war and in the years between 1967 and 1973.

Between the cease-fire of 1949 and the weeks immediately preceding the 1967 war, Egypt did not consider going to war against Israel. In the early days of May 1967, when Nasser began moving large numbers of troops across the Canal, the available evidence indicates that he did not intend to provoke a war.[204] It soon became clear to Nasser and his lieutenants, however, that their actions were very likely to lead to a war with Israel. They recognized that continued escalation of the crisis would provoke an Israeli strike. Nevertheless, they continued to escalate the crisis. The Egyptians actually welcomed an Israeli attack because they were confident that they could stop it and could inflict heavy losses on the Israelis.

There are a number of important parallels between Egyptian behavior in this crisis and in 1973. In neither case is there any evidence that the Egyptians thought that they could take the offensive against Israel and could score a decisive victory. The Egyptians have had a long-standing respect for Israeli military prowess. In both cases the Egyptians considered their strong suit to be defensive warfare, or more specifically, holding fixed positions. The Egyptians did, of course, take limited offensive action in 1973 before assuming the defensive.[205] Nevertheless, there are more similarities than differences between Egyptian military strategy in 1967 and in 1973.

In a strict definitional sense, it would be inaccurate to label the 1967 Egyptian plan a limited aims strategy. After all, the Egyptians did not take the offensive, and they did not capture any Israeli territory. They did, however, move large numbers of forces into an area that adjoined Israel and had hitherto been free of large troop formations. This offensive act was not altogether unlike crossing the Canal in 1973. Then, having moved deep into the Sinai, the Egyptians assumed defensive positions to await an Israeli attack. In 1967, as in 1973, the Egyptians wanted to avoid engagements in which Egyptian forces were on the offensive. Instead, the objective was to create a situation in which the Israelis would suffer significant casualties in their futile efforts to dislodge the Egyptians from their well-entrenched positions. It is clear that Egypt's strategy in 1967 bears marked resemblance to the limited aims strategy employed in 1973.

Although the Egyptians were dealt a staggering military defeat in 1967, they remained convinced that some form of military action against Israel was necessary. They were, in fact, under significant political pressure to find a way to use the military instrument against Israel.[206] That the Egyptians had to resort to the war of attrition is evidence that they were deterred from starting a conventional war. As a result of the 1967 war, Israel had created a situation in which the Egyptians would not dare provoke another conventional war. The Egyptians recognized that they were not even in a position to pursue a limited aims strategy. Thus they resorted to the war of attrition, which was characterized by air strikes, artillery exchanges, and commando raids.

Although the details of the conflict are not revelant here, some general points are noteworthy. First, the Egyptians were confident that should the Israelis mount large-scale attacks across the Canal, the Egyptians would be able to defeat them. Certainly, the fact that the Canal was such a formidable barrier would make this task somewhat easier. Nevertheless, the Egyptians' attitude indicates Egypt's confidence in its ability to fight on the defensive. Furthermore, an important element of Egyptian strategy was the belief that Israel was extremely sensitive to casualties. As in 1967 and 1973, the Egyptians sought to engage Israel in a costly conflict. Finally, both sides were very much aware of the influence that the superpowers might have on the conflict's outcome.

The war of attrition ended in August 1970, and Israel remained firmly entrenched in the Sinai. Again, there was widespread pressure on the Egyptian leaders to do something militarily to alter the status quo. As I showed in the previous section, they eventually decided to pursue a limited aims strategy. By then, significant reforms had been instituted in the Egyptian army. Nonetheless, Egyptian leaders were guardedly optimistic about the capabilities of their army. Although the decision to strike in 1973 was the first offensive against Israel that the Egyptians had launched since 1948, it did not represent a fundamental shift in Egyptian thinking on how best to wage war with the Israelis.

With respect to the Israelis, two general points are in order. Although the Israelis have scored three very convincing military victories in the past three decades, in no sense have they been eager to go to war against the Arabs. The evidence does not support the notion that the IDF has been an instrument primed for war. Furthermore, when the possibility of launching a conventional strike was first mentioned in 1955, the Israelis rejected it. And they decided to strike in the following year only after lengthy deliberation. In May 1967, the Egyptian move into the Sinai and the closing of the Straits of Tiran caught the Israelis by surprise, and again, only after lengthy debate did the Israelis strike. In 1973, the Israelis were again caught off guard.[207] This time, however, the Israelis did not land the first blow. In fact, during the early hours of 6 October, when it was clear that an Arab attack was imminent, the Israelis decided against preemption.[208]

The principal reason that the Israelis did not strike on the morning of 6 October was diplomatic. They feared a negative American reaction. Like the Egyptians, the Israelis have consistently paid serious attention to the views of outside actors, as we see from their actions in the 1956 and 1967 wars as well as in the war of attrition.

[6]

The Prospects for Conventional Deterrence in Central Europe

In the previous three chapters, I have used my theory to explain past deterrence failures and successes. I shall now analyze the prospects for deterrence in Central Europe, where the armed forces of NATO and the Warsaw Pact face each other. More specifically, this chapter will seek to determine the prospects for deterring the Soviets from launching a conventional attack in a future crisis.

Certainly the Allies do not rely exclusively on conventional forces to deter the Soviets. Soviet decision makers contemplating a conventional attack would have to consider the possibility that the numerous tactical nuclear weapons in Europe might be used or that strategic nuclear forces might be deployed against the Soviet Union. This chapter, however, will investigate only the prospects for conventional deterrence in Europe. Actually, with the emergence of strategic parity and the Allies' manifest lack of enthusiasm for tactical nuclear weapons, the importance of the conventional element in the overall deterrence equation has increased significantly within the past decade.[1]

Whether or not deterrence obtains in a future crisis will depend, in large part, on whether the Soviets think that they can launch a successful blitzkrieg. Their aim will be complete and rapid destruction of NATO's capability to wage war; this objective is reflected in the Soviets' military literature as well as in the organization of their ground forces.[2] The Soviets have no intention of engaging in a lengthy war of attrition.[3] Nor is it likely that they would pursue a limited aims strategy. Even if the Soviets were to achieve their objectives, NATO would not be defeated and would still be capable of continuing the war. In fact, it is very likely that the conflict would turn into a war of attrition, an outcome the Soviets certainly want to avoid.

Could the Soviets effect a successful blitzkrieg against NATO? Any analysis must address two closely related issues. First, it must determine whether the Soviets have the force structure, the doctrine, and the raw ability to implement such a strategy. Second, when NATO's capabilities and the theater's terrain are considered, what are the prospects for Soviet success? It may very well be that the Soviet military is well primed to launch a blitzkrieg but that NATO in turn has the capability to thwart it.[4]

Any assessment of the NATO-Pact balance will depend on certain assumptions about the preparatory moves both sides would take before the war starts. Although the possibilities are many, observers most often posit three scenarios. The first is the *standing start* attack,[5] in which the Soviets launch an attack after hardly any mobilization and deliver a knockout blow against an unsuspecting NATO.[6] This eventuality is not, however, likely. Without significantly improving the readiness of their standing forces, the Soviets would not have the capability to score a decisive victory. Instead they would have to settle for capturing a portion of West German territory. As I have noted, such a limited victory is hardly an attractive option.[7] Second, for a war in Europe to become a realistic possibility, there would have to be a significant deterioration in East-West relations. Given such a development, both sides would very probably take some steps, however limited, to increase the readiness of their forces. It is difficult to imagine that an alert Pact could catch NATO completely unprepared.

The second scenario is more realistic and more dangerous. In the midst of a crisis, NATO detects a Pact mobilization but does not mobilize its forces for fear of triggering a Soviet attack.[8] Surely, if NATO fails to respond quickly to a Pact mobilization, as posited in this second scenario, the Pact would soon be in a position to inflict a decisive defeat on NATO.

In the third scenario, NATO's mobilization begins immediately after the Pact starts to mobilize. In this case the Pact does not gain an overwhelming force advantage as a result of NATO's failure to mobilize. I shall concern myself principally with this third scenario. My focus will thus be on a conflict in which both sides are alerted and in which neither enjoys an advantage as a result of the other's failure to mobilize.

I do not deny that strategic warning and especially the political decision to mobilize are important issues. On the contrary—and they will have a significant influence on the outcome of any future conflict in Europe. The assumption here is that strategic warning and mobilization are acted upon by NATO; the raw capabilities of the opposing forces will thus be examined under those clearly defined conditions.

Before directly assessing Soviet prospects for launching a blitz-krieg, we must briefly examine the balance of forces on the central front and the doctrines of the two sides.

THE BALANCE OF FORCES ON THE CENTRAL FRONT

The Pact has fifty-seven and one-third divisions located in Central Europe, while NATO has twenty-eight and one-third, giving the Pact slightly more than a 2:1 advantage in divisions.[9] Comparison of these numbers, however, distorts our view of the balance, since the numbers alone do not indicate the significant differences, both qualitative and quantitative, among each nation's divisions. There are generally two alternative ways of assessing the balance: one focuses on the manpower on each side, while the other compares weaponry.[10]

Robert Lucas Fischer, in his 1976 study of the conventional balance in Europe (which is one of the unfortunately few comprehensive studies on the subject), notes that NATO has 414,000 men in its divisions, while the Pact has 564,000.[11] If we compare divisional manpower, then, the Soviet advantage shrinks to 1.36:1. Fischer calculates that when overall manpower levels on the central front are considered, the Pact's advantage shrinks even further to 1.09:1. The reason is that NATO has traditionally assigned more men to combat units, which are not organic to divisions. Since Fischer's study was published, the Pact has added approximately 50,000 men, raising the overall advantage in manpower to 1.15:1—hardly an alarming figure.[12] In the British government's recent *Statement on Defence Estimates, 1981*, the Soviet advantage in overall manpower is placed at 1.2:1.[13] Under the category of "soldiers in fighting units," the Soviets are again given a 1.2:1 advantage. These figures are clear evidence that NATO is not hopelessly outnumbered.[14] Perhaps the most important problem with comparisons of manpower levels, however, is that they do not take into account weaponry.

It is not difficult to compare numbers of specific weapons on each side. For example, the Pact has approximately a 2.5:1 advantage in tanks and about a 2.8:1 advantage in artillery.[15] Such comparisons, however, do not indicate qualitative differences within the same category of weapons (that is, NATO's artillery is significantly better than Pact artillery); nor do they allow for different categories of weapons (that is, tanks versus artillery). To counter this problem, the Defense Department has devised a system of weighing weapons within the same category as well as across different categories.[16] Three principal characteristics of each weapon are considered: mobility, survivability, and firepower. Using this system, the Defense Department weighs all the weaponry in every division on the central front and then arrives at a composite figure, known as armored division equivalents (ADEs), for both NATO and the Warsaw Pact. Unfortunately, the number of armored division equivalents on each side is classified information. Very significantly, however, the ratio is not. Where standing forces are concerned, the Pact has a 1.2:1 advantage.[17] Again, it is clear that NATO is not hopelessly outnumbered.

Now let us consider the critical matter of comparative reinforcement capabilities. Although NATO's reinforcement capability is not as great as the Soviets' in an absolute sense, NATO has the potential to keep the overall ratio of forces very close to the premobilization ratio. The notion that the Soviets can rely on some massive second echelon that NATO cannot match is false. The ratio of forces in any future mobilization, however, will be heavily influenced by the timeliness of each side's efforts to mobilize. If NATO begins mobilizing its forces before the Pact does, or simultaneously, then the force ratios will remain close to 1.2:1 (in armored division equivalents) and 1.36:1 (in divisional manpower)—the ratios that obtained before mobilization.[18] If NATO starts mobilizing a few days after the Pact, then the balance of forces should approach but not exceed a 2:1 ratio in the very early days of mobilization and should then fall to a level close to the premobilization ratios. But once the gap in mobilization starting times reaches seven days (in the Pact's favor), NATO begins to face serious problems that become even more pronounced as the mobilization gap widens further. As I have noted, the assumption here is that NATO starts mobilizing immediately after the Pact, thus ensuring that the overall force ratios never reach 2:1 and in fact remain reasonably close to the premobilization ratios.

As I emphasized in Chapter 2, there are definite limits to the utility of measuring force levels. After all, even a cursory study of military history would show that it is impossible to explain the outcome of many important military campaigns by simply comparing the number of forces on each side. Nevertheless, it is clear that if one side has an overwhelming advantage in forces, the glaring asymmetry is very likely to portend a decisive victory.[19] In essence, the larger force will simply overwhelm the smaller one—as, for example, the Germans did the Poles in September 1939. The previous analysis of the balance of forces in Europe indicates that the Soviets do not enjoy an equally great advantage. They do not have the numerical superiority simply to crush NATO. In a conventional war in Europe, whether or not the Soviets prevail will depend on how they employ their forces against NATO's defenses. In other words, success will be a function of strategy, not of overwhelming numbers. I do not deny that the Soviets would be better served with an overall advantage in armored division equivalents of 1.8:1 rather than, say, 1.2:1. But regardless of which ratio obtains, ultimate success will turn on the issue of strategy. More specifically, success will depend on the Soviets' capability to effect a blitzkrieg.[20]

Doctrine

NATO's forces are divided into eight corps sectors, which are aligned in layer-cake fashion along the inter-German border (see figure 6.1).[21] There are four corps sectors each in the Northern Army Group (NORTHAG) and the Central Army Group (CENTAG). There are also German and Danish forces located in Schleswig-Holstein, which is adjacent to the northern portion of the central front.

NATO's forces are arrayed to support a strategy of forward defense. In other words, to meet a Pact offensive, the forces in each of NATO's corps sectors are deployed very close to the border between the two Germanies. The objective is to meet and to thwart an attack right at this boundary. Political as well as military considerations dictate the choice of this strategy. A number of defense analysts in the West, however, argue that NATO's chances of thwarting a Pact attack are negligible as long as NATO employs a forward defense. They claim that the Soviets can mass their forces at points of their choosing along NATO's extended front, can achieve overwhelming force ratios, and can blast through NATO's forward defense. It would then be very easy to effect deep strategic penetrations, since NATO has few reserves that could be used to check the Soviets' armored spearheads. These analysts favor a maneuver-oriented defense.[22] The subsequent discussion will address the charge that NATO's strategy of forward defense is fundamentally flawed.

How do the Soviets plan to fight a nonnuclear war in Europe? What, in other words, is their doctrine for fighting a conventional war? Western analysts often assume that the Soviets have one neatly packaged. As we shall see, however, such is not the case. It is frequently assumed that they will employ a blitzkrieg. Although the

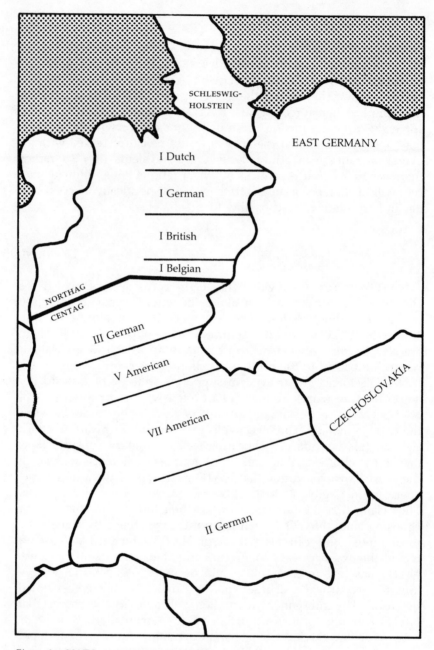

Figure 6.1. NATO corps sectors, West Germany

Soviets do not use the term *blitzkrieg*, it is clear that they pay serious attention to the question of how to effect a blitzkrieg against NATO. They continually emphasize the importance of massing large tank forces on narrow fronts, breaking through NATO's forward defenses, and then racing deep into NATO's rear so as to bring about the rapid collapse of NATO's forces. Furthermore, the Soviets have shown considerable interest in studying the lessons of their 1945 offensive against the Japanese army in Manchuria.[23] That operation was a classic blitzkrieg.

Although my focus here is on the Soviets' capability to effect a blitzkrieg, they might alternatively employ an attrition strategy, as they did against the Germans on the eastern front in World War II.[24] Instead of relying on deep strategic penetrations to bring about the collapse of the German army, Soviet strategy called for wearing the German army down by slowly pushing it back along a broad front. Massive firepower, as we know, is the key ingredient with an attrition strategy.

There is no doubt that the Soviets want to use a blitzkrieg in any future war in Europe. Doubt is growing in the Soviet Union, however, as to whether such a strategy is possible on the modern battlefield.[25] The matter has been debated at length in Soviet military journals, but there has apparently been no clear consensus of opinion. The important question, which I shall address later, is: What effect does such doctrinal uncertainty have on the Soviets' ability to effect a blitzkrieg?

SOVIET PROSPECTS FOR EFFECTING A BLITZKRIEG IN CENTRAL EUROPE

By choosing a forward defense strategy, NATO has effectively determined that a war in Europe will be won or lost along the inter-German border. It is thus imperative that NATO thwart the Pact in initial battles along the border. This point is evident from the opening page of *FM 100-5*, which describes basic U.S. Army doctrine: "The first battle of our next war could well be its last battle. . . . the U.S. Army must, above all else, *prepare to win the first battle of the next war.*"[26] If the Soviets win those initial battles and penetrate with large armored forces deep into NATO's rear, NATO's fate is sealed, since it has neither the reserve strength necessary to counter such penetrations nor the strategic depth that would allow for retreat and the establishment of a new front.

[171]

To determine whether the Soviets can successfully launch a blitz-krieg against NATO's forward defense, two key questions must be answered. First, can the Soviets achieve the necessary force ratios on their main axes of advance so that they can then open gateways into NATO's rear? In other words, given the deployment of NATO's forces as well as the terrain, how likely is it that the Soviets will be able to repeat the German achievement opposite the Ardennes Forest in 1940? Is it true, as advocates of a maneuver-oriented de-fense claim, that the Pact can choose any point on the NATO front and can achieve the superiority of forces necessary to effect a break-through? The answer to these questions will be determined largely by matching NATO's deployment pattern, which is well known, against the deployment patterns that would most likely be used as part of a Soviet blitzkrieg.

Second, if the Soviets are able to tear open a hole or two in NATO's defensive front, will the Soviets be able to exploit the open-ings and to penetrate into the depths of the NATO defense before NATO has a chance to shift forces and to slow the penetrating spearheads? It is difficult to effect a deep strategic penetration in the "fog of war," when the defender is doing everything possible to seal off the gaps in his defense, and the task requires a first-rate army. How capable is the Soviet army of accomplishing this difficult objective? Although it is not possible to provide definitive answers to these questions, there is good reason to believe that NATO is capable of thwarting a Soviet blitzkrieg and turning the conflict into a war of attrition.

The Initial Deployment Patterns

With regard to Soviet deployment patterns for a conventional war, the most basic question is: How will the Soviets apportion their forces across the front? More specifically, will the Soviets disperse their forces rather evenly across the front, mounting attacks along numerous axes, or will they concentrate their forces at one, two, or three points along the inter-German border? In many of the accounts by Western analysts, it is assumed that a Soviet offensive will be multipronged. John Erickson, for example, expects that the Soviets will attempt "eight to ten breakthrough operations."[27] In effect, NATO will be faced with numerous attacks across its entire front. Equally important, it is frequently assumed that the Soviets will achieve overwhelming superiority in forces on each of these avenues of attack.

[172]

It is possible that the Soviets might choose to launch an offensive along multiple axes of advance. This course of action would be consistent with their doctrine for fighting a nuclear war, in which the emphasis is on keeping the attacking forces widely dispersed so that they are not vulnerable to nuclear attacks. Still, such a deployment pattern would hardly facilitate employment of a blitzkrieg, simply because it would be virtually impossible for the Soviets, given the present overall balance of forces, to achieve overwhelming force ratios on any of the axes. To see this point, let us consider a *hypothetical* but realistic model of the central front.

Let us assume that the Pact has sixty-four armored division equivalents, while NATO has thirty-two; in other words, the Pact has a 2:1 force advantage across the front.[28] Furthermore, let us assume that the Soviets plan to employ a multipronged attack, aiming to strike along six main axes. In keeping with the dictates of a forward defense, NATO divides its thirty-two divisions evenly among its eight corps sectors (see figure 6.2). It is usually believed that to overwhelm the defense, an attacking force needs more than a 3:1 advantage in forces on the main axes of advance; suppose, then, in the first instance, that the Soviets decide they require a 5:1 advantage.[29] They would therefore need twenty divisions per axis, which would allow them only three main axes of advance (see figure 6.3).[30] Moreover, they would be quite vulnerable to NATO in the remaining five corps sectors.

If we assume that the Soviets require only a 4:1 advantage on the main axes, they would then need sixteen divisions per axis. This number would allow them only four main axes; however, they would not have any forces left with which to defend the remaining corps

Figure 6.2. Initial distribution of NATO divisions

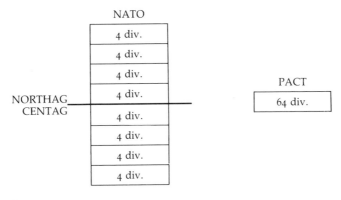

[173]

Figure 6.3. Distribution of forces when Soviets desire 5:1 advantage

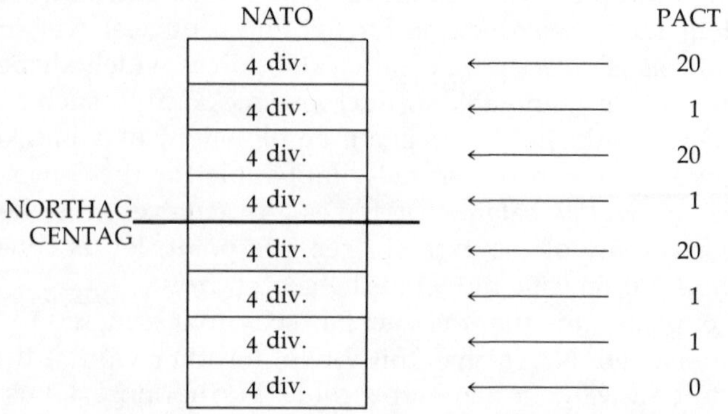

	NATO		PACT
	4 div.	←	20
	4 div.	←	1
	4 div.	←	20
NORTHAG	4 div.	←	1
CENTAG	4 div.	←	20
	4 div.	←	1
	4 div.	←	1
	4 div.	←	0

sectors (see figure 6.4). If the Soviets were to aim for the projected six axes, they would be able to place approximately ten divisions on each main axis (see figure 6.5). They would then have a force ratio on each axis of 2.5:1, which is hardly satisfactory in light of the widely recognized assumption that an attack requires more than a 3:1 advantage on each main axis to succeed. Obviously, the more axes you have, the smaller the advantage you achieve on each axis. Finally, the point is reached, in this case with eight main axes of advance, where the distribution of forces on each axis is the same as the overall 2:1 ratio (see figure 6.6).

It is apparent from this *hypothetical* model that as long as NATO keeps the overall force ratio under 2:1, it is impossible for the Soviets to have six-ten axes of advance and at the same time to have an overwhelming advantage in forces on each axis (that is, a ratio of 4:1

Figure 6.4. Distribution of forces when Soviets desire 4:1 advantage

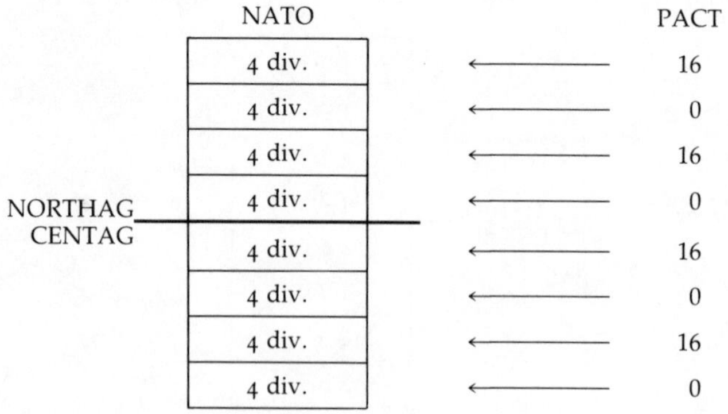

	NATO		PACT
	4 div.	←	16
	4 div.	←	0
	4 div.	←	16
NORTHAG	4 div.	←	0
CENTAG	4 div.	←	16
	4 div.	←	0
	4 div.	←	16
	4 div.	←	0

[174]

Figure 6.5. Distribution of forces when Soviets aim for six main axes

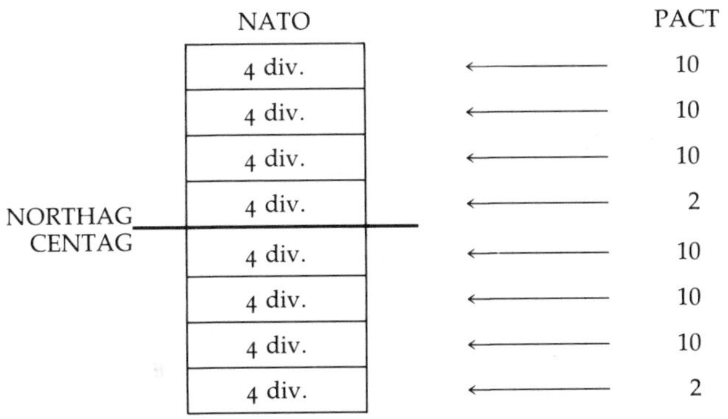

	NATO		PACT
	4 div.	←	10
	4 div.	←	10
	4 div.	←	10
NORTHAG	4 div.	←	2
CENTAG	4 div.	←	10
	4 div.	←	10
	4 div.	←	10
	4 div.	←	2

or more). The Soviets simply do not have a great enough overall force advantage to allow them to spread out their forces on numerous widely dispersed axes. The matter of force ratios aside, from NATO's viewpoint, a multipronged attack is the most desirable Pact deployment pattern. If so, NATO, whose forces are evenly spread out along a wide front, need not concern itself with shifting forces to counter massive concentrations of force by the Pact. From NATO's perspective, a multipronged attack results in a propitious meshing of the offensive and defensive deployment patterns.[31]

If the Pact does choose a multipronged attack, it will, at best, in the end push NATO back across a broad front, much as the Soviets pushed the Germans westward across Europe in World War II. This is not a blitzkrieg but an attrition strategy. If the Soviets hope to defeat NATO with a blitzkrieg, they will have to concentrate mas-

Figure 6.6. Distribution of forces when Soviets aim for eight main axes

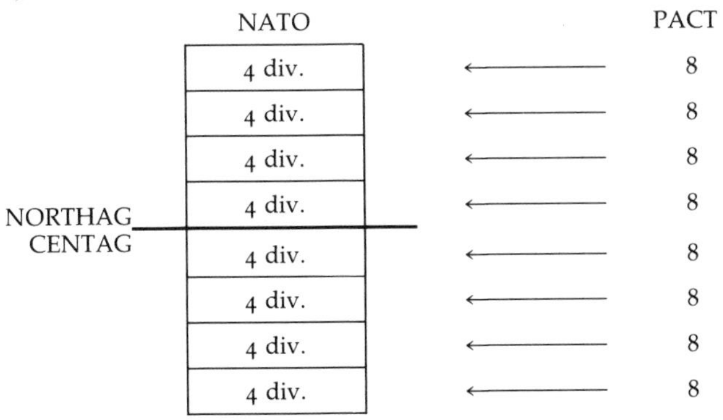

	NATO		PACT
	4 div.	←	8
	4 div.	←	8
	4 div.	←	8
NORTHAG	4 div.	←	8
CENTAG	4 div.	←	8
	4 div.	←	8
	4 div.	←	8
	4 div.	←	8

sive amounts of armor on one, two or, at most, three major axes of advance. This requirement suggests certain obvious questions: Where are those axes likely to be? How well-positioned is NATO to deal with the most likely Pact deployment patterns? More specifically, are NATO's forces positioned so that they can, first, stymie the initial onslaughts on the various potential axes of advance, and second, give NATO time to move reinforcements to threatened positions and, in effect, to erase the temporary superiority in forces that the Pact has achieved by massing its forces at specific points?[32] These questions are best answered by closely examining, corps sector by corps sector, both the terrain and the deployment of NATO's forces.

It is most unlikely that the Pact would place a major axis of advance in either the far north or the far south of the NATO front. In the south, in other words, a major attack against II German Corps would not be feasible simply because it would not result in a decisive victory. The Allies could afford to lose almost the entire corps sector, reaching back to the French border, and they would still be able to continue the war. Moreover, the mountainous terrain in this part of Germany would impede the movement of large armored forces. In the north, a major offensive against Schleswig-Holstein is unlikely. Although the terrain is not mountainous in this sector, there are still enough obstacles (bogs, rivers, urban sprawl around Hamburg) to hinder the movement of a large armored force. Furthermore, a Pact success in this region would not constitute a mortal blow to NATO. The main body of NATO's forces would still be intact and capable of conducting a vigorous defense.

Channeling Forces: The Pact's Axes of Attack in CENTAG

The Soviets are most likely to locate their main attacks along the front stretching from the I Dutch Corps Sector in the north to the VII American Corps Sector in the south. Let us first consider the three key corps sectors in CENTAG (III German, V American, and VII American). Generally, the terrain in the CENTAG area is very obstacle-ridden. In addition to mountains there are numerous rivers and forests. Consequently CENTAG affords a small number of natural avenues of attack. Actually, there are three potential axes on which the Soviets are likely to advance.

The most threatening possibility would be an attack from the Thuringian Bulge through the Fulda Gap, aimed at Frankfurt (see figure 6.7). Except for the Fulda River, the terrain on this axis should not greatly hinder the movement of large armored forces. This axis

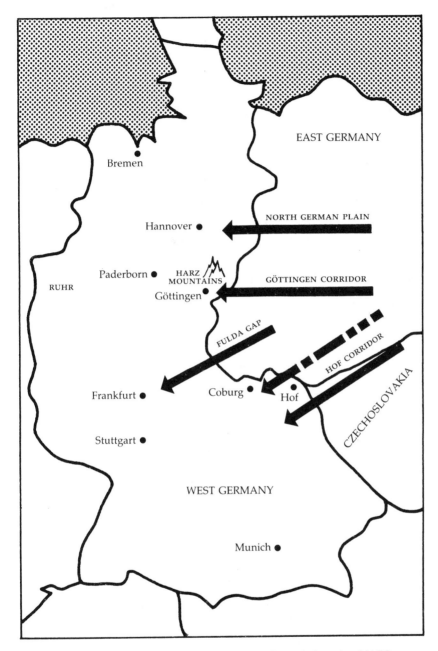

Figure 6.7. Most likely axes of advance in a Warsaw Pact attack against NATO

cuts across the "wasp-waist," or narrowest, section of Germany. The distance from the inter-German border to Frankfurt is a mere 100 kilometers. Frankfurt, because of its central location in Germany's communications network, would be a most attractive target. Its capture would effectively cut Germany in half and, given the importance of north-south lines of communication, would leave NATO's forces in southern Germany isolated.

The second potential axis of advance is located in the sector covered by the III German Corps. The attacking forces would move through the Göttingen Corridor, just south of the Harz Mountains. The industrialized Ruhr is located due west of Göttingen. Although the terrain on the western half of this axis (between Paderborn and the Ruhr) is suitable for the large-scale employment of tanks, the terrain on the eastern half of the axis, which the attacker must traverse first, is not obstacle-free. There are a number of forests in the region, and the attacking forces would have to cross the Leine River and then the Weser River.

A third potential axis of advance in CENTAG is less attractive than the axes that run through the Fulda Gap and the Göttingen Corridor. This axis runs from Bohemia through the area around the city of Hof toward Stuttgart: the Hof Corridor.[33] The terrain that an attacking force would have to traverse in this region is considerably more obstacle-ridden than that along the other axes. Moreover, Stuttgart is a far less attractive target than either Frankfurt or the Ruhr. Aside from these three axes, there are no attractive alternatives.

NATO's forces in CENTAG should be able to contain a major Soviet attack in this region. There are only a limited number of potential axes of advance, each of which is quite narrow and well defined and each of which NATO is well prepared to defend. Moreover, NATO has contingency plans to shift forces to combat Soviet efforts designed to achieve overwhelming force ratios at the points of main attack.[34] NATO's prospects of successfully halting a Soviet attack are further strengthened by the terrain, which not only limits the number of potential axes but also channels the attacking forces across the width of Germany. In other words, the potential axes of advance are rather narrow and do not allow the attacker to spread his forces after the initial breakthrough.[35] In 1940, once the Germans crossed the Meuse River, they came upon the open, rolling plains of northeastern France, which was ideal terrain for armored forces. Such would not be the case in CENTAG, where the attacking forces would be canalized by the terrain throughout their movement across Germany.

Considerations of geography should contribute to NATO's prospects for stopping a Soviet penetration before a decisive blow could be landed.

Another reason for optimism is that the NATO corps sectors in CENTAG are manned by German and American forces, which are the best in NATO.[36] Furthermore, there are reinforcements in CENTAG. The United States has prepositioned material for two divisions in CENTAG's rear.[37] Also, French and Canadian forces (three small French armored divisions and one Canadian brigade) are located in CENTAG and can serve as an operational reserve for this half of NATO's defense.[38]

The North German Plain

Now, consider NATO's prospects for containing a Soviet attack directed against NORTHAG. It is widely held that NATO is more vulnerable in this region than in CENTAG. The terrain in NORTHAG, which is not mountainous or heavily forested, is generally held to be more favorable to the movement of large armored formations. Frequent reference is made to the suitability of the North German Plain for a blitzkrieg.[39] Second, there are doubts about whether the Dutch and the Belgians, and even the British, have the capability to withstand a Soviet attack. There is only one German corps sector in NORTHAG and there is no American corps sector, although prepositioned material for an American corps, which will serve as an operational reserve for NORTHAG, is being deployed near Bremen.[40] Notwithstanding that NATO is more vulnerable in this region than in CENTAG, the prospects for thwarting a major Soviet attack in NORTHAG are quite good. The terrain is not obstacle free by any means, and as we shall see, the Belgian and Dutch corps sectors are not the weak links that they are often said to be.

NORTHAG covers a front of only 225 kilometers, while CENTAG defends a front that is more than two times as long (500 kilometers).[41] Appropriately, the corps sectors in NORTHAG are smaller than those in CENTAG. The I Belgian Corps occupies the southernmost and smallest sector in NORTHAG, measuring only thirty-five kilometers. Approximately one-third of the front is covered by the Harz Mountains, while the terrain throughout the depth of the corps sector is laden with obstacles. Belgium's two divisions, small as they are, are adequate for defending this short front in the initial stages of an attack.[42] Although it is unlikely that the Pact would place a main axis through this corps sector, if it did do so, forces from the III German Corps, immediately to the south, could be moved north to reinforce the Belgians, and forces from the American corps in reserve could be moved forward.

The North German Plain, above the Belgian corps sector, is covered by the I British and I German corps. There is widespread agreement that the Pact will place a single main axis against NORTHAG and that that axis will be located on the North German Plain. Although there are no mountains and few forests in this region, there are obstacles in both the German and British corps sectors. In the heart of the British corps sector, there is significant urban sprawl centered on Hannover.[43] Armored forces simply will not be able to move rapidly through those urban areas that NATO chooses to defend. Since urbanization continues in this area, it will become increasingly difficult, if not impossible, to avoid large-scale urban fighting in the event of war. There are also a number of rivers in the British sector. The terrain in the I German Corps Sector, on the other hand, is covered, in large part, by the Lüneberger Heath, which is a formidable impediment to the rapid movement of masses of armor. For this reason the North German Plain is usually identified with the British corps sector.

The British Army of the Rhine (BAOR) comprises four small divisions, a force that is adequate for covering the seventy-kilometer corps sector front.[44] There are, however, thirteen brigades—or four and one-third formidable divisions—in the I German Corps Sector.[45] Aside from the fact that these German forces are more than adequate for defending their assigned corps sector, they can be rapidly moved to the south to augment the BAOR, and of course they can also move northward to help the Dutch. This contingent in the I German Corps Sector represents the largest concentration of forces in all of the sectors. Given its central location in NORTHAG as well as the excellent north-south lines of communication in that region, this force is a formidable instrument for thwarting a Pact attack across the North German Plain.[46] Furthermore, there will be an American corps, part of which is already deployed, in NORTHAG's rear.[47] In sum, NATO has the wherewithal to deal with a Pact attack across the North German Plain.

Finally, there is the Dutch corps sector, which is manned by two Dutch divisions. Should the Soviets place a main axis through this sector, the Dutch forces, like their British and Belgian counterparts, should be capable of defending their front in the initial stages of the conflict. Then forces from the adjacent I German Corps can be moved north to assist the Dutch. Moreover, the American corps will be located directly to the rear of the Dutch corps sector. The terrain within the Dutch corps sector is not conducive to the rapid movement of armored forces. In addition to the Elbe River, which forms the inter-German border in this sector, a number of other rivers, canals, and bogs are liberally sprinkled throughout this sector. The Lüneberger Heath, which is such a prominent feature in the adjacent I German Corps Sector, extends northward across the Dutch corps sector. To add to the woes of the attacker, there is significant urban sprawl around Bremen and Bremerhaven.[48] Finally, even if the attacking forces were able to penetrate through this sector rapidly, it is unlikely that NATO would be mortally wounded. Certainly NATO would feel the loss of the ports in northern Germany. Since the attacking forces would go from Germany into the northern part of the Netherlands, however, NATO would still have access to the most important Belgian, Dutch, and French ports.

Force-to-Space Ratios

A number of additional points concerning Soviet and NATO deployment patterns merit attention. The discussion has so far focused on the matter of how the Pact might achieve overwhelming superiority on specific axes of advance. If we are examining prospects for a breakthrough at the point of main attack, however, we cannot simply focus on the balance of forces. It is also necessary to consider force-to-space ratios, or the number of divisions that the defender requires to hold a specific sector of territory,[49] as well as the crossing-the-T phenomenon.[50] It is generally agreed that a brigade can hold a front approximately seven to fifteen kilometers long.[51] With seven kilometers, which is obviously the more desirable figure, a brigade should be able to hold its position for an extended period of time before it needs reinforcement. As the figure approaches fifteen kilometers, the defender should be able to cope with the initial onslaughts without any problem. It will, however, be necessary to bring in reinforcements after a day or so, since the attacker's forces will have begun to wear down the defender by that time. Since the length of the NORTHAG front is 225 kilometers, if one assumes that each brigade could hold 15 kilometers, then a minimum of 15 brigades would be needed to cover the front. There are actually 30 brigades within the four NORTHAG corps sectors.[52] Given that there are 30 brigades and a 225-kilometer front, this means that each brigade will have to cover 7.5 kilometers, which is extremely close to the most desirable force-to-space ratio for a brigade.

[181]

Now let us assume that NATO deploys its 30 brigades along the NORTHAG front in the traditional "two brigades up, one back" configuration. The remaining 20 brigades would then have to cover 225 kilometers (11 kilometers per brigade), with 10 brigades in immediate reserve. NATO would be in very good shape. Two other points are noteworthy. First, because there are a number of obstacles along the NORTHAG front, NATO would not have to worry about covering every section of the 225 kilometers. Second, the American corps in NORTHAG's rear, when fully operational, will provide an additional 9 brigades. Also, at least 6 armored infantry brigades in the German Territorial Army could be assigned to NORTHAG.[53] In short, NORTHAG does not have force-to-space problems.[54]

The length of the CENTAG front is 500 kilometers. Assuming 15 kilometers per brigade, 33 brigades would be required to cover this front. NATO has 33 brigades in the four CENTAG corps sectors, a figure that is hardly alarming in light of the obstacle-ridden terrain along this portion of the NATO front and the fact that the brigades in these corps sectors are the heaviest in NATO and will therefore have the least amount of trouble covering 15 kilometers of front.[55] Furthermore, there are 21 brigades (including the French, but not including the German Territorials) available for reinforcement in CENTAG's rear.[56]

Consider briefly the crossing-the-T phenomenon, which further highlights the problems that the Soviets will have breaking through NATO's forward positions. In one of the U.S. Army's standard scenarios for a major Soviet attack against one of the two American corps sectors in CENTAG, a Soviet force of five divisions is pitted against two American divisions.[57] In the opening battle, three Soviet divisions attack across about forty to fifty kilometers of front against two U.S. divisions.[58] The remaining two Soviet divisions are held in immediate reserve. Thus in that opening battle the ratio of forces directly engaged is 3:2 in the Pact's favor, not 5:2. (It should be noted that these ratios would be even more favorable to NATO if they were translated into armored division equivalents.) The key question is, of course: Can those three Soviet divisions so weaken the two American divisions that the remaining two Soviet divisions will be able to effect a breakthrough? In this regard, the matter of force-to-space ratios is of crucial importance. Since two divisions, or six brigades, are defending forty to fifty kilometers, each of these powerful American brigades will be holding approximately seven kilometers. Without a doubt, the Soviets would have a great deal of difficulty penetrating that American front.

Now let us assume that the Soviets start with ten or even fifteen divisions, instead of the five employed in the above scenario. Only a very few of these additional divisions could be placed at the point of main attack, simply because there would be limited room on the front to accommodate them. They would have to be located behind the attacking forces, where they would have little impact on the initial battles.[59] Certainly, the forces in each NATO corps sector should be capable of blunting the initial Soviet attack and of providing adequate time for NATO to shift forces from other corps sectors and its operational reserves to threatened points along the front.[60]

In sum, given the initial deployment patterns of both NATO and the Pact, it appears that NATO is reasonably well deployed to meet a Soviet blitzkrieg. Although both Pact and NATO deployment patterns have been examined, attention has been focused, for the most part, on examining NATO's capability to thwart a blitzkrieg. Let us now shift our focus and examine Soviet capabilities in detail.

SOVIET CAPABILITIES

To ascertain whether the Soviet army has the capacity to effect a blitzkrieg, it is necessary to examine that army on three levels. First, one must consider how the Soviet army is organized. In other words, are the forces structured to facilitate a blitzkrieg? Second, it is necessary to consider doctrine, a subject that has already received some attention. Finally, there is the matter of raw skill. Assuming that the problems with force structure and doctrine are minimal, is the Soviet army capable of performing the assigned task? These questions have, of course, no simple answers. They are nonetheless extremely important and have received little serious attention in the West, where it is all too often assumed that the Soviets have only strengths and no weaknesses.

Since almost all the Pact divisions that would be used in a European war are either armored or mechanized infantry, it seems reasonable to assume that the Pact is appropriately organized to launch a blitzkrieg. On close inspection, however, there are potential trouble spots in the Pact's force structure. During the past decade, Soviet divisions have become extremely heavy units. Western analysts pay a great deal of attention to the large and growing number of tanks, infantry fighting vehicles, artillery pieces, rocket launchers, surface-to-air missiles, air defense guns, antitank guided missiles, and assorted other weapons that are found in Soviet divisions as well as in other Pact divisions.[61] Past a certain point, however, there is an inverse relationship between the mass and the velocity of an attacking force. As the size of the attacking force increases, the logistical difficulties as well as the command and control problems increase proportionately. It then becomes very difficult to move that force rapidly—an essential requirement when the attacker is seeking to strike deep into the defender's rear before the defender can shift forces to deal with the penetrating forces. Although the notion is perhaps counterintuitive, bigger divisions are not necessarily better divisions when an attacking force is attempting to effect a blitzkrieg.[62]

There is a second organizational problem facing the Soviets. As noted, in a blitzkrieg, the attacker seeks to combine arms (infantry, artillery, armor) within his divisions at as high a level as possible.[63] The attacker wants to maximize the size of his pure tank units. There is evidence, however, that because of the need to be prepared to fight a nuclear war and because of the growing firepower available to NATO, the Soviets are being forced to mix arms at lower levels than heretofore.[64] This trend must disturb the Soviets.

Consider now the matter of doctrine. As I noted earlier, it is not possible to determine exactly how the Soviets plan to fight a conventional war in Europe. The Soviets themselves are not sure; there is presently doctrinal uncertainty in their military circles. Certainly, they continue to emphasize the necessity of rapidly defeating NATO should a war in Europe break out. The Soviets recognize, however, that it is becoming increasingly difficult to effect rapid defeat, especially because of the proliferation of ATGMs.[65] Moreover, they are well aware of how the organizational problems just described compound their task. They realize that it will be difficult to effect deep strategic penetrations against prepared defenses.[66] Although the Soviets have made a considerable effort to solve this problem, if anything, they appear to be moving closer to an attrition strategy. This trend is reflected in their growing reliance on artillery and dismounted infantry.[67] There is no evidence that the Soviets have made a conscious decision to fight a war of attrition. Instead, it appears that they are being inexorably drawn in this direction by their efforts to neutralize the growing firepower, both ground based and air delivered, available to NATO.

Blitzkrieg and the Nuclear Battlefield

The Soviets continue to pay serious attention to the possibility that NATO will use nuclear weapons. Thus they devote much time to training for a nuclear war which, by their own admission, would be fundamentally different from a conventional war and would require a different doctrine. For example, whereas a blitzkrieg concentrates the armor in massive formations, in nuclear war the armor would be widely dispersed across the front so as not to present NATO with lucrative targets for its nuclear weapons.[68] Moreover, given the firepower provided by nuclear weapons, piercing NATO's front would not require the high concentration of forces that is necessary to achieve the same objective in a conventional conflict; the role of artillery would be greatly diminished on a nuclear battlefield. In sum, the time and resources the Soviets spend preparing their forces to fight a nuclear war could be spent training those forces to fight a conventional war. A crisis will force the Soviets to decide between the two—a difficult choice indeed. In this regard, NATO's plethora of tactical nuclear weapons serves a valuable purpose. The nuclear-conventional dichotomy aside, however, the Soviets still have not found a satisfactory strategy for fighting a conventional war. As long as they are not confident that they have a sound doctrine for inflicting a rapid and decisive defeat on NATO, the Soviets are not likely to initiate conflict in a crisis.

Soviet Training and Initiative

Finally, there is the question of whether the Soviet army has the necessary raw skills. An army that intends to implement a blitzkrieg should have a highly flexible command structure as well as officers and NCOs at every level of the chain of command who are capable of exercising initiative.[69] A blitzkrieg is not a steamroller: success is ultimately a consequence of commanders' ability to make rapid-fire decisions in the fog of battle that enable the attacking forces to make the crucial deep strategic penetrations. Should the Soviets attack NATO, there is a chance that the Soviets will open one or more holes in the NATO front. Naturally, NATO will try to close those holes and to seal off any penetrations as quickly as possible. The key question is: Can the Soviets exploit such opportunities before NATO, which is well prepared for such an eventuality, shuts the door? In this battle, the crucial determinant will be not the amount of firepower the Soviets have amassed for the breakthrough but the ability of highly skilled officers and NCOs to make decisions that will enable the armored spearheads to outrun NATO's defenses. A blitzkrieg depends on split-second timing, since opportunity on the battlefield is so fleeting.

[185]

There is substantial evidence that Soviet officers and NCOs are sadly lacking in individual initiative and, furthermore, that the Soviet command structure is rigid. Christopher Donnelly notes:

It is hard for a western officer to appreciate what a difficult concept this [initiative] is to reconcile with a normal Soviet upbringing. There has never been a native Russian word for initiative. The idea of an individual initiating unilateral action is anathema to the Soviet system. The Soviet army has always considered as one of its strengths its iron discipline and high-level, centralised command system combined with a universal tactical doctrine. The run-of-the-mill officer, particularly a sub-unit officer, has never had to do other than obey orders.[70]

The Soviets are keenly aware of the need for initiative and flexibility, and they stress the importance of these qualities in their military journals.[71] These attributes cannot, however, be willed into existence. Their absence is largely the result of powerful historical forces.[72] Fundamental structural change in Soviet society and the Soviet military would be necessary before flexibility and initiative would increase significantly.

Certain analysts in the West argue that the Soviets have obviated this problem by relying on "steamroller tactics at the divisional level." Steven Canby, one of the leading proponents of this view, writes:

Steamroller tactics, at the divisional level, are characterized by a relatively inflexible command system and a rigid system of echeloned forces. . . . As formations are exhausted by fighting they are replaced rapidly by other echelons. . . . By maintaining momentum with large numbers of formations, Soviet forces plan to saturate enemy defences and offset the need for flexibility and initiative at the company level, where their tactics tend to be rigid. Having large numbers available gives higher commanders considerable flexibility.

Combat divisions and *even armies* can be used like drill tips on a high-speed drill—to be ground down and replaced until penetration occurs. [Emphasis added][73]

This approach has major problems. First, the Pact lacks the overall superiority in forces needed for such "steamroller tactics."[74] Second, the process of removing shattered divisions from the front and replacing them with fresh divisions is complex and time consuming. Third, even if steamroller tactics enable the Pact to open a hole in NATO's front in the initial stages of the conflict, the Pact forces

[186]

must still effect a deep strategic penetration while NATO is moving forces into its path. This task is most demanding and requires both flexibility and initiative. Continued use of steamroller tactics after the breakthrough battle will not suffice.[75]

Other deficiencies in the Soviet army cast doubt on the Soviets' capacity to launch a successful blitzkrieg. For example, the Soviets have significant problems with training.[76] Overreliance on training aids and simulators is often reported, and there is widespread feeling among Soviet military leaders that the training process does not satisfactorily approximate actual combat conditions. Training is of special importance for the Soviets, since their army is composed largely of conscripts who serve a mere two years. Moreover, since new conscripts are trained in actual combat units, more than half of the troops in the nineteen Soviet divisions in East Germany are soldiers with less than two years of experience. At any one time, a significant number of those troops is either untrained or partially trained. It should also be noted that Soviet soldiers are deficient in map reading, a skill that is of much importance for an army attempting to launch a blitzkrieg.[77]

Finally we must consider the capabilities of the non-Soviet divisions, which compose approximately half of the Pact's fifty-seven and one-third standing divisions. Although the Soviet divisions will certainly perform the critical tasks in any offensive, the non-Soviet divisions will have to play a role in the operation. Otherwise the offensive would have to be scaled down significantly in size. We cannot say with any degree of certainty that the East Europeans would be militarily incapable of performing their assigned task or that they would not commit themselves politically to supporting a Soviet-led offensive. The Soviets, however, would have to assess the reliability of the East Europeans carefully.[78] If the Soviets indeed pay as careful attention to the lessons of the Great Patriotic War as observers widely claim, they recall what happened opposite Stalingrad in 1942 when the Soviets were able to inflict a stunning defeat on the Germans by ripping through those sectors of the front covered by the Rumanians, the Hungarians, and the Italians.[79]

Although the Soviet army has important deficiencies, it would still be a formidable opponent in a war in Europe; the Soviet army is not by any means a hapless giant. Neither, however, is it an army that is well prepared to defeat NATO with a blitzkrieg. The shortcomings noted in the foregoing discussion cast extreme doubt on the claim that the Soviets have the capability to launch a blitzkrieg with confidence of success. Their army is definitely not a finely tuned instrument capable of overrunning NATO at a moment's notice. The claim, then, that the Soviets have "adopted and improved the German *blitzkrieg* concept"[80] has a hollow ring. Most important, the evidence indicates that the Soviets recognize these shortcomings and their implications for winning a quick victory.

CONCLUSION

Even if we were to discount the apparent weaknesses of the Soviet army, the task of quickly overrunning NATO's defenses would be formidable. A Pact offensive would need to traverse the obstacle-ridden terrain that covers almost all of Germany and restricts the movement of large armored units. Moreover, there is good reason to believe that NATO has the wherewithal to thwart such an offensive. Certainly, NATO does not have the capability to win a conventional war on the Continent against the Soviets. NATO does have, however, the wherewithal to deny the Soviets a quick victory and then to turn the conflict into a lengthy war of attrition, where NATO's advantage in population and GNP would not bode well for the Soviets. In short, NATO is in relatively good shape at the conventional level. Since, as former defense secretary Donald Rumsfeld noted, "the burden of deterrence has once again fallen on the conventional forces," this news is welcome.[81]

[7]

Precision-Guided Munitions and
Conventional Deterrence

During the past fifteen years, a revolution of sorts has been taking place in the realm of conventional weaponry, the principal result of which has been the proliferation of extremely accurate and therefore lethal weapons.[1] Attention has been focused on a type of weapon known as precision-guided munitions (PGMs), although a number of key developments do not fall under the PGM rubric.[2] When PGMs first began to attract public attention, some analysts claimed that these new weapons would favor the defense over the offense and would thus improve the prospects for deterrence.[3] There was even talk about the "death of the tank."[4] Others argued, however, that the claims made on behalf of the new weapons were greatly exaggerated and that PGMs could be used effectively by both sides—and therefore might diminish the chances for deterrence.[5]

The effect of PGMs on conventional deterrence can best be understood by examining the relationship between PGMs and the blitzkrieg. More specifically, does the presence of these weapons on the battlefield facilitate the launching of a blitzkrieg, or do they enhance the defender's capability to thwart a blitzkrieg? Before considering this question, we should recall that although a potential attacker, when viewed in isolation, may have the capability to launch a blitzkrieg, his success is not guaranteed. Contrary to the popular opinion of the time, the fall of France did not signify the ascendance of the offense. As I have already noted, a defender skilled in the art of mobile armored warfare can stymie a blitzkrieg. The issue is whether PGMs benefit the attacker or the defender, not whether they finally provide a means for thwarting a blitzkrieg.

In the paragraphs below I shall focus on the PGMs that impact directly on the battlefield—weapons like TOW, Sagger, Dragon,

Milan, Maverick, and the various surface-to-air missiles. Long-range PGMs such as the cruise missile that can strike important targets in an opponent's rear and air-to-air PGMs fall outside the scope of this book, as outlined in Chapter 1.

The recent developments in precision guidance have significantly enhanced the capability of a defense to thwart an offensive based on the blitzkrieg. Deterrence is enhanced because PGMs increase the number of weapons systems capable of destroying armored vehicles and also because the new systems are extremely accurate. In addition to using tanks and artillery, the defense can rely on shoulder-launched antitank guided missiles, crew-served ATGMs, helicopters and infantry-fighting vehicles equipped with ATGMs, "smart artillery," and aircraft carrying a variety of "smart bombs." An attacking force that confronts a defender who has intelligently employed such weapons would have great difficulty making progress.

PGMs present two broad problems for the attacking forces. First, a blitzkrieg requires the attacker to concentrate his armored forces at a specific point(s) of attack to accomplish the initial breakthrough. Should the defender subsequently establish new defensive lines, the attacking forces would have to concentrate again to pierce them. It is dangerous, however, to mass forces against an opponent armed with PGMs, especially when obstacle-ridden terrain has canalized the attacking force. In this situation, only the attacker's lead forces would be able to engage a defense armed with a plethora of lethal weapons. The remainder of the offensive forces (the second and third echelons) would be unable to engage the defense directly—the crossing-the-T phenomenon.[6] Therefore, those few set-piece battles (especially the initial breakthrough) that have traditionally been required for the blitzkrieg have become increasingly difficult to win. The great increase in firepower resulting from the proliferation of new conventional weapons has raised the price that the offense must pay to pierce the defender's fixed positions.

Second, and more important, the notion that tanks can drive deep into the defender's rear largely unsupported by infantry and artillery is anachronistic in the face of a defense armed with PGMs. The record of Israel's 190th Armored Brigade in the 1973 Middle East war demonstrates this point.[7] That brigade, which had little infantry and artillery support, was completely destroyed as it attempted to overtake an Egyptian force heavily armed with PGMs. It is important to emphasize that, historically, armored forces that did not have to concern themselves to any significant degree with supporting infantry and artillery were responsible for effecting the deep strategic penetration of the blitzkrieg.[8] Not that close coordination between the various combat arms was eschewed by practitioners of the blitzkrieg; certainly, combined arms operations were necessary during the initial breakthrough and for subduing the defensive strong points that the main armored force could not ignore. On a battlefield pervaded with PGMs, however, armored units will have to be supported by infantry and artillery virtually all the time. The tank is simply too vulnerable to operate unsupported for long periods, as it frequently did in the past.

The proliferation of systems capable of destroying armored vehicles has obviously made tanks more vulnerable. Yet the heart of the new development is the asymmetrical vulnerability of the tank and of the individual soldier. Before the appearance of PGMs, the infantryman was a minor threat to the tank, since antitank weapons such as the 90mm recoilless rifle were of limited value on the battlefield. Consequently, armored columns driving deep into the defense's rear could virtually ignore pockets of infantrymen; ensuing forces would deal with such threats. Now, however, tanks cannot ignore infantry strong points. Shoulder-launched ATGMs such as Sagger and Dragon, as well as crew-served ATGMs such as TOW and HOT, must be suppressed before the tank can advance.

At the same time that the proliferation of extremely accurate weapons has done much to increase the combat effectiveness of the infantryman, it has done little to increase his vulnerability. The PGMs being deployed on the battlefield are designed primarily for use against weapon systems, not against infantrymen. The same relationship obtains between an infantryman and an aircraft. An SA-7 or a Stinger represents a serious threat to an attacking aircraft, while a laser-guided Maverick missile is of little value against an infantryman.

I do not mean to suggest that the battlefield of the future will feature a defensive force of PGM-armed infantrymen pitted against an offensive force dominated by tanks and aircraft. On the contrary, any successful defense against a blitzkrieg will require large numbers of tanks and aircraft, as well as some type of infantry fighting vehicle armed with a PGM, a matter to which I shall return.[9] The key point is that a blitzkrieg places a high premium on armored vehicles moving forward at a rapid pace without extensive reliance on infantrymen for support. The defense, on the other hand, depends heavily on both infantry and armored vehicles. Since the ability of the individual soldier to "kill" armored vehicles has increased significantly, while the ability of the tank, or any PGM-armed vehicle for that

[191]

matter, to "kill" infantrymen has not increased correspondingly, the defense benefits more than the offense. In his autobiography, Moshe Dayan explains how this asymmetry manifested itself in the 1973 war:

> The principal combat factor was that in the north, most of the fighting took place with Syrian tanks on the attack and on the move, while our tanks were deployed in defensive positions. Thus . . . the Syrian *Sagger* anti-tank missiles had no special influence on the outcome of the battle.
>
> This was not the case in the south. In the first two days, our tanks were on the attack, hurrying toward the Canal, while the Egyptians—primarily infantry equipped with anti-tank missiles—were in defensive emplacements. And indeed, our tank losses in the south were caused by the defensive Egyptian deployment.[10]

This development can be contrasted with another advance in conventional weaponry. During the past decade, the ability of tanks to "kill" tanks with their main guns has increased notably.[11] Since both the offense and the defense rely heavily on tanks, it is difficult to say which side benefits from such a development. Such is not the case with the PGM-armed infantrymen; they clearly strengthen the hand of the defense.

The defense against a blitzkrieg is further fortified because PGMs permit a reduction in the size of the force necessary to hold a particular defensive line against an attack (the force-to-space ratio). The increased firepower available to the individual soldier, coupled with such developments as smart artillery, reduces the number of troops required to hold a front and releases them for use in a strategic reserve or for deployment as part of a defense in depth. Other recent developments in conventional weapons technology that are not related to improved accuracy (improved conventional munitions, air-scatterable mines, fuel-air explosives, and so forth) also contribute to the increased firepower available to the defense and thus further lower the force-to-space ratio.[12]

RESCUING THE BLITZKRIEG

PGMs clearly favor the defense, thus making it increasingly difficult for an attacker to implement a blitzkrieg. Still, a variety of arguments have been offered to rebut the claim that the utility of the blitzkrieg has decreased as a consequence of PGMs. One frequently mentioned means of counteracting them is increased coordination between armor and its sister branches—artillery and infantry. One analyst notes that "infantry sweeps preceding armor may be a very effective means of dealing with a spread defense relying on PGMs."[13] This tactic has little redeeming value. First, World War I demonstrated that the machine gun makes infantry sweeps prohibitive. The vulnerability of the exposed infantryman has been further increased by the development of sophisticated antipersonnel devices. Second, placing infantry in front of armor threatens the very essence of the blitzkrieg, since the mobility and speed of the attacking armor then depend on the pace established by foot soldiers.

Nor can the antipersonnel devices that are so effective against attacking infantrymen be employed with equal effectiveness against the defender's PGM-armed infantrymen. The reason is that the attacker must move forward, while the defender can fight from fixed positions. Therefore, the attacker's infantrymen will be either standing or at best in a prone position for limited periods of time, while the defender's infantrymen will undoubtedly be in protected positions or at worst in prone positions. An infantryman in a standing position is much more vulnerable than one in a foxhole.[14]

A more realistic solution to the problem of PGMs would be closer coordination between simultaneously advancing infantry and armor supported by artillery and air power. The U.S. Army refers to such a force as the "combined arms team" and sees its operations as a necessity on a battlefield permeated with PGMs.[15] More important, all evidence indicates that the Soviets accept the need for placing greater reliance on combined arms operations. This approach has striking limitations, however, a point not lost on the Soviets.[16]

First, a coordinated attack involving such a diversity of forces is complex. The coordination of artillery fire with advancing infantry and armor is especially so, since mobile artillery does not have the luxury of making extensive fire preparations, and to be effective its fire must be laid down very close to the advancing troops.[17] Second, whereas a blitzkrieg requires relatively little logistical support, a campaign based on the sustained use of combined arms operations would require a good deal more. There would be a need for more ammunition, especially artillery rounds, and for more petroleum-oil lubrication (POL), since the number of vehicles necessary to transport the infantry, the artillery, and the ammunition would increase. Third, the maximum range at which PGMs can engage targets varies from 1,000 meters for Dragon to 3,000 meters for TOW.[18] Infantry armed with rifles and machine guns advancing simultaneously with tanks would not be able to engage PGM-armed soldiers effectively until the distance was somewhat less than 500 yards. Obviously, the PGM force would be at a decisive advantage, since it would have first draw in the fight. Fourth, and most important, the pace of the attack would be slowed, because tanks would still be required to keep pace with advancing infantry. If heavy reliance was placed on artillery, the time spent preparing for and engaging in artillery exchanges would further hinder the rate of advance.[19] On a battlefield ridden with sophisticated tank-killing systems, slowing down the speed and therefore increasing the exposure time of the tank are clearly most undesirable. There is little doubt that although placing greater reliance on combined arms operations may be an effective way of dealing with PGMs, such tactics greatly hinder efforts to effect a blitzkrieg.

It is interesting to note that in the past the defender's infantry had to rely heavily on armored forces for support. At one time infantry had no effective means of dealing with tanks. As a result of PGMs, however, which provide infantry with the capability to engage tanks, the defender's infantrymen are now able to act independently of armor—although there would certainly be a need to coordinate the efforts of the two branches.[20] On the other hand, the presence of PGMs has forced the attacking forces to increase their reliance on infantry-armor coordination. Infantry are expected to deal with the defender's PGMs and, in essence, to protect the tank. Given that coordinated operations between any elements of an army are demanding, this development works to the advantage of the defense.

To combat the slowness and vulnerability of dismounted infantry, armored personnel carriers (APCs) have been developed and deployed. The objective is to develop a balanced attacking force using mechanized infantry that can keep pace with tanks, dismounting only when necessary. These personnel carriers, which usually carry a squad of soldiers, are becoming increasingly sophisticated. They are no longer being designed merely to transport troops from point A to point B, but instead are being designed with enough firepower, mobility, and armor protection to function as what is commonly termed an infantry fighting vehicle (IFV). In other words, an infantry squad can now conduct combat operations without dismounting. The Soviet Union began developing IFVs and began integrating them into its force structure well before the United States. The Soviet BMP, which is equipped with a 73mm gun, an ATGM system, and a coaxial 7.62mm machine gun, was originally designed to operate on a nuclear battlefield, where it was expected to exploit the many gaps in the defense resulting from the use of nuclear weapons. Although the BMP is relatively thin skinned (it was not intended for use against fixed positions), it is an integral part of Soviet strategy for a non-nuclear war.

Evidence from the 1973 Middle East war indicates, however, that IFVs are very vulnerable on a battlefield dense with accurate antitank weaponry.[21] Their weakness is basically the armor, which is not nearly as thick as the armor on a tank. An added disadvantage for the IFV is that a direct hit would probably result in the elimination of an entire infantry squad. Very significantly, the implications of the IFV's vulnerability are different for the offense and the defense. Since an offensive force must move forward, and since there are real limits on the amount of protection afforded an attacker by the terrain, the attacking IFV will be very vulnerable to enemy fire. For this reason the Soviets place their BMPs in the second echelon of the attacking forces and require the attacking infantry to dismount when engaging fixed positions.[22] So used, the IFV is of questionable value to the offense. It might actually make more sense for an offensive-minded army to abandon the IFV concept and instead to procure more tanks and to build cheap APCs that simply transport infantry from one point to another.[23]

Because a defensive force usually fights from fixed positions, however, it is possible for an IFV to use man-made or natural obstacles for protection. Although doing so will not mean total invulnerability, an IFV's ability to survive is certainly greater in a defensive position than when it is rolling forward in the open as part of a strike force. And an IFV can significantly strengthen a defense. First, a defensive force on the modern battlefield will have to be mobile. Given the large size of PGMs, such as TOW, it is necessary to mount a proportion of such weapons on mobile platforms. An IFV provides the capability to transport TOWs as well as infantrymen carrying shoulder-launched PGMs. Second, an IFV affords infantrymen and mounted PGMs a degree of protection when the attacker employs artillery and other antipersonnel devices. The importance of this service cannot be exaggerated, since an attacking force will undoubtedly attempt to destroy those infantrymen who threaten tanks. Clearly the IFV favors the defense and not the attacking force. Still, two caveats should be considered. First, a defender will be required to counterattack—to go on the offensive—from time to time. In such instances, the value of the IFV to the defense becomes questionable. Second, in encounter battles that do not permit the defense to fight from fixed positions (battles that manifest little distinction between offense and defense), the IFV is of little value to either side. In general, the IFV is a stabilizing system because it benefits the defense more than the offense.

The most serious threat to PGMs is the development of "special armor," or what is referred to in the West as *Chobham* armor. Reports indicate that Chobham provides a threefold increase in protection over conventional steel armor and that at present no PGM—Soviet or American—can penetrate it.[24] Although we have no reason to doubt these reports, there are problems associated with this new technology. First, it is very expensive, and the number of armored vehicles that can be outfitted with Chobham is therefore limited. After all, Britain could not afford to incorporate Chobham into its Chieftain tanks. For the foreseeable future, it seems highly unlikely that IFVs will be equipped with the new armor, and it would not be surprising if only a portion of a nation's tank force was protected by Chobham. Survivability has an expensive price tag. Second, although there are rumors that the new Soviet tank (T-80) might have special armor, all evidence indicates that the Soviet Union is behind the West in developing this technology.[25] It will take the Soviets considerable time to equip a significant portion of the Warsaw Pact's huge tank inventory with special armor.

Moreover, while special armor is being developed and deployed, advances are being made in ATGM technology.[26] Many of those systems used so effectively in Vietnam and in the 1973 Middle East war are essentially first-generation weapons.[27] They represent the cutting edge of the PGM revolution. Future versions will be designed with Chobham armor in mind. Importantly, the speed at which technological innovations are incorporated into new generations of weapons favors the PGM over the tank. The tank's greater complexity gives rise to technical problems and also to a protracted development process. Although no one can predict developments in weaponry with great accuracy, we have no reason to believe that the effectiveness of PGM has largely been nullified by advances in armor protection.

Should the balance continue to shift in favor of special armor, however, the battlefield equation will be significantly affected. The only PGM capable of penetrating special armor would be the larger ones such as Hellfire; shoulder-launched PGMs and possibly even crew-served PGMs such as TOW would be largely ineffective against equipped vehicles.[28] Obviously, the value to the defense of such infantry-borne PGMs will be inversely proportional to the number of special-armor-equipped vehicles in the attacking force. If the trend is toward larger PGMs, they will have to be mounted on IFVs or on some other mobile platform. As I noted earlier, such a development certainly benefits the defense more than the offense. Nevertheless, the elimination of PGM-armed infantrymen as a salient influence on the battlefield would be detrimental to the defense. In general, it seems likely that if advances in PGM technology are not forthcoming (other than to increase the size of the missile), the offense-defense equation will shift back toward the offense.

Given the rapidly escalating cost of increasingly vulnerable tanks, some observers argue that instead of procuring a limited number of expensive tanks, nations should deploy greater numbers of less expensive and less sophisticated tanks.[29] This approach has its shortcomings, however. First, inexpensive tanks are very vulnerable, and it is doubtful whether enough extra tanks could be procured to offset the higher losses that would result from the increased vulnerability of such an armored force.[30] The cost-exchange ratio between tanks and PGMs clearly favors the latter. Second, the true cost of a tank force cannot be measured simply by multiplying the number of tanks by the hardware cost per tank. Tanks require manpower, and in NATO countries, at least, the cost of additional tank crews makes it very difficult to increase the size of an armored force. The British Army of the Rhine, for example, had to place approximately fifty Chieftain tanks in storage because there were not enough crews to operate them.[31] It is highly unlikely that the trend will be toward larger numbers of cheaper and less sophisticated tanks,[32] but such a trend would in any case not reduce the utility of PGMs such as Dragon and TOW.

With regard to the IFV's vulnerability, some observers will undoubtedly argue for placing special armor on the IFV so as to convert it into a small tank with a missile instead of a gun. Such a scheme lacks utility, since it is widely recognized that, for a variety of reasons, tanks should be equipped with guns, not missiles.[33] For the defense, the attraction of an IFV equipped with a PGM is its inexpensiveness relative to a tank. (The two systems also complement each other nicely on the battlefield.) Placing special armor on the IFV would raise the price of an IFV to a level commensurate with the cost of a tank. The key assumption is that the protection the terrain affords the defender is supposed to compensate for the IFV's vulnerability. In any case, when the defense is forced to go on the offensive, primary reliance will be placed on the tank force. If either the offense or the defense must increase its offensive punch, building additional tanks would be more desirable than placing special armor on the IFV, especially in view of the limited resources available for the purchase of armored vehicles.

Some analysts argue that the attacker can negate the effectiveness of PGMs by resorting to night attacks. There is abundant evidence that Soviet forces are well trained in night operations.[34] This approach too has drawbacks, however. First, although it might be possible to achieve certain limited objectives with night attacks, it is hard to imagine any military force relying exclusively on them to inflict total defeat. The problems of coordination and poor visibility make such a strategy highly questionable.[35] Furthermore, the assumption that PGMs are ineffective in the dark because they cannot see the target is doubtful. The United States is developing thermal-imaging night sights that will allow Dragon, TOW, and Maverick to pinpoint targets in the dark. Finally, there is no reason why NATO forces cannot be trained to fight at night. Night fighting does not inherently favor the offense.

PRECISION-GUIDED MUNITIONS AND THE AIR-GROUND BALANCE

Both the German and Israeli blitzkriegs relied heavily on close air support instead of land-based artillery for firepower. The defense can also use close air support, of course, to help thwart an armored offensive. For both the defense and the offense, the extent to which reliance on close air support is possible depends on who controls the air space above the battlefield—on who has air superiority. In World War II, air superiority was largely a function of the balance between the air forces of the opposing sides. With the well-publicized appearance of highly accurate, ground-based air defense systems, first in Vietnam and then in the 1973 Middle East war, it became apparent that the matter of air superiority is greatly influenced by ground-based systems.

The deployment of air-launched PGMs such as the Maverick has increased the combat effectiveness of close air support aircraft. At the same time, however, the effectiveness of ground-based air defense systems such as SAMs and air defense guns has also increased. In addition to evolutionary improvements in systems such as Hawk, the SA-2, and the SA-3, new developments such as the highly mobile SA-6 and the shoulder-launched Stinger have appeared on the battlefield. The deployment of radar-controlled air defense guns such as the ZSU/23/4 has further complicated the ability of aircraft operating above the battlefield to survive.[36]

In providing firepower for the offense, ground attack aircraft are ideal weapons. Given the inherent mobility of an airplane, it is a most flexible weapon. Moreover, aircraft do not present the logistical problems or command and control problems that artillery does for the ground forces. An attacking force that confronts a defense lacking both an effective ground-based air defense system and fighter aircraft could take maximum advantage of its ground attack aircraft —as of course the Germans did in May 1940 and the Israelis did in June 1967.

Conversely, ground attack aircraft that encounter a defense with a belt of SAMs and air defense guns, as well as a reliable fighter force, would have considerable difficulty assisting the advancing armored columns. Very importantly, it is now possible for a defender with no aircraft to speak of to parry attack aircraft with SAMs and air defense guns, as the Egyptians clearly demonstrated in the 1973 Middle East war when they exacted a heavy toll in Israeli close air support aircraft.[37] The evidence indicates that in the battle between ground-based air defense systems and close air support aircraft, the former has a distinct advantage. When those ground-based systems are complemented by a formidable air force, it becomes well nigh impossible for attack aircraft to influence the outcome on the battlefield. For this reason there is a growing belief that the traditional notion of close air support may be obsolete.[38]

What effect do the recent developments have on the offense-defense equation with respect to the blitzkrieg? Assuming that the proliferation of the new conventional weapons technologies continues, and that both the offense and the defense maintain ground-based air defense systems and close air support aircraft, the blitzkrieg's chances for success will be further complicated. First, when the defense employs an extensive network of SAMs and air defense guns, the offense finds it increasingly difficult to rely on close air support as the principal source of firepower. As a result, the main source of firepower will have to be artillery. Not surprisingly, in the wake of the 1973 war, Israel has significantly increased the artillery in its army,[39] a development that is much more detrimental to the offense than to the defense because it creates logistical problems as well as coordination problems that will slow the blitzkrieg and will lead to set-piece battles. Second, the offense's reliance on SAMs and on air defense guns also creates logistical and coordination problems, which add to the woes resulting from an increased reliance on artillery. Furthermore, the pace of the attacking armored columns could be slowed, since these forces absolutely must not outrun their air defense systems. The problem could be obviated by relying on fighter aircraft to provide air defense for the offensive forces and by abandoning reliance on a ground-based air defense system. For a variety of reasons, the major military establishments (especially the Soviets) do not appear to be moving in this direction.

Third, in instances when attack aircraft are able to bring Mavericks and other sophisticated weapons to bear, the key problem will be target acquisition.[40] The difficulties will be especially acute on the European battlefield, where visibility is limited for long periods of the year. The problem of target acquisition is more serious for the attacker's aircraft, since the defense will be, for the most part, fighting from fixed positions. Because the offense must abandon cover and move forward it will provide greater targets of opportunity for the defender's attack aircraft. Even so, the defense will *not* be able to rely heavily on attack aircraft to destroy armored vehicles in the attacking force. (This fact has caused American policy makers to express great concern about the A-10, which is designed to provide air support directly over the battlefield.) Attack aircraft will simply not survive over a battlefield laden with SAMs and with air defense guns. The defender's aircraft are most likely to be effective against fast-moving armored forces that penetrate the defensive front and have no time to set up their antiair systems or against the attacker's second-echelon forces.[41] In sum, the evidence indicates that the advances in weapons technology relating to the air-ground balance will contribute to the defender's capability to thwart a blitzkrieg.

CONCLUSION

There is little doubt that the development of PGMs and assorted other new conventional weapons has not produced any radical change in the nature of the conventional battlefield. There has not been and probably will not be in the foreseeable future a revolution in the conduct of warfare such as that which occurred after the tank appeared on the battlefield. Nevertheless, as a result of developments in precision-guided technologies, it is clearly much more difficult to implement a blitzkrieg—a development with significant implications for deterrence.

To adjust to the proliferation of PGMs, the offense has been forced to increase the mass of its attacking force. An offensive must now place heavy reliance on artillery, SAMs, air defense guns, and mechanized infantry. The tank-dominated offensive, which relied on ground attack aircraft for firepower support, has no place on the modern battlefield. The new emphasis on combined arms operations creates severe logistical problems as well as myriad problems of battlefield coordination, both of which rob the blitzkrieg of mobility and speed. The increased reliance of the offense on artillery also contributes to the demise of the blitzkrieg. We must recognize that the fundamental question is not whether an attacker can deal with PGMs but what changes in offensive strategy are necessary to overcome these weapons.

At the same time that PGMs have compounded the attacker's task, they have worked to benefit the defense. The increased firepower available to the defense makes it possible to turn each major defensive position into a "wall of fire" that the offense can penetrate only by paying an exceedingly high price.[42] If a potential attacker perceives that a blitzkrieg is likely to fail and to evolve into a chain of set-piece battles, he will be very reluctant to initiate hostilities.

As we have seen, any attack involves some combination of offense and defense. When the objective is to inflict total military defeat on an opponent, the attacking force is primarily concerned with the offensive ingredient. The blitzkrieg is such a strategy. An attacker who pursues a limited aims strategy, however, pays much greater attention to defensive tactics. After a quick offensive surge, the offense shifts to the defensive and prepares for a counterattack by the opposition. The attacker-turned-defender can then employ PGMs to strengthen his defensive position. If the victim chooses to launch a counterattack, he will be forced to attack a well-fortified and alert defense.

An offensive with limited objectives will undoubtedly attempt to use the element of surprise to achieve its objectives before the defense has the opportunity to establish the wall of fire described above. In this regard, surprise is a key means for dealing with PGMs. But although surprise can provide the key to success in limited operations, it can offer only significantly limited benefits when the objective is total defeat of the opponent's armed forces.[43]

The value of PGMs to an offensive based on limited objectives was clearly demonstrated by Egypt in the 1973 Middle East war. The Israeli army suffered heavy losses in the first period of the war when it attacked Egyptian defensive positions buttressed with PGMs. Only after Egypt abandoned its first strategy on 14 October to launch a new offensive did its position begin to deteriorate. Even then, the margin between Israel's ultimate success and possible failure was narrow. For the Israelis, who rely on a reserve army, the possibility that the Arabs will achieve surprise and will capture some territory before the Israeli defense force can mobilize remains a threat. Should an Arab state successfully pursue such a strategy, then Israel, which has traditionally relied on armor instead of infantry, must deal with a PGM-armed defense ideally suited to counter armor-heavy forces. In short, the limited aims strategy, rather than the blitzkrieg, will be well served by PGMs.

[8]

Conclusion

We may identify three theories of conventional deterrence. The first contends that deterrence is likely to fail when one side enjoys a significant numerical advantage in forces; the second focuses on the nature of the weaponry on each side, arguing that deterrence is least likely to obtain when offensive weapons dominate; and the third views deterrence as a function of the specific strategy available to the potential attacker. I have discussed important shortcomings of the first two theories. In considering the third—my own—I have stressed that decision makers are concerned primarily with determining how their forces will be employed to achieve the desired objective. As I have noted, an attacker can generally employ any of three strategies on the modern battlefield, and each affects the prospects for deterrence differently.

DETERRENCE AND THE BLITZKRIEG

My central proposition in this book is that, in a crisis, if one side has the capability to launch a blitzkrieg, deterrence is likely to fail. As I have noted, it did so in 1940 when the Germans attacked the Allies and in 1956 and 1967 in the Middle East. In a number of other cases, some of which have been briefly mentioned, deterrence broke down because one side had the capability to effect a blitzkrieg: the German invasion of the Soviet Union (1941); the Soviet offensive against Japan's Kwantung Army in Manchuria (1945); the North Korean invasion of South Korea (1950); the Indian offensive against East Pakistan (1971); and the Vietnamese drive into Cambodia (1979). It is appropriate to outline each of these cases briefly.

Shortly after the German victory in France, Hitler turned his attention toward the East.[1] He met little resistance from his generals when he announced his intention of going to war against the Soviet Union; German military leaders were confident that they could employ against the Soviets the basic strategy that had served them so well in the West. This supposition is clearly reflected in the OKW directive for Operation Barbarossa: "The mass of the army stationed in Western Russia is to be destroyed in bold operations involving deep penetrations by armored spearheads, and the withdrawal of elements capable of combat into the extensive Russian land spaces is to be prevented."[2]

The other World War II case involving a blitzkrieg was the Soviet decision, after the defeat of Germany, to launch an attack against the Japanese in Manchuria. As Soviet literature on the campaign shows, the Soviets made a conscious decision to abandon the attrition strategy employed against Germany and instead to employ a blitzkrieg.[3] An important Soviet account of the Manchurian campaign notes: "In essence, the question revolved around a plan for a truly lightning defeat of the opposing enemy. As circumstances would have it, the Soviet Armed Forces had to put in practice the very kind of a 'lightning operation,' to the description of which vaunted German military theoreticians in their time devoted a multitude of their works to no particular avail."[4] The Soviets massed their armor on narrow fronts to effect deep strategic penetrations that quickly produced the collapse of Japan's Kwantung Army. Not surprisingly, artillery played a minor role in the Soviet victory; instead, the Soviets relied heavily on tactical air power.[5]

It is important to note that except for the Soviet invasion of Finland in 1939, when the Finns were hopelessly outmatched, the post–1917 Soviet Union has opted to start a conventional war on only one other occasion: against the Japanese in Manchuria.[6] And in this case the decision rested on the assumption that a blitzkrieg would lead to a rapid and decisive victory.

The first of the three post–World War II cases of deterrence failure relating to the blitzkrieg is the North Korean invasion of South Korea. Although there is no evidence available on the actual decision to initiate war, it is clear from our knowledge of North Korean strategy and tactics of the period and from events on the battlefield that the North Koreans employed a blitzkrieg. Field manuals captured during the war provide abundant evidence that the North Koreans were heavily influenced by the World War II experiences of the Soviet Union.[7] More specifically, North Korean doctrine called for concentrating armor at specific points and then using it to drive into the depths of the defense.

Not surprisingly, the actual strategy adopted by the North Koreans was wholly consistent with their doctrine. Although they did not have a very large armored force, they concentrated their available armored units on a narrow front opposite the Uijongbu Corridor, the traditional invasion route leading to Seoul.[8] The attack was led by rapidly moving T-34 tanks and by self-propelled artillery that consistently bypassed South Korean strong points in the drive toward Seoul.[9] Not only were the South Koreans caught completely by surprise, but they had also chosen to employ a forward defense.[10] Once the North Koreans had pierced the South Korean's forward positions, the South Koreans could do little to stop the North Koreans, who would have scored a decisive victory if the United States had not intervened with massive force.

Turning to the Vietnamese invasion of Cambodia, we lack information not only on the decision-making process but also on the course of the battle. Since the United States had advisers on the ground in Korea in June 1950, Americans were present to witness the North Korean onslaught. Such was obviously not the case in Cambodia; there were not even any Western journalists in Cambodia during the war.[11] Nevertheless, the available evidence indicates that the Vietnamese, who were also influenced by Soviet military practices, employed a blitzkrieg.[12] The Vietnamese brought about the rapid collapse of the Cambodian army by driving armored spearheads deep into Cambodia. The advancing Vietnamese tank columns received extensive close air support. These armored forces, which bypassed Cambodian strong points at every opportunity, advanced so quickly that Cambodia was overrun in fifteen days.

The third post–World War II case of a blitzkrieg is the 1971 Indian attack against East Pakistan. As early as April 1971, when refugees from East Pakistan began moving into India in large numbers, it was apparent to India's leaders that a war with Pakistan was likely.[13] The Indians began making preparations, assuming that India would launch an offensive into East Pakistan. The original plan called for a limited aims strategy.[14] The Indian army would capture a large section of East Pakistani territory and would establish a provisional government for the insurgents in East Pakistan. General Manekshaw, a chief of staff of the Indian army, however, firmly opposed a limited aims strategy. He maintained that even if it succeeded, it would lead to an endless war; the Pakistani army would be able to attack this occupied zone at will.[15] Sometime between late July and early August 1971, Indian military leaders reached the conclusion that they could decisively defeat the Pakistani forces located in East Pakistan.[16] Henceforth opposition to military action ceased. It is clear that the emergence of the blitzkrieg as a viable option convinced the Indian leadership that they could win a decisive victory.

In the wake of the 1965 India-Pakistan war, when the Chinese threatened to intervene on Pakistan's behalf, the Indians recognized that they might be forced to fight a three-front war.[17] In such a case they could not afford to involve themselves in a protracted war on any front. Thus a high premium was placed on winning quick victories. Gen. D. K. Palit notes that "by training and tradition the Indian Army's normal methods of operation had always been the set-piece battle, phased programmes to capture strong points—and venturing on further advance only after due regrouping and re-inforcement."[18] Such a modus operandi was hardly consistent with the notion of a quick victory. Under the leadership of officers like Manekshaw and Gen. J. S. Aurora, the head of the Eastern Command, the Indian army was reconstituted so that it could win a quick victory.[19] Much emphasis was placed on developing highly mobile forces that could rapidly thrust into the enemy's rear. To facilitate this task, the Indian air force was trained to provide the ground forces with extensive close air support and also to transport supplies to the fast-moving ground units.[20]

The actual Indian plan for a war in the East was a classical blitzkrieg against the Pakistani army.[21] The objective was to attack East Pakistan on all three of its exposed flanks, driving armored columns into the "Dacca Bowl," which was centrally located in the rear of each of the three fronts (see figure 8.1). The Indians recognized that commanders up and down the chain of command would have to make bold decisions to maintain the necessary rapid movement.[22] Significantly, the Indians recognized that the Pakistanis had decided to employ a forward defense to meet an Indian offensive,[23] because they expected the Indians to pursue a limited aims strategy. With a forward defense, the Pakistanis would be well positioned to thwart an Indian attempt to capture territory along the India-Pakistan border. The Indians recognized that the Pakistanis, with their forces thinly spread across a broad front and no operational reserve, were very vulnerable to a blitzkrieg—and immediately the last barrier to war disappeared.

THE ATTRITION STRATEGY, THE LIMITED AIMS STRATEGY, AND DETERRENCE

As we have seen, deterrence is likely to hold when a potential attacker is faced with the prospect of employing an attrition strat-

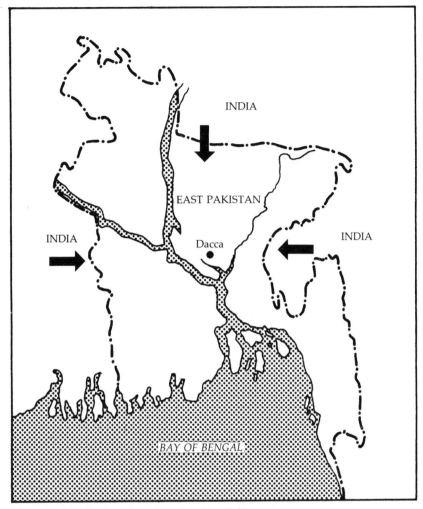

Figure 8.1. India's plan of attack against East Pakistan

egy, largely because of the associated exorbitant costs and because of the difficulty of accurately predicting ultimate success in a protracted war. The deterrent value of an attrition strategy is apparent from Allied decision making during the Munich crisis and from events during the early months of World War II. Surely the possibility of becoming engaged in a long, costly war, even if success could be guaranteed, is a powerful deterrent to military action.

There is, of course, a third military option: the limited aims strategy. Although it is the least ambitious and the least difficult to implement, it is not likely to lead to war in a crisis. One reason is the powerful tendency of modern nation-states to favor decisive victories; in the discussions between Sadat and Syria's Hafez al-Assad leading to the October 1973 attack on Israel, Sadat had to convince a doubting al-Assad that a limited aims strategy was worth pursuing.[24]

Another reason is the possibility that the conflict will turn into a war of attrition. This second reason largely explains why the German military adamantly opposed launching an offensive in the West during the period from October 1939 to February 1940. It also accounts in large part for the failure of the British and the French to consider a limited aims strategy seriously. And finally, as I noted earlier in this chapter, India's General Manekshaw opposed a limited aims strategy because he believed that the Pakistanis would not accept the resulting change in the status quo and that a protracted war would ensue. Undoubtedly the same calculation would lead the Soviets to avoid employing a limited aims strategy against NATO.

It is not axiomatic, however, that a limited aims strategy will result in a protracted slugging match, especially in regional conflicts, in which the superpowers invariably have an abiding interest. Superpower involvement significantly reduces the likelihood of a lengthy war of attrition between client states, because the superpowers have the means to terminate conflicts between warring client states by curtailing the supply of resources for waging war. When regional strife threatens to escalate into a global war, the superpowers are very likely, although not certain, to intervene to restore peace. In past regional conflicts, then, the decision makers of the warring states have hardly concerned themselves with the threat of a prolonged, costly war resulting from a limited aims strategy. Manekshaw's concern that a limited victory in East Pakistan would lead to a constant state of war is clearly an exception.[25] There is invariably great concern, however, about the possibility of superpower interference.[26] In short, when a limited victory does not threaten to turn into a protracted war, decision makers have a viable alternative to an attrition strategy.

THE POLITICAL-MILITARY CONTEXT

As I have emphasized throughout this book, conventional deterrence is ultimately based on the interaction between the broadly defined political considerations that move a nation toward war and the potential costs and risks of military action. In light of the crises that I have examined, what conclusions can we draw about the relationship between the two?

The cases can be divided into two broad categories. In the first, a satisfactory military strategy emerges early in the decision-making process, and whether or not deterrence obtains is basically a consequence of political considerations. For obvious reasons, military calculations will not deter the decision makers. A number of my cases belong to this category. In each, the attacker believed that, specific strategies aside, the two armies were unevenly matched, with the attacker enjoying the advantage. Moreover, in each case save one, the attacker planned to launch a blitzkrieg. The German decision to invade the Soviet Union (1941), the Soviet decision to attack Japan's Kwantung Army (1945), and the Israeli decision to strike in the Sinai (1956) were all predicated on the belief that the attacking forces could effect a blitzkrieg. Both the Soviets (1945) and the Israelis (1956) enjoyed significant numerical superiority; and in the 1941 case, the Germans considered the Soviet army to be a qualitatively inferior foe likely to collapse quickly. Although little information is available on the Vietnamese decision to attack Cambodia (1979), and on the North Korean decision to strike in the South (1950), these two cases have the earmarks of the three just described. Both the North Koreans and the Vietnamese were quantitatively and qualitatively superior to their foes, and both were prepared to launch a blitzkrieg. The German decision to invade Poland (1939) is the single example in this first category of an attacker who did not employ a blitzkrieg. As I have noted, the choice was an attrition strategy, which the Germans believed would result in a quick and decisive victory.[27] The basis for their confidence was the belief that their army was, from both a qualitative and a quantitative point of view, far superior to that of the Poles.

None of these cases displays evidence of significant pressure not to go to war because of dissatisfaction with the military plan. By this statement I do not mean that the enterprise was considered risk free or that the political elites did not carefully study the proposed plan of operations. On the contrary, the decision to go to war is never taken lightly, as was evident in the one case in this broad category that I examined in detail, the 1956 Israeli decision. As we saw, Ben-Gurion was very concerned about the efficacy of Dayan's plan for defeating the Egyptians, and he carefully reviewed it before making his final decision. Nevertheless, and this is my key point, military considerations did not serve as a deterrent, simply because the Israelis were generally confident from the start that they could achieve their objectives on the battlefield. Before deterrence could have obtained, political, not military, considerations would have had to prevail.

In the second group of cases, although a political rationale for going to war exists, there is initially either no military solution or only an extremely risky one. Naturally, in this category we are likely to find a potential attacker deterred for military reasons, but tremendous pressure will be generated to find an acceptable military solution. Examples include fall 1939, when Hitler informed his generals that he planned to strike in the West, and 1967, when the Israelis were being pushed toward war. These two cases, both of which have been discussed at length, show striking parallels. Although in both there was great pressure to go to war, the military was initially unable to find a satisfactory plan. Since the balance of forces was roughly equal on both occasions, the particular strategy chosen was of great importance. In each instance, military planners first called for a limited aims strategy, which generated much dissatisfaction—especially in the German case; it was widely believed that this strategy would lead to a war of attrition. Eventually, both the Germans and the Israelis adopted a blitzkrieg, which was generally regarded as an excellent answer to each nation's predicament. Not surprisingly, war broke out shortly thereafter both times. Again, military considerations no longer served as a brake.

Despite the pressure on the military to develop an attractive strategy, one is not always found. Often the military is able to produce only a plan that entails considerable risks and is therefore not particularly attractive. Thus at such moments decision makers must carefully weigh the political risks of not striking against the risks associated with the military proposal. Here, for the first time, we see decision makers pondering not attacking because of military considerations.

Invariably, such hesitancy occurs when the attacker is considering a limited aims strategy. Such was the case after Sadat decided in 1972 to strike against Israel. The Egyptians, who had been soundly trounced by the Israelis in 1967 and who had not considered starting a conventional war in the years after 1967, recognized that their planned offensive involved significant risks. The political circumstances, however, made the Egyptian leadership feel that the risks were worth taking. A similar situation existed in Germany between October 1939 and January 1940 when the Germans planned to implement a limited aims strategy. Unlike the generals, who were adamantly opposed to that plan, Hitler was willing, for political reasons, to accept the risks associated with an attack on the Allies. In the 1967 Israeli case, prior to 1 June, a number of Israelis were willing to launch a limited attack against Egypt, even though the existing operational plan did not seem particularly attractive. Finally, there was much dissatisfaction in India (1971) with the original plan of operations—a limited aims strategy—against East Pakistan.

In the Israeli, German, and Indian cases, a much more attractive military solution was eventually discovered. Although we can never be certain, it appears that had the Germans, the Indians, and the Israelis not discovered the blitzkrieg, they would have launched limited offensives. Surely the risks would have been considerable (especially in the German case), but given the pressure in each instance to take some military action, war probably could not have been avoided. Although a limited aims strategy is hardly ever an attractive option, it is usually not so unattractive that deterrence obtains in a crisis.

Finally, there are the cases in which, despite the pressure to find an acceptable military plan, none is forthcoming. In essence, if the attacker chooses to go to war, he is likely either to lose or to find himself engaged in a lengthy war of attrition. Given such circumstances, deterrence is almost certain to hold, as it did for the Allies at Munich and again during the months immediately preceding and following the start of the Second World War. The Allies, however, did formally declare war against Germany, although it seems clear that they would never have attacked Germany had Germany not attacked first. Their decision to declare war highlights the intensity of the pressure to take military action against Germany.

After their humiliating defeat in 1967, the Egyptians soon came to believe that some form of military action against Israel would be necessary. The Egyptians, however, were deterred from starting a conventional war because they feared that they would be defeated. They therefore turned to the war of attrition.[28] Conventional deterrence obtained in the Middle East between 1967 and 1973, although this state of affairs certainly did not constitute peace. Throughout the period the Egyptians were preparing themselves to fight against Israel. By late 1972, they had reached the point where they could seriously consider engaging the Israelis in a conventional war. Recognizing that such a course of action entailed serious risks, the Egyptians nevertheless struck in October 1973. Their behavior clearly shows that when a nation is dissatisfied with the status quo, the long-term prospects for deterrence are not promising. The pressure to find an acceptable military solution will be too intense.

THE NATO BALANCE

From our analysis of the conventional balance in Central Europe, we may conclude that the prospects for conventional deterrence in some future crisis are quite good. The conventional wisdom notwithstanding, assessment of the balance of forces and the capabilities of each side makes plain that the Pact could not presently expect to score a quick and decisive victory against NATO. Moreover, the ongoing proliferation of PGMs appears likely to enhance NATO's position in the immediate future. Although these weapons are clearly not "super weapons" that will render the tank extinct, they make it more difficult for the Soviets to effect a blitzkrieg and thus can only increase the likelihood of deterrence.

NATO policy makers have good reason, however, to be very cautious when assessing their position in some future crisis. For the cases examined here show that, when a nation has a powerful motive for war, it will go to great lengths to find a suitable military strategy. Military planners will be subjected to unremitting pressure. Furthermore, a defender who becomes complacent is likely to be surprised, as were the Israelis in 1973 and the Allies in May 1940. The central message for status quo powers is clear: beware in a crisis, because your opponent is seeking a way to defeat you.

Notes

Abbreviations

CAB   cabinet papers
COS   chiefs of staff
DMO and I director of military operations and intelligence
MI   military intelligence
WO   War Office

1. *Introduction*

1. This trend has been clearly reflected in the annual *Posture Statements* of the secretaries of defense since the early 1960s. Also see Helmut Schmidt's October 1977 speech before the International Institute for Strategic Studies, a copy of which can be found in *Survival*, 20 (January-February 1978), 2–10; and *White Paper 1979: The Security of the Federal Republic of Germany and the Development of the Federal Armed Forces* (Bonn: Federal Minister of Defence, 4 September 1979), 112 (hereafter cited as *1979 German White Paper*).

2. See Col. Graham D. Vernon, *Soviet Options for War in Europe: Nuclear or Conventional?* National Security Affairs Monograph 79-1 (Washington, D.C.: National Defense University, January 1979).

3. Traditionally studies in the field of international relations have treated the nation as a unitary actor capable of making calculated, rational choices. See Graham T. Allison, *Essence of Decision* (Boston: Little, Brown, 1971), chap. 1. As Allison and others correctly note, however, nations per se do not measure the impact of those factors acting on a nation contemplating military action, nor do nations per se design foreign policies. Individual decision makers are responsible for such calculations and formulations. Appropriately, when I use terms such as *nation* and *attacker*, I intend them merely to denote the collection of decision makers responsible for formulating policy. Concerning the issue of rationality, "the basic assumption . . . [is that] of a calculating individual with a multiplicity of values, aware of cost and risk as well as of advantage, and capable of drawing significant inferences from symbolic acts" (William W. Kaufmann, "Limited Warfare," in *Military Policy and National Security*, ed. William W. Kaufmann [Princeton: Princeton University Press, 1956], 117).

[213]

4. As will become evident in Chapter 2, this book starts with the assumption that nations go to war for *political* reasons. I use the term *political,* however, in its broadest sense. For example, a nation might go to war because it foresees a decline in its position in the international system. That decline, however, might be largely a consequence of *economic* considerations (Japan in 1941) or *military* considerations (Israel in 1956). Furthermore, domestic political considerations, rather than international ones, sometimes push a nation toward war.

5. The principal works on nuclear deterrence similarly restricted the scope of their analyses. See, for example, Glenn Snyder, *Deterrence and Defense* (Princeton: Princeton University Press, 1961), v, 11.

6. See Thomas C. Schelling, *Arms and Influence* (New Haven: Yale University Press, 1972); and Snyder, *Deterrence and Defense.* There is not, however, complete agreement on the use of terminology in the deterrence literature. Some analysts prefer to confine use of the term *deterrence* to the threat of punishment. Concepts such as dissuasion and defense are then used to denote what I have labeled conventional deterrence. See Robert J. Art, "To What Ends Military Power?" *International Security,* 4 (spring 1980), 3–35; Barry R. Posen, "The Systemic, Organizational, and Technological Origins of Strategic Doctrine: France, Britain, and Germany between the World Wars" (Ph.D. diss., University of California, Berkeley, 1981). Another distinction in the literature bears mentioning. It is possible to identify a third notion of deterrence, one based on an *offensive,* or disarming, strategy. If Nation A wants to deter Nation B, Nation A, by inflicting a decisive and painful defeat on B or by threatening to launch a preemptive attack against B, will make clear to Nation B the cost of war—and will thus deter Nation B from striking or even from mobilizing. See Posen, *Origins of Strategic Doctrine.* This offensively oriented notion of deterrence, which falls outside the scope of this book, has received much attention in Israel. See Saadia Amiel, "Deterrence by Conventional Forces," *Survival,* 20 (March-April 1978), 58–62; and Yoav Ben-Horin and Barry Posen, *Israel's Strategic Doctrine,* R-2845-NA (Santa Monica: Rand, September 1981), 12–16.

7. Dean Acheson, *Power and Diplomacy* (New York: Atheneum, 1962), 85.

8. See George H. Quester, *Deterrence before Hiroshima* (New York: John Wiley, 1966).

9. See Bernard Brodie, *Escalation and the Nuclear Option* (Princeton: Princeton University Press, 1966); Samuel T. Cohen, "Tactical Nuclear Weapons and U.S. Military Strategy," *Orbis,* 15 (spring 1971), 178–93; Colin S. Gray, "Mini-nukes and Strategy," *International Journal,* 29 (spring 1974), 216–41; Henry A. Kissinger, *Nuclear Weapons and Foreign Policy* (New York: Harper and Row, 1957); and John P. Rose, *The Evolution of U.S. Army Nuclear Doctrine, 1945–1980* (Boulder: Westview, 1980).

10. For a discussion of changes in the conduct of war in the nineteenth century, see Michael Howard, *War in European History* (Oxford: Oxford University Press, 1976); and Theodore Ropp, *War in the Modern World* (Durham: Duke University Press, 1959).

11. Carl von Clausewitz, *On War,* ed. and trans. Michael Howard and Peter Paret (Princeton: Princeton University Press, 1976), 593. Also see pp. 170–74.

12. The point made in this paragraph needs careful elaboration. My argument should not be interpreted to mean that no elements of continuity in the general nature of war apply throughout time. Certainly, general phenomena such as friction and surprise, to name just two, are not peculiar to any single historical period. And such phenomena would definitely be considered in the decision-making process. My main point is, however, that the more detailed calculations having to do with the conduct of war—those based on possibilities relating to the kind of weaponry on

hand and the size and composition of the army—change with time. So despite these continuities in the general nature of war, significant changes in its conduct that occur in the course of time alter the military calculations on which deterrence is based. Now, some writers argue that it is possible to make meaningful universal generalizations (focusing on the military element of deterrence) by moving to a higher level of abstraction. This attitude is apparent in arguments that focus on the "principles of war." Many students of war maintain that certain timeless principles must be understood and applied by all commanders if they hope to be successful. Yet such principles are too abstract to be of any value. No one argues that the principles of war are wrong, simply because they are so general and so obviously true that it is impossible to reject them. In a similar vein, but one more relevant for this study, some argue that deterrence is a function of a broad offense-defense relationship. (I shall discuss this matter in Chapter 2.) Unfortunately, such abstractions are invariably so vague that they have no real explanatory power. Only by limiting the scope to a specific period can we develop meaningful propositions. Finally, my discussion to this point has been concerned with only the military aspects of conventional deterrence. Regarding the broader relationship between military and political considerations, we can make generalizations with wider application. For a discussion of this matter, see n. 18 and the attendant text.

13. See Bernard Brodie's discussion of this matter in *The American Scientific Strategists*, P-2979 (Santa Monica: Rand, 1964), 20–22. The problem is compounded by the fact that American scholars have traditionally ignored the study of military history. See Peter Paret, "The History of War," *Daedalus*, 100 (spring 1971), 376–96; and Richard H. Kohn, "The Social History of the American Soldier: A Review and Prospectus for Research," *American Historical Review*, 86 (June 1981), 553–67.

14. One very reputable historian went so far as to argue that "to project its past history [i.e., that of the institution of war] into the future is not merely to invite but to make certain a total catastrophe of civilization" (Walter Millis, *Military History*, Publication 39 [Washington, D.C.: American Historical Association, Service Center for Teachers of History, 1961], 16).

15. See Brodie, *Scientific Strategists*, 22; Samuel P. Huntington, *The Soldier and the State* (New York: Vintage, 1964), 198–200; Jeffrey Record, "The Fortunes of War," *Harper's*, 260 (April 1980), 19–23; Richard Swain to Editor, *Harper's*, 260 (June 1980), 4–5; and Russell F. Weigley, ed., *New Dimensions in Military History* (San Rafael: Presidio, 1975), 1–16. More specifically, the American military has paid little attention to the lessons of World War II. See Gen. William DePuy's comments in his *Generals Balck and Von Mellenthin on Tactics: Implications for NATO Military Doctrine*, BDM/W-81-077-TR (McLean: BDM, 19 December 1980), 1.

16. This interest is reflected in the significant number of translations of books about World War II issued by the Israeli army publishing house (*Ma'archot*). Also see Maj. Geoffrey G. Prosch, "Israeli Defense of the Golan: An Interview with Brigadier General Avigdor Kahalani," *Military Review*, 59 (October 1979), 7.

17. For examples of the great influence of World War II on contemporary Soviet thinking, see V. Y. Savkin, *The Basic Principles of Operational Art and Tactics*, trans. U.S. Air Force (Washington, D.C.: GPO, 1976; originally published, Moscow, 1972); A. A. Sidorenko, *The Offensive*, trans. U.S. Air Force (Washington, D.C.: GPO, 1976; originally published, Moscow, 1970); and V. D. Sokolovskiy, *Soviet Military Strategy*, ed. Harriet Fast Scott, 3rd ed. (New York: Crane, Russak, 1968).

18. Nevertheless, history has limited usefulness in this broader realm for two basic reasons. First, as soon as we attempt to introduce a degree of specificity into the

discussion of the relationship between military and political considerations, we are forced to deal with the specifics of the military element—a constraint that obviously causes problems. Second, and more important, although the relationship between war and politics shows some constants, much does change when the nature of the political system undergoes fundamental alteration. The rise of the modern nation-state, for example, had a profound effect on this relationship.

19. Some of the more prominent works in this category are: Bernard Brodie, *Strategy in the Missile Age* (Princeton: Princeton University Press, 1959); Herman Kahn, *On Thermonuclear War* (Princeton: Princeton University Press, 1960); Snyder, *Deterrence and Defense*; and Albert Wohlstetter, "The Delicate Balance of Terror," *Foreign Affairs*, 37 (January 1959), 211–34. The extensive literature dealing with strategic arms control also fits in this category. For an excellent example, see John Newhouse, *Cold Dawn: The Story of SALT* (New York: Holt, Rinehart and Winston, 1973).

20. Nuclear deterrence and the theory of conventional deterrence that I have outlined here show one important similarity. As I have noted, nuclear deterrence is largely a function of specific targeting *strategies*. My central argument in this book is that conventional deterrence is basically a function of military strategy. There are of course significant differences between nuclear and conventional strategies.

21. Some of the more prominent works in this category are: Alexander L. George and Richard Smoke, *Deterrence in American Foreign Policy* (New York: Columbia University Press, 1974); Robert Jervis, *The Logic of Images in International Relations* (Princeton University Press, 1970); Stephen Maxwell, *Rationality in Deterrence*, Adelphi Paper 50 (London: International Institute for Strategic Studies, 1968); Schelling, *Arms and Influence*; and Schelling, *The Strategy of Conflict* (New York: Oxford University Press, 1960). It should be noted that a number of the works cited in n. 19 also address the credibility-of-commitment issue.

22. The most comprehensive study of this subject is George and Smoke, *Deterrence in American Foreign Policy*, which examines "the effort of the United States to deter *limited* conflicts" by threatening to use different levels of force (p. 1). Because the overriding concern of their book is with credibility of American commitments, these authors pay little attention to the battlefield itself and to the question of how an opponent's objectives on the battlefield may be denied. In other words, George and Smoke say very little about the conduct of war and its relationship to deterrence. And when they do address military matters, they are concerned with either the employment of nuclear weapons or the sending of small-scale detachments of marines, infantry, or airborne forces into trouble spots. These particular elements of the American military are involved when credibility is a serious concern. American forces trained to fight a conventional war on the modern battlefield (the armored and mechanized infantry divisions) either are deployed in NATO or are located in the United States and are earmarked for immediate commitment to NATO. The book includes little discussion of the American commitment to helping NATO fight a conventional war. In short, George and Smoke are not directly concerned with the modern battlefield, and in consequence they do not explain why deterrence fails or succeeds in cases involving it.

23. See Schelling, *Arms and Influence*, chaps. 2 and 3.

24. The importance of these two questions is reflected in Glenn Snyder's *risk calculus*, which details the four factors a potential aggressor must consider: "They are (1) his valuation of his war objectives; (2) the cost which he expects to suffer as a result of various possible responses by the deterrer; (3) the probability of various responses, including 'no response'; and (4) the probability of winning the objectives

[216]

with each possible response" (Snyder, *Deterrence and Defense*, 12). The third factor relates to the issue of credibility. Snyder's terse phrase incorporates the essence of each of the two questions.

25. Returning to Snyder's risk calculus (see n. 24) it is possible, using my assumptions about the probability of response and the nature of the response, to excise the third factor ("probability of various responses, including 'no response'"). This deletion accomplished, then the potential aggressor must weigh the political utility of his war objectives (factor 1) against the cost of military action (factor 2) and the probability of success (factor 4).

26. See the sources cited in n. 21.

27. I do not deny that the problem could arise. If, for example, a third party's commitment to come to the defense of an ally appeared to be equivocal, and that third party had none of its own troops stationed in the potential victim's territory, then the issue of credibility would have to be addressed.

28. There is, however, significant doubt about the United States' commitment to use nuclear weapons to defend Europe.

29. For a discussion of the methodology used in this study, see: Alexander L. George, "Case Studies and Theory Development: The Method of Structured, Focused Comparison," in *Diplomacy*, ed. Paul G. Lauren (New York: Free Press, 1979), 43–68; and Arend Lijphart, "Comparative Politics and the Comparative Method," *American Political Science Review*, 65 (September 1971), 682–93.

30. I did not include these crises for a variety of reasons. The Iraq-Iran case, for example, was too recent. I completed almost all of my research before that conflict began. It is not clear that the North Vietnamese invasion of South Vietnam can be classified as a modern armored war—even allowing for a liberal definition of that term. These points aside, there are two general reasons why I omitted these cases from consideration. First, I simply did not have enough time to do the necessary research. Second, little information is available, and it is, moreover, not readily available.

31. Although the Allies were deterred throughout the time that I examine in Chapter 3, the decision-making process showed distinct periods. Moreover, in this case we can compare the thinking of the two Allies, France and Britain.

32. For a comprehensive discussion of the maneuver-attrition debate, see John J. Mearsheimer, "Maneuver, Mobile Defense, and the NATO Central Front," *International Security*, 6 (winter 1981–82), 104–22.

2. Conventional Deterrence

1. Two additional points are noteworthy. First, it is difficult to feel fully confident about the final outcome of a protracted conflict, simply because that outcome is likely to be influenced by unforeseen events. This likelihood would enhance deterrence. Second, many post–World War II conflicts have been characterized by superpower-client relationships such that the superpowers replace lost equipment and back their client states. Thus we might argue that in this circumstance the costs of a failed offensive would be relatively low, weakening deterrence.

2. See Richard N. Rosecrance, *Defense of the Realm* (New York: Columbia University Press, 1968), chap. 4.

3. See Marion W. Boggs, *Attempts to Define and Limit "Aggressive" Armament in Diplomacy and Strategy* (Columbia: University of Missouri, 1941); B. H. Liddell Hart, *Memoirs*,

vol. 1 (London: Cassell, 1967), chap. 8; Robert Jervis, "Cooperation under the Security Dilemma," *World Politics*, 30 (January 1978), 167–214; and George Quester, *Offense and Defense in the International System* (New York: John Wiley, 1977). For slight variations on this theme, see Frederick Engels, *Herr Eugen Dühring's Revolution in Science (Anti-Dühring)*, trans. Emile Burns (New York: International, 1939), 184–92; J. F. C. Fuller, *Armament and History* (New York: Scribner's, 1945); and Tom Wintringham and J. N. Blashford-Snell, *Weapons and Tactics* (Baltimore: Penguin, 1973).

4. Quester, *Offense and Defense*, 7. Also see Boggs, *Attempts*, 94–95.

5. Although a number of the works of this genre treat technology as clearly the most important variable, they also consider changes in social structure (i.e., the rise of the modern nation-state) that affect the shape and size of the military (i.e., the rise of the mass army). See, for example, Quester, *Offense and Defense*, 2, 66–83.

6. See Boggs, *Attempts*, 93; Liddell Hart, *Memoirs*, vol. 1, pp. 185–90; and Quester, *Offense and Defense*, 138–46.

7. See Quester, *Offense and Defense*, 3. Also see Boggs, *Attempts*, 84–85, 90–93.

8. For an excellent discussion of the proceedings of this conference, see Boggs, *Attempts*.

9. It is interesting to note that Liddell Hart, who argued in 1932 that the tank was clearly an offensive weapon (*Memoirs*, vol. 1, pp. 185–90), was arguing by 1937 that a tank-dominated defense could stop a tank-dominated offensive. See his *Europe in Arms* (London: Faber and Faber, 1937). In 1937, when Lord Gort (who later commanded the British forces in France in 1940) outlined a German attack through Belgium that bore uncanny resemblance to the actual German plan of 1940 (See Brian Bond, *Liddell Hart: A Study of His Military Thought* [London: Cassell, 1977], 118, n. 41), Liddell Hart retorted: "I agree that it is possible, if *not* probable, that a breach may be achieved in the way you suggest. But even the fulfilment of the possibility will not necessarily mean that 'the war will pass into open country.' Mechanization brings preponderant possibilities of rapid reinforcement to close a breach, and air power such a means of hindering the attacker's passage through it, while I can see lines of defence multiplying" (from a memorandum in Liddell Hart's personal papers dated 6 November 1937 and titled "Defence or Attack—Notes on Gort's Notes" [1/322/54]).

10. This entire subject, as it relates to the tank, will be discussed at length in subsequent sections of this chapter.

11. B. H. Liddell Hart, *Deterrent or Defense* (New York: Praeger, 1960), chap. 10.

12. See Erich von Manstein, *Lost Victories* (Chicago: Regnery, 1958); F. W. von Mellenthin, *Panzer Battles* (New York: Ballantine, 1976).

13. This theory of conventional deterrence is basically deductive and has not been tested in specific cases. Also, we should note that proponents of this theory approach technological determinism. For an excellent discussion of the matter, see Posen, "Origins of Strategic Doctrine," 121–32.

14. Actually, no single composite indicator encompasses all of these elements. The two best measures are a comparison of manpower on each side and a comparison of overall weaponry on each side (as reflected in armored division equivalents). See Chapter 6 ("The Balance of Forces on the Central Front"), where I discuss these measures in the context of the NATO–Warsaw Pact balance. For a discussion of the problems associated with measuring the balance of forces, see J. A. Stockfish, *Models, Data, and War: A Critique of the Study of Conventional Forces*, R-1526-PR (Santa Monica: Rand, March 1975); and U.S. Comptroller General, *Models, Data, and War: A Critique of the Foundation for Defense Analyses*, PAD-80-21 (Washington, D.C.: General Accounting Office, 12 March 1980).

15. For an example of an ambitious attempt to use quantitative indicators to determine battlefield outcomes, see Trevor N. Dupuy, *Numbers, Predictions, and War* (New York: Bobbs-Merrill, 1979).

16. See Chapter 4 of this book for a discussion of differing views of the balance of forces in May 1940. Regarding the decision to invade the Soviet Union, see Seweryn Bialer, ed., *Stalin and His Generals: Soviet Military Memoirs of World War II* (New York: Pegasus, 1969), 182.

17. See Steven L. Canby, "Mutual Force Reductions: A Military Perspective," *International Security*, 2 (winter 1978), 122–35, which provides an excellent critique of the NATO position.

18. These three strategies are "ideal types"—logically precise concepts abstracted from reality that include all the requisite characteristics of a specific strategy. It is therefore unrealistic to expect an actual case to have all the earmarks of any single one. As Max Weber explains, "In order to give a precise meaning to these terms, it is necessary . . . to formulate pure ideal types of the corresponding forms of action which in each case involve the highest possible degree of logical integration by virtue of their complete adequacy on the level of meaning. But precisely because this is true, it is probably seldom if ever that a real phenomenon can be found which corresponds exactly to one of these ideally constructed pure types" (Max Weber, *The Theory of Social and Economic Organization*, trans. and ed. A. M. Henderson and Talcott Parsons [New York: Free Press, 1964], 110). Although there is no one-to-one correspondence between an ideal type and any specific cases, the ideal type, as Talcott Parsons notes, functions as "a generalized rubric within which an indefinite number of particular cases may be classified." (ibid., 13). Using the rubric, it is possible to make generalizations about deterrence. As Weber observes "Theoretical analysis in the field of sociology is only possible in terms of such pure types" (ibid., 110).

19. The distinction between unlimited military objectives and unlimited political objectives is especially relevant today because of superpower involvement in regional conflicts. A nation may render an opponent militarily impotent but, because of superpower involvement, may not be in a position to dictate peace terms.

20. Clausewitz noted, in a plan for revising *On War* dated 10 July 1827, "The revision will bring out the two types of war with greater clarity at every point. . . . War can be of two kinds, in the sense that either the objective is to *overthrow the enemy*— to render him politically helpless or militarily impotent, thus forcing him to sign whatever peace we please; or *merely to occupy some of his frontier-districts* so that we can annex them or use them for bargaining. . . . the fact that the aims of the two types are quite different must be clear at all times" (*On War*, 69). Also see *On War*, bk. 1, chap. 2.

21. As I use the term here, *strategy* is a means to achieve a specific objective. Thus a blitzkrieg could be used in pursuit of either limited or unlimited objectives. The same is true of a strategy predicated on either attrition or surprise. In this regard, strategy has no direct link with a specific objective, although the three types will be directly tied to specific objectives. The attrition and blitzkrieg strategies are used in pursuit of decisive victory, while surprise is linked with the pursuit of limited objectives (the limited aims strategy). In essence, the term *strategy* will be broadened to include the desired objective.

22. I do not mean that policy makers automatically recognize these three strategies and then simply choose the one that best suits them. As my case studies will show, the decision-making process is far more complex.

23. The importance that commanders such as Frederick the Great and Napoleon

placed on maneuver is clearly reflected in Jay Luvaas, ed., *Frederick the Great on the Art of War* (New York: Free Press, 1966); and David G. Chandler, *The Campaigns of Napoleon* (New York: Macmillan, 1966), especially 161–201.

24. For a discussion of this distinction between penetration and maneuver, see Wilhelm Balck, *Development of Tactics—World War*, trans. Harry Bell (Fort Leavenworth: General Service Schools Press, 1922); and Hermann Foertsch, *The Art of Modern Warfare* (New York: Oskar Piest, 1940). It should be emphasized that tactical maneuver is still commonplace on the battlefield, but it involves maneuver on a much smaller scale than does the classical concept, which is in essence strategic maneuver.

25. For an excellent discussion of these tactics, see Timothy T. Lupfer, *The Dynamics of Doctrine: The Changes in German Tactical Doctrine during the First World War*, Leavenworth Paper 4 (Fort Leavenworth: U.S. Army Command and General Staff College, July 1981), 37–54. Also see Balck, *Development of Tactics*, 260–93.

26. The following discussion on the use of tanks in World War I is based on: B. H. Liddell Hart, *The Tanks*, vol. 1 (New York: Praeger, 1959); and J. F. C. Fuller, *Tanks in the Great War* (New York: Dutton, 1920).

27. This plan, which later came to be known as "Plan 1919," was devised by J. F. C. Fuller. A copy can be found in his *Memoirs of an Unconventional Soldier* (London: Nicholson and Watson, 1936), 322–36.

28. For a detailed discussion of these different schools of thought, see Richard M. Ogorkiewicz, *Armor* (New York: Praeger, 1960), chap. 2.

29. See, for example, V. W. Germains, "The Limitations of the Tank," *Journal of the Royal United Services Institute*, 75 (February 1930), 124–29.

30. For a discussion of the conflict between the various schools of thought in each industrialized nation, see Charles Messenger, *The Blitzkrieg Story* (New York: Scribner's, 1976), chaps. 3, 4.

31. In this section as well as in "The Blitzkrieg Strategy" and "The Limited Aims Strategy," I assume that both sides are somewhat evenly matched in terms of numbers of forces—neither one has an overwhelming force advantage. In a later section ("Strategy and Numbers"), I shall consider the case in which there is a great disparity.

32. Clausewitz, *On War*, 75.

33. Ibid., 228. As I noted earlier, Clausewitz emphasized the key distinction between limited and unlimited objectives. (See n. 20.) Moreover, he recognized that when the attacker is pursuing limited objectives, he does not have to engage in bloody battles. Therefore it is wrong to argue that Clausewitz simply advocated using brute force to annihilate the opposition. When the objective is total defeat of the opponent's armed forces, however, Clausewitz clearly believed that success could result only from winning bloody set-piece battles.

34. Clausewitz, *On War*, 228.

35. A copy of "Montgomery's Address to Senior Officers of Eighth Army before the Battle of El Alamein," no date, appears in Liddell Hart's correspondence with the author Chester Wilmot (1/753). Not surprisingly, Eisenhower described Montgomery as "a master in the methodical preparation of forces for a formal, set-piece attack" (cited in Chester Wilmot, *The Struggle for Europe* [London: Collins, 1965], 466).

36. It is important to note that the attacking forces would attempt to penetrate the defender's extended front. The penetrations would be limited in depth (tactical penetrations), however, and would most likely be spread across a broad front. As I shall note later, the blitzkrieg relies on the massing of forces at one or two specific points to effect a deep strategic penetration.

37. In the wake of El Alamein, Rommel commented to his wife, "We're simply

being crushed by enemy weight" (*The Rommel Papers*, ed. B. H. Liddell Hart [New York: Harcourt, Brace, 1953], 320).

38. An important assumption here is that the weaponry and the troops engaged on each side are of roughly equivalent quality. Regarding the advantages that accrue to the defender in set-piece battles, see n. 48.

39. For example, see Messenger, *Blitzkrieg Story*. Messenger simply does not attempt to detail the specific elements of the blitzkrieg in order to integrate them into a coherent framework. Also see F. O. Miksche, *Blitzkrieg* (London: Faber and Faber, 1941), which does attempt to provide a precise and comprehensive description of the blitzkrieg. Unfortunately, however, this book contains a number of inaccuracies that are obviously the result of the fact that it was written in the immediate aftermath of the German victory in France (1940).

40. A copy of the memorandum, which was endorsed by Gen. Heinz Guderian, can be found in Liddell Hart, *Memoirs*, vol. 1, pp. 164–65. Although it is not comprehensive, the memorandum does succinctly summarize the basic elements of the strategy. A good description can be found in the German army's current field manual detailing basic doctrine (*Command and Control in Battle*, German Army Regulation 100/100 [Bonn: Federal Ministry of Defense, 28 September 1973), hereafter referred to as 100/100). Readers who have reservations about the continuity of the modern battlefield will find that this document illustrates the marked similarities between the contemporary battlefield and that of World War II. For another good discussion of the blitzkrieg, see Edward N. Luttwak, "The Operational Level of War," *International Security*, 5 (winter 1980–81), 61–79.

41. See J. F. C. Fuller, *Lectures on F.S.R. III* (London: Sifton Praed, 1932), which was slightly revised and was issued as *Armoured Warfare* (Harrisburg: Military Service, 1943).

42. Soon after publication of Fuller's *Lectures on F.S.R. III*, Liddell Hart analyzed Fuller's views on armored warfare. The major points of his critique highlight those points in Fuller's argument that are inconsistent with the blitzkrieg. A summary of Liddell Hart's critique can be found in Liddell Hart, *Memoirs*, vol. 1, pp. 90–91. A qualified defense against Liddell Hart's criticisms can be found in Anthony J. Trythall, *"Boney" Fuller* (New Brunswick: Rutgers University Press, 1977), 226–28.

43. See Heinz Guderian, *Panzer Leader* (New York: Ballantine, 1972); and Manstein, *Lost Victories*. In a letter to Liddell Hart, Guderian noted that "it is very difficult to give a definition of the blitzkrieg method" (Heinz Guderian to B. H. Liddell Hart, 1 May 1949 [9/24/62]).

44. See Hans Rothfels, "Clausewitz," in *Makers of Modern Strategy*, ed. Edward Mead Earle (Princeton: Princeton University Press, 1973), 98. Also see Chandler, *Campaigns of Napoleon*, 141.

45. Clausewitz, *On War*, 231.

46. At the 16 May 1940 meeting of the Allied Supreme War Council (six days after the Germans launched their blitzkrieg in the West), General Gamelin, the Allied commander, said, "French feeling was that we simply must stop the present advance of the armored force. It was getting at our rear where we were completely vulnerable" (CAB 99/3, minutes of 16 May 1940 meeting of Supreme War Council).

47. It is absolutely essential that an attacker effect a deep strategic penetration if the blitzkrieg strategy is to be successful. See Liddell Hart's memorandum on the blitzkrieg in *Memoirs*, vol. 1, pp. 164–65. Gen. Hasso von Manteuffel, one of the most skilled armored commanders in the World War II German army, told Liddell Hart; "According to my experiences only *the push in the depth* can paralyze the *enemy's*

defense system. One must never turn sideways too early. The success is the greater the deeper the push penetrates into the rear of the enemy" (Gen. Hasso von Manteuffel to B. H. Liddell Hart, 15 May 1950 [9/24/72]). Also see 100/100, chaps. 30 and 31.

48. It is important to recognize the difference between the overall force ratio and the ratio of forces needed at the point(s) of the main attack. There is widespread agreement on the rule of thumb that the attacking forces must achieve somewhat more than a 3:1 advantage at the point(s) of main attack because of the natural advantages that accrue to the defender. See Gen. William E. DePuy, "Technology and Tactics in Defense of Europe," *Army*, 29 (April 1979), 14–23; and *Operations: FM 100-5* (Washington, D.C.: U.S. Army, (1976), p. 3–4, hereafter cited as *FM 100-5*. (The army released an updated version of *FM 100-5* in 1982, but the edition I used, to which I refer throughout this book, is that published in 1976.) Also see Savkin, *Basic Principles*, 201–29; and Sidorenko, *The Offensive*, chap. 1. Obviously an attacker can achieve a 4:1 or 5:1 advantage at specific points along a front without having an overall advantage of 3:1. In fact, he could achieve a 4:1 or 5:1 advantage on one axis without having an overall advantage, as the Germans did in May 1940. Although there was an overall balance of forces, the Germans achieved a decisive superiority in the area of the Ardennes Forest. The greater the overall ratio, of course, the easier it is to achieve those overwhelming advantages on the main axes of attack.

49. This discussion of the blitzkrieg focuses almost exclusively on the attacker. As I shall show in the next section, the defender is not without recourse against a blitzkrieg.

50. It is very important to recall the distinction between maneuver and penetration that I noted earlier. The blitzkrieg is *not* a maneuver-oriented strategy. The objective is to penetrate the defender's front and then to enlarge the penetration as rapidly as possible by continuing directly into the depths of the defense.

51. Before the start of the 1967 Middle East war, Gen. Israel Tal, one of Israel's foremost experts on armored war, told his subordinate commanders that in the breakthrough battle "everybody shall attack without paying heed to any number of casualties and it will therefore be a battle of life or death." He then said, however, "in the battles to come, after this victorious break-through encounter, we shall try to avoid further attrition-engagements" (quoted in a Jehuda Wallach to B. H. Liddell Hart, 22 January 1968 [2/81]). Current German doctrine states: "Wherever possible, the foremost elements will bypass enemy resistance and look for a route into his depth without becoming unnecessarily engaged in combat which causes heavy losses" (100/100, p. 30–25).

52. As the attacker's armored spearheads push into the depths of the defense, his flanks continuously lengthen. The attacker's forces take on the form of a finger-shaped mass. The defender can try to thwart the offensive by placing forces in front of that moving finger and/or by cutting into the sides or flanks of the finger and cutting it off from its base. The following section will discuss at length the ways in which a defender deals with a blitzkrieg.

53. See Liddell Hart, *Memoirs*, vol. 1, pp. 41–49.

54. See Martin Van Creveld, *Supplying War* (Cambridge: Cambridge University Press, 1977), chap. 5.

55. Concerning this point, a British intelligence report examining the disasters of May 1940 notes that "the French who had always shown themselves to be adept at improvization, failed to put any measures into operation to stem the advancing Ger-

man columns" (WO 193/176, "Causes of French Collapse," memorandum prepared by British army [MI3a], 7 June 1940).

56. The importance of psychological damage is captured in the diary of Gen. Sir Edmund Ironside, the chief of the British Imperial General Staff for the first nine months of World War II. He noted on 18 August 1940 that "France was defeated by terror and not by the slaughter of numbers of her soldiers. The mobile columns, having broken through, simply eat out the guts of the country, and this they did in France" (*Time Unguarded: The Ironside Diaries, 1937–1940,* ed. Roderick Macleod and Denis Kelly [New York: David McKay, 1962], 389). In a memorandum prepared by British intelligence ("Causes of French Collapse") in the immediate aftermath of Dunkirk, it was noted that as a result of the German attack, "French plans were . . . thrown out of gear and a feeling of complete helplessness seemed to overcome the troops."

57. Paul Carell, *Hitler Moves East, 1941–1943* (New York: Ballantine, 1971), 86–102; Guderian, *Panzer Leader,* 138–62; B. H. Liddell Hart, *The German Generals Talk* (New York: William Morrow, 1948), 175–87; and Van Creveld, *Supplying War,* chap. 5.

58. See Manstein, *Lost Victories,* 177.

59. Current German doctrine still reflects uncertainty about this matter. See 100/100, p. 31–1.

60. Manstein as quoted in Carell, *Hitler Moves East,* 28. Also see B. H. Liddell Hart, "Strategy of a War," *Encounter,* 30 (February 1968), 17.

61. The Germans, after deciding not to push directly toward Moscow, trapped 600,000 Soviet soldiers in the Kiev pocket and 600,000 more in the Vyasma pocket (Liddell Hart, *History of the Second World War* [New York: Putnam, 1970], 167).

62. From "Maxims of Napoleon," in *Jomini, Clausewitz, and Schlieffen* (West Point: U.S. Military Academy, Department of History, 1969), 62.

63. Liddell Hart, *History of the Second World War,* 73.

64. See Chaim Herzog, *The War of Atonement* (Boston: Little, Brown, 1975), chap. 18; Edward Luttwak and Dan Horowitz, *The Israeli Army* (New York: Harper and Row, 1975), 217, 289–90, 368; Miksche, *Blitzkrieg,* chap. 9; Ogorkiewicz, *Armor,* 122; Fred K. Vigman, "The Theoretical Evaluation of Artillery after World War I," *Military Affairs,* 16 (1952), 115–18; and Martin Van Creveld, "Two Years After: The Israeli Defense Forces, 1973–1975," *Journal of the Royal United Services Institute* (March 1976), 29–34.

65. Gen. Israel Tal notes that Genghis Khan's Mongol army "averaged a distance of 27km. a day," while "the German Blitzkrieg averaged a distance of 10km. a day." He attributes this difference to the different logistical requirements facing the two armies (Israel Tal, "Modern Tank Warfare," speech delivered at Air War College, Maxwell Air Force Base, 9 March 1978). Also see Martin Van Creveld, "Supplying an Army: An Historical View," *Journal of the Royal United Services Institute,* 123 (June 1978), 60–62.

66. In a number of contemporary armies, many of the infantry divisions have been so mechanized that they scarcely differ from armored divisions. Obviously, such mechanized infantry divisions might be used to effect a blitzkrieg. My concern here, however, is with preserving a clear distinction between armored divisions and the more traditional, nonmechanized infantry divisions.

67. Regarding the organization of German armored divisions, which changed somewhat in the course of the war, see Ogorkiewicz, *Armor,* chap. 7.

68. See Ogorkiewicz, *Armor,* 121–22. For a corresponding description of the Israeli blitzkrieg, see Luttwak and Horowitz, *Israeli Army,* 292–95, 363.

69. Gen. Israel Tal, one of Israel's foremost experts on armored warfare, told me that he considers this matter to be of the greatest importance when designing an armored force that can win quick and decisive victories (personal communication, 6 October 1978). Also see the comments of the German generals in DePuy, *Generals Balck and Von Mellenthin on Tactics*, 42–43.

70. See DePuy, *Generals Balck and Von Mellenthin on Tactics*, 16–23, 54–55; Manstein, *Lost Victories*, 63, 284; and Martin Van Creveld, *Fighting Power: German Military Performance, 1914–1945* (Washington, D.C.: Department of Defense, Office of Net Assessment, December 1980), chap. 5. This emphasis is also apparent in 100/100 (especially p. 10-2).

71. This aphorism embodies the Israeli army's view of the specific value of operational plans. Dan Horowitz, "Flexible Responsiveness and Military Strategy: The Case of the Israeli Army," *Policy Sciences*, 1 (summer 1970), 196.

72. See 100/100, chap. 10.

73. See Manstein, *Lost Victories*, 189. It should be emphasized that all commanders, not only those charged with armored forces, must be capable of making instantaneous decisions. For a discussion of how infantry forces were trained in the pre–World War II German army, see Anthony Farrar-Hockley, *Infantry Tactics* (London: Almark, 1976), 14–16.

74. See 100/100, chaps. 10, 30–31; and Horowitz, "Flexible Responsiveness."

75. See Mildred H. Gillie, *Forging the Thunderbolt* (Harrisburg:Military Service, 1947); Kent Roberts Greenfield, Robert R. Palmer, and Bell I. Wiley, *The Organization of Ground Combat Troops* (Washington, D.C.: U.S. Army, Historical Division, 1947); and Ogorkiewicz, *Armor*, chaps. 5 and 8.

76. See H. Essame, *Patton* (New York: Scribner's, 1974), 250–51; Siegfried Westphal, *The German Army in the West* (London: Cassell, 1951), 170–76; and Russell F. Weigley, *Eisenhower's Lieutenants* (Bloomington: Indiana University Press, 1981), 4.

77. See Field Marshal The Viscount Montgomery of Alamein, *Normandy to the Baltic* (Boston: Houghton Mifflin, 1948), chap. 11; and Wilmot, *Struggle for Europe*, chaps. 24–25.

78. See Essame, *Patton*, chap. 13; and George S. Patton, Jr., *War as I Knew It* (Boston: Houghton Mifflin, 1947), 89–137. Liddell Hart maintains that "the best chance of a quick finish" rested with Patton, who "had a keener sense than anyone else on the Allied side of the key importance of persistent pace in pursuit" (Liddell Hart, *History of the Second World War*, 567).

79. Roland G. Ruppenthal, "Logistics and the Broad-Front Strategy," in *Command Decisions*, ed. Kent Roberts Greenfield (Washington, D.C.: U.S. Army, Office of the Chief of Military History, 1960), 420–21.

80. See Ruppenthal, "Logistics"; and Van Creveld, *Supplying War*, chap. 7.

81. "By 11 September [1944] the Allies had reached a general line which pre–D-Day planners had expected would be gained about D plus 330 (2 May 1945)." They were 233 days ahead of schedule. Charles B. MacDonald, *The Siegfried Line Campaign* (Washington, D.C.: U.S. Army, Office of the Chief of Military History, 1963), 4.

82. Liddell Hart, *History of the Second World War*, 567. Also see Weigley, *Eisenhower's Lieutenants*, especially 727–30.

83. As I noted earlier, the tank is not inherently an offensive weapon; the defender may derive the greater advantage from highly mobile forces.

84. See Martin Blumenson, *Breakout and Pursuit* (Washington, D.C.: U.S. Army, Office of the Chief of Military History, 1961), chaps. 4–9.

85. For an excellent discussion of the concept of force-to-space ratios, see Liddell Hart, *Deterrent or Defense*, chap. 10.

86. On the eastern front in World War II, the Germans did not have enough divisions to cover the entire front adequately. The Soviets, by massing their forces at specific points, were almost always able to break through the overstretched German defense.

87. I shall discuss this matter in greater detail later in this section.

88. See Guderian, *Panzer Leader*, 396.

89. See Erich von Manstein, "The Development of the Red Army, 1942–1945," in *The Soviet Army*, ed. B. H. Liddell Hart (London: Weidenfeld and Nicolson, 1956), 141; and Earl F. Ziemke, *Stalingrad to Berlin* (Washington, D.C.: U.S. Army, Office of the Chief of Military History, 1968), 29–31.

90. See Liddell Hart, *History of the Second World War*, 163, 169; and Robert Cecil, *Hitler's Decision to Invade Russia, 1941* (New York: David McKay, 1975), chap. 8.

91. See Carell, *Hitler Moves East*, chap. 4; and Guderian, *Panzer Leader*, 152–62.

92. See n. 61.

93. Regarding the extraordinary problems that arose as the German lines of communication lengthened, see Van Creveld, *Supplying War*, chap. 5. Regarding the Soviet learning process, see Savkin, *Basic Principles*, 51.

94. Of course, the Germans had to launch another offensive to deal with the French and British armies located on the southern portion of the defensive line that were not trapped by the initial blitzkrieg. Similarly, in the case of Barbarossa, the Germans were well aware that it would be necessary to conduct subsequent operations after defeating the Soviets west of the Dnieper. These operations, however, were envisioned as finishing touches on campaigns that had been decided earlier.

95. See Winston Churchill's comments quoted in the final section of Chapter 3.

96. Alexander Werth, *Russia at War, 1941–1945* (New York: Dutton, 1964), 133.

97. See John Erickson, *The Soviet High Command* (London: Macmillan, 1962), 510–87; Ogorkiewicz, *Armor*, 98–99.

98. I shall discuss this matter in Chapter 5.

99. See n. 85 and the attendant text for a discussion of this matter. Also see "Force-to-Space Ratios" in Chapter 6.

100. See n. 48.

101. Quester, *Offense and Defense*, 92. Also see "Force-to-Space Ratios" in Chapter 6.

102. The terms used for each form of defense in the subsequent discussion are commonplace. Because there is no widespread agreement on their meaning, however, they are often loosely applied. Former army chief of staff Gen. Bernard Rogers, for example, argues that "a forward defense . . . could be static, linear, active, or mobile" (U.S. Congress, Senate, Armed Services Committee, *Hearings on Department of Defense Authorization for Appropriations for Fiscal Year 1979*, pt. 2, 95th Cong., 2nd sess. [Washington, D.C.: GPO, 1978], 1573). J. R. Alford, who has written a superb study on mobile defense, notes that "one of the great difficulties in conducting a study such as this has been the absence of a really coherent set of definitions and the rather loose way in which terms are used" (Col. J. R. Alford, *Mobile Defence: The Pervasive Myth* [London: King's College, Department of War Studies, 1977], 7). It is therefore imperative that I carefully define the terms used in the following discussion.

103. Although tactical and strategic mobility are difficult to differentiate clearly, they must nevertheless be carefully defined. Strategic mobility obtains when a nation has the capability to move a significant number of forces to virtually all parts of the

theater of battle to engage the attacking forces. A force with strategic mobility has an unlimited radius of movement within the theater of battle. Tactical mobility, on the other hand, is the ability to move to a limited number of parts of the theater of battle to engage the attacking forces. J. R. Alford provides different definitions of strategic and tactical mobility that complement the above definitions nicely. For Alford, tactical mobility is the freedom to move forces that are in direct contact with the enemy, while strategic mobility is the capability to move forces that are not in contact with the enemy (Alford, *Mobile Defence*, 28).

104. Thus it is not surprising that German doctrine, which places very little emphasis on using nuclear weapons in defense against a Soviet attack, maintains that "if there is danger that the defense will be penetrated on a large scale, it may be practical to annihilate penetrating enemy with nuclear weapons" (100/100, p. 27–24).

105. Miksche, *Blitzkrieg*, 183.

106. See Steven Canby, *The Alliance and Europe*, pt. 4: *Military Doctrine and Technology*, Adelphi Paper 109 (London: International Institute for Strategic Studies, 1974–75). Also see Alford, *Mobile Defence*, 18–22.

107. See Canby, *The Alliance and Europe*, 24; and Miksche, *Blitzkrieg*, 176.

108. See Miksche, *Blitzkrieg*, 176.

109. See *FM 100-5*, p. 1-1.

110. See *Great Patriotic War of the Soviet Union, 1941–1945: A General Outline* (Moscow: Progress, 1974), 179–80; and Martin Caidin, *The Tigers Are Burning* (New York: Hawthorn, 1974).

111. For a more comprehensive discussion of the concept of mobile defense, see Alford, *Mobile Defence*; and Mearsheimer, "Maneuver, Mobile Defense, and the NATO Central Front."

112. The forces kept in the strategic reserve do not serve the purpose of reinforcing the units on the forward edge of the battlefield that are absorbing the main attacks. Such a strategy would be a forward defense, not a mobile defense. It is important to note that, although a forward defense requires placement of the majority of the defender's forces on the front line, the defender may still maintain reserves that can be used to augment his beleaguered units.

113. For this reason Alford refers to mobile defense as "the pervasive myth" in the title of his study.

114. See Liddell Hart, *The German Generals Talk*, chap. 15; Percy E. Schramm, *Hitler: The Man and the Military Leader* (Chicago: Quadrangle, 1971), chap. 2; and Ziemke, *Stalingrad to Berlin*, 217.

115. Alford, in his study of the mobile defense, was able to find only three examples of a defender employing a mobile defense based on the use of a counterstroke. They were: the Germans at Tannenberg in 1914; Rommel's defensive action at Sollum in 1941; and the Chinese strategy against the United Nations forces in 1950 (Alford, *Mobile Defence*, 2).

116. See n. 48.

117. See Christopher Donnelly, "The Soviet Ground Forces," in *The Soviet War Machine*, ed. Ray Bonds (New York: Chartwell, 1976), 166–71.

118. Proponents of a mobile defense often argue that it is excellent when the defender is outnumbered by the attacking forces (see Edward Luttwak, "The American Style of Warfare and the Military Balance," *Survival*, 21 [March–April 1979], 58). Actually, the opposite is true, since this defensive strategy relies so heavily on offensive action. See Alford, *Mobile Defence*, 12–16, for further discussion of this matter.

119. It should be emphasized that although a forward defense, as defined here,

does not involve large numbers of reserves, the defender's best interests require that he maintain as many reserves as possible for use, as I observed in n. 112, in reinforcing threatened points. I shall discuss this matter in Chapter 6 when I analyze NATO's prospects for thwarting a Soviet offensive.

120. Manstein, "Development of the Red Army," 140.

121. Heinz Guderian, "Unification or Coordination: The Armed Forces Problem (MS #T-113)," in *World War II German Military Studies*, ed. Donald S. Detwiler, vol. 6 (New York: Garland, 1979), 11.

122. Given the natural advantages enjoyed by the defender, the attacker would most likely suffer higher casualties. We should also note that only a strong feeling of hostility toward the opponent would make a nation willing to accept the casualty levels associated with such a strategy of punishment. Once such hostility is present, there will be great pressure to pursue a decisive victory, rendering moot any discussion of a limited conflict.

123. See Fred C. Iklé, *Every War Must End* (New York: Columbia University Press, 1971).

124. Whereas strategic surprise obtains when the defense does not expect an attack, tactical surprise starts from the assumption that the defense knows an attack to be imminent. Tactical surprise is possible because the attacker can still choose the location and the time of the attack.

125. As I noted in discussing the blitzkrieg, for the attacking forces, vulnerable flanks are an accepted risk. The attacker assumes that his penetrating armored columns will deliver the decisive blow before the defender is able to take advantage of the lightly defended flanks. Halting the attacking forces before they can deliver the knockout blow therefore obviously destroys the blitzkrieg. In the case of the limited aims strategy, because there is no emphasis on effecting a deep strategic penetration, the attacker can quickly consolidate his gains, thus eliminating the danger of weakly defended flanks.

126. As I have noted, if the depth of the battlefield is great, it may be necessary for the attacker to launch two blitzkriegs to defeat the enemy decisively, as happened in 1941 when the Germans invaded the Soviet Union. After the first blitzkrieg failed to prove decisive, the Germans needed to launch a second blitzkrieg against the remaining Soviet forces east of the Dnieper to inflict defeat.

127. In a more contemporary vein, a conflict between the Soviet Union and China would present opportunities for either side to employ a blitzkrieg for limited objectives.

128. See Chapter 3, n. 32 and the attendant text.

129. See Chapter 6, nn. 5, 6, and 7 and the attendant text.

130. See n. 31.

131. See n. 48 and the attendant text.

132. For a discussion of the Polish campaign, see Matthew Cooper, *The German Army, 1933–1945* (New York: Stein and Day, 1978), chap. 13; Robert M. Kennedy, *The German Campaign in Poland* (Washington, D.C.: U.S. Army, 1956); and Liddell Hart, *History of the Second World War*, chap. 3. Also see Chapter 4, n. 26 and the attendant text.

133. For an excellent discussion of this matter, see Cooper, *The German Army*, chap. 13.

134. As I noted in Chapter 1, consideration of the nonmilitary risks and costs of military action is beyond the scope of the theory developed here.

135. Clausewitz, *On War*, 605.

136. For a discussion of this matter, see John J. Mearsheimer, "The Theory and Practice of Conventional Deterrence" (Ph.D. diss., Cornell University, 1981), 102–15.

137. Ibid., 115–25; Morton H. Halperin, *Limited War in the Nuclear Age* (New York: John Wiley, 1963); and Robert E. Osgood, *Limited War* (Chicago: University of Chicago Press, 1957).

138. At the risk of further complicating matters, it should be noted that decision makers must also consider the political value of defeat, or, in other words, the political consequences of losing on the battlefield. Thus along with the probability of achieving one's objectives (P_v), decision makers must consider the value of continued peace (V_p), the political benefits of a successful military campaign (V_v), and the value of defeat (V_d). Translating this statement into mathematical form, deterrence is likely to fail when $V_v(P_v) + V_d(1 - P_v) > V_p$.

139. See Michael E. Brown, *Deterrence Failures and Deterrence Strategies*, P-5842 (Santa Monica: Rand, March 1977); Daniel Ellsberg, *The Crude Analysis of Strategic Choices*, P-2183 (Santa Monica: Rand, 15 December 1960); and Richard N. Rosecrance, "Deterrence and Vulnerability in the Pre-Nuclear Era," in *The Future of Strategic Deterrence*, pt. 1, Adelphi Paper 160 (London: International Institute for Strategic Studies, autumn 1980), 24–30.

140. Quoted in Fritz Fischer, *War of Illusions*, trans. Marian Jackson (New York: Norton, 1975), 377.

141. B. H. Liddell Hart, *The Current of War* (London: Hutchinson, 1941), 55.

142. See my earlier discussion of this matter in "Strategy and Numbers."

143. See Richard K. Betts, *Soldiers, Statesmen, and Cold War Crises* (Cambridge: Harvard University Press, 1977); and Huntington, *The Soldier and the State*, chap. 3.

144. If a potential attacker enjoys a significant superiority in numbers, he is very unlikely to consider a limited aims strategy.

145. See the discussion of this matter in "Strategy and Numbers."

146. I discuss this matter at greater length in "The Final Decision."

3. The Allied Decision Not to Attack Germany, March 1939–May 1940

1. The French, after declaring war on Germany, did launch an extremely limited offensive against the Siegfried Line. After making contact with the Germans, they quickly pulled back behind the Maginot Line. See Gamelin's description of the offensive in CAB 99/3, minutes of 12 September 1939 meeting of Supreme War Council.

2. The principal works on this subject, which this section draws upon heavily, are: Richard D. Challener, *The French Theory of the Nation in Arms, 1866–1939* (New York: Russell and Russell, 1965); Jeffrey J. Clarke, "Military Technology in Republican France" (Ph.D. diss., Duke University, 1969); Alvin D. Coox, "French Military Doctrine, 1919–1939" (Ph.D. diss., Harvard University, 1951); Robert A. Doughty, "The Evolution of French Army Doctrine, 1919–1939" (Ph.D. diss., University of Kansas, 1979); Fred Greene, "French Military Leadership and Security against Germany, 1919–1940" (Ph.D. diss., Yale University, 1950); Donald J. Harvey, "French Concepts of Military Strategy (1919–1939)" (Ph.D. diss., Columbia University, 1953); Robert J. Young, *In Command of France* (Cambridge: Harvard University Press, 1978); Robert J. Young, "Preparations for Defeat: French War Doctrine in the Inter-war Period," *Journal of European Studies*, 2 (June 1972), 155–72; and Robert J. Young, "La Guerre de Longue Durée: Some Reflections on French Strategy and Diplomacy in the 1930s," in *General Staffs and Diplomacy before the Second World War*, ed. Adrian Preston (London: Croom

Helm, 1978), 41–64. Although each of these works has a somewhat different focus, all the authors agree on the essential elements of French military thought during the interwar period. Unfortunately, few official French documents from this period have been made available to scholars.

3. See Challener, *Nation in Arms*, 139. Also see Enno Kraehe, "The Motives Behind the Maginot Line," *Military Affairs*, 8 (1944), 111–15; and Arnold Wolfers, *Britain and France between Two Wars* (New York: Harcourt, Brace, 1940), chap. 1.

4. Because the French were so decisively defeated in May 1940, it is frequently assumed that they did not seriously address the matter of national defense. As Robert Young notes, "the popular conception" of France in the 1920s and 1930s portrayed the nation as "directionless and defeatist, paralyzed by indecision" (Young, *Command*, 3). For an excellent discussion of this phenomenon, see: John C. Cairns, "Along the Road back to France, 1940," *American Historical Review*, 64 (April 1959), 583–603; and John C. Cairns, "Some Recent Historians and the 'Strange Defeat' of 1940," *Journal of Modern History*, 46 (March 1974), 60–85. This was not the case, however, as Young explains at great length. "One need not be blind to the shortcomings of the fallen Republic to recognize within it a seriousness of purpose toward the perils at hand . . . [and] a willingness to devote enormous care and effort to the cause of national defense" (Young, *Command*, 2).

5. Dudley Kirk, "Population and Population Trends in Modern France," in *Modern France: Problems of the Third and Fourth Republics*, ed. Edward Mead Earle (Princeton: Princeton University Press, 1951), 314. Also see Joseph J. Spengler, *France Faces Depopulation* (Durham: Duke University Press, 1938).

6. Kirk, "Population Trends," 314, 316. Also see H. C. Hillmann, "Comparative Strengths of the Great Powers," in *The World in March 1939*, ed. Arnold Toynbee and Frank T. Ashton-Gwatkin (Oxford: Oxford University Press, 1952), 370–75.

7. See Spengler, *Depopulation*, 53; and Harvey, "French Concepts," 64.

8. See Hillmann, "Comparative Strengths," 431–91.

9. See ibid., 431–40; and W. Arthur Lewis, *Economic Survey, 1919–1939* (London: Allen and Unwin, 1949).

10. For a vivid description of this problem, see Charles DeGaulle, *The Army of the Future* (London: Hutchinson, n.d.), 12–13.

11. See Young, *Command*, 15–19; Doughty, "Evolution," 111–19; and Harvey, "French Concepts," 61–63.

12. Cited in Young, *Command*, 22.

13. See John C. Cairns, "A Nation of Shopkeepers in Search of a Suitable France, 1919–1940," *American Historical Review*, 79 (June 1974), 710–43; Neville Waites, ed., *Troubled Neighbors* (London: Weidenfeld and Nicolson, 1971); and Wolfers, *Britain and France*.

14. It is important to note that in the early 1920s, when the German army was unable to defend Germany and when some of the offense-oriented French generals of World War I (Foch, Joffre) still wielded influence, the French army did pay some attention to planning for offensive operations. By the late 1920s, however, the last vestiges of an offensive orientation had disappeared from French military thinking. See Doughty, "Evolution," chap. 3.

15. See Stefan T. Possony and Étienne Mantoux, "DuPicq and Foch: The French School," in *Makers*, ed. Earle, 206–33.

16. See Doughty, "Evolution," chap. 5.

17. See Clarke, "Military Technology," chap. 4; and Greene, "Military Leadership," 49–53.

18. DeGaulle's views are presented in his controversial book, *The Army of the Future*.

Also see Harvey, "French Concepts," chap. 5. DeGaulle's command of center stage should not obscure the fact that there were other proponents of the blitzkrieg in the French army. See Challener, *Nation in Arms*, 246–47.

19. See Paul Reynaud, *In the Thick of the Fight, 1930–1945*, trans. James D. Lambert (New York: Simon and Schuster, 1955), chap. 7; and Harvey, "French Concepts," chap. 5.

20. DeGaulle's views on the use of armor were not responsible for the failure of his proposal to win acceptance, although there was undoubtedly massive resistance to them. His proposal was rebuffed because of his advocacy of a professional army with a potent offensive capability. Although he claimed that the proposed force would be an addition to the mass army (see *Army of the Future*, 36), critics maintained that he was attempting to create a Praetorian Guard, which for historical reasons caused great concern among many French politicians. DeGaulle was not very successful in rebutting these charges. Also, many French politicians, especially those on the left, were not enthusiastic about creating a force that could be used for "preventive intervention" (*Army of the Future*, 115). Finally, the vast majority of military leaders joined forces against him because they believed that, since all wars are wars of attrition, it would be essential to have a mass army. Thus there was widespread agreement among military leaders and political leaders of all persuasions that the French should rely on the nation in arms, not on a small professional army. For a discussion of the failure of DeGaulle's proposal, see P. C. F. Bankwitz, *Maxime Weygand and Civil-Military Relations in Modern France* (Cambridge: Harvard University Press, 1967), chap. 4; Challener, *Nation in Arms*, 225–26; Clarke, "Military Technology," 154–57; and Robert A. Doughty, "DeGaulle's Concept of a Mobile, Professional Army: Genesis of French Defeat?" *Parameters*, 4:2 (1974), 23–34.

21. In 1936, the French army issued its *Instruction sur l'emploi tactique des grandes unités*. The new *Instructions*, which outlined basic French doctrine, replaced the 1921 version. The relationship between these two versions is evident from the following passage in the 1936 document: "Without misunderstanding the importance of the progress realized since this epoch [World War I] in the means of combat and transport, the Commission nonetheless estimated that this technical progress would not essentially modify the tactical rules established by our predecessors. Thus, it affirmed that the body of doctrine objectively determined after the victory by our eminent military leaders . . . ought to remain the charter for the tactical employment of our divisional-sized units" (quoted in Clarke, "Military Technology," 184).

22. Quoted in Harvey, "French Concepts," 29.

23. Young, "Preparations for Defeat," 159.

24. Quoted in Clarke, "Military Technology," 184–85.

25. Quoted in Reynaud, *Thick of the Fight*, 246.

26. In his study of the development of the French armored force, Jeffrey Clarke concludes that "technology was used to bolster the existing concepts rather than serving as the basis for something new" (Clarke, "Military Technology," 244). This theme is also clearly reflected in Doughty, "Evolution."

27. "On 1 January 1940, 1 and 2 Armored Divisions were formed; 3 Armored was activated on 16 March 1940 and 4 Armored on 11 April 1940. The latter two were incompletely formed, and lacked sufficient training and material when the Germans attacked" (Greene, "Military Leadership," 69). When the Germans finally struck on 10 May 1940, approximately 30 percent of France's 4,688 tanks were assigned to tank battalions that provided direct support to larger infantry formations (R. H. S. Stolfi,

"Equipment for Victory in France in 1940," *History*, 52 [February 1970], 6, 12). The remaining tanks were assigned to: seven motorized *infantry* divisions; *cavalry* formations (four light mechanized divisions and four light cavalry divisions); and four *armored* divisions (see Stolfi). Less than one-sixth of the French armor was assigned to these four armored divisions (Greene, "Military Leadership," 71), which, as I noted earlier, were not formed until after the war had begun. The Germans, on the other hand, placed virtually all their tanks in their ten armored divisions.

28. See Doughty, "Evolution," 170–71.

29. See Henry Guerlac, "Vauban: The Impact of Science on War," in *Makers*, ed. Earle, 26–48; and Kraehe, "Maginot Line."

30. See Irving M. Gibson [A. Kovacs], "Maginot and Liddell Hart: The Doctrine of Defense," in *Makers*, ed. Earle, 369–70; and Harvey, "French Concepts," 66–68.

31. Harvey, "French Concepts," 66. Also see DeGaulle, *Army of the Future*, 32. Of course, DeGaulle was advocating that France develop the same capability. See DeGaulle, *Army of the Future*, 119; and E. W. Sheppard, "Two Generals, One Doctrine," *Army Quarterly*, 61 (October 1940), 105–18.

32. It should be emphasized that the attaque brusquée is not synonymous with the blitzkrieg strategy. (See the discussion of this matter in Chapter 2, "Employing the Blitzkrieg and Attrition Strategies for Limited Objectives".) As I have noted, in the case of the attaque brusquée, success is predicated on the scoring of a knockout blow before the victim has a chance to establish his defenses. For this reason the French placed great emphasis on rapid mobilization. For the attacker, strategic surprise is the key to success. The blitzkrieg, on the other hand, is a strategy designed to defeat a prepared defense, although the attacker would certainly attempt to achieve surprise when possible. Now consider the specifics of the French case. After 1933, the enhanced capability of the French to protect themselves while mobilizing and the transformation of the German army from a small, professional force to a mass army resulted in a lessening of French concern about an attaque brusquée. In September 1939, once the French had their forces in place, the threat of an attaque brusquée disappeared. The ensuing German blitzkrieg caught the French completely by surprise.

33. See Young, "La Guerre de Longue Durée," 56.

34. For an excellent discussion of the French concept of the nation in arms, see Challener, *Nation in Arms*, chaps. 4–7. Also, see Doughty, "Evolution," chap. 3; and Greene, "Military Leadership," 218–34. The French decision to rely on the nation in arms of course meant that the French military would be a very inflexible instrument. As an investigating commission noted after the war, "to chase three regiments of the Wehrmacht, it would have been necessary to put all the French army on a war footing" (quoted in Challener, *Nation in Arms*, 264).

35. See Young, *Command*, 23–28.

36. See Doughty, "Evolution," chap. 4; Greene, "Military Leadership," 14–28; and Young, "Preparations for Defeat," 156–57.

37. See Brian Bond, *France and Belgium, 1939–1940* (London: Davis-Poynter, 1975). For a discussion of the Maginot Line and its implications, see: Judith M. Hughes, *To the Maginot Line* (Cambridge: Harvard University Press, 1971); Kraehe, "Maginot Line"; and Vivian Rowe, *The Great Wall of France* (London: Putnam, 1959).

38. Quoted in Harvey, "French Concepts," 22.

39. This awareness is apparent throughout Young's *Command* and in his "La Guerre de Longue Durée," 48–50.

40. See Young, *Command*, 28, 34.

41. Gen. Maxime Weygand, "How France Is Defended," *International Affairs*, 18 (July–August 1939), 476.

42. This contradiction is readily apparent in Weygand, "How France Is Defended," 472–73. Also see Greene, "Military Leadership," 28–44, 324–54.

43. DeGaulle, *Army of the Future*, 70. Also see 69–73.

44. Young, *Command*, 201.

45. Although the French were concerned about their lack of a short-term offensive capability, this concern was diminished by the widespread belief that France would be Germany's first victim (Greene, "Military Leadership," 28, 231). In such a case, the key question would be whether the East European allies had an offensive capability.

46. In his diary, Gen. Sir Edmund Ironside nicely expressed the difference between the French and British approaches to war resulting from their different geopolitical circumstances. He writes: "The French have much more definite problems to solve than we have. They love order in their plans. . . . We cannot make hypothetical plans to meet uncertain circumstances. We are arch-improvisers. We hate jumping fences before there is any necessity. Our problems are so vague that we must keep our plans liquid" (*Ironside Diaries*, 51).

47. For a discussion of this matter, see Paul M. Kennedy, *The Rise and Fall of British Naval Mastery* (New York: Scribner's, 1976), chaps. 7–12; and Harold and Margaret Sprout, *Toward a New Order of Sea Power* (Princeton: Princeton University Press, 1943), chaps. 1–3.

48. This is one of the principal arguments in Michael Howard's *The Continental Commitment* (London: Pelican, 1974), 17.

49. See Hillmann, "Comparative Strengths," 398–99, 406–9.

50. Quoted in Howard, *Continental Commitment*, 77.

51. For a detailed discussion of the DRC and its proposals, see N. H. Gibbs, *Grand Strategy*, vol. 1 (London: HMSO, 1976), pt. 2.

52. See F. Coghlan, "Armaments, Economic Policy, and Appeasement: Background to British Foreign Policy, 1931–7," *History*, 57, (June 1972), 205–16; G. C. Peden, *British Rearmament and the Treasury: 1932–1939* (Edinburgh: Scottish Academic Press, 1979); and Robert P. Shay, Jr., *British Rearmament in the Thirties* (Princeton: Princeton University Press, 1977).

53. See Gibbs, *Grand Strategy*, 285–87.

54. CAB 23/90A, minutes of 22 December 1937 cabinet meeting 48(37), hereafter cited as Cab. Mtg. 48(37). See also Gibbs, *Grand Strategy*, 468–71.

55. For an excellent discussion of the impact of this cabinet decision on the army, see Brian Bond, *British Military Policy between the Two World Wars* (New York: Oxford University Press, 1980), chaps. 9–11. Also see Gibbs, *Grand Strategy*, chap. 12.

56. And as we know, it did not do so. See Bond, *British Military Policy*, 144–45, 321–26; and *Ironside Diaries*, chap. 9 and 158–59.

57. Cab. Mtg. 48(37); Gibbs, *Grand Strategy*, 465–83; and *Ironside Diaries*, 46.

58. This is a central conclusion of two of the key volumes in *Britain's Official History of the War*: Gibbs, *Grand Strategy*; and M. M. Postan, *British War Production* (London: HMSO, 1952). The story of army unpreparedness is also outlined in Bond, *British Military Policy*; Brian Bond, ed., *Chief of Staff: The Diaries of Lieutenant-General Sir Henry Pownall*, vol. 1 (London: Leo Cooper, 1972); *Ironside Diaries*; and Ronald Lewin, *Man of Armour: A Study of Lieut.-General Vyvyan Pope and the Development of Armoured Warfare* (London: Leo Cooper, 1976), chaps. 7–10.

59. *Ironside Diaries*, 61; Postan, *War Production*, 57, 70.

60. Bond, *British Military Policy*, 262–65, 270; Gibbs, *Grand Strategy*, 460–68, 474; Postan, *War Production*, 28–33; *Pownall Diaries*, 136, 141, 166; and *Ironside Diaries*, 47, 58.

61. Postan, *War Production*, 6.

62. CAB 53/37, COS 698, Committee of Imperial Defence, Chiefs of Staff Subcommittee, "Military Implications of German Aggression against Czechoslovakia," 28 March 1938.

63. J. R. M. Butler, *Grand Strategy*, vol. 2: *September 1939–June 1941* (London: HMSO, 1957), 28. Also see Bond, *British Military Policy*, 328; and Gibbs, *Grand Strategy*, 525–26. By May 1940, the British had 286 tanks on the Continent. The French had 4,688. Stolfi, "Equipment for Victory," 6, 16.

64. See *Ironside Diaries*, 54.

65. Gibbs, *Grand Strategy*, 524. This is also the central conclusion of Bond's *British Military Policy*.

66. *Ironside Diaries*, 55. Also see pp. 56, 86, 242; and Bond, *British Military Policy*, 180–81. Interestingly, after Gort delivered his talk on the attaque brusquée, he informed the assembled officers "that there was going to be a reduction of 1,500 officers in the establishment of the Army" (*Ironside Diaries*, 55).

67. See Gibbs, *Grand Strategy*, chap. 13.

68. See Postan, *War Production*, chaps. 2–3; and Peden, *British Rearmament*.

69. See Gibbs, *Grand Strategy*, 518; and *Pownall Diaries*, 201.

70. *Ironside Diaries*, 76, 86, 243.

71. Ibid., 133–34.

72. Also, the army leaders of 1939–1940 were victims of a self-fulfilling prophecy that they and their predecessors had helped perpetuate. British opposition to a Continental commitment was predicated on the assumption, unquestioned by the army throughout the 1920s and 1930s, that another European war would be a war of attrition. This was of course one of the principal reasons why the army leadership was always so equivocal about a Continental commitment. Once such a commitment had been accepted, it was natural to think that it would result in a war of attrition, since the conventional wisdom for years had been that World War II would begin where the Great War had left off.

73. See Farrar-Hockley, *Infantry Tactics*, 7–12.

74. The essentials of the British plan for fighting a war against Germany can be found in the following documents: CAB 53/40, COS 754, Committee of Imperial Defence, Chiefs of Staff Subcommittee, "Draft Appreciation of the Situation in the Event of War against Germany in April 1939," July 1938; CAB 53/45, COS 843, Committee of Imperial Defence, Chiefs of Staff Subcommittee, "European Appreciation, 1939–40," 20 February 1939; and CAB 53/49, COS 915, Committee of Imperial Defence, Chiefs of Staff Subcommittee, "Covering Memorandum to the Chiefs of Staff, European Appreciation, 1939–40," 25 May 1939.

75. See Coghlan, "Armaments," 216; and Postan, *War Production*, 76–80.

76. See W. N. Medlicott, *The Economic Blockade*, vol. 1 (London: HMSO, 1952), 1–40.

77. *Pownall Diaries*, 255.

78. Gibbs, *Grand Strategy*, 701–702.

79. *Pownall Diaries*, 197. Furthermore, on 13 April 1939, the British and the French gave guarantees to Greece and Romania.

80. Young, *Command*, 232–33; and Greene, "Military Leadership," 346–48.

[233]

81. See: CAB 53/49, COS 909, Committee of Imperial Defence, Chiefs of Staff Subcommittee, "Staff Conversations with Poland," 18 May 1939; CAB 16/209, Committee of Imperial Defence, Strategical Appreciation Subcommittee, minutes of 13 March 1939 meeting; and Gibbs, *Grand Strategy*, 679–80.

82. CAB 53/11, Committee of Imperial Defence, Chiefs of Staff Subcommittee, minutes of 10 May 1939 meeting.

83. See CAB 53/49, COS 905, Committee of Imperial Defence, Chiefs of Staff Subcommittee, "Memorandum on Anglo-French Action in Support of Poland," 3 June 1939.

84. See Gibbs, *Grand Strategy*, 703–704.

85. See Young, *Command*, chap. 8; and Greene, "Military Leadership," chap. 11.

86. See John Kennedy, *The Business of War* (New York: William Morrow, 1958), 8. The British recognized that any Allied offensive in the immediate aftermath of a German attack on Poland would have involved only French ground forces. See COS 905.

87. WO 193/196, "Minutes of Anglo-French Staff Conversations," thirteenth meeting (3 May 1939).

88. See minutes of 10 May 1939 meeting, Chiefs of Staff Subcommittee (n. 82).

89. CAB 53/49, COS 913, Committee of Imperial Defence, Chiefs of Staff Subcommittee, British military attaché in Paris to DMO and I, 18 May 1939.

90. CAB 53/50, COS 916, Committee of Imperial Defence, Chiefs of Staff Subcommittee, 26 May 1939 memorandum from French delegation to British delegation.

91. CAB 53/49, COS 877, Committee of Imperial Defence, Chiefs of Staff Subcommittee, "Report on Staff Conversations with the French," 13 April 1939; CAB 16/209, Committee of Imperial Defence, Strategical Appreciation Subcommittee, minutes of 17 April 1939 meeting.

92. See *Ironside Diaries*, 78–79. Also see 80, 85; and *Pownall Diaries*, 204–205.

93. See CAB 53/11, Committee of Imperial Defence, Chiefs of Staff Subcommittee, minutes of 1 June 1939 meeting. It should be noted that although the British and the French had not discussed strategy during the interwar period, the British military was maintaining as early as July 1938 that "the initial French strategy would probably be defensive" (COS 754). The British were well aware of the basic assumptions underlying French strategy.

94. COS 905. The chiefs had a draft of this memorandum before them at the 1 June meeting.

95. John Slessor, *The Central Blue* (New York: Praeger, 1957), 229–31. Also see 234, 238.

96. It should also be noted that the British and the French considered the possibility of attacking Germany from the air to support Poland, but they were deterred on this front also. See COS 905; Gibbs, *Grand Strategy*, 669–70; CAB 99/3, minutes of 17 November 1939 meeting of Supreme War Council.

97. COS 843. Also see COS 754; and CAB 53/49, COS 872, Committee of Imperial Defence, Chiefs of Staff Subcommittee, "Report on Military Implications of an Anglo-French Guarantee of Poland and Rumania," April 1939.

98. COS 872.

99. As I noted in Chapter 2 (see "Strategy and Numbers"), when an attacker enjoys overwhelming numerical superiority, he can employ his forces as called for by the attrition strategy and can yet win a quick victory.

100. *Ironside Diaries*, 117.

101. See Williamson Murray, "Munich, 1938: The Military Confrontation," *Journal*

of Strategic Studies, 2 (December 1979), 288–89. The following discussion on the Czecho-slovakian crisis is based largely on this article.

102. COS 698. Also see CAB 23/93, minutes of cabinet meeting 15(38), 22 March 1938.

103. For further elaboration on the change in the military balance between 1938 and 1939 (which favored Germany, not the Allies), see Telford Taylor, *Munich* (Garden City: Doubleday, 1979), 978–1004; and Williamson Murray, "The Change in the European Balance of Power, 1938–1939" (Ph.D. diss., Yale University, 1975).

104. See WO 193/196, "Minutes of Anglo-French Staff Conversations," third meeting (30 March 1939); COS 877; COS 915; Slessor, *Central Blue,* 231; Butler, *Grand Strategy,* 10–11; and Gibbs, *Grand Strategy,* 668.

105. Slessor, *Central Blue,* 231.

106. CAB 53/51, COS 939, Committee of Imperial Defence, Chiefs of Staff Subcommittee, "Report on the Attitude of Italy in War and the Problem of Anglo-French Support to Poland," 18 July 1939. Also see Bond, *British Military Policy,* 312–19.

107. The importance of the Ruhr to the German war effort, coupled with its vulnerability to Allied attack, greatly concerned Hitler. In fact, to gain support for his plan to strike in the West, he argued that it was imperative for Germany to strike the Allies before they captured the Ruhr. See Hitler's "Memorandum and Directives for Conduct of the War in the West," 9 October 1939, a copy of which can be found in *Nazi Conspiracy and Aggression,* vol. 7 (Washington, D.C.: GPO, 1948), 800–14, hereafter cited as *NCA.* The memorandum is hereafter cited as 9 October Memorandum.

108. Murray, "Munich," 291.

109. For an interesting discussion of the Allied decision not to assume the offensive in September 1939, see Jon Kimche, *The Unfought Battle* (New York: Stein and Day, 1968).

110. See Greene, "Military Leadership," 338.

111. CAB 99/3, minutes of 12 September 1939 meeting of Supreme War Council.

112. See WO 193/157, "Strategy: Siegfried Line"; WO 106/1684, "Strategy—Western Europe: Conferences and Discussions with General Gamelin"; and WO 106/1664, "Possible Future Operations, 10 Sept. 39–17 April 40."

113. The "Appreciation of German Possibilities in the Spring 1940 and the Possibilities of a Resumption of the Offensive on Our Side" (which can be found in WO 193/157) was forwarded to Ironside by Gamelin in mid-December 1939 and is hereafter cited as "French Appreciation." It was prepared in response to Ironside to Gamelin, 3 December 1939 (which can be found in WO 106/1664).

114. "French Appreciation." All subsequent statements of French views in this section are from "French Appreciation" unless otherwise noted.

115. It should also be noted that in the "Appreciation," the French emphasized that their view of an offensive "demand[ed] the employment of considerable material in proportion to the numbers engaged."

116. For an indication of this emphasis, see section 4 of the "French Appreciation," which is entitled "Resources Necessary."

117. In addition to the "French Appreciation," see the French study, "Note on the Attack on Fortified Towns," 7 July 1939 (with a 10 September 1939 addition), which is signed by Gamelin. A copy can be found in WO 193/157.

118. In a memorandum written in response to the "French Appreciation," the British argued that "it would be very difficult, if not impossible, to attain surprise because you [will] tip the defender off with your massive preparations." This memorandum,

titled "Answers to Questionnaire," is undated and unsigned. A copy can be found in WO 193/157. The memo is hereafter cited as "British Answers."

119. See also "Note on the Attack on Fortified Towns."

120. *Ironside Diaries*, 174.

121. See "British Answers" and the 12 March 1940 memorandum on the "French Appreciation" that the British army's director of military operations and plans sent to General Ironside. A copy can be found in WO 193/157. The 12 March memo is hereafter cited as "DMO & P Memo."

122. "British Answers." Also see COS 872.

123. For example, on 29 September 1939, Ironside wrote to Gamelin, "I have been considering means of surmounting the obstacle of the Siegfried Line, and I am driven to conclude that the most promising line to pursue is to develop a special tank for the purpose." A copy of this letter can be found in WO 106/1684. Churchill relates that during the months between September 1939 and May 1940, he "gave much thought and compelled much effort to the development of . . . a machine . . . which would cut a groove in the earth sufficiently deep and broad through which assaulting infantry and presently assaulting tanks could advance in comparative safety" (Winston S. Churchill, *The Gathering Storm* [Boston: Houghton Mifflin, 1948], 713). For Ironside's favorable comments on Churchill's idea, see *Ironside Diaries*, 171–72.

124. See *Ironside Diaries*, 243; and Gibbs, *Grand Strategy*, 38.

125. See Churchill's 16 December 1939 memorandum arguing for an offensive against Norway, a copy of which can be found in Churchill, *Gathering*, 544–47.

126. See Medlicott, *The Economic Blockade*, vol. 2, p. 634.

127. See Weygand, "How France Is Defended," 474; Greene, "Military Leadership," 321.

128. See Ironside's summary of French President Daladier's comments on an offensive made at the 19 December 1939 meeting of the Supreme War Council (*Ironside Diaries*, 173).

129. CAB 53/41, COS 764, C. L. N. Newall to the Secretary, Committee of Imperial Defence, 9 September 1938.

130. See n. 105.

131. See especially the discussion in n. 145.

132. See "French Appreciation"; and Gamelin's estimates cited in Greene, "Military Leadership," 150–51.

133. In June 1944, the German army had a total of 307 divisions. *Supplemental Readings for HM 401–2*: Subcourse V (West Point: U.S. Military Academy, Department of History, 1970), 107. A number of these divisions were of course understrength. That would not, however, have been the case had the Germans remained behind the Siegfried Line awaiting an Allied attack. It should also be noted that there were small differences in the size of each nation's divisions.

134. Greene, "Military Leadership," 148.

135. Ibid., 144–50.

136. *Ironside Diaries*, 104.

137. Ibid., 103.

138. Butler, *Grand Strategy*, 32.

139. Winston Churchill, *Their Finest Hour* (Boston: Houghton Mifflin, 1949), 5.

140. Ibid.

141. "DMO & P Memo."

142. The balance of divisions aside, in 1939, the British had 5.7 million males between the ages of twenty and thirty-four, which, when added to France's 4.3 million males in the same category, totals 10 million. Greater Germany (which includes Aus-

tria and the Sudeten territories) had 9.4 million males in the twenty-to-thirty-four age group in 1939. These figures come from Hillmann, "Comparative Strengths," 373. The small Allied advantage did not translate into essential parity on the battlefield because, proportionally, the British raised far fewer divisions than the French and the Germans.

143. Correlli Barnett, *The Swordbearers* (New York: New American Library, 1963), 302.

144. It should also be noted that the American divisions were approximately twice as large as the European divisions.

145. As I have noted, neither the French nor the British ever explained the reasoning behind the assumption that the Allies would be much stronger than Germany in a long war. Indeed, they may have realized that such would not be the case with regard to manpower. In their "Appreciation," for example, the French make it clear that they expected the Allies to be outnumbered by the Germans when the Allied offensive was finally launched. ("Thus the grand total of our requirements amounts to: 130 to 140 divisions, opposed by 150 to 160 German divisions.") Also see *Ironside Diaries*, 174. Evidence indicates that the Allies believed that their real strength vis-à-vis Germany was in the economic sphere, although it was recognized that ground forces would have to deliver the final and decisive blow. See *Pownall Diaries*, 139; and Kennedy, *British Naval Mastery*, chaps. 10–11.

146. CAB 16/209, Committee of Imperial Defence, Strategic Appreciation Subcommittee, minutes of 6 April 1939 meeting.

147. Postan, *War Production*, 224. In late 1941, Churchill reassured Stalin that the British intended to return to the Continent, possibly in the spring of 1942, with a force of eight to ten divisions (Postan, *War Production*, 128). In fairness to the British, it should be noted that, as a result of their defeat on the Continent, they lost the equipment for approximately ten divisions.

148. Ibid., 243.

149. Ibid., 113–14.

150. See ibid., chap. 5, especially the charts on 239, 247.

151. For comparative figures on the French and British navies, see Hillmann, "Comparative Strengths," 394. The French air force was the "cinderella service" of the French military, a position much like that of the army in Britain. See Robert J. Young, "The Strategic Dream: French Air Doctrine in the Inter-War Period, 1919–1939," *Journal of Contemporary History*, 9 (October 1974), 57–76.

152. Young, *Command*, 23.

153. Hillmann, "Comparative Strengths," 431–91.

154. See Medlicott, *The Economic Blockade*, vol. 2, p. 630.

155. See Slessor, *Central Blue*, 238. Despite the fact that Britain devoted a significant amount of its defense monies to the Royal Air Force, it was not capable of outproducing Germany in aircraft in a long war. See Kennedy, *British Naval Mastery*, 309.

156. See Charles Webster and Noble Frankland, *The Strategic Air Offensive against Germany, 1939–1945*, 4 vols. (London: HMSO, 1961). See especially: vol. 1, pp. 299, 313, 473; vol. 2, p. 90. Also see U.S. Strategic Bombing Survey, Overall Economic Effects Division, *The Effects of Strategic Bombing on the German War Economy* (Washington, D. C.: GPO, 31 October 1945), chap. 1.

157. See Kennedy, *British Naval Mastery*, chap. 11; Medlicott, *The Economic Blockade*, vol. 2, chap. 22; and Alan S. Milward, *War, Economy, and Society, 1939–1945* (Los Angeles: University of California Press, 1977), chap. 9.

158. See the sources cited in n. 157.

159. See *The Effects of Strategic Bombing on the German War Economy*.

160. See Young, *Command*, 14; and WO 190/683, "Note on Possible Action by the French against the Western Frontier of Germany," MI3b, 26 September 1938. Appropriately, the "French Appreciation" indicates that the projected Allied offensive would be launched "between the Rhine and the Moselle."

161. This consideration also influenced the Allied decision not to pursue a limited aims strategy (Churchill, *Gathering*, 478).

162. The conversation is recorded in Churchill, *Finest*, 42. Also see *Finest*, 42–51; Churchill, *Gathering*, 473–76; and Slessor, *Central Blue*, 236–37.

163. CAB 99/3, minutes of the 16 May 1940 meeting of the Supreme War Council.

164. Churchill, *Finest*, 43.

165. The Americans and the British, and to a much lesser extent the French, also contributed to Germany's final defeat. It was the Soviets, however, who bore the costly burden of wearing down the powerful German army. At El Alamein, for example, which is widely regarded as one of the British army's great victories of World War II, the British engaged 4 1/2 German divisions. At the same time, the Soviets were facing 190 German divisions on the eastern front (Correlli Barnett, *Britain and Her Army, 1509–1970* [Harmondsworth: Penguin, 1970], 425).

4. The German Decision to Attack in the West, 1939–1940

1. See, for example: André Beaufre, *1940*, trans. Desmond Flowers (London: Cassell, 1967); Marc Bloch, *Strange Defeat*, trans. Gerard Hopkins (Oxford: Oxford University Press, 1949); Bond, *France and Belgium*; Guy Chapman, *Why France Collapsed* (London: Cassell, 1968); Theodore Draper, *The Six Weeks' War* (New York: Book Find Club, 1944); L. F. Ellis, *The War in France and Flanders, 1939–1940* (London: HMSO, 1953); A. Goutard, *The Battle of France, 1940*, trans. A. R. P. Burgess (London: Frederick Muller, 1958); Alistair Horne, *To Lose a Battle* (London: Macmillan, 1969); André Maurois, *Tragedy in France*, trans. Denver Lindley (New York: Harper, 1940); William L. Shirer, *The Collapse of the Third Republic* (New York: Simon and Schuster, 1969); Edward Spears, *Assignment to Catastrophe*, 2 vols. (London: Heinemann, 1954); and John Williams, *The Ides of May* (New York: Knopf, 1968). It should be noted that some of these studies do discuss the German planning process (Ellis, Goutard, Horne) although not at great length.

2. Two excellent studies of the German planning process are Hans-Adolf Jacobsen, "Dunkirk 1940," trans. Edward Fitzgerald, in *Decisive Battles of World War II*, ed. H. A. Jacobsen and J. Rohwer (New York: Putnam, 1965), 29–68; and Telford Taylor, *The March of Conquest* (New York: Simon and Schuster, 1958), chaps. 2, 5. Manstein, *Lost Victories*, chaps. 4 and 5, also provides a detailed discussion of the matter, although it is a personal account by one of the participants in the process.

3. Of the three schools of thought, this first one is the least well defined, although its influence is widespread. In much of the literature dealing with the Battle of France, writers often do not deal with the specifics of the German planning process but instead focus on the question of why the Germans won, letting the reader infer that the Germans attacked for that same reason. Such is clearly the case with the first school of thought. Nobody says that the Germans attacked because they had material superiority. The reader may draw that conclusion, however, upon being told that success was a result of the overpowering military strength of Germany.

4. For example, see J. Benoist-Méchin, *Sixty Days That Shook the West* (London: Jonathan Cape, 1963), 43.

5. See Telford Taylor, *Munich*, xv.

6. Cited in Goutard, *Battle of France*, 14. Since the French before 1940 placed so much emphasis on the need for material superiority, it is hardly surprising that the cause of failure was frequently attributed to the Germans' advantage in material.

7. For an excellent description of the crucial balance of armored forces immediately prior to the May 1940 attack, see Stolfi, "Equipment for Victory." For a more general overview of the balance, see Goutard, *Battle of France*, chap. 2; Westphal, *The German Army in the West*, 69–72; Cooper, *German Army*, 214–15; and Liddell Hart, *History of the Second World War*, chap. 2. Aside from the fact that there was essentially parity between the opposing forces, the level of preparedness in the German army was not high in either September 1939 or May 1940. See Cooper, *German Army*, 159–66, 209–16; and Goutard, *Battle of France*, chap. 1.

8. For a description of the German economy before and during World War II, see: Berenice A. Carroll, *Design for Total War* (The Hague: Mouton, 1968); Hillmann, "Comparative Strengths," 366–507; Burton H. Klein, *Germany's Economic Preparation for War* (Cambridge: Harvard University Press, 1959); T. W. Mason, "Some Origins of the Second World War," *Past and Present*, 29 (December 1964), 67–87; and Alan S. Milward, *The German Economy at War* (London: Athlone, 1965).

9. Despite what we now know about the actual balance, the myth of German superiority has shown remarkable staying power. Churchill's account of the Second World War is an excellent example. See Churchill, *Finest*, 27–43; and Churchill, *Gathering*, 480. For further evidence of this myth, see Reynaud, *Thick of the Fight*, 264–66, 283; Ellis, *France and Flanders*, 333; and Edward W. Fox, *History in Geographic Perspective: The Other France* (New York: Norton, 1971), 155–56.

10. In late March 1940, Gen. Franz Halder, the chief of staff of the German army, estimated that the Germans would have "about 100 Divs" ready for a May offensive, while the Allies would also have "about 100." See the entry for 28 March 1940 in *The Private War Journals of Generaloberst Franz Halder, Chief of the General Staff of the Supreme Command of the German Army (OKH), 14 August 1939 to 24 September 1942*, 8 vols., trans. Arnold Lissance (Nuremberg: Office of the Chief of Counsel for War Crimes of the American Military Government, 1948). Hereafter cited as *HD*. Also see Westphal, *The German Army in the West*, 70.

11. See Alan Alexandroff and Richard Rosecrance, "Deterrence in 1939," *World Politics*, 29 (April 1977), 404–24; Liddell Hart, *History of the Second World War*, 65–66; Liddell Hart, *The German Generals Talk*, chap. 10; and John W. Wheeler-Bennett, *The Nemesis of Power* (New York: St. Martin's, 1954), 496–97.

12. Liddell Hart writes: "The heads of the German army had little faith in the prospects of the offensive, which they had unwillingly launched on Hitler's insistence" (*History of the Second World War*, 65).

13. A. J. P. Taylor, *The Origins of the Second World War* (Greenwich: Fawcett, 1961), 287.

14. See, for example: Manstein, *Lost Victories*; Guderian, *Panzer Leader*; and Walter Warlimont, *Inside Hitler's Headquarters, 1939–1945*, trans. R. H. Barry (London: Weidenfeld and Nicolson, 1964).

15. For an interesting discussion of this phenomenon, see David Irving, *Hitler's War*, vol. 1 (New York: Viking, 1977), xix–xxii.

16. For example, see: Miksche, *Blitzkrieg*; Larry H. Addington, *The Blitzkrieg Era and the German General Staff, 1865–1941* (New Brunswick: Rutgers University Press, 1971); John Strawson, *Hitler as Military Commander* (London: Batsford, 1971); Messenger, *Blitzkrieg*; S. L. A. Marshall, *Blitzkrieg* (New York: William Morrow, 1940); and Beaufre, *1940*.

17. For example, Alan Milward writes: "German *strategic* and *economic* thinking before the war revolved around the concept of the Blitzkrieg" (Milward, *German Economy*, 7; emphasis added). Also see Carroll, *Design for Total War*; Hillmann, "Comparative Strengths," 488–91; and Kimche, *Unfought Battle*, 65–66, 68.

18. For an elaboration of the various viewpoints on this issue, see: William Roger Louis, ed., *The Origins of the Second World War: A. J. P. Taylor and His Critics* (New York: John Wiley, 1972); and Milan Hauner, "Did Hitler Want a World Dominion?" *Journal of Contemporary History*, 13 (1978), 15–32.

19. Although Hitler's decision was officially announced on 27 September, there is evidence that certain key individuals knew of his intentions a few days before the announcement.

20. See *HD*, 10 September 1939 and 17 September 1939, as well as Halder's testimony in *NCA*, Supplement B, 1566–67. It is significant that Halder's principal assistant, Heinrich von Stülpnagel, had just completed (on 24 September) a detailed memorandum arguing "that Germany for years to come would not be in a position to survive a conflict with the Western powers, except for the defense of the Western wall" (see Walter Warlimont's testimony in Nuremberg Military Tribunals, High Command Case, *Official Transcript at Trials of War Criminals*, Law School Library, Harvard University, 6485, hereafter cited as *NMT Transcript*). Also see Manstein, *Lost Victories*, 82–84. Hitler had recently guaranteed the Low Countries that he would respect their neutrality. Therefore it was not unreasonable to assume that an offensive would have to be directed at the Maginot Line (as Stülpnagel supposed), which the German military greatly respected. This assumption was important in discouraging offensive action and in encouraging a defensive posture. See Helmuth Greiner, "The Campaigns in the West and North (MS #C-065d)," in *World War II German Military Studies*, ed. Detwiler, vol. 7, pp. 4–5; and Manstein, *Lost Victories*, 82–83.

21. *Trial of the Major War Criminals before the International Military Tribunal*, vol. 15 (Nuremberg: Allied Control Authority for Germany, 1948), 379–80, hereafter cited as *IMT*. Also see *Excerpts from Jodl's Diary (1811-PS)* (hereafter cited as *Jodl's Diary*), 15 October 1939 and 25 October 1939, a copy of which can be found in Book 15 of Exhibits and Documents for Nuremberg Military Tribunals Case 12. It is important to emphasize that the fact that the Allies declared war against Germany when the Germans invaded Poland did not mean that the Germans had to attack in the West. The generals had no evidence that the Allies were planning military operations, and it was therefore reasonable to assume that the war would remain "phoney" for an indefinite period.

22. See Hitler's comments in his 9 October Memorandum; his 23 November 1939 speech to his military leaders, a copy of which can be found in *Trials of War Criminals before the Nuremberg Military Tribunals*, vol. 10 (Washington, D.C.: GPO, 1951), 823–31 (hereafter cited as *NMT*; the speech is hereafter cited as 23 November Speech); "Directive No. 6 for the Conduct of the War," 9 October 1939, a copy of which can be found in *NMT*, vol. 10, 805–807 (hereafter cited as OKW Directive No. 6); *Jodl's Diary*, 25 October 1939; and Gen. Franz Halder, "Operational Basis for the First Phase of the French Campaign in 1940 (MS #P-151)," *World War II German Military Studies*, ed. Detwiler, vol. 12, pp. 7–8.

23. See Hitler's 9 October Memorandum; and his 23 November Speech. Also see the minutes of Hitler's 23 May 1939 conference with his generals, a copy of which can be found in *NMT*, vol. 10, pp. 671–79; and Hitler's 22 August 1939 speech to his military leaders, a copy of which can be found in *NMT*, vol. 10, pp. 698–703 (hereafter cited as 22 August Speech).

24. It should be noted that there is a school of thought, of which Timothy Mason is the chief proponent, that argues that Hitler had to pursue a policy of continual war because of severe internal political and economic problems.

25. *HD*, 29 September 1939. Also see Greiner, "Campaigns in the West," 4.

26. For a discussion of the Polish campaign, see the sources cited in Chapter 2, n. 132. See especially Cooper, *German Army*, chap. 13.

27. General Brauchitsch (the commander in chief of the army), General Halder (the army chief of staff), and General Bock (the commander of Army Group B) all expressed reservations about the infantry's performance in Poland. See *HD*, 24 September 1939; Manstein, *Lost Victories*, 86; and Barry Leach, *The German General Staff* (New York: Ballantine, 1973), 81. Concerning the German economy and a long war, see nn. 97 and 98 and the attendant text.

28. Greiner, "Campaigns in the West," 5; Halder's testimony in *NMT Transcript*, 1887; *Jodl's Diary*, 25 October 1939; and Manstein, *Lost Victories*, 92.

29. OKW Directive No. 6, pp. 805–806. It should be noted that OKW was not an important organization. In fact, it was little more than Hitler's personal staff. Also see nn. 39, 73.

30. As I shall show, when the military was forced to devise a plan for an offensive, it chose to concentrate German forces in northern Belgium, where they could attend to the task of quickly capturing the Channel coast. It was Hitler who mandated that the main axis of attack be moved further south so that the German army could defeat a greater number of Allied forces. See n. 83 and the attendant text.

31. On the day when OKW Directive No. 6 was issued, Hitler released a lengthy document detailing his views on a war in the West (9 October Memorandum). In it, Hitler argues that "the German war aim *can consist only* in the annihilation of Anglo-French forces" (9 October Memorandum, 807, emphasis added). He qualifies his position (on more than one occasion, however, by noting that "if this [offensive] should not succeed for reasons not clear at the moment, then the secondary objective will be to attempt to secure an area possessing favorable conditions for the successful conduct of a long drawn-out war" (9 October Memorandum, 811). Despite the rhetoric of this memorandum, it is clear from subsequent developments (OKW's Directive No. 6 is only the first piece of evidence) that Hitler, when forced to deal with the harsh realities of war planning, recognized that the "secondary objective" was the only realistic course to pursue. It is also important to note that Hitler recognized that such a limited aims strategy would lead to "a long drawn-out war."

32. Hitler claimed in early October, for example, that "the passing of every further month represents a loss of time unfavorable to the German power of offensive" (9 October Memorandum, 809). Also see Hitler's 23 November Speech and his 22 August Speech.

33. Gen. Wilhelm Keitl, chief of the OKW, writes that Hitler believed one British division was the equivalent of three or four French divisions (*The Memoirs of Field Marshal Keitl*, trans. David Irving [London: William Kimber, 1965], 99). Also see Hitler's 9 October Memorandum; his 23 November Speech; and Greiner, "Campaigns in the West," 15.

34. Directive No. 6, p. 805. It should be noted that Hitler was even willing to risk attacking with unprepared troops to facilitate an immediate strike. He states in his 9 October Memorandum: "Most important is the maximum speed in setting-up the new formations already envisaged, risking the danger that they will not come up to standard of normal first-rate troops" (9 October Memorandum, 813).

35. Directive No. 6, p. 805.

36. For a copy of the plan, see "Aufmarschanweisung 'Gelb' vom 19/10/1939," in *Dokumente zur Vorgeschichte des Westfeldzuges, 1939–1940*, ed. H. A. Jacobsen (Göttingen: Musterschmidt, 1956), 41–45. Also see Manstein, *Lost Victories*, 95–98; Taylor, *Conquest*, 159–60; and Ellis, *France and Flanders*, 335–37.

37. For a succinct but excellent discussion of this matter, see Taylor, *Conquest*, 161. Also see Manstein, *Lost Victories*, 98–99.

38. From "Notes to the War Diary," a copy of which can be found in *NCA*, vol. 4, pp. 370–74.

39. The chain of command ran from Hitler to Brauchitsch and Halder at OKH. Keitl and Jodl wielded little influence with Hitler. In short, OKW was not a weighty force in the planning process. For a detailed discussion of this matter, see Warlimont, *Hitler's Headquarters*.

40. It should be emphasized that these were not formal coalitions of a long-standing nature. On the contrary, the alliances were loose and have relevance only in the context of this case.

41. In general, German military leaders had much respect for both the French and the British armies. For example, see: Gen. Ritter von Leeb's 11 October 1939 Memorandum (p. 868), a copy of which can be found in *NMT*, vol. 10, pp. 865–72 (hereafter cited as Leeb's 11 October Memorandum); Jacobsen, "Dunkirk 1940," 32; Manstein, *Lost Victories*, 102; and Guenther Blumentritt, *Von Rundstedt*, trans. Cuthbert Reavely (London: Odhams, 1959), 65–69.

42. Leeb's 11 October Memorandum, 869. This memorandum, which is filled with references to World War I, reflects the prevailing view among members of this coalition that World War II would be a repeat of World War I.

43. In the mid-1930s Leeb published a series of articles on the nature of modern warfare that were subsequently issued (1938) as a book: Ritter von Leeb, *Defense*, trans. Stefan T. Possony and Daniel Vilfroy (Harrisburg: Military Service, 1943). In this influential book, which starts from the assumption that a future war would look much like the Great War, Leeb argues the case for remaining on the defensive until the enemy exhausts itself by launching futile attacks, thereafter assuming the offensive. Although it would be wrong to claim that Brauchitsch and Halder were disciples of Leeb, they did share his views on the basic nature of warfare and agreed that a defensive posture was desirable.

44. For an excellent discussion of this matter, see Cooper, *German Army*, chap. 10. *Conservative*, as used here to describe the political and military views of these German officers, has a specific meaning that reflects Samuel Huntington's definition of conservatism as a situational ideology (Samuel P. Huntington, "Conservatism as an Ideology," *American Political Science Review*, 51 [June 1957], 455).

45. See: Cooper, *German Army*, chap. 10; Hans von Seeckt, *Thoughts of a Soldier*, trans. Gilbert Waterhouse (London: Ernest Benn, 1930); Hajo Holborn, "Moltke and Schlieffen: The Prussian-German School," in *Makers*, ed. Earle, 172–205; and Robert E. Harkavy, *Preemption and Two-Front Conventional Warfare*, Jerusalem Paper 23 (Jerusalem: Hebrew University, 1977).

46. This is apparent in Leeb's *Defense*.

47. As noted in Chapter 2, large-scale, or classical, maneuver is largely an anachronistic concept on the modern battlefield. Thus the German military believed that attempting to employ a strategy based on maneuver would lead to a war of attrition—as it had in the case of Schlieffen Plan in 1914.

48. Leeb's 11 October Memorandum, 868. Halder of course made essentially the same statement when he observed: "Techniques of Polish campaign no recipe for the West. No good against a well-knit Army" (*HD*, 29 September 1939).

49. See Manstein, *Lost Victories*, 101–102. This belief is also clearly reflected in the various soon-to-be-discussed memorandums that Army Group A forward to OKH.

50. The Germans did not use the term *blitzkrieg* to describe this strategy. For an etymology of the word, see Cooper, *German Army*, 116; and Len Deighton, *Blitzkrieg* (New York: Knopf, 1980), 102–103.

51. Although Guderian advocated using large-scale armored units independently of infantry divisions, he was a strong proponent of integrating elements of infantry and artillery into those large-scale armored units, but only as support for the armored forces.

52. For a compilation of his prewar writings see: Heinz Guderian, *Achtung-Panzer!* (Stuttgart: Union Deutsche Verlagsgesellschaft, 1937); also see Cooper, *German Army*, chap. 11.

53. See Kenneth Macksey, *Guderian* (New York: Stein and Day, 1975), chaps. 3–5; and Guderian, *Panzer Leader*, chap. 2.

54. See Cooper, *Germany Army*, chap. 11; Guderian, *Panzer Leader*, chap. 2; Guderian, "Unification or Coordination"; and Macksey, *Guderian*, chaps. 3–5. Those who maintain that the Germans entered World War II with a clearly defined blitzkrieg strategy in hand often point to Guderian's prewar writings and lectures as evidence of the blueprint. For example, see Miksche, *Blitzkrieg*, 97. Still, Guderian's ideas were not widely accepted.

55. Liddell Hart, *The German Generals Talk*, 63.

56. There is no doubt that Manstein was the actual author of the various proposals forwarded to OKH by Army Group A, while Rundstedt served as the principal spokesman for Manstein's ideas. Guenther Blumentritt, the chief of operations for Army Group A and a devoted admirer of both Manstein and Rundstedt, makes this point clear in *Von Rundstedt*, 59.

57. Manstein recognized this fact. See Manstein, *Lost Victories*, 94–95. It should also be noted that both Guderian and Manstein were outspoken officers who were not on good terms with Halder and Brauchitsch, the two generals they sought to influence with their ideas. See Jacobsen, "Dunkirk 1940," 36–37; and Macksey, *Guderian*, 99.

58. As I shall note shortly, there is evidence that Hitler learned about Army Group A's proposal in December 1939 through an informal channel (see n. 144 and the attendant text), and the evidence indicates that this channel remained open (see n. 146 and the attendant text). Yet it is very difficult to determine exactly how much Army Group A communicated with Hitler throughout the entire period.

59. In his biography of Hitler, Joachim Fest writes that "with some justice he has been called the 'most informed and versatile specialist in military technology of his age'" (*Hitler*, trans. Richard Winston and Clara Winston [New York: Harcourt Brace Jovanovich, 1974], 634). Also see Irving, *Hitler's War*, 93–94; *Memoirs of Keitl*, 108–10; and Schramm, *Hitler*, 103–10.

60. See, for example, the citation from *Mein Kampf* in Cecil, *Hitler's Decision to Invade Russia*, 49. Also see J. F. C. Fuller, *Machine Warfare* (London: Hutchinson, 1943), 14.

61. See Guderian, *Panzer Leader*, 42–44; and Macksey, *Guderian*, 97–103.

62. 9 October Memorandum, 808–10.

63. It should be emphasized that although we know much about Hitler's *Weltanschauung*, we know little about his reasons for taking specific actions. He left behind few records, and even those individuals who were closest to him during the war admitted afterward that they really knew little about the man they served. See comments by Jodl and Ribbentrop in Irving, *Hitler's War*, xii, xxiv. Also see Schramm, *Hitler*, 107. In this regard, it is interesting to note that when Halder became chief of staff of the army, Hitler told him: "My true intentions you will never know. Even

those in my closest circle who feel quite sure they know my intentions, will not know about them" (Halder's testimony in *NMT Transcript*, 1833).

64. I do not deny that in fall 1939 Hitler's views on the employment of armor were closer to Guderian's position than were the views of the generals in the first coalition.

65. See n. 31. In his 23 November Speech, Hitler argued, "Wars are always ended only by the destruction of the opponent" (p. 827).

66. This understanding is apparent throughout the 9 October Memorandum. Also see Hitler's 22 August Speech, 701.

67. See n. 32.

68. 23 November Speech, 829.

69. 23 November Speech, 829. Hitler's 22 August Speech, which was delivered right before the attack on Poland, provides further evidence of the risks that Hitler was willing to take because of overriding political considerations.

70. 9 October Memorandum, 811.

71. Another possible interpretation of Hitler's actions during fall 1939 that bears mentioning starts with the assumption that Hitler had no intention of attacking at that time. Although he certainly wanted to knock France out of the war and to drive the British from the Continent, he recognized that a limited aims strategy was likely to lead to catastrophe. He kept the military in a high state of readiness and constantly threatened to attack for two reasons. First, since he believed that the Allies were planning to move into Belgium and Holland, he wanted the military to be ready to respond to their first move. Second, he wanted to defeat the French decisively, and he recognized that his military leaders would produce a satisfactory plan only if he placed significant pressure on them. According to this explanation, Hitler was actually deterred from attacking in fall 1939 because he feared a war of attrition. This argument, which does not square with the available evidence, is elaborated in Irving, *Hitler's War*, 56; and in *Memoirs of Keitl*, 103–104.

72. Wheeler-Bennett, *Nemesis of Power*, 463. See HD, 29 September 1939 and 30 September 1939.

73. HD, 4 October 1939. Despite the fact that Generals Jodl and Keitl occupied key positions at OKW, they wielded little real influence and thus did not figure prominently in the decision to attack in the West. Hitler chose them because he knew that they would be pliant subordinates who would give him little trouble.

74. HD, 7 October 1939.

75. Ibid.

76. HD, 10 October 1939. Regarding the memorandum, see n. 22.

77. Leeb's 11 October Memorandum, 865.

78. Ibid., 866.

79. HD, 17 October 1939.

80. To register their disapproval of an offensive, the OKH leaders sent the plan in draft form to OKW and then allowed General Keitl, the chief of OKW, to present it to the OKW staff. See Warlimont, *Hitler's Headquarters*, 51.

81. The following discussion of the first OKH plan is based on the sources cited in n. 36.

82. Ellis, *France and Flanders*, 335.

83. *Jodl's Diary*, 25 October 1939.

84. HD, 25 October 1939. Also see Leach, *General Staff*, 83.

85. *Jodl's Diary*, 25 October 1939. It should be emphasized that Bock, who was the commander of the army group that would make the main attack, opposed the plan.

See the testimony in *NMT Transcript* of General von Salmuth, Bock's chief of staff (pp. 3925–27); General Halder (p. 1887); and General Leeb (pp. 2309–10).

86. Taylor, *Conquest*, 50; Leach, *General Staff*, 83.

87. As a consequence of his opposition to an attack in fall 1939, Reichenau's stock with Hitler was badly eroded. See Guderian, *Panzer Leader*, 65.

88. *Memoirs of Keitl*, 100. Even the commanders of the Luftwaffe, the service most sympathetic to Nazism, were opposed to striking in fall 1939. See Wheeler-Bennett, *Nemesis of Power*, 465.

89. *Jodl's Diary*, 27 October 1939. Also see *HD*, 27 October 1939.

90. *HD*, 28 October 1939. Also see *Jodl's Diary*, 26, 27, 28 October 1939.

91. For a copy of the plan, see "Aufmarschanweisung 'Gelb' vom 29/10/1939," in *Dokumente*, ed. Jacobsen, 46–53. Also see Ellis, *France and Flanders*, 336–37; Manstein, *Lost Victories*, 97–98; and Taylor, *Conquest*, 160–61.

92. The disenchantment with such a frontal attack is clearly reflected in the first memorandum (and in the accompanying cover letter) that Army Group A forwarded to OKH. See "Schreiben des Oberbefehlshabers der HGr. A an den Oberbefehlshaber des Heeres vom 31/10/1939" and "Vorschlag zur Kriegführung im Westen vom 31/10/1939," in *Dokumente*, ed. Jacobsen, 119–24 (hereafter cited as Army Group A/First Memorandum).

93. A copy of Leeb's 31 October 1939 memorandum can be found in *NMT*, vol. 10, pp. 872–74. Also see Leeb's testimony in *NMT Transcript*, 2316.

94. Army Group A/First Memorandum; and Manstein, *Lost Victories*, 105–106.

95. *The Von Hassell Diaries* (Garden City: Doubleday, 1947), 87.

96. *HD*, 3 November 1939.

97. *HD*, 4 November 1939.

98. *HD*, 29 September 1939; and Warlimont's testimony in *NMT Transcript*, 6486.

99. *HD*, 5 November 1939 (postwar clarification).

100. After the war, Halder told Allied interrogators, "In order to deter Hitler, Von Brauchitsch deliberately exaggerated what was merely slackness and bad behavior as a result of the prolonged alert, into incipient mutiny reminiscent of 1918" (*HD*, 5 November 1939 [postwar clarification]).

101. See Manstein, *Lost Victories*, 87. In addition, this meeting dealt the growing conspiracy against Hitler a blow. See Leach, *General Staff*, 86–87; and Wheeler-Bennett, *Nemesis of Power*, 470–72.

102. Leach, *General Staff*, 86–87. Halder remarked in his diary after the meeting: "Any sober discussion of these things is impossible with him" (*HD*, 5 November 1939).

103. *NMT*, vol. 10, p. 177.

104. For an example of the tactics used to delay an offensive, see Halder's testimony in *NMT Transcript*, 1887.

105. See Army Group A/First Memorandum.

106. Six of these memorandums are reprinted in Jacobsen, ed., *Dokumente* (see Documents 32/33, 35, 36, 37, 38, 41). For an excellent discussion of these memorandums and Army Group A's efforts to win acceptance of its plan, see Manstein, *Lost Victories*, chap. 5.

107. See, for example, Manstein's discussion of the key meetings on 2–3 November, 21 November, and 22 December (*Lost Victories*, 107–15).

108. See Manstein, *Lost Victories*, 107–15. Also see "Schreiben des Chefs des Generalstabes des Heeres an Gen. Lt. v. Manstein vom 5/12/39," in *Dokumente*, ed. Jacobsen, 57.

109. See Army Group A/First Memorandum.

110. In describing the drawbacks of the existing plan, for example, Rundstedt writes, "the means of attack which could give us superiority, i.e., the *Luftwaffe* and the *Panzerwaffe*, will, for reasons of weather and terrain, be neutralized in part or hampered in the rapidity of their movements" (Army Group A/First Memorandum, 120).

111. Jacobsen, "Dunkirk 1940," 34–35.

112. *Jodl's Diary*, 30 October 1939.

113. For a copy of the actual order assigning the Nineteenth Panzer Corps to Army Group A, see "Fernschreiben des OKH an die Heeresgruppen A und B vom 11/11/1939," in *Dokumente*, ed. Jacobsen, 53–55. It should also be noted that at this time Brauchitsch was just beginning to come under pressure from Manstein and Rundstedt to assign armored forces to Army Group A. So from Brauchitsch's viewpoint, the Nineteenth Panzer Corps's new assignment placated not only Hitler but Manstein and Rundstedt as well.

114. The second memorandum is not included in Jacobsen, ed., *Dokumente*. It is clear from Manstein's *Lost Victories* (p. 108) that it was basically the same as the first memorandum.

115. A copy of OKW Directive No. 8 can be found in *NCA*, vol. 3, pp. 397–99.

116. Manstein, *Lost Victories*, 110.

117. The following account of the meeting is based on Guderian, *Panzer Leader*, 67–68; and Manstein, *Lost Victories*, 109.

118. In *Panzer Leader*, Guderian writes of telling Manstein that, if possible, all of the armored and motorized divisions should be assigned to Army Group A (p. 68).

119. See n. 137.

120. "Absicht der Heeresgruppe für die Führung der Angriffsoperation vom 21/11/1939," in *Dokumente*, ed. Jacobsen, 126 (the translation is mine). This was actually Army Group A's third memorandum.

121. Although it has no direct bearing on the discussion here, Army Group A was also deeply interested in acquiring a third army to help protect its southern flank during the offensive.

122. This intent is clearly reflected in the fourth memorandum, which was forwarded to OKH on 6 December. See the summary of this memorandum in "Denkschrift der Heeresgruppe A über die Durchführung der Operationen im Sinne einer die volle Entscheidung zu Lande suchenden Führung der Westoffensive vom 12/1/1940," in *Dokumente*, ed. Jacobsen, 136. Hereafter cited as "Denkschrift, 12/1/1940."

123. Army Group A continued to lobby for control of the Fourteenth Motorized Corps. See Manstein, *Lost Victories*, 114; and "Vortragsnotiz des Chefs des Generalstabes der HGr. A vom 24/1/1940," in *Dokumente*, ed. Jacobsen, 150–51. Hereafter cited as "Vortragsnotiz, 24/1/1940." It is worth noting that Army Group A never formally requested that the main body of armor be shifted from Army Group B to Army Group A. It is possible that it was assumed that the transfer would occur as a matter of course, once the location of the main attack had been changed.

124. *NCA*, vol. 6, p. 900; *HD*, 27 December 1939.

125. *NCA*, vol. 6, p. 902; *HD*, 10 January 1940.

126. *Jodl's Diary*, 12 January 1940.

127. *NCA*, vol. 6, p. 903.

128. Halder remarked in his diary on 20 January, for example, the "situation compels us to adopt new methods" (*HD*, 20 January 1940).

129. See Manstein, *Lost Victories*, 116–19. For copies of the final two memorandums, see "Denkschrift, 12/1/1940"; and "Vortragsnotiz, 24/1/1940." A copy of OKH's reply to the seventh memorandum can be found in *NMT*, vol. 10, pp. 838–39.

130. Manstein, *Lost Victories*, 118–19; *HD*, 25 January 1940. Also see "Denkschrift, 12/1/1940," which was originally prepared as a talking paper for this conference.

131. Manstein, *Lost Victories*, 119–20.

132. Ellis, *France and Flanders*, 341; *HD*, 7 February 1940; Manstein, *Lost Victories*, 119; Taylor, *Conquest*, 170–71.

133. See "Schreiben der HGr. A an das OKH vom 1/2/1940," in *Dokumente*, ed. Jacobsen, 151–53, hereafter cited as "Schreiben, 1/2/1940."

134. Guderian, *Panzer Leader*, 67; *HD*, 7 February 1940.

135. Manstein, *Lost Victories*, 119.

136. *HD*, 14 February 1940. Also see Guderian, *Panzer Leader*, 69.

137. Commenting on this meeting in his memoirs, Guderian writes, "Now was the time when we needed Manstein!" (*Panzer Leader*, 70).

138. Cited in Ellis, *France and Flanders*, 340.

139. Cited in Taylor, *Conquest*, 171.

140. Ellis, *France and Flanders*, 340. Both Heusinger and Grieffenberg were favorably disposed toward Manstein's proposal. See Horne, *To Lose a Battle; 137*, and Charles B. Burdick, "German Military Planning for the War in the West, 1935–1940" (Ph.D. diss., Stanford University, 1954), 220.

141. For a detailed account of this meeting, see Manstein, *Lost Victories*, 120–22.

142. Manstein, *Lost Victories*, 122.

143. *HD*, 18 February 1940.

144. The subsequent discussion of this meeting is from Burdick, "German Military Planning," 197–98.

145. Concerning the grand strategic decisions that can lead to war, Hitler was certainly audacious. His actions during the late 1930s and his initial decision to strike in the West all involved great risks. In the realm of military strategy, however, he tended to be cautious. Absence of daring was evident during the offensive in May 1940 when he sought to brake the surging armored forces. His caution also was apparent during the German invasion of the Soviet Union in 1941.

146. In late January 1940, Schmundt made another visit to the headquarters of Army Group A and was again briefed on Manstein's plan. He returned to Berlin on 1 February and briefed Hitler (Irving, *Hitler's War*, 87; and Jacobsen, "Dunkirk 1940," 37). In his memoirs, Manstein speculated that his meeting with Hitler on 17 February was the result of Schmundt's intervention (Manstein, *Lost Victories*, 120). Finally, it should be noted that Schmundt was a close friend of Col. Henning von Tresckow, another of Manstein's trusted lieutenants who believed fervently in the Army Group A plan. See Manstein, *Lost Victories*, 68, 120.

147. Liddell Hart, *History of the Second World War*, 40; Jacobsen, "Dunkirk 1940," 37; and Ellis, *France and Flanders*, 341.

148. *HD*, 24 February 1940; and Taylor, *Conquest*, 173. For a copy of the final plan, see "Neufassung der Aufmarschanweisung 'Gelb' vom 24/2/1940," in *Dokumente*, ed. Jacobsen, 64–68. Also see Taylor, *Conquest*, 180–86.

149. Taylor, *Conquest*, 172. Also see Ellis, *France and Flanders*, 344.

150. The Allies made the decision to move into Belgium in mid-November 1939. See Bond, *France and Belgium*, chap. 1. By January 1940 the Germans had knowledge of Allied plans. Guderian, *Panzer Leader*, 73; Halder, "Operational Basis," 14; Blumentritt, *Rundstedt*, 60; Jacobsen, "Dunkirk 1940," 35–37. It should be emphasized that this information played a major role in the decision to opt for Army Group A's plan.

151. See "Schreiben, 1/2/1940."

152. See "Schreiben, 1/2/1940"; and "Schreiben des Ia der HGr. A an General v. Manstein vom 16/2/1940," in *Dokumente*, ed. Jacobsen, 153–55, hereafter cited as "Schreiben, 16/2/1940."

153. Guderian, *Panzer Leader*, 69–70.

154. Taylor, *Conquest*, 173.

155. "Schreiben des Chefs des Generalstabes der HGr. A, Gen. Lt. v. Sodenstern, an den Chef des Generalstabes des Heeres vom 5/3/1940," in *Dokumente*, ed. Jacobsen, 157–61.

156. "Schreiben des Chefs des Generalstabes des Heeres an den Chef des Generalstabes der Heeresgruppe A, Gen. Lt. v. Sodenstern, vom 12/3/1940," in *Dokumente*, ed. Jacobsen, 68–71. Halder also had a telephone conversation with Sodenstern on this matter. Afterward, Halder wrote in his diary, "It seems Army Gp. [A] has caught on to our ideas" (*HD*, 6 March 1940).

157. Guderian, *Panzer Leader*, 70–71.

158. Guderian, summing up the conflict within the German army about the strategy to be employed against the West, writes: "After years of hard struggle, I had succeeded in putting my theories into practice before the other armies had arrived at the same conclusions" (Guderian, *Panzer Leader*, 71–72).

159. *Von Hassell Diaries*, 137.

160. See n. 156.

161. In early February, when the question of how to employ the armor became a controversial issue, Blumentritt wrote a letter to Manstein expressing his doubts about the wisdom of assigning the panzer divisions an independent role (see "Schreiben, 16/2/1940"). It is clear, however, that Blumentritt failed to convince Manstein (see Manstein's notes from his 17 February meeting with Hitler, a copy of which can be found in *Lost Victories*, 121–22. This meeting took place after Blumentritt had written to Manstein), and moreover, once the new plan was finalized, Blumentritt was fully confident that it would lead to a decisive victory.

162. See Guderian, *Panzer Leader*, 75.

163. *HD*, 25 February 1940.

164. Ibid.

165. Quoted in Leach, *General Staff*, 93. Also see Taylor, *Conquest*, 178; and a memorandum that Bock wrote in March 1940, "Beurteilung der Lage der HGr. B nach dem Stande vom 8/3/1940," in *Dokumente*, ed. Jacobsen, 112–18.

166. *HD*, 17 March 1940.

167. Ibid. Also see Greiner, "Campaigns in the West," 37–38.

168. *HD*, 14 April 1940.

169. See n. 140.

170. On 27 March, Leeb met with Hitler to discuss the forthcoming offensive. The positive tone of the meeting is reflected in Hitler's concluding remarks (see *HD*, 27 March 1940).

171. Wheeler-Bennett, *Nemesis of Power*, 496.

172. Warlimont, *Hitler's Headquarters*, 55. Also see Taylor, *Conquest*, 64, 180.

173. The weather during the fall and winter of 1939–40 was particularly harsh and complicated Hitler's efforts to launch an offensive.

174. See Cecil, *Hitler's Decision to Invade Russia*; Rudolf Hofmann, "The Battle for Moscow," in *Decisive Battles*, ed. Jacobsen and Rohwer, 137–78; Barry K. Leach, *German Strategy against Russia, 1939–1941* (Oxford: Clarendon Press, 1973); Albert Seaton, *The Russo-German War* (New York: Praeger, 1970); and Van Creveld, *Supplying War*, chap. 5.

5. Conventional Deterrence and the Arab-Israeli Conflict

1. The literature on the Israeli decision-making process leading to the 1956 war is not extensive. See Michael Brecher, *Decisions in Israel's Foreign Policy* (New Haven: Yale University Press, 1975), 225, n. 1. Brecher's study (see *Decisions*, chap. 6) is certainly the best analysis of the 1956 decision, although little attention is paid to military considerations. One of the principal reasons for this dearth of literature is that only a very small number of individuals were involved in the decision-making process. Since no official documents relating to the decision have been made public, the analyst is forced to rely, for the most part, on a small number of memoirs. Moreover, the principal participant in the decision, David Ben-Gurion, did not reveal his thoughts at the time and even later did not describe them in any detail.

2. For detailed discussions of Israeli military doctrine, see Ben-Horin and Posen, *Israel's Strategic Doctrine*; Michael I. Handel, *Israel's Political-Military Doctrine*, Occasional Paper 30 (Cambridge: Harvard University, Center for International Affairs, 1973); Dan Horowitz, *Israel's Concept of Defensible Borders*, Jerusalem Paper 16 (Jerusalem: Hebrew University, 1975); Luttwak and Horowitz, *Israeli Army*; Zeev Schiff, *A History of the Israeli Army (1870–1974)*, trans. Raphael Rothstein (San Francisco: Straight Arrow, 1974), chap. 12; and Israel Tal, "Israel's Doctrine of National Security: Background and Dynamics," *Jerusalem Quarterly*, 4 (summer 1977), 44–57.

3. Quoted in Horowitz, *Defensible Borders*, 6. Also see Simha Flapan, "The Theory of Interceptive War," review of *Masach Shel Chol [Curtain of Sand]*, by Yigal Allon, *New Outlook: Middle East Monthly*, 3 (April 1960), 42–53. It should be noted that, after the 1967 war, Israel's geographic position improved dramatically; consequently, Israeli decision makers no longer strongly believed that they must deal the first blow in a conflict. This change in attitude was clearly reflected in Israeli behavior immediately before the start of the 1973 war.

4. See Dayan's comments in his *Diary of the Sinai Campaign* (New York: Shocken, 1967), 39. Although the populations of Israel and its Arab enemies are asymmetrical in size, the Arab states are presently not able to put nearly as large a percentage of their population under arms as do the Israelis. See Steven J. Rosen, *Military Geography and the Military Balance in the Arab-Israeli Conflict*, Jerusalem Paper 21 (Jerusalem: Hebrew University, 1977), 45–58.

5. For an interesting discussion of this subject, see Harkavy, *Preemption and Two-Front Conventional Warfare*.

6. See Handel, *Military Doctrine*, chap. 2; and Luttwak and Horowitz, *Israeli Army*, chap. 3.

7. Yadin, as well as a number of other Israelis, did claim to be a staunch proponent of B. H. Liddell Hart's "strategy of the indirect approach." See Yadin's "A Strategical Analysis of Last Year's Battles," in Liddell Hart, *Strategy* (New York: Praeger, 1968), 396–401. The strategy of the indirect approach, however, is such a loosely defined concept that it has no real meaning. See Brian Bond, "Further Reflections on the Indirect Approach," *Journal of the Royal United Services Institute*, 116 (December 1971), 69–70; Bond, *Liddell Hart*, chap. 2; and John Terraine, "History and the 'Indirect Approach,'" *Journal of the Royal United Services Institute*, 116 (June 1971), 44–49. For a discussion of the relationship between Liddell Hart and the Israelis, see Bond, *Liddell Hart*, chap. 9; and Tuvia Ben-Moshe, "Liddell Hart and the Israel Defence Forces—A Reappraisal," *Journal of Contemporary History*, 16 (April 1981), 369–91.

8. See Handel, *Military Doctrine*, chaps. 3 and 4; Luttwak and Horowitz, *Israeli*

Army, chaps. 4 and 5; and Moshe Dayan, *Story of My Life* (London: Sphere, 1976), chap. 12.

9. For a detailed description of the events leading up to the Israeli decision to strike in the Sinai, see Brecher, *Decisions*, chap. 6.

10. Actually, Israeli intelligence knew about "the impending agreement . . . towards the end of August" (Brecher, *Decisions*, 257).

11. Dayan, *Diary*, 12.

12. Ibid.

13. Ibid., 13–15; also see Dayan, *My Life*, 191–92.

14. See Shimon Peres, *David's Sling* (London: Weidenfeld and Nicolson, 1970), chap. 10; and Dayan, *My Life*, 196.

15. As Michael Brecher notes, the "internal political-ideological balance was drastically changed by the resignation of . . . Sharett . . . and his replacement by a devoted Ben Gurionist, Mrs. Meir" (*Decisions*, 232). Also see Michael Brecher, *The Foreign Policy System of Israel* (New Haven: Yale University Press, 1972), 379–91.

16. See Brecher, *Foreign Policy System*, 391–94.

17. Brecher, *Decisions*, 233.

18. Ibid., 233, n. 1.

19. Peres's lack of expertise about purely military matters is reflected in his own account of the 1956 decision. Aside from the fact that the operational aspects of the proposed plan are hardly discussed, he provides evidence that he avoided such matters. First, in May 1956, when the French defense minister asked him how long it would take the IDF to capture Sinai, he responded, *"our army people* estimated that" (*David's Sling*, 186; emphasis added). Second, after returning from France on 25 September 1956, he rode with Ben-Gurion and Dayan from the airport to Jerusalem. He reveals that he did not participate in the discussion that took place during "the first half of the journey," since Ben-Gurion and Dayan were discussing the military aspects of a possible campaign (*David's Sling*, 191).

20. As Michael Handel notes, Peres "acted as Prime Minister Ben Gurion's foreign minister in all policy matters related to France" (Handel, *Military Doctrine*, 81, n. 15). For this reason Golda Meir, the foreign minister in the crucial months before the war, was not a central actor in the process.

21. Dayan, *Diary*, 38.

22. Ibid., 35.

23. Ibid., 39.

24. Ibid., 39. Also see 206.

25. Ibid., 36.

26. Ibid., 39.

27. Ibid., 35. Also see 124–26.

28. Ibid., 35.

29. Ibid.

30. Ibid., 35–36.

31. Ibid., 40. Also see 122.

32. For a discussion of Dayan's views, see: Handel, *Military Doctrine*, 25–27; Luttwak and Horowitz, *Israeli Army*, 118, 126–32, 138–53; and Shabtai Teveth, *Moshe Dayan*, trans. Leah Zinder and David Zinder (Boston: Houghton Mifflin, 1973), 261–64. Although Israel's infantry units employed tracked or mechanized vehicles, the majority of the force was composed of motorized vehicles.

33. See Dayan, *Diary*, 31.

34. Handel, *Military Doctrine*, 26; Teveth, *Dayan*, 263.

35. There were no significant numbers of tanks in the Middle East before the 1956 war; the Tripartite Declaration (1950) had limited the number shipped into the area. Also, armor was scarce among the Egyptian forces in the Sinai, a fact that undoubtedly helps account for Dayan's skeptical attitude toward the tank.

36. Teveth, *Dayan*, 264. Also see Luttwak and Horowitz, *Israeli Army*, 150.

37. Handel maintains that the switch took place "one week prior to the launching of the campaign" (Michael I. Handel, "The Yom Kippur War and the Inevitability of Surprise," *International Studies Quarterly*, 21 [September 1977], 465).

38. See Trevor N. Dupuy, *Elusive Victory* (New York: Harper and Row, 1978), 146–47.

39. Brecher, *Decisions*, 248; Dayan, *My Life*, 215.

40. See, for example, Ben-Gurion's comments on the proposed Israeli-Franco-British plan in Brecher, *Decisions*, 271.

41. See Dayan, *My Life*, 216, 237; Teveth, *Dayan*, 254–55. It should be noted that the contrasting views of Dayan and Ben-Gurion on this matter of diplomatic isolation account in part for Ben-Gurion's abject pessimism during the 1967 crisis (when Israel was isolated) and for Dayan's optimistic assessment of Israel's prospects during that same crisis.

42. Dayan, *Diary*, 68. Dayan appears to have underestimated Israel's need for the trucks from France; in July 1956 Dayan had told Ben-Gurion that Israel could defeat the Egyptians without the arms that France had promised. See Dayan, *My Life*, 194–95. Also see n. 48 and the attendant text.

43. Dayan, *My Life*, 245.

44. Dayan, *Diary*, 20.

45. Ibid., 22.

46. Ibid., 31. Also see n. 49.

47. Ibid., 32.

48. Ibid., 36. These reservations were undoubtedly linked to the lack of reliable Israeli trucks (see n. 42 and the attendant text). It seems reasonable to conclude that Dayan was able to dispel the doubts by referring to the French truck deal, whose importance, as noted above, he apparently underestimated at the time.

49. The French believed that the Israeli operational plan was particularly ambitious (Dayan, *My Life*, 217), although they were confident that the IDF would accomplish the task at hand (Dayan, *My Life*, 214).

50. Dayan, *Diary*, 38–41.

51. See, for example, Dayan, *Diary*, 64–65, 75.

52. For a discussion of events at these meetings and a description of the final plan, see Brecher, *Decisions*, 268–74; and Hugh Thomas, *Suez* (New York: Harper and Row, 1967).

53. Peres, *David's Sling*, 202.

54. Dayan, *Diary*, 61. Also see Dayan, *My Life*, 249.

55. Brecher, *Decisions*, 248.

56. Quoted in ibid., 248.

57. Quoted in ibid., 271–72.

58. See the excerpt from Peres's *Diary* in Brecher, *Decisions*, 254.

59. See Dayan, *My Life*, 241. The fear of engaging in attrition warfare was given expression in Ben-Gurion's 15 October speech before the Knesset, when he expressed his confidence in the IDF's ability to win a decisive victory. See Teveth, *Dayan*, 252.

60. Dayan, *My Life*, 245. As I have noted, there is evidence that a number of the IDF armor advocates assumed that the tanks would engage in "prolonged tank battles

over every locality." It is interesting to consider whether Dayan would have persuaded Ben-Gurion to opt for war had Dayan employed the reported arguments of the armor enthusiasts.

61. Brecher, *Decisions*, 273.

62. See Handel, *Military Doctrine*, 38–44; Luttwak and Horowitz, *Israeli Army*, chap. 6; and Shabtai Teveth, *The Tanks of Tamuz* (New York: Viking, 1969), pt. 2.

63. See David Kimche and Dan Bawly, *The Six-Day War* (New York: Stein and Day, 1968), 137; Luttwak and Horowitz, *Israeli Army*, 221; Nadav Safran, *Israel: The Embattled Ally* (Cambridge: Harvard University Press, Belknap Press, 1978), 408; and Schiff, *History*, 157, 183. There were sharp differences of opinion among political as well as military leaders about the desirability of going to war.

64. This split basically resulted from a personal feud between Ben-Gurion and Eshkol, who had succeeded Ben-Gurion as prime minister in June 1963. Two years later, Ben-Gurion quit Mapai and formed a new party (Rafi). Although Dayan and Peres joined Ben-Gurion, Rafi was not very successful at the polls, and by 1968 the two parties were one again. During the 1967 crisis, this split not only affected military expertise but also had important political ramifications. In short, Eshkol's competence was openly questioned by the Rafi party.

65. The *overall* balance of forces in the 1956 war provided the Egyptians with an acceptable explanation for their defeat on the battlefield. In 1956, unlike 1967, they found it quite easy to rationalize their losses. This rationalization undoubtedly contributed to the Egyptians' bold actions during the crisis preceding the 1967 war. Surely the Israelis were influenced by the same reasoning.

66. Regarding the balance of forces, see Dupuy, *Elusive Victory*, 239–44, 338–39; Luttwak and Horowitz, *Israeli Army*, 214–23; and Schiff, *History*, 169, 180.

67. Concerning the omnipresent pessimism in Israel during the weeks before the 1967 war, see: Randolph S. Churchill and Winston S. Churchill, *The Six Day War* (London: Heinemann, 1971), 52, 59; Abba Eban, *Abba Eban: An Autobiography* (New York: Random House, 1977), 382; Benjamin Geist, "The Six Day War" (Ph.D. diss., Hebrew University, 1974), 303; Kimche and Bawly, *Six-Day War*, 140; Luttwak and Horowitz, *Israeli Army*, 224; and Teveth, *Tanks*, 26.

68. My discussion of events at this meeting and at the following one is based on: Brecher, *Decisions*, 378–80; Dayan, *My Life*, 318–20; Eban, *Eban*, 333–35; Geist, "Six Day War," 188–95; and Yitzhak Rabin, *The Rabin Memoirs* (Boston: Little, Brown, 1979), 78–79.

69. Quoted in Geist, "Six Day War," 190.

70. It should be noted that the Israelis had been attempting to solve the crisis diplomatically since its inception in mid-May. See Brecher, *Decisions*, 361–77; and Geist, "Six Day War," chap. 5.

71. At this meeting and throughout the crisis, Eban was clearly the most forceful advocate of the diplomatic route. Although we might argue that it is natural for a diplomat to favor such a course of action, it seems clear that Rabin's assessment of the military situation, which Rabin personally gave to Eban on 21 May and reiterated at the two meetings on 23 May, added to Eban's conviction that it was imperative to solve the crisis diplomatically. For a discussion of the 21 May meeting and its impact on Eban, see his *Eban*, 333; and Robert Slater, *Rabin of Israel* (London: Robson, 1977), 127. Slater believes that this meeting occurred on 22 May.

72. Rabin, *Memoirs*, 79. Also see Schiff, *History*, 160.

73. Dayan, *My Life*, 322–23.

74. Although the Israelis adopted a number of different plans for dealing with the

Egyptian army, each of these plans called for destruction of the Egyptian air force by surprise. See Geist, "Six Day War," 363–64.

75. See Rabin, *Memoirs*, 75–76. Ben-Gurion contributed greatly to the atmosphere of despair that pervaded Israeli society in the weeks before the 1967 war. See Moshe Carmel's comments in Brecher, *Decisions*, 333. Also see Geist, "Six Day War," 166–67 (especially n. 171), 302–303, 387–88; and my n. 41 above.

76. See Rabin, *Memoirs*, 80–81.

77. Ibid., 81.

78. Ibid.

79. See ibid., 82–83; Ezer Weizman, *On Eagles' Wings* (New York: Berkley, 1979), 202–203; and Slater, *Rabin*, chap. 5.

80. See Weizman, *Eagles' Wings*, 202.

81. See Geist, "Six Day War," 158; and Slater, *Rabin*, 125.

82. See Geist, "Six Day War," 201, n. 43.

83. See ibid., 201, n. 43; and Slater, *Rabin*, 127.

84. See Dayan, *My Life*, 325.

85. See Geist, "Six Day War," 213–15, 363–64.

86. Weizman, *Eagles' Wings*, 204.

87. Ibid., 206.

88. Ibid., 172.

89. See Brecher, *Decisions*, 327.

90. Dayan, *My Life*, 330. Also see Schiff, *History*, 164. The matter of how the different senior commanders within the Southern Command viewed the various operational plans requires some elaboration at this point. Gavish was the commanding officer, and his principal subordinates were Generals Sharon, Tal, and Yoffe. The latter two were not present at the 24 May meeting of the General Staff, when the revised plan was discussed with Eshkol (Geist, "Six Day War," 215). All evidence indicates that Gavish was satisfied with the updated plan. It is clear that Sharon and Tal were the individuals displeased with the limited nature of the existing operational plan (see n. 94). Gavish has said that he did not change his views in favor of pursuing a decisive victory until approximately 1 June (see n. 117 and the associated text). This statement squares with Dayan's account of Gavish's views (see n. 73 and the associated text).

91. Dayan, *My Life*, 330.

92. Rabin, *Memoirs*, 92–93.

93. Ibid., 92.

94. Brecher, *Decisions*, 385; and Geist, "Six Day War," 233–34. It is also important to note that at this meeting with Eshkol, Sharon voiced the opinion that Israel should reject a limited aims strategy and instead should plan to inflict a decisive defeat on the Egyptian army (see Geist, "Six Day War," 233, especially n. 125). Sharon reported that he "was the only speaker on this matter." Although he was present, Gavish apparently did not offer an opinion.

95. Brecher, *Decisions*, 327.

96. This role is apparent in Rabin's *Memoirs* (see pp. 84–92).

97. Brecher, *Decisions*, 385; Geist, "Six Day War," 291; and Michael Brecher with Benjamin Geist, *Decisions in Crisis* (Los Angeles: University of California Press, 1980), 130.

98. It should be noted that the influence of these two advocates of military action was limited. Weizman's opinions were not widely respected by either the political leadership or the military leadership (see Weizman, *Eagles' Wings*, 193–96, 207–209).

For this reason Chaim Bar-Lev was appointed deputy chief of staff in the midst of the crisis. See Geist, "Six Day War," 201 n. 43. Yariv, on the other hand, was highly regarded but was not in the operational chain of command. He was a staff officer whose primary responsibility was the evaluation of enemy capabilities.

99. Quoted in Brecher, *Decisions*, 334.

100. It is important to emphasize, however, that there is no evidence that any individual in a position of responsibility thought that Israel would suffer a defeat on the battlefield.

101. See n. 65.

102. Quoted in Geist, "Six Day War," 182.

103. See Schiff, *History*, 160.

104. See Rabin, *Memoirs*, 84–86.

105. See Brecher, *Decisions*, 417; Eban, *Eban*, 384–92; and Rabin, *Memoirs*, 95.

106. Brecher, *Decisions*, 326–27. Regarding the various steps Israel took to mobilize its reserves, see Geist, "Six Day War," 114–41.

107. Two points are noteworthy. First, there were two candidates for defense minister: Yigal Allon and Dayan. Although Allon was Eshkol's preferred choice, Dayan was the candidate of the more right-wing parties that were outside the government. (These parties were by no means Dayan's only base of support.) By choosing Dayan, Eshkol went a long way toward silencing some of his most ardent foes (see n. 64). Second, Dayan's appointment was one step toward the formation of a national unity government, which certainly worked to end the political squabbling in Israel. See Brecher, *Decisions*, 415–16; and Geist, "Six Day War," 299–359. This discussion indicates that Israeli military officers, aside from their purely professional functions, serve important political purposes. For a discussion of their role, see Dani Zamir, "Generals in Politics," *Jerusalem Quarterly*, 20 (summer 1981), 17–35.

108. Rabin, *Memoirs*, 76.

109. See Dayan, *My Life*, 349.

110. Furthermore, Eshkol's overall credibility had diminished significantly by 1 June. His 28 May speech to the country, explaining the cabinet's decision to continue pursuing the diplomatic route, had a devastating effect on the country (Dayan, *My Life*, 333; Eban, *Eban*, 374–75; Rabin, *Memoirs*, 92) and greatly contributed to the image of Eshkol as a weak leader. This image was partially responsible for the appointment of Dayan as defense minister.

111. Dayan, *My Life*, 349–50. Also see Dayan's discussion of his relationship with Eshkol on 340–41.

112. Churchill and Churchill, *Six Day War*, 72. This relationship is reflected in Rabin, *Memoirs*, 98.

113. Weizman, *Eagles' Wings*, 210. Also see Geist, "Six Day War," 362.

114. See Dayan, *My Life*, 339; Geist, "Six Day War," 360; Teveth, *Dayan*, 329; and Weizman, *Eagles' Wings*, 210–11.

115. Dayan, *My Life*, 339.

116. There is some controversy concerning Eban's position on military action at this point. Dayan maintains, "It was clear from Eban's general remarks that he was not enthusiastic about military action" (Dayan, *My Life*, 340). Eban disputes this view, arguing that Dayan and those urging military action were merely "preaching to the converted" (Eban, *Eban*, 392; also see Geist, "Six Day War," 345).

117. Luttwak and Horowitz, *Israeli Army*, 231–32. As previously noted (see n. 73 and associated text, and nn. 90 and 94), Gavish had supported a limited aims strategy. He maintains that he changed his mind in favor of pursuing a decisive victory

just before his conversation with Rabin. His shift is not surprising, since he had discussed the matter with Dayan (see n. 73 and the associated text) and since two of his own subordinates, Tal and Sharon, advocated pursuing a decisive victory (see n. 94).

118. Rabin, *Memoirs*, 97–98. Also see Teveth's description of how the plan was changed in his *Dayan*, 331–32.

119. Dayan, *My Life*, 341. There was some debate (mainly between Allon and Dayan) as to whether the Israelis should move up to the Canal after defeating the Egyptians. This dispute was tangential to the Israeli decision to adopt a blitzkrieg.

120. See Kimche and Bawly, *Six-Day War*, 155; Rabin, *Memoirs*, 98–99; and Weizman, *Eagles' Wings*, 210.

121. Weizman, *Eagles' Wings*, 210. Also see Alouph Hareven, "Disturbed Hierarchy: Israeli Intelligence in 1954 and 1973," *Jerusalem Quarterly*, 9 (fall 1978), 3–19 (especially p. 19).

122. See sources cited in n. 62.

123. Weizman, *Eagles' Wings*, 210. Also see Churchill and Churchill, *Six Day War*, 72, for a description of Dayan's role at the 4 June cabinet meeting when the air plan was discussed.

124. Dayan, *My Life*, 342.

125. Geist, "Six Day War," 377–78.

126. Dayan, *My Life*, 346.

127. After their experience in the 1956 war, the Israelis were acutely aware of the danger of alienating the United States. Opting to give diplomacy a chance at this early stage of the crisis allowed the Israelis to determine where they stood vis-à-vis the Americans.

128. Technically, if Dayan had been defense minister at the time of the 28 May cabinet meeting, his vote for war would have tipped the balance (10–9) in favor of that course of action. Eshkol, although he was both prime minister and defense minister, cast only one vote.

129. See Eban, *Eban*, 335.

130. Golda Meir, *My Life* (New York: Putnam, 1975), 363–64. Also see Terence Prittie, *Eshkol* (New York: Pitman, 1969), 260.

131. Eban, who was the most influential proponent of reliance on diplomacy, had changed his viewpoint on 1 June. See Eban, *Eban*, 384–92. Also see n. 116.

132. See Brecher, *Decisions*, 333–35. As Brecher notes, Bar-Lev was firmly convinced that the Egyptians had no intention of attacking Israel. His attitude in this respect may help explain why Bar-Lev was not enthusiastic about attacking Egypt.

133. See n. 117.

134. Brecher makes this point very nicely when he writes that the "primary focus of concern [among those advocating the appointment of Dayan to a high government position] was the *management* of Israel's military capability, not the issue of war or peace" (*Decisions*, 328; also see my n. 107).

135. This section is limited to discussion of the Egyptian decision to go to war in October 1973. The Syrian decision will not be examined simply because there is negligible information on the subject available in the West. Even in the Egyptian case, there is relatively little material.

136. Anwar el-Sadat, *Anwar el-Sadat: In Search of Identity* (New York: Harper and Row, 1978), 174. Also see 172–74. For a brief discussion of Egyptian decision making prior to the 1967 war, see n. 204 and the associated text.

137. Mohamed Heikal, *The Road to Ramadan* (New York: Ballantine, 1976), 38.

Heikal, who was the editor of the influential newspaper *Al Ahram*, was a confidant of Nasser and Sadat.

138. Sadat, *Sadat*, 181. Also see 179–80, 184.

139. See Lt. Gen. Saad el Shazly, *The Crossing of the Suez* (San Francisco: American Mideast Research, 1980), 24–25.

140. Mohamed Heikal, *The Sphinx and the Commissar* (New York: Harper and Rów, 1978), 218.

141. Heikal, *Ramadan*, 38–48; Heikal, *Sphinx*, 250–51; Herzog, *War of Atonement*, 13–14, 32–38, 273–76; and Shazly, *Crossing*, chaps. 1–3.

142. For an excellent discussion of the war of attrition and the events leading to it, see Yaacov Bar-Siman-Tov, *The Israeli-Egyptian War of Attrition, 1969–1970* (New York: Columbia University Press, 1980); and Avi Shlaim and Raymond Tanter, "Decision Process, Choice, and Consequences: Israel's Deep-Penetration Bombing in Egypt, 1970," *World Politics*, 30 (July 1978), 483–516.

143. See Edward R. F. Sheehan, "Sadat's War," *New York Times Magazine*, 18 November 1973, pp. 35, 112–30; and Insight Team of the London *Sunday Times*, *The Yom Kippur War* (Garden City: Doubleday, 1974), 46–62.

144. Sadat, *Sadat*, 238.

145. Sadat, *Sadat*, 232; Hassan el Badri, Taha el Magdoub, and Mohammed Dia el Din Zohdy, *The Ramadan War, 1973* (Dunn Loring, Va.: T. N. Dupuy, 1978), 18.

146. Badri et al., *Ramadan*, 15. Throughout this section, Badri's name is used to represent the joint views of the three authors of *The Ramadan War, 1973*.

147. Badri et al., *Ramadan*, 15. Also see Insight Team, *Yom Kippur War*, 60.

148. Badri et al., *Ramadan*, 18. For a more detailed description of the Egyptian plan, see chap. 2 of this same book; Shazly, *Crossing*, chaps. 2–3; and Mohamad el Gamasy, "The Military Strategy of the October 1973 War," in *October 1973 War*, proceedings of an international symposium held on 27–31 October 1975 (Cairo: Ministry of War, 3 October 1976), 31–43. Gamasy was chief of operations prior to and during the 1973 War, while Shazly was the army chief of staff.

149. Badri et al., *Ramadan*, 17–18; Insight Team, *Yom Kippur War*, 88; and Sadat, *Sadat*, 244.

150. Because of the prestige that the Israeli military gained after their resounding victory in the 1967 war, the impact of even a minor Egyptian victory on the battlefield was found to be great. For the Arabs, not losing was the equivalent of winning a monumental victory. See n. 193 and the attendant text.

151. Badri et al., *Ramadan*, 17. Also, see Shazly, *Crossing*, 26–27, 262. Heikal writes of Nasser that in choosing an Egyptian commander for a war, "he wanted a Montgomery and not a Rommel" (Heikal, *Ramadan*, 41).

152. See Herzog, *War of Atonement*, 15; and Insight Team, *Yom Kippur War*, 60, 86.

153. Shazly, *Crossing*, 22–23, 245–246.

154. See, for example, Heikal, *Ramadan*, 219–20. Also see Herzog, *War of Atonement*, 233–34.

155. Badri et al., *Ramadan*, 17–18; Shazly, *Crossing*, chap. 2, pp. 245–46.

156. Badri et al., *Ramadan*, 21; Shazly, *Crossing*, 25–26, 34.

157. Heikal, *Ramadan*, 225.

158. Ibid. Also see Insight Team, *Yom Kippur War*, 221–32.

159. See Herzog, *War of Atonement*, 205–207; Insight Team, *Yom Kippur War*, 289–99; and Shazly, *Crossing*, 243–51. Sadat maintained during the war that "we can lose three tanks for every one Israel loses. . . . But they will reach bottom before we do" (Insight Team, *Yom Kippur War*, 319). Although this statement might have been true,

the 14 October battle demonstrated that, for every IDF tank lost, *far more* than three Egyptian tanks were destroyed.

160. See Heikal, *Ramadan*, 216–25.

161. Badri et al., *Ramadan*, 23. Also see 19; and Dupuy, *Elusive Victory*, 389.

162. Badri et al., *Ramadan*, 23.

163. For example, Heikal writes that the Egyptians were "prepared for 26,000 casualties" in the attack across the Canal (Heikal, *Ramadan*, 33). Herzog maintains that Sadat "estimated that the crossing of the Canal would cost Egypt some 10,000 soldiers killed" (Herzog, *War of Atonement*, 37).

164. Although the Egyptians were willing to accept high casualties, they were chiefly concerned with maintaining the integrity of their army. See Insight Team, *Yom Kippur War*, 222. Thus there were limits to how many casualties the Egyptians could accept. Clearly they too were unprepared for a lengthy war of attrition.

165. See Shlaim and Tanter, "Deep-Penetration Bombing," 499–516.

166. See Heikal, *Ramadan*, 5–6; Gamasy, "Military Strategy," 38; and Shazly, *Crossing*, 34–35, 58–59, 225–26.

167. Badri et al., *Ramadan*, 19.

168. For a full discussion of the implications of ATGMs, see Chapter 7 of this book.

169. Badri et al., *Ramadan*, 21.

170. Insight Team, *Yom Kippur War*, 63–76; and Shazly, *Crossing*, chap. 2.

171. Badri et al., *Ramadan*, 18, 20; Heikal, *Ramadan*, 247; Insight Team, *Yom Kippur War*, 66–67; and Shazly, *Crossing*, 47.

172. Heikal, *Sphinx*, 256–57. Also see Insight Team, *Yom Kippur War*, 224; and Shazly, *Crossing*, chap. 3.

173. See Badri et al., *Ramadan*, chap. 4; Heikal, *Ramadan*, pt. 1; and Shazly, *Crossing*, 202–13.

174. Insight Team, *Yom Kippur War*, 68.

175. Badri et al., *Ramadan*, 16.

176. Sadat, *Sadat*, 234–37.

177. See Shazly, *Crossing*, chap. 4, for a discussion of this matter.

178. Badri et al., *Ramadan*, 29.

179. See Shazly, *Crossing*, 7–9, 53–57. After the war, "Ahmed Ismail [the Egyptian minister of war and the commander of the army] recounted the story that upon viewing the Israeli-built Canal embankments a few weeks prior to the war, a Soviet General commented that 'not even an atom bomb' could eliminate this obstacle" (Galia Golan, *Yom Kippur and After* [Cambridge: Cambridge University Press, 1977], 64). Moshe Dayan was also greatly impressed by the difficulty of crossing the Canal. See Insight Team, *Yom Kippur War*, 139.

180. For a description of the Bar-Lev Line and the Israeli plan for fighting a war in the Sinai, see Herzog, *War of Atonement*, 5–12; and Dupuy, *Elusive Victory*, 394–401. It was largely because the Israelis employed a forward defense that the Egyptians placed such importance on achieving surprise. The Egyptians hoped to accomplish their territorial objectives before the IDF was fully mobilized and could bring reinforcements up to the Bar-Lev Line.

181. Badri et al., *Ramadan*, 29. Also see Gamasy, "Military Strategy," 40.

182. Shazly, *Crossing*, 27. Also see 206, 216.

183. Chaim Bar-Lev, "Surprise and the Yom Kippur War," in *Military Aspects of the Israeli-Arab Conflict*, ed. Louis Williams (Tel Aviv: University Publishing Projects, 1975), 262.

184. Leslie H. Gelb, "Why Did the Mideast Erupt Again? The Experts Offer Some

Theories," *New York Times*, 9 October 1973, p. 17. As Gelb notes, this view enjoyed widespread support in the United States during the war.

185. See, for example, Brown, *Deterrence Failures*, 7–9.

186. It should be stressed that this account only partially explains why the Israelis were surprised in October 1973. Other important reasons fall beyond the scope of this study.

187. Michael Brecher refers to this phenomenon as the "holocaust syndrome." See Brecher, *Decisions*, 333–34.

188. Schiff, *History*, 210. Also see Schiff as quoted in Brecher, *Decisions*, 324.

189. Sraya Shapiro, "Begin's Ismailiya Trip Almost Caused a War," *Jerusalem Post*, 28 September 1978, p. 3.

190. Sharon as quoted in Amos Perlmutter, "The Covenant of War," *Harper's*, 248 (February 1974), 57. This viewpoint is also clearly reflected in Dayan, *My Life*, chap. 40.

191. Certainly there were exceptions to this rule. See Yigal Allon's prescient comment in *The Making of Israel's Army* (London: Sphere, 1971), 101. Also see Tal, "Israel's Doctrine," 49–50.

192. See, for example, Gen. Ariel Sharon's prewar comments in "Israel's Combat Arms," *Armed Forces Journal International*, 111 (October 1973), 70. Also see Safran, *Embattled*, 327; and Avi Shlaim, "Failures in National Intelligence Estimates: The Case of the Yom Kippur War," *World Politics*, 28 (April 1976), 362.

193. Badri et al., *Ramadan*, 19. Also see 17. This is a constant theme in Egyptian writings on the 1973 conflict, as is clearly reflected by the comments of Egyptian participants at the International Symposium referred to in n. 148. Also see n. 150.

194. Dayan, *Diary*, 124; Herzog, *War of Atonement*, 273.

195. Dayan, *Diary*, 126.

196. See Weizman, *Eagles' Wings*, 280.

197. As quoted in Avigdor Haselkorn, *Israeli Intelligence Performance in the Yom Kippur War*, Hudson Institute Discussion Paper 2033 (Croton, N.Y.: Hudson Institute, 17 July 1974), 7.

198. See William B. Quandt, *Decade of Decisions* (Los Angeles: University of California Press, 1977), 168–69. Also see Heikal, *Ramadan*, 8.

199. Quandt, *Decade*, 176.

200. Heikal, *Sphinx*, 187.

201. Ibid., 256.

202. Sheehan, "Sadat's War," 115. The Jordanians were also skeptical about Egypt's chances for success. See Insight Team, *Yom Kippur War*, 86.

203. It should be emphasized that the Egyptians came very close to accomplishing their objective. If they had not left a large gap between their two armies, or even if they had moved quickly to close the gap once the IDF had moved into it, the Israelis very probably would not have been able to dislodge Egyptians from their position on the Canal's east bank.

204. This account of Egyptian decision making prior to the 1967 war is based on Geist, "Six Day War," 101–102, 125–26, 163–65, 176–80, 202–203, 247–48, 292–95, 599–600; Sadat, *Sadat*, 172–74; and Janice G. Stein and Raymond Tanter, *Rational Decision-Making* (Columbus: Ohio State University Press, 1980), 136, 229, 328–29.

205. In addition, the 1973 offensive was carefully planned, while the 1967 strategy was improvised in the weeks before the start of the conflict.

206. This discussion of the Egyptian decision to resort to the war of attrition is based on Bar-Siman-Tov, *War of Attrition*, chap. 3.

207. Regarding the various Egyptian-Israeli conflicts examined here, it is interesting to note the extent to which Egyptian initiatives have shaped events. Except for 1956, and even here the issue is debatable, the Israelis have acted in response to specific Egyptian actions. This pattern is of course manifested in Sadat's visit to Jerusalem (1977).

208. For a discussion of this matter, see Dayan, *My Life*, chap. 28.

6. *The Prospects for Conventional Deterrence in Central Europe*

1. See Chapter 1, nn. 1 and 2 and the attendant text.

2. See, for example, Savkin, *Basic Principles*; Sidorenko, *The Offensive*; and Sokolovskiy, *Soviet Military Strategy*. Concerning the organization of Soviet ground forces, see Donnelly, "The Soviet Ground Forces"; and John Hemsley, "The Soviet Ground Forces," in *Soviet Military Power and Performance*, ed. John Erickson and E. J. Feuchtwanger (Hamden: Archon, 1979), 66–68.

3. Aside from the obvious and important reason that the Soviets do not want to suffer the tremendous costs associated with a lengthy conventional war, there are a number of other reasons why the Soviets would want to avoid such a conflict. First, in a war of attrition, when manpower and economic strength are the key indicators of success, NATO would have the upper hand. Second, the Soviet army does not have the necessary configuration for a long war (see the sources cited in n. 2). Although the Soviets could remedy this problem, the fact remains that they have not done so. Third, because of the Sino-Soviet split, the Soviets must consider the possibility of a war on two fronts. Even if there was no imminent threat of war with China, a war of attrition in the West would threaten to weaken the Soviets to such an extent that they might consider themselves vulnerable to a Chinese attack. Fourth, there is the real threat of unrest in Eastern Europe should the Pact find itself engaged in a bloody war. (See A. Ross Johnson, Robert W. Dean, and Alexander Alexiev, "The Armies of the Warsaw Pact Northern Tier," *Survival*, 23 [July-August 1981], 174–82.) Finally, there is the danger that nuclear weapons will be used if the Soviets do not win a quick and decisive victory. Also see n. 66 of this chapter.

4. This study does not consider the impact of air forces on the balance. Although it is possible that NATO's airpower will not have the decisive influence on the land battle that many expect, it is clear that the air balance, when qualitative and quantitative factors are considered, does not favor the Pact. See Carnegie Panel on U.S. Security and the Future of Arms Control, *Challenges for U.S. National Security, Assessing the Balance: Defense Spending and Conventional Forces*, Preliminary Report, pt. 2 (Washington D.C.: Carnegie Endowment for International Peace, 1981), 69–73.

5. The two most prominent discussions of this scenario are Gen. Robert Close, *Europe without Defense?* (New York: Pergamon, 1979); and U.S. Congress, Senate, Armed Services Committee, *NATO and the New Soviet Threat*, report by Sens. Sam Nunn and Dewey F. Bartlett, 95th Cong., 1st sess. (Washington, D.C.: GPO, 24 January 1977), hereafter cited as *Nunn-Bartlett Report*. For the best critique of this scenario, see Les Aspin, "A Surprise Attack on NATO: Refocusing the Debate," a copy of which can be found in *Congressional Record*, 7 February 1977, pp. H911–14.

6. It should be emphasized that, given NATO's intelligence-gathering capabilities, the Pact would not be able to mobilize its forces in any significant way without being detected, so that surprise would be impossible. See Adm. Bobby Inman, deputy director of Central Intelligence, speech delivered before the ninety-sixth annual con-

vention of the American Newspaper Publishers Association, San Francisco, 27 April 1982. Therefore, the notion of "an immense blitzkrieg preceded by little warning" (*Nunn-Bartlett Report*, 16) or a "gigantic operation [that] would have the advantage of complete surprise" (Robert Close, "The Feasibility of a Surprise Attack against Western Europe," typescript [Rome: NATO Defence College, 24 February 1975]), is unrealistic. A massive surprise attack is a contradiction in terms. For a very good discussion of the difficulties the Soviets would have achieving surprise against NATO, see Peter Vigor, "Doubts and Difficulties Confronting a Would-Be Soviet Attacker," *Journal of the Royal United Services Institute*, 125 (June 1980), 32–38.

7. With an attack from a standing start, the Soviets would not be able to employ all of the Pact's fifty-seven and one-third standing divisions. Undoubtedly they would rely on the nineteen Soviet divisions stationed in East Germany and the five Soviet divisions stationed in Czechoslovakia. They would probably not, however, upgrade these divisions significantly prior to an attack for fear that such an action would alert NATO. Given that non-Soviet divisions in the Pact are three-quarters manned or less and that their awareness of a forthcoming offensive might result in a security breach, these forces would most likely not be used for a surprise attack. The Pact would then have twenty-four Soviet divisions, which would be striking against NATO's twenty-eight divisions. The 24:28 ratio would shrink even further if it was translated into either armored division equivalents or divisional manpower. Although NATO's forces would not be in their forward positions in this scenario, the Pact would still have to defeat them to gain a decisive victory. Such an outcome is hardly likely, given the balance of forces in this case and the fact that the Pact would not overrun NATO's forces at the outset of the conflict. Instead, a majority of NATO's forces would be located behind their forward defensive positions, where they would have ample time to identify the Pact's main thrusts. A number of analysts note that an attack on such short warning would invariably result in a limited victory. See, for example, Aspin, "A Surprise Attack on NATO," H912–13; Alain C. Enthoven, "U.S. Forces in Europe: How Many? Doing What?" *Foreign Affairs*, 53 (April 1975), 517–18; and Gen. James H. Polk, "The North German Plain Attack Scenario: Threat or Illusion?" *Strategic Review*, 8 (summer 1980), 60–66.

8. For an excellent discussion of this matter, see Richard K. Betts, "Surprise Attack: NATO's Political Vulnerability," *International Security*, 5 (spring 1981), 117–49. Also see his "Hedging against Surprise Attack," *Survival*, 23 (July-August 1981), 146–56; and the letter from Jeremy J. Stone to Gen. Robert Close, found in the latter's *Europe without Defense?* 251.

9. These figures come from Robert L. Fischer, *Defending the Central Front: The Balance of Forces*, Adelphi Paper 127 (London: International Institute for Strategic Studies, 1976), 8. Fischer's calculations are based on the assumption that the Pact has fifty-eight and one-third divisions in Central Europe. Actually, the Soviets recently removed a division from East Germany, so fifty-seven and one-third divisions remain. Since the Soviets have increased the size of these divisions somewhat, and since my argument does not rest on precise calculations (see n. 20), the minor discrepancy poses no problems. Regarding the balance of divisions on the central front, also see James Blaker and Andrew Hamilton, *Assessing the NATO/Warsaw Pact Military Balance* (Washington, D.C.: Congressional Budget Office, December 1977); and *The Military Balance, 1980–1981* (London: International Institute for Strategic Studies, 1980). Although the Fischer and Blaker/Hamilton studies are somewhat dated, no shifts in the force levels have occurred on either side that would alter the figures in any significant way. It should be noted that, throughout this article, French forces located in Ger-

many are counted in the NATO totals (see n. 14). Regarding this assumption, see *1979 German White Paper*, 118.

10. The available data base on the conventional balance is relatively primitive. Certainly, in a number of simple assessments, numbers of tanks or numbers of divisions are counted. Very few comprehensive studies attempt to examine the balance of forces in a detailed manner, however, especially with regard to weaponry. There is an acute need for studies that attempt to judge the balance overall, following consideration of all the weapon systems on each side and all of the various indexes by which their effectiveness is measured.

11. See Fischer, *Defending the Central Front*, 10–15.

12. This increase has been apparent in the annual *Military Balance*. Also see Robert Shishko, *The European Conventional Balance: A Primer*, P-6707 (Santa Monica: Rand, 24 November 1981), 18.

13. Quoted in Shishko, *Balance*, 18.

14. It should be noted that if the entire French army were counted, instead of just the French forces stationed in West Germany, NATO forces *would* outnumber Pact forces. See Blaker and Hamilton, *Assessing the Balance*, 11.

15. These figures are from Shishko, *Balance*, 18.

16. For further discussion of the concept of armored division equivalents, see Blaker and Hamilton, *Assessing the Balance*; and U.S. Army, Concepts Analysis Agency, *Weapon Effectiveness Indices/Weighted Unit Values (WEI/WUV)*, Study Report CAA-SR-73-18 (Bethesda, April 1974).

17. Regarding the balance of armored division equivalents, see Pat Hillier, *Strengthening NATO: POMCUS and Other Approaches* (Washington, D.C.: Congressional Budget Office, February 1979), 53–57; and Pat Hillier and Nora Slatkin, *U.S. Ground Forces: Design and Cost Alternatives for NATO and Non-NATO Contingencies* (Washington, D.C.: Congressional Budget Office, December 1980), 23–24. We should note that this figure was calculated on the basis of fifty-eight and one-third Pact divisions rather than fifty-seven and one-third divisions (see n. 9). Also, it is not possible to ascertain whether NATO and Pact nondivisional assets have been incorporated into this 1.2:1 ratio. If not, the ratio would shift further in NATO's favor when they were added to the balance.

18. See Fischer, *Defending the Central Front*, 20–25; and Hillier, *Strengthening NATO*, 53–57. Also see Hillier's more recent study (*U.S. Ground Forces*), in which he makes the highly questionable assumption that the Soviets will have 120 divisions in Central Europe thirty days after mobilization starts. Even so, the overall ratio of armored division equivalents never exceeds 2:1 (see p. 24 of his study). In fact, at its peak, the ratio for the 120-division figure is 1.7:1.

19. For a discussion of this matter, see "Strategy and Numbers" in Chapter 2.

20. This discussion of the importance of strategy highlights the key point that my argument does not depend on precise calculations about the balance of forces. In other words, whether or not the balance of armored division equivalents is 1.2:1 or 1.3:1 is not, in and of itself, of great consequence. There is no doubt, of course, as I have just noted, that a balance of 1.2:1 differs from one of 1.8:1. See the discussion in nn. 32 and 60.

21. A corps normally controls two to three divisions as well as a number of nondivisional assets. In NATO, corps comprise forces from only one nation.

22. For a discussion of the views of the maneuver advocates, see Mearsheimer, "Maneuver, Mobile Defense, and the NATO Central Front."

23. See John Despres, Lilita I. Dzirkals, and Barton Whaley, *Timely Lessons of History:*

The Manchurian Model for Soviet Strategy, R-1825-NA (Santa Monica: Rand, July 1976); Lilita I. Dzirkals, *"Lightning War" in Manchuria: Soviet Military Analysis of the 1945 Far East Campaign*, P-5589 (Santa Monica: Rand, January 1976); and Peter Vigor and Christopher Donnelly, "The Manchurian Campaign and Its Relevance to Modern Strategy," *Comparative Strategy*, 2:2 (1980), 159–78.

24. For a good description of Soviet strategy on the eastern front, see Manstein, "Development of the Red Army"; and Ziemke, *Stalingrad to Berlin*.

25. See Christopher N. Donnelly's very important article "Tactical Problems Facing the Soviet Army: Recent Debates in the Soviet Military Press," *International Defense Review*, 11:9 (1978), 1405–12. This article challenges the widely held belief that the Soviets have a well-designed strategy for defeating NATO (see the sources cited in n. 80 for evidence of this belief). Also see A. A. Grechko, *The Armed Forces of the Soviet Union*, trans. Yuri Sviridov (Moscow: Progress, 1977), 160; Phillip A. Karber, "The Soviet Anti-Tank Debate," *Survival*, 18 (May-June 1976), 105–11; V. Kulikov, "Soviet Military Science Today," *Strategic Review*, 5 (winter 1977), 127–34; and Vigor and Donnelly, "The Manchurian Campaign."

26. *FM 100-5*, p. 1-1.

27. John Erickson, "Soviet Breakthrough Operations: Resources and Restraints," *Journal of the Royal United Service Institute*, 121 (September 1976), 75. Also see the scenario described by John Hackett et al., *The Third World War: A Future History* (London: Sidgwick and Jackson, 1978), 127.

28. It should be emphasized that in light of the balance of standing forces in Central Europe (1.2:1 in terms of armored division equivalents) and the fact that NATO has the capability to match the Pact as it brings in reinforcements, this 2:1 force advantage is a conservative figure. Unless otherwise specified, the unit of measure in all subsequent discussion of force ratios is armored division equivalents.

29. The Soviets emphasize the importance of achieving overwhelming superiority on the main axes of advance in a conventional war. See Savkin, *Basic Principles*, 119–52, 201–29; and Sidorenko, *The Offensive*, chap. 1. Following the lessons of World War II, the Soviets estimate that "a decisive superiority . . . [is] 3–5 times for infantry, 6–8 times for artillery, 3-4 times for tanks and self-propelled artillery, and 5–10 times for aircraft" (Sidorenko, *The Offensive*, 81–82). These ratios are consistent with the American army's view on the matter. See *FM 100-5*, p. 3–4. For further discussion of this matter, see Chapter 2, n. 48 and the attendant text.

30. This hypothetical model is based on the important assumption that the Soviets can place only one main axis in each corps sector. As will become evident in the subsequent discussion, the terrain features along the inter-German border force the attacker to think in terms of a single axis per corps sector. Moreover, in light of the length of the various NATO corps sectors and the length of front that the Soviets allot their attacking divisions and armies, it is most likely that the Soviets would locate only one axis in each corps sector. For a discussion of Soviet attack frontages, see Donnelly, "The Soviet Ground Forces," 166–70; John Erickson, "Soviet Theatre-Warfare Capability: Doctrines, Deployments, and Capabilities," in *The Future of Soviet Military Power*, ed. Lawrence L. Whetten (New York: Crane, Russak, 1976), 148; and n. 57 and the attendant text of this chapter.

31. The claim is frequently made that the Soviets will monitor progress along the various axes and will move second-echelon armies (those forces moving up from the western Soviet Union) onto the axes where they are making the most progress. This maneuver is hardly conducive to effecting a blitzkrieg. First, NATO will also be moving its reinforcements onto those same axes, since the Pact is threatening to break

through there. Moreover, it takes time to move second-echelon forces into an attacking position, time during which NATO will make important adjustments. A blitzkrieg, by effecting a rapid breakthrough and then immediately exploiting it, seeks to deny the defender the time to make such adjustments. Finally, the divisions in the Pact's second-echelon armies will not be the Pact's most capable divisions. The twenty-six divisions in Central Europe, and specifically the nineteen Soviet divisions in East Germany, are the best divisions in the Pact. They will have to make the key breakthroughs and conduct the deep strategic penetrations. The second-echelon armies may be of crucial importance in a war of attrition, but they will not play a major role in a blitzkrieg.

32. It is assumed in this case that, even if the Pact has only a small overall force advantage, it can still establish a significant superiority on at least one axis. NATO must then shift its forces so as to reestablish the overall balance at the points of main attack before the Pact is able to effect a deep strategic penetration. It is widely accepted that the attacking forces need more than a 3:1 advantage at the points of main attack (see n. 29 and the attendant text). If we bear in mind that the overall balance will be significantly less than 3:1, we see that NATO will be in excellent shape if it has the capability to stop the initial onslaughts and then to shift NATO forces to threatened points. Some analysts argue that, if the overall balance of forces is greater than 1.5:1, NATO's chances of accomplishing this task will be slim. See Hillier, *Strengthening NATO*; Hillier and Slatkin, *U.S. Ground Forces*, chap. 2; and U.S. Department of Defense, *Fiscal Year 1976* and *197T Posture Statement*, p. III-15. See also the discussion of this matter in n. 60.

33. This axis could be shifted somewhat by moving the axis of advance 50 kilometers to the west of Hof, toward the city of Coburg. Therefore we might argue that there are actually two potential axes of advance in the VII American Corps Sector.

34. Furthermore, given the sophisticated intelligence-gathering devices in the service of NATO, it should be possible to locate the Pact's main forces as they move to concentrate for the attack (see n. 6). Certainly NATO should know where to look for Soviet troop concentrations.

35. We should note, however, that the Göttingen Corridor covers only the eastern half of West Germany. (It is approximately 100 kilometers in length.) To the west of Paderborn, the terrain is open and is generally well suited for armored warfare.

36. In terms of the quality of the fighting forces, NATO military leaders generally recognize that the German army is the best in Europe, not excluding the Soviets. Regarding equipment, the German and American armies are the best equipped in NATO.

37. This equipment for U.S. forces is commonly referred to as POMCUS (*prepositioned material configured to unit sets*). In a crisis, the United States will fly the designated units (only the troops) to Europe, where the necessary equipment will be waiting for them. POMCUS solves the difficult problem of how rapidly to transport a unit's equipment across the Atlantic. A POMCUS division is expected to be ready to fight ten days after mobilization. For a discussion of POMCUS, see Hillier, *Strengthening NATO*.

38. The Germans are in the process of significantly upgrading the fighting capability of the Territorial Army. The core of this force is six armored infantry brigades, although numerous other units (including six more armored infantry brigades) are also being upgraded. See *1979 German White Paper*, 154–56.

39. For example, see Close, *Europe without Defense?* 172; John M. Collins, *U.S.-Soviet Military Balance* (New York: McGraw-Hill, 1980), 312–14; Hackett et al., *Third World*

War, 101–102; and Richard D. Lawrence and Jeffrey Record, *U.S. Force Structure in NATO* (Washington, D.C.: Brookings Institution, 1974), 28. For an excellent discussion of this matter that directly challenges this view, see Polk, "The North German Plain Attack Scenario."

40. The corps will comprise three divisions. It is important to note that only two brigades will actually be stationed in Europe. These two brigades will serve as forward elements for two of the divisions, the remainder of which will be flown in from the United States. All of the third division will be stationed in the United States. The POMCUS (see n. 37) for one of these three divisions is in place. The POMCUS for the remaining two is presently being deployed (see *Fiscal Year 1983 Posture Statement*, III-96–97). The presence of these three POMCUS divisions in NORTHAG, plus the two POMCUS divisions in CENTAG, shows the importance for NATO of immediate mobilization in a crisis.

41. Polk, "The North German Plain Attack Scenario," 61. It is somewhat difficult to reach a precise agreement on these distances because they may correspond to the actual contour of the inter-German border, to the straight-line distance of the corps sector front, or to some combination of the two.

42. I shall discuss force-to-space ratios later in greater detail. It is generally agreed that a brigade can hold a front of seven to fifteen kilometers (see n. 51 and the attendant text). Since the Belgians have four brigades in their corps sector (a good portion of which is covered by the Harz Mountains), they should be able to hold thirty-five kilometers of front long enough for NATO to bring in reinforcements.

43. See Paul Bracken, "Urban Sprawl and NATO Defence," *Survival*, 18 (November-December 1976), 256; and *FM 100-5*, p. 14-17. The Soviets are fully cognizant of the difficulties of conducting offensive operations in urban areas. See C. N. Donnelly, "Soviet Techniques for Combat in Built Up Areas," *International Defense Review*, 10:2 (1977), 238–42. For a general discussion of the terrain in NORTHAG, see Polk, "The North German Plain Attack Scenario," 61–62.

44. There are the equivalent of seven brigades in the BAOR. Assuming that a brigade can cover a front of seven to fifteen kilometers (see n. 51 and the attendant text), the BAOR should be able to hold its front long enough for NATO to bring in reinforcements.

45. Furthermore, those thirteen brigades are 10 percent "over strength" (Daniel Schorr, "The Red Threat and NATO Today," *Norfolk Virginian-Pilot*, 2 October 1978, p. 19). Also see Polk, "The North German Plain Attack Scenario," 61.

46. The German forces are divided among three corps sectors and Schleswig-Holstein. None of these sectors is adjacent to any of the others, which means that the Germans, by bumping forces up or down the line, can move German brigades into every non-German corps sector on the front. When an attacking force executes a blitzkrieg, the attacker's flanks are usually vulnerable. The Soviets would have to keep in mind that if they penetrate into the rear of a non-German corps, the Germans will undoubtedly drive into their exposed flanks, attempting to sever the penetrating forces from their base.

47. Furthermore, German units from CENTAG can be moved to NORTHAG. See Ulrich de Maizière, *Rational Deployment of Forces on the Central Front* (London: Western European Union, 2 April 1975), 40. There are also the forces in the German Territorial Army (see n. 38), a portion of which will undoubtedly be assigned to NORTHAG in a conflict.

48. See Bracken, "Urban Sprawl and NATO Defence," 256; and *FM 100-5*, p. 14-17.

49. For a discussion of the concept of force-to-space ratios, see Chapter 2, nn. 85 and 99 and the attendant texts.

50. See Chapter 2, n. 101 and the attendant text for a discussion of this concept.

51. It is difficult to provide an exact figure for the optimum number of kilometers that a brigade can hold. A force-to-space ratio of this sort varies with the size and quality of the forces on each side as well as with the nature of the terrain. If we bear in mind this qualification, it is generally estimated that a brigade can hold seven to fifteen kilometers of front. I suggest these figures on the basis of discussions with American, German, and Israeli military officers and on the basis of the following sources: J. R. Angolia and Donald B. Vought, "The United States Army," in *The U.S. War Machine*, ed. Ray Bonds (New York: Crown, 1978), 74; Hillier and Slatkin, *U.S. Ground Forces*, 25; Liddell Hart, *Deterrent or Defense*, chap. 10; Hans-Joachim Löser, "Vorneverteidigung der Bundesrepublik Deutschland?" *Österreichische Militärische Zeitschrift*, 18 (March-April 1980), 121; and U.S. Army Training and Doctrine Command, *Division Restructuring Study*, Phase 1 Report, Executive Summary, vol. 1 (Fort Monroe, 1 March 1977), 3.

52. There are: six brigades in the I Dutch Corps Sector; thirteen brigades in the I German Corps Sector; the equivalent of seven brigades in the I British Corps Sector; and four brigades in the I Belgian Corps Sector. These figures are from de Maizière, "Rational Deployment of Forces," 11–12.

53. See the discussion of the German Territorial Army in n. 38.

54. It should be noted that after a lengthy mobilization involving both sides, NATO's position, regardless of the overall balance of forces, would be extremely favorable with respect to the force-to-space ratio. In other words, with regard to the adequacy of forces to cover the entire front, NATO's position, which is favorable before mobilizing, improves even more as large numbers of additional forces are moved to the central front.

55. There are: seven brigades in the III German Corps Sector; seven brigades in the V American Corps Sector; seven brigades in the VII American Corps Sector; and twelve brigades in the II German Corps Sector. These figures are from de Maizière, "Rational Deployment of Forces," 12–13.

56. Also, given the nature of the terrain along the inter-German border in CENTAG, NATO would not have to be very concerned with protecting sizable segments of the front. The twenty-one brigades include a Canadian brigade and three French divisions (six brigades) stationed in West Germany as well as two American-based divisions (six brigades) with POMCUS in CENTAG and four French divisions (eight brigades) stationed in France.

57. See U.S. Congress, Senate, Armed Services Committee, *Hearings on Department of Defense Authorization for Appropriations for Fiscal Year 1981*, pt. 5, 96th Cong., 2nd sess. (Washington, D.C.: GPO, 1980), 3053–78. It should be noted that the Americans would actually have two and one-third divisions, not two divisions, in each of their corps sectors. The discrepancy results from the fact that the armored cavalry regiment that would be in each corps sector is not counted in this scenario.

58. These three attacking divisions would not be spread out evenly across the forty to fifty kilometers of front but would concentrate at specific points.

59. The Soviets could attempt to spread out their forces and attack across a broad front. Doing so, however, they would encounter serious problems. First, the terrain along the inter-German border is such that the natural avenues of attack are relatively narrow and well defined. Second, and more important, once the attacking forces are spread out, the key principle of concentrating forces on narrow fronts to

effect a breakthrough is violated. Not surprisingly, all evidence indicates that the Soviets intend to concentrate their attacking forces on narrow fronts, placing large numbers of their divisions in echelons behind the main body of attacking divisions (see the sources cited in nn. 30 and 73). During the past decade the United States has devoted considerable attention to developing weaponry specifically designed to attack second- and third-echelon forces. (See, for example, the discussion in the document cited in n. 57.)

60. A number of defense analysts argue that NATO must prevent the overall ratio of forces on the central front from exceeding 1.5:1 in the Pact's favor (see n. 32). Once the Pact has such an advantage, they argue, it can very easily achieve overwhelming force advantages at specific points along the front. Although an overall ratio of 1.5:1 or less is certainly desirable, the foregoing discussion plainly suggests that even if the overall ratio reaches 2:1 (certainly a worst case assumption, with NATO mobilizing immediately after the Pact), and the Pact thus achieves overwhelming superiority on two or three axes, NATO should be able to hold at the points of main attack long enough to allow NATO to shift its forces and to establish at these points ratios that reflect the overall 2:1 ratio. It is clear, however, that NATO would have significant problems should the overall ratio surpass 2:1. See U.S. Department of Defense, *Fiscal Year 1982 Posture Statement*, 74.

61. See, for example, Richard Burt, "Soviet Said to Add to Its Bloc Troops," *New York Times*, 8 June 1980, p. 4.

62. See the comments of the German General Balck in DePuy, *Generals Balck and Von Mellenthin on Tactics*, 46–48.

63. See Chapter 2, n. 69 and the attendant text.

64. See "GSFG Ground Force Reorganization," *International Defense Review*, 14:6 (1981), 701; and Vigor and Donnelly, "The Manchurian Campaign," 172.

65. See the sources cited in n. 25, especially Donnelly's "Tactical Problems," which examines in detail Soviet thinking on strategy and tactics in a European land war. Also see his "Soviet Tactics for Overcoming NATO Anti-Tank Defenses," *International Defense Review*, 12:7 (1979), 1099–1106. For a general discussion of ATGMs and the blitzkrieg, see Chapter 7.

66. Christopher Donnelly writes: "[I]f the victory is not achieved quickly, the Russians believe, no meaningful victory can be achieved at all. It is not surprising, therefore, that Soviet officers have applied themselves to the problem of how to ensure their rapid rate of advance in war. . . . What is of particular interest is that no single straightforward answer to this problem has yet emerged and that it is still the subject of intense discussion" (Donnelly, "Tactics for Overcoming," 1099). He then continues to say, "in general, their identification and dissection of the problem is excellent. Their suggestions as to what should be done usually appear quite sound, but are often tinged with lack of confidence or an excess of bland enthusiasm, hiding uncertainty. Sometimes they are contradictory in detail" (ibid., 1100).

67. See Christopher Donnelly, "Modern Soviet Artillery," *NATO's Fifteen Nations*, 24 (June-July 1979), 48–54; Donnelly, "Tactical Problems"; Donnelly, "Tactics for Overcoming"; and Karber, "Anti-Tank Debate."

68. See Savkin, *Basic Principles*, chap. 3. Also see Sokolovskiy, *Soviet Military Strategy*.

69. See Chapter 2, nn. 70–74 and the attendant text.

70. Christopher Donnelly, "The Soviet Soldier: Behavior, Performance, Effectiveness," in *Soviet Military Power and Performance*, ed. Erickson and Feuchtwanger, 115. Also see Joshua M. Epstein, "On Conventional Deterrence in Europe: Questions of Soviet Confidence," *Orbis*, 26 (spring 1982), 71–86.

71. Interestingly, Donnelly notes that when the Soviets discuss the problem of achieving a quick victory on the battlefield, "not infrequently the panacea of 'initiative' is invoked as a *deus ex machina*" (Donnelly, "Tactics for Overcoming," 1100).

72. See Norman Stone, "The Historical Background of the Red Army," in *Soviet Military Power and Performance*, ed. Erickson and Feuchtwanger, 3–17.

73. Canby, *The Alliance and Europe*, 10–11. Also see John Erickson, "Soviet Ground Forces and the Conventional Mode of Operations," *Journal of the Royal United Services Institute*, 121 (June 1976), 46.

74. The overall force ratios described earlier in this chapter make this point plain.

75. With regard to a Soviet offensive, Canby ironically criticizes NATO for preparing for a firepower-oriented battlefield while the Pact "is oriented towards an armoured-style conflict based on manoeuvre." He continues: "This means the United States fights battles to wear down opponents. The Soviet Union fights battles to *avoid further battles*" (Steven Canby, "NATO: Reassessing the Conventional Wisdoms," *Survival*, 19 [July-August 1977], 165). This view of Soviet strategy hardly squares with Canby's discussion of the use of divisions and *even armies* in support of steamroller tactics.

76. See Donnelly, "Soviet Soldier," 117–20; Keith A. Dunn, "Soviet Military Weaknesses and Vulnerabilities: A Critique of the Short War Advocates," memorandum (Carlisle Barracks: U.S. Army War College, Strategic Studies Institute, 31 July 1978), 15–16; Herbert Goldhamer, *Soviet Military Management at the Troop Level*, R-1513-PR (Santa Monica: Rand, May 1974), chaps. 2–4; Leon Gouré and Michael J. Deane, "The Soviet Strategic View," *Strategic Review*, 8 (winter 1980), 84–85; and Karber, "Anti-Tank Debate," 108.

77. Dunn, "Soviet Military Weaknesses," 16–17.

78. See Johnson et al., "The Armies of the Warsaw Pact"; Dale R. Herspring and Ivan Volgyes, "Political Reliability in the Eastern European Warsaw Pact Armies," *Armed Forces and Society*, 6 (winter 1980), 270–96; and Vigor, "Doubts and Difficulties," 32–38.

79. As John Erickson notes, it is very unlikely "that any non-Soviet national force would be alloted an independent operational role on any scale" (Erickson, "Soviet Military Capabilities in Europe," *Journal of the Royal United Services Institute*, 120 [March 1975], 66). The Soviets might thus have problems because they were forced to disperse their own divisions, thus limiting the number available for the principal attacks.

80. Canby, *The Alliance and Europe*, 9. This view is also reflected in: Eugene D. Bétit, "Soviet Tactical Doctrine and Capabilities and NATO's Strategic Defense," *Strategic Review*, 4 (fall 1976), 96; Erickson, "Soviet Ground Forces," 46; and Daniel Gouré and Gordon McCormick, "PGM: No Panacea," *Survival*, 22 (January-February 1980), 16.

81. U.S. Department of Defense, *Fiscal Year 1978 Posture Statement*, 85.

7. *Precision-Guided Munitions and Conventional Deterrence*

1. For a discussion of the broad aspects of these developments in conventional weaponry, see Johan J. Holst and Uwe Nerlich, eds., *Beyond Nuclear Deterrence* (New York: Crane, Russak, 1977); *New Conventional Weapons and East-West Security*, pts. 1 and 2, Adelphi Papers 144 and 145 (London: International Institute for Strategic Studies, spring 1978); and Geoffrey Kemp, Robert L. Pfaltzgraff, and Uri Ra'anan, eds., *The Other Arms Race* (Lexington: D. C. Heath, 1976).

2. A PGM is generally defined as a missile that is extremely accurate because it has a terminal guidance system. An example of a similar significant development that is not PGM-related in a strict definitional sense is the greatly improved accuracy of main tank guns.

3. See Col. Edward B. Atkeson, "Is the Soviet Army Obsolete?" *Army*, 24 (May 1974), 10–16; James Digby, *Precision Guided Weapons*, Adelphi Paper 118 (London: International Institute for Strategic Studies, 1975); Col. Stanley D. Fair, "Precision Weaponry in the Defense of Europe," *NATO's Fifteen Nations*, 20 (August-September 1975), 17–26; Kenneth Hunt, "New Technology and the European Theater," in *The Other Arms Race*, ed. Kemp et al., 109–23; Michael L. Nacht, "Technology and Strategy," *National Defense*, 61 (November-December 1976), 199–201; Jeffrey Record, "The October War: Burying the Blitzkrieg," *Military Review*, 56 (April 1976), 19–21; Peter A. Wilson, "Battlefield Guided Weapons: The Big Equalizer," *U.S. Naval Institute Proceedings*, 101 (February 1975), 18–25; and Albert Wohlstetter, "Threats and Promises of Peace: Europe and America in the New Era," *Orbis*, 17 (winter 1974), 1107–44.

4. See, for example, John H. Morse, "Advanced Technology in Modern War," *Journal of the Royal United Services Institute*, 121 (June 1976), 12; and Paul F. Walker, "Precision-Guided Weapons," *Scientific American*, 245 (August 1981), 37–45.

5. See Richard Burt, *New Weapons Technologies: Debate and Directions*, Adelphi Paper 126 (London: International Institute for Strategic Studies, summer 1976); James L. Foster, *The Future of Conventional Arms Control*, P-5489 (Santa Monica: Rand, August 1975); Gouré and McCormick, "No Panacea," 15–19; Colin Gray, "The Blitzkrieg: A Premature Burial?" *Military Review*, 56 (October 1976), 15–18; Richard M. Ogorkiewicz, "The Future of the Battle Tank," in *The Other Arms Race*, ed. Kemp et al., 43–45; Uri Ra'anan, "The New Technologies and the Middle East: 'Lessons' of the Yom Kippur War and Anticipated Developments," in *The Other Arms Race*, ed. Kemp et al., 79–90; and Jeffrey Record, "Outwitting 'Smart' Weapons," *Washington Review of Strategic and International Studies*, 1 (April 1978), 83–85.

6. See Chapter 2, n. 101 and the attendant text. The United States is developing and deploying a variety of weapons to deal with the Soviet's second-echelon forces. See, for example, the discussion in the document cited in Chapter 6, n. 57.

7. See Herzog, *War of Atonement*, chap. 13. Although the experience of the 190th Brigade is the most frequently cited example of the impact of PGMs on the battlefield, the use of massive numbers of PGMs by the Egyptians greatly influenced events over the entire battlefield until the Israelis crossed the Canal. See my "Rejoinder" to Gouré and McCormick, in *Survival*, 22 (January-February 1980), 20–22.

8. See "The Blitzkrieg Stategy," in Chapter 2.

9. Since tank guns are most effective inside 1,000 yards, while most ATGMs are best used against targets more than 1,000 yards away, these two types of systems nicely complement each other. Thus Phillip Karber talks about "the synergistic relationship between the tank and the ATGM" (Phillip A. Karber, "Anti-Tank Weapons and the Future of Armor," *Armed Forces Journal International*, 114 [November 1976], 23). Also see *Range and Lethality of U.S. and Soviet Anti-Armor Weapons*, TRADOC Bulletin 1 (Fort Monroe: U.S. Army, Training and Doctrine Command, 30 September 1975), 5–23 (hereafter cited as TRADOC Bulletin 1); and the prepared statement of Dr. Percy A. Pierre and Lt. Gen. Donald R. Keith in U.S. Congress, House, Armed Services Committee, *Hearings on Military Posture and H.R. 10929*, pt. 3, bk. 1, 95th Cong., 2nd sess. (Washington, D.C.: GPO, 1 March 1978), 534–602. It should be noted that there is also a synergistic relationship between air defense guns and SAMs. See Lt. Col. J. Viksne, "The Yom Kippur War—in Retrospect," pt. 2, "Technology," *Army Journal*, 324 (May 1976), 33–35.

10. Dayan, *My Life*, 516. Also see Prosch, "Israeli Defense of the Golan," 11.

11. See *FM 100-5*, chap. 2; and TRADOC Bulletin 1, 20–23.

12. For a description of these technologies, see Cecil I. Hudson, Jr., and Peter H. Haas, "New Technologies: The Prospects," in *Beyond Nuclear Deterrence*, ed. Holst and Nerlich, 107–48; and C. Ivan Hudson, "New Conventional Munitions," in *New Conventional Weapons and East-West Security*, pt. 1, 45–50.

13. Foster, *Conventional Arms Control*, 10. Also see Burt, *New Weapons Technologies*, 13.

14. *FM 100-5* states, for example, "Individual foxholes provide a 10-fold or greater reduction in casualties against impact fuzed artillery ammunition" (p. 3-12).

15. See TRADOC Bulletin 1, 20, 24.

16. See the sources cited in Chapter 6, nn. 25 and 65 and the attendant texts.

17. It is questionable whether Soviet artillery is capable of adjusting to the demands of a fast-moving attack that relies on the use of extensive artillery fire. See Donnelly, "Modern Soviet Artillery."

18. See TRADOC Bulletin 1 for a discussion of the ranges of various ATGMs.

19. The Soviets clearly recognize this problem. See Karber, "Anti-Tank Debate," 108.

20. The Israelis, for example, have organized special tank killer teams of infantrymen. See Hirsch Goodman, "The Tank Killers," *Jerusalem Post Magazine*, 23 February 1979, pp. 8–9.

21. This development has been a cause of great concern for Soviet defense specialists. Phillip Karber writes that the Soviets "had previously assessed APC to be twice as vulnerable as tanks. Apparently, in exercises and field tests since the Middle East War, the army has found that BMP is even more vulnerable to the new generation of anti-tank weapons than was previously believed " (Karber, "Anti-Tank Debate," 108).

22. See Donnelly, "Tactical Problems," 1406–407; and Hemsley, "The Soviet Ground Forces," 71.

23. Karber notes that some Soviet writers consider the BMP so vulnerable that they suggest "forgetting the BMP and mounting the troops on the backs of tanks as in World War II" (see Karber, "Anti-Tank Debate," 108).

24. See Richard Ogorkiewicz, "Tanks and Anti-Tank Weapons," in *New Conventional Weapons and East-West Security*, pt. 1, pp. 38–44.

25. There is, however, some evidence that the T-80 will have better armor protection than its predecessor, the T-72. Furthermore, some analysts argue that the present generation of U.S. ATGMs will not be capable of penetrating the T-80. The new armor on the T-80 is not the Chobham armor developed in the West. See Drew Middleton, "Soviet Introducing New Tank in Europe," *New York Times*, 16 March 1980, p. 7; and "AUSA '79: Crash Programs to Counter Deployed Soviet Armour," *International Defense Review*, 13:1 (1980), 89–91. Some experts argue, however, that Soviet capabilities have been exaggerated. See R. D. M. Furlong, "Europeans Oppose Single-Type Standardization of NATO Anti-Tank Missiles," *International Defense Review*, 14:2 (1981), 141–42.

26. The United States is taking steps to offset these improvements in Soviet armor (see sources in n. 25). Furthermore, the United States is developing a new generation of ATGMs. For an optimistic assessment of the future of ATGMs, see William J. Perry, *The FY 1981 Department of Defense Program for Research, Development, and Acquisition* (Washington, D.C.: GPO, 1 February 1980), I-10-15; Walker, "Precision-Guided Weapons"; and George C. Wilson, "Defense Getting the Upper Hand," *Astronautics and Aeronautics*, 18 (May 1980), 26–27. For a more pessimistic assessment, see the testi-

mony of two U.S. Army spokesmen in U.S. Congress, House, Armed Services Committee, *Hearings on Military Posture and H.R. 6495, Department of Defense Authorization for Appropriations for Fiscal Year 1981,* pt. 2, 96th Cong., 2nd sess. (Washington, D.C.: GPO, 1980), 598–615.

27. Generally, first-generation ATGMs are those such that "the gunner must fly the missile visually to his target, visually tracking both [the missile and the target] simultaneously throughout the firing sequence." The Soviet systems are first-generation ATGMs. Second-generation ATGMs require "the gunner to track only the target, while the system automatically follows the missile and issues appropriate commands to fly it into the intersection of his cross hairs." The U.S. systems are second-generation ATGMs. Third-generation ATGMs, which are now being developed in the United States, are essentially "fire and forget" systems. These definitions are given in TRADOC Bulletin 1, p. 5.

28. It appears that modification of the TOW will enable it to penetrate virtually all types of new armor (see sources cited in n. 25). The future of Dragon and similar ATGMs, however, which are designed for use by individual infantrymen (as opposed to TOW, which is a crew-served weapon), is more problematic. See the sources cited in n. 26 for differing views on the matter. Also see "Tank Breaker/IMAAWS Situation Still Confused," *International Defense Review,* 14:6 (1981), 703; and Deborah M. Kyle and Benjamin F. Schemmer, "Technology Won't Save Us If We Don't Field It," *Armed Forces Journal International,* 118 (August 1981), 26–28.

29. See, for example, U.S. Comptroller General, *Critical Considerations in the Acquisition of a New Main Battle Tank,* PSAD-76-113A (Washington, D.C.: General Accounting Office, 22 July 1976); and Walther Stutzle, "The Impact of New Conventional Weapons Technology on NATO Military Doctrine and Organization," in *New Conventional Weapons and East-West Security,* pt. 1, p. 24.

30. See Ogorkiewicz, "Tanks and Anti-Tank Weapons," 43.

31. "Rearming without Tears," *Economist,* 268 (19 August 1978), 10–11.

32. See Richard M. Ogorkiewicz, "Trends in Tank Technology," *Armor,* 89 (July-August 1980), 8–14. Also see "The Merkava MK 1," *International Defense Review,* 11:7 (1978), 1049–52.

33. See Ogorkiewicz, "Tanks and Anti-Tank Weapons," 40.

34. See Eugene D. Bétit, "Soviet Technological Preparations for Night Attack," *Military Review,* 55 (March 1975), 89–93.

35. John Hemsley notes that current Soviet doctrine "tends to the view that the problems of control make it undesirable to launch night attacks for formations above regimental levels" (Hemsley, "The Soviet Ground Forces," 58).

36. Steven Canby notes that in the 1973 Middle East war, the ZSU/23/4, "though few in number, accounted for about 30 percent of Israel's aircraft losses in the October War" (Steven L. Canby, "Tactical Air Power in Armored Warfare," *Air University Review,* 30 [May-June 1979], 14–15). Also see Viksne, "Yom Kippur War," 33–35. Viksne estimates that the ZSU/23/4 accounted for 43 percent of Israeli losses.

37. Herzog, *War of Atonement,* 251–61.

38. See Canby, "Tactical Air Power"; Herzog, *War of Atonement,* 261; and U.S. Congress, House, Armed Services Committee, *Hearings on Military Posture,* pt. 3, bk. 2, 96th Cong., 1st sess. (Washington, D.C.: GPO, 19 March 1979), 1707–42.

39. See Irvine Cohen, "Israel Rebuilds Her Army," *Army,* 25 (June 1975), 23; and Van Creveld, "Two Years After," 31.

40. Johannes Steinhoff, the former chairman of the NATO Military Committee, notes that "target acquisition has now fallen behind weapon effectiveness; our ability

to destroy targets, especially tactical targets in enemy territory, is generally greater than our ability to locate them" (Steinhoff, "The Scope and Direction of New Conventional Weapons Technology," in *New Conventional Weapons and East-West Security*, pt. 1, p. 16).

41. This is basically the principal role that Europeans envision for close air support aircraft. See Canby, "Tactical Air Power."

42. Regarding the increased firepower resulting from the proliferation of PGMs, Mohamed Heikal writes concerning the 1973 Egyptian attack: "It was this last-minute 'overdose' of weapons [extra Strellas and Saggers given to the attacking forces] that enabled the infantry to hold out, and General Dayan was later to admit that it was not so much the novelty of the weapons that took the Israelis by surprise as the sheer numbers in which they were available to the Egyptians at the outset of the battle" (Heikal, *Ramadan*, 6). Phillip Karber notes, "What seems to bother Soviet writers about anti-tank weapons is less their specific technological characteristics than the growing density of their deployment" (Karber, "The Impact of New Conventional Technologies on Military Doctrine and Organization in the Warsaw Pact," in *New Conventional Weapons and East-West Security*, pt. 1, p. 31).

43. See "Employing the Blitzkrieg and Attrition Strategies for Limited Objectives," in Chapter 2.

8. Conclusion

1. For a list of the best available sources dealing with this subject, see Chapter 4, n. 174.

2. Guderian, *Panzer Leader*, 396.

3. For a list of the best available sources dealing with this subject, see Chapter 6, n. 23.

4. Cited in Dzirkals, *"Lightning War" in Manchuria*, 22.

5. Despres et al., *Timely Lessons*, 51–53, 61–66; Dzirkals, *"Lightning War" in Manchuria*, 69–72, 79–85.

6. The Soviet moves into Hungary (1956), Czechoslovakia (1968), and Afghanistan (1979) were mere police actions. The Soviet advance into Poland (1939) was largely unopposed, since it took place after the Germans had destroyed the Polish army. The Finnish and Manchurian cases are the only examples of the Soviets moving against an opposing military that was prepared to contest them in large-scale battles. In the Finnish case, the disparity in forces was so great that the concept of deterrence really does not apply. See the relevant discussion in "Strategy and Numbers," in Chapter 2.

7. For a thorough discussion of this matter, see Daniel Stelmach, "The Influence of Russian Armored Tactics on the North Korean Invasion of 1950" (Ph.D. diss., St. Louis University, 1973).

8. Roy E. Appleman, *South to the Naktong, North to the Yalu, (June-November 1950)* (Washington, D.C.: U.S. Army, Office of the Chief of Military History, 1961), 20. It is important to note that the North Korean army was both quantitatively and qualitatively superior to the South Korean army. See ibid., chap. 2. In fact, the North Koreans had 150 excellent tanks, while the South Koreans had none.

9. Appleman, *South to the Naktong*, 20, 69–72; and J. Lawton Collins, *War in Peacetime* (Boston: Houghton Mifflin, 1969), 50–51.

10. Appleman, *South to the Naktong*, 20–21.

11. See Angus Deming, "Hanoi's Power Play," *Newsweek*, 43 (22 January 1979), 31.

12. See Deming, "Hanoi's Power Play," 31–34; and Nayan Chanda, "Cambodia: Fifteen Days That Shook Asia," *Far Eastern Economic Review*, 103 (19 January 1979), 10–13.

13. Pran Chopra, *India's Second Liberation* (Cambridge: M.I.T. Press, 1974), 69–101.

14. Ibid., 93–103.

15. Ibid., 94–95.

16. Ibid., 98.

17. Maj. Gen. D. K. Palit, *The Lightning Campaign* (New Delhi: Thomson, 1972), 38–39.

18. Ibid., 100. The Indian army had of course been trained by the British army.

19. D. R. Mankekar, *Pakistan Cut to Size* (New Delhi: Indian Book, 1972), 51–52; and Palit, *Lightning Campaign*, 39–40, 100–101.

20. Chopra, *India's Second Liberation*, 126–27, 139–42; Mankekar, *Pakistan Cut to Size*, 37.

21. For a description of the plan, see Chopra, *India's Second Liberation*, 120–27. Also see Mankekar, *Pakistan Cut to Size*, 53–54, 78–79; and Palit, *Lightning Campaign*, 100–105.

22. Palit, *Lightning Campaign*, 101.

23. See Chopra, *India's Second Liberation*, 96–98, 120, 186–88; Mankekar, *Pakistan Cut to Size*, 158; and Palit, *Lightning Campaign*, 94–95, 120.

24. Insight Team, *Yom Kippur War*, 72–73, 303–304. Also see Shazly, *Crossing*, 27–28, 109–111.

25. Furthermore, it should be noted that Manekshaw was willing to pursue a limited aims strategy against West Pakistan in the 1971 war. See Chopra, *India's Second Liberation*, 133–34, 146–47; and Palit, *Lightning Campaign*, 42, 85, 152.

26. The record shows that the threat of superpower interference has been a major consideration in past Indian, Pakistani, Israeli, and Arab decisions. Undoubtedly the North Koreans and Vietnamese have also paid careful attention to this matter.

27. See Chapter 2, n. 132, and Chapter 4, n. 26, and the attendant texts.

28. See Bar-Siman-Tov, *War of Attrition*.

Select Bibliography

1. Unpublished Sources

Liddell Hart, B. H. Personal papers. Liddell Hart Centre for Military Archives. University of London, King's College, London.
British Cabinet Papers and War Office Papers, 1918–40. Public Records Office, Kew, England.

Dissertations

Burdick, Charles B. "German Military Planning for the War in the West, 1935–1940." Ph.D. diss., Stanford University, 1954.
Burke, Richard T. "The German 'Panzerwaffe,' 1920–1939: A Study in Institutional Change." Ph.D. diss., Northwestern University, 1969.
Clarke, Jeffrey J. "Military Technology in Republican France: The Evolution of the French Armored Force, 1917–1940." Ph.D. diss., Duke University, 1969.
Coox, Alvin D. "French Military Doctrine, 1919–1939: Concepts of Ground and Aerial Warfare." Ph.D. diss., Harvard University, 1951.
Doughty, Robert A. "The Evolution of French Army Doctrine, 1919–1939." Ph.D. diss., University of Kansas, 1979.
Geist, Benjamin. "The Six Day War." Ph.D. diss., Hebrew University, 1974.
Greene, Fred. "French Military Leadership and Security against Germany, 1919–1940." Ph.D. diss., Yale University, 1950.
Harvey, Donald J. "French Concepts of Military Strategy (1919–1939)." Ph.D. diss., Columbia University, 1953.
Murray, Williamson. "The Change in the European Balance of Power, 1938–1939." Ph.D. diss., Yale University, 1975.
Posen, Barry R. "The Systemic, Organizational, and Technological Origins of Strategic Doctrine: France, Britain, and Germany between the World Wars." Ph.D. diss., University of California, Berkeley, 1981.
Stelmach, Daniel. "The Influence of Russian Armored Tactics on the North Korean Invasion of 1950." Ph.D. diss., St. Louis University, 1973.

2. Published Sources

General Theory

Acheson, Dean. *Power and Diplomacy*. New York: Atheneum, 1962.

Alford, J. R. *Mobile Defence: The Pervasive Myth*. London: Department of War Studies, King's College, 1977.

Allison, Graham T. *Essence of Decision: Explaining the Cuban Missile Crisis*. Boston: Little, Brown, 1971.

Art, Robert J. "To What Ends Military Power?" *International Security*, 4 (spring 1980), 3–35.

Balck, Wilhelm. *Development of Tactics—World War*. Trans. Harry Bell. Fort Leavenworth: General Service Schools Press, 1922.

Barnett, Correlli. *The Desert Generals*. London: William Kimber, 1960.

Bell, J. Bowyer. "National Character and Military Strategy: The Egyptian Experience, October 1973." *Parameters*, 5:1 (1975), 6–16.

Betts, Richard K. *Soldiers, Statesmen, and Cold War Crises*. Cambridge: Harvard University Press, 1977.

———. *Surprise Attack: Lessons for Defense Planning*. Washington, D.C.: Brookings Institution, 1982.

Bialer, Seweryn, ed. *Stalin and His Generals: Soviet Military Memoirs of World War II*. New York: Pegasus, 1969.

Bidwell, Shelford. *Modern Warfare: A Study of Men, Weapons, and Theories*. London: Allen Lane, 1973.

Blumenson, Martin. *Breakout and Pursuit*. Washington, D.C.: U.S. Army, Office of the Chief of Military History, 1961.

Boggs, Marion W. *Attempts to Define and Limit "Aggressive" Armament in Diplomacy and Strategy*. Columbia: University of Missouri, 1941.

Bond, Brian. "Further Reflections on the Indirect Approach." *Journal of the Royal United Services Institute*, 116 (December 1971), 69–70.

———. *Liddell Hart: A Study of His Military Thought*. London: Cassell, 1967.

Boulding, Kenneth E. *Conflict and Defense: A General Theory*. New York: Harper, Harper Torchbooks, 1963.

Brodie, Bernard. *The American Scientific Strategists*. P-2979. Santa Monica: Rand, 1964.

———. *Escalation and the Nuclear Option*. Princeton: Princeton University Press, 1966.

———. *War and Politics*. New York: Macmillan, 1973.

Brown, Harold. Speech delivered at the Commonwealth Club of California, San Francisco, 23 June 1978.

Brown, Michael E. *Deterrence Failures and Deterrence Strategies*. P-5842. Santa Monica: Rand, March 1977.

Carell, Paul. *Hitler Moves East, 1941–1943*. New York: Ballantine, 1971.

Cecil, Robert. *Hitler's Decision to Invade Russia, 1941*. New York: David McKay, 1975.

Clausewitz, Carl von. *On War*. Trans. Michael Howard and Peter Paret. Princeton: Princeton University Press, 1976.

Cole, Hugh M. *The Ardennes: Battle of the Bulge*. Washington, D.C.: U.S. Army, Office of the Chief of Military History, 1965.

Command and Control in Battle. German Army Regulation 100/100. Bonn: Federal Ministry of Defense, 28 September 1973.

de Maizière, Ulrich. *Rational Deployment of Forces on the Central Front*. London: Western European Union, 2 April 1975.

DePuy, Gen. William E. *Generals Balck and Von Mellenthin on Tactics: Implications for NATO Military Doctrine*. BDM/W-81-077-TR. McLean, Va.: BDM, 19 December 1980.

———. "Technology and Tactics in Defense of Europe." *Army*, 29 (April 1979), 14–23.

Detwiler, Donald S., ed. *World War II German Military Studies*. 24 vols. New York: Garland, 1979.

Dumas, Samuel, and K. O. Vedel-Petersen. *Losses of Life Caused by War*. Oxford: Clarendon Press, 1923.

DuPicq, Ardant. *Battle Studies*. Trans. John N. Greely and Robert C. Cotton. New York: Macmillan, 1921.

Dupuy, Trevor N. *Numbers, Prediction, and War*. New York: Bobbs-Merrill, 1979.

Earle, Edward Mead, ed. *Makers of Modern Strategy*. Princeton: Princeton University Press, 1973.

Ellsberg, Daniel. *The Crude Analysis of Strategic Choices*. P-2183. Santa Monica: Rand, 15 December 1960.

Engels, Frederick. *Herr Eugen Dühring's Revolution in Science (Anti-Dühring)*. Trans. Emile Burns. New York: International, 1939.

Enthoven, Alain C., and K. Wayne Smith. *How Much Is Enough?* New York: Harper and Row, 1971.

Erickson, John. *The Soviet High Command: A Military-Political History, 1918–1941*. London: Macmillan, 1962.

Essame, H. *Patton: A Study in Command*. New York: Scribner's, 1974.

Farrar-Hockley, Anthony. *Infantry Tactics*. London: Almark, 1976.

Foch, Ferdinand. *The Principles of War*. Trans. J. de Morinni. New York: H. K. Fly, 1919.

Foertsch, Hermann. *The Art of Modern Warfare*. Trans. Theodore W. Knauth. New York: Oskar Piest, 1940.

Fuller, J. F. C. *Armament and History*. New York: Scribner's, 1945.

———. *Armoured Warfare: Lectures on Field Service Regulation III*. Harrisburg: Military Service, 1943.

———. *The Conduct of War, 1789–1961*. New Brunswick: Rutgers University Press, 1961.

———. *Machine Warfare: An Enquiry into the Influence of Mechanics on the Art of War*. London: Hutchinson, 1943.

———. *Memoirs of an Unconventional Soldier*. London: Nicholson and Watson, 1936.

———. *Tanks in the Great War*. New York: Dutton, 1920.

George, Alexander L. "Case Studies and Theory Development: The Method of Structured, Focused Comparison." In *Diplomacy*, ed. Paul G. Lauren. New York: Free Press, 1979.

George, Alexander L., and Richard Smoke. *Deterrence in American Foreign Policy: Theory and Practice*. New York: Columbia University Press, 1974.

Germains, V. W. "The Limitations of the Tank." *Journal of the Royal United Services Institute*, 75 (February 1930), 124–29.

Gillie, Mildred H. *Forging the Thunderbolt: A History of the Development of the Armored Force*. Harrisburg: Military Service, 1947.

Goldhamer, Herbert. *Reality and Belief in Military Affairs: A First Draft (June 1977)*. R-2448-NA. Santa Monica: Rand, February 1979.

Great Patriotic War of the Soviet Union, 1941–1945: A General Outline. Moscow: Progress, 1974.

Greenfield, Kent Roberts, Robert R. Palmer, and Bell I. Wiley. *The Organization of Ground Combat Troops*. Washington, D.C.: U.S. Army, Historical Division, 1947.

Guderian, Heinz. *Achtung-Panzer! Die Entwicklung der Panzerwaffe, ihre Kampftaktik, und ihre operativen Möglichkeiten*. Stuttgart: Union Deutsche Verlagsgesellschaft, 1937.

———. *Panzer Leader*. New York: Ballantine, 1972.

Halperin, Morton H. *Limited War in the Nuclear Age.* New York: John Wiley, 1963.

Harkabi, Y. "Basic Factors in the Arab Collapse during the Six-Day War." *Orbis,* 11 (fall 1967), 677–91.

Harkavy, Robert E. *Preemption and Two-Front Conventional Warfare.* Jerusalem Paper 23. Jerusalem: Hebrew University, 1977.

Heilbrunn, Otto. *Conventional Warfare in the Nuclear Age.* London: Allen and Unwin, 1965.

Herzog, Chaim. *The War of Atonement.* Boston: Little, Brown, 1975.

Horowitz, Dan. "Flexible Responsiveness and Military Strategy: The Case of the Israeli Army." *Policy Sciences,* 1 (summer 1970), 191–205.

Howard, Michael. "The Forgotten Dimensions of Strategy." *Foreign Affairs,* 57 (summer 1979), 975–86.

———. *The Franco-Prussian War.* London: Hart-Davis, 1961.

———. *War in European History.* Oxford: Oxford University Press, 1976.

Huntington, Samuel P. *The Soldier and the State.* New York: Vintage, 1964.

Iklé, Fred C. *Every War Must End.* New York: Columbia University Press, 1971.

Jervis, Robert. "Cooperation under the Security Dilemma." *World Politics,* 30 (January 1978), 167–214.

Jomini, Baron Antoine Henri. *The Art of War.* Westport: Greenwood, n.d.

Jomini, Clausewitz, and Schlieffen. West Point: U.S. Military Academy, Department of History, 1969.

Kaufmann, William W., ed. *Military Policy and National Security.* Princeton: Princeton University Press, 1956.

Keegan, John. *The Face of Battle.* New York: Vintage, 1977.

Kissinger, Henry A. *The Necessity for Choice.* New York: Harper and Row, 1960.

———. *Nuclear Weapons and Foreign Policy.* New York: Harper and Row, 1957.

Knorr, Klaus, ed. *NATO and American Security.* Princeton: Princeton University Press, 1959.

Kohn, Richard H. "The Social History of the American Soldier: A Review and Prospectus for Research." *American Historical Review,* 86 (June 1981), 553–67.

Lanchester, F. W. *Aircraft in Warfare: The Dawn of the Fourth Arm.* London: Constable, 1916.

Leeb, Ritter von. *Defense.* Trans. Stefan T. Possony and Daniel Vilfroy. Harrisburg: Military Service, 1943.

Liddell Hart, B. H. *The Current of War.* London: Hutchinson, 1941.

———. *Deterrent or Defense.* New York: Praeger, 1960.

———. *Europe in Arms.* London: Faber and Faber, 1937.

———. *The German Generals Talk.* New York: William Morrow, 1948.

———. *The Ghost of Napoleon.* New Haven: Yale University Press, 1934.

———. *History of the Second World War.* New York: Putnam, 1970.

———. *Memoirs.* 2 vols. London: Cassell, 1967.

———. *Paris, or The Future of War.* London: Paul Kegan, 1925.

———. *Strategy.* New York: Praeger, 1967.

———. "Strategy of a War." *Encounter,* 30 (February 1968), 16–20.

———. *The Tanks.* 2 vols. New York: Praeger, 1959.

———, ed. *The Rommel Papers.* Trans. Paul Findlay. New York: Harcourt, Brace, 1953.

———, ed. *The Soviet Army.* London: Weidenfeld and Nicolson, 1956.

Lijphart, Arend. "Comparative Politics and the Comparative Method." *American Political Science Review,* 65 (September 1971), 682–93.

Lupfer, Timothy T. *The Dynamics of Doctrine: The Changes in German Tactical Doctrine during the First World War.* Leavenworth Paper 4. Fort Leavenworth: U.S. Army Command and General Staff College, July 1981.

Luttwak, Edward N. "The Operational Level of War." *International Security,* 5 (winter 1980–81), 61–79.

Luttwak, Edward, and Dan Horowitz. *The Israeli Army.* New York: Harper and Row, 1975.

Luvaas, Jay, ed. and trans. *Frederick the Great on the Art of War.* New York: Free Press, 1966.

MacDonald, Charles B. *The Siegfried Line Campaign.* Washington, D.C.: U.S. Army, Office of the Chief of Military History, 1963.

Macksey, Kenneth. *Tank Warfare: A History of Tanks in Battle.* London: Hart-Davis, 1971.

Manstein, Erich von. *Lost Victories.* Chicago: Henry Regnery, 1958.

Mearsheimer, John J. "Maneuver, Mobile Defense, and the NATO Central Front." *International Security,* 6 (winter 1981–82), 104–22.

Mellenthin, F. W. von. *Panzer Battles: A Study of the Employment of Armor in the Second World War.* New York: Ballantine, 1976.

Messenger, Charles. *The Blitzkrieg Story.* New York: Scribner's, 1976.

Miksche, F. O. *Blitzkrieg.* London: Faber and Faber, 1941.

Ogorkiewicz, Richard M. *Armor: A History of Mechanized Forces.* New York: Praeger, 1960.

Operations: FM 100-5. Washington, D.C.: U.S. Army, 1976.

Osgood, Robert E. *Limited War: The Challenge to American Strategy.* Chicago: University of Chicago Press, 1957.

Paret, Peter. "The History of War." *Daedalus,* 100 (spring 1971), 376–96.

——. "Nationalism and the Sense of Military Obligation." *Military Affairs,* 34 (February 1970), 2–6.

Patton, George S. *War as I Knew It.* Boston: Houghton Mifflin, 1948.

Preston, Adrian, ed. *General Staffs and Diplomacy before the Second World War.* London: Croom Helm, 1978.

Prosch, Maj. Geoffrey G. "Israeli Defense of the Golan: An Interview with Brigadier General Avigdor Kahalani." *Military Review,* 59 (October 1979), 2–13.

Quester, George H. *Deterrence before Hiroshima.* New York: John Wiley, 1966.

——. *Offense and Defense in the International System.* New York: John Wiley, 1977.

Ropp, Theodore. *War in the Modern World.* Durham: Duke University Press, 1959.

Rosecrance, Richard N. "Deterrence and Vulnerability in the Pre-Nuclear Era." In *The Future of Strategic Deterrence.* Pt. 1. Adelphi Paper 160. London: International Institute of Strategic Studies, autumn 1980.

Ruppenthal, Roland G. "Logistics and the Broad-Front Strategy." *Command Decisions.* Ed. Kent Roberts Greenfield. Washington, D.C.: U.S. Army, Office of the Chief of Military History, 1960.

Savkin, V. Y. *The Basic Principles of Operational Art and Tactics.* Trans. U.S. Air Force. Washington, D.C.: GPO, 1976. Originally published in Moscow, 1972.

Schelling, Thomas C. *Arms and Influence.* New Haven: Yale University Press, 1972.

——. *The Strategy of Conflict.* New York: Oxford University Press, 1960.

Sidorenko, A. A. *The Offensive.* Trans. U.S. Air Force. Washington, D.C.: GPO, 1976. Originally published in Moscow, 1970.

Sinnreich, Richard H. "NATO's Doctrinal Dilemma." *Orbis,* 19 (summer 1975), 461–76.

Snyder, Glenn H. *Deterrence and Defense: Toward a Theory of National Security.* Princeton: Princeton University Press, 1961.

Stockfish, J. A. *Models, Data, and War: A Critique of the Study of Conventional Forces.* R-1526-PR. Santa Monica: Rand, March 1975.

Tal, Israel. "Modern Tank Warfare." Speech delivered at the Air War College, Maxwell Air Force Base, 9 March 1978.

Terraine, John. "History and the 'Indirect Approach.'" *Journal of the Royal United Services Institute,* 116 (June 1971), 44–49.

Trythall, Anthony J. *"Boney" Fuller.* New Brunswick: Rutgers University Press, 1977.

U.S. Comptroller General. *Models, Data, and War: A Critique of the Foundation for Defense Analyses.* PAD 80–21. Washington, D.C.: General Accounting Office, 12 March 1980.

U.S. Congress. House. Subcommittee on Europe and the Middle East of the Committee on International Relations. *Hearings on Western Europe in 1977: Security, Economic, and Political Issues.* 95th Cong., 1st sess. Washington, D.C.: GPO, 1977.

——. Senate. Armed Services Committee. *Hearings on Department of Defense Authorization for Appropriations for Fiscal Year 1979.* Pt. 2. 95th Cong., 2nd sess. Washington, D.C.: GPO, 1978.

U.S. Department of Defense. Secretary of Defense. *Posture Statements.* Fiscal years 1961–83. Washington, D.C.: GPO, 1960–82.

Vagts, Alfred. *A History of Militarism: Civilian and Military.* New York: Free Press, 1959.

Van Creveld, Martin. *Fighting Power: German Military Performance, 1914–1945.* Washington, D.C.: Department of Defense, Office of Net Assessment, December 1980.

——. "Supplying an Army: An Historical View." *Journal of the Royal United Services Institute,* 123 (June 1978), 56–63.

——. *Supplying War: Logistics from Wallenstein to Patton.* Cambridge: Cambridge University Press, 1977.

——. "Two Years After: The Israeli Defence Forces, 1973–1975." *Journal of the Royal United Services Institute,* 121 (March 1976), 29–34.

Vigman, Fred K. "The Theoretical Evaluation of Artillery after World War I." *Military Affairs,* 16 (1952), 115–18.

Weigley, Russell F. *The American Way of War: A History of United States Military Strategy and Policy.* New York: Macmillan, 1973.

——. *Eisenhower's Lieutenants.* Bloomington: Indiana University Press, 1981.

——, ed. *New Dimensions in Military History.* San Rafael: Presidio, 1975.

Werth, Alexander. *Russia at War, 1941–1945.* New York: Dutton, 1964.

Westphal, Siegfried. *The German Army in the West.* London: Cassell, 1951.

Wilmot, Chester. *The Struggle for Europe.* London: Collins, 1965.

Wintringham, Tom, and J. N. Blashford-Snell. *Weapons and Tactics.* Baltimore: Penguin, 1973.

Ziemke, Earl F. *Stalingrad to Berlin: The German Defeat in the East.* Washington, D.C.: U.S. Army, Office of the Chief of Military History, 1968.

French-British Decision Making, 1939–1940

Adamthwaite, Anthony. *France and the Coming of the Second World War, 1936–1939.* London: Cass, 1977.

Bankwitz, P. C. F. *Maxime Weygand and Civil-Military Relations in Modern France.* Cambridge: Harvard University Press, 1967.

Barnett, Correlli. *Britain and Her Army, 1509–1970: A Military, Political, and Social Survey.* Harmondsworth: Penguin, 1970.

Beaufre, André. *1940: The Fall of France*. Trans. Desmond Flowers. London: Cassell, 1967.

Bloch, Marc. *Strange Defeat*. Trans. Gerard Hopkins. Oxford: Oxford University Press, 1949.

Bond, Brian. *British Military Policy between the Two World Wars*. New York: Oxford University Press, 1980.

————. *France and Belgium, 1939–1940*. London: Davis-Poynter, 1975.

————, ed. *Chief of Staff: The Diaries of Lieutenant-General Sir Henry Pownall*. Vol. 1. London: Leo Cooper, 1972.

Butler, J. R. M. *Grand Strategy*. Vol. 2, *September 1939–June 1941*. London: HMSO, 1957.

Cairns, John C. "Along the Road back to France 1940." *American Historical Review*, 64 (April 1959), 583–603.

————. "A Nation of Shopkeepers in Search of a Suitable France, 1919–1940." *American Historical Review*, 79 (June 1974), 710–43.

————. "Some Recent Historians and the 'Strange Defeat' of 1940." *Journal of Modern History*, 46 (March 1974), 60–85.

Challener, Richard D. *The French Theory of the Nation in Arms, 1866–1939*. New York: Russell and Russell, 1965.

Chapman, Guy. *Why France Collapsed*. London: Cassell, 1968.

Chauvineau, Narcisse. *Une invasion est-elle encore possible?* Paris: Berger Levrault, 1939.

Churchill, Winston. *The Gathering Storm*. Boston: Houghton Mifflin, 1948.

————. *Their Finest Hour*. Boston: Houghton Mifflin, 1949.

Coghlan, F. "Armaments, Economic Policy, and Appeasement: Background to British Foreign Policy, 1931–7." *History*, 57 (June 1972), 205–16.

DeGaulle, Charles. *The Army of the Future*. London: Hutchinson, n.d.

Doughty, Robert A. "DeGaulle's Concept of a Mobile, Professional Army: Genesis of French Defeat?" *Parameters*, 4:2 (1974), 23–34.

Draper, Theodore. *The Six Weeks' War*. New York: Book Find Club, 1944.

Gamelin, Maurice G. *Servir*. 3 vols. Paris: Plon, 1946–47.

Gibbs, N. H. *Grand Strategy*. Vol. 1, *Rearmament Policy*. London: HMSO, 1976.

Gibson, Irving [A. Kovacs]. "Maginot and Liddell Hart: The Doctrine of Defense." In *Makers of Modern Strategy*, ed. Edward Mead Earle. Princeton: Princeton University Press, 1973.

Hillmann, H. C. "Comparative Strengths of the Great Powers." In *The World in March 1939*, ed. Arnold Toynbee and Frank T. Ashton-Gwatkin. Oxford: Oxford University Press, 1952.

Horne, Alistair. *To Lose a Battle*. London: Macmillan, 1969.

Howard, Michael. *The Continental Commitment: The Dilemma of British Defence Policy in the Era of Two World Wars*. London: Pelican, 1974.

Hughes, Judith M. *To the Maginot Line: The Politics of French Military Preparation in the 1920's*. Cambridge: Harvard University Press, 1971.

Kennedy, John. *The Business of War*. New York: William Morrow, 1958.

Kennedy, Paul M. *The Rise and Fall of British Naval Mastery*. New York: Scribner's, 1976.

Kimche, Jon. *The Unfought Battle*. New York: Stein and Day, 1968.

Kirk, Dudley. "Population and Population Trends in Modern France." In *Modern France: Problems of the Third and Fourth Republics*, ed. Edward Mead Earle. Princeton: Princeton University Press, 1951.

Kraehe, Enno. "The Motives behind the Maginot Line." *Military Affairs*, 8 (1944), 111–15.

Lewin, Ronald. *Man of Armour: A Study of Lieut.-General Vyvyan Pope and the Development of Armoured Warfare*. London: Leo Cooper, 1976.

Lewis, W. Arthur. *Economic Survey, 1919–1939*. London: Allen and Unwin, 1949.

Liddell Hart, B. H. *The British Way in Warfare*. London: Faber and Faber, 1932.

Macleod, Roderick, and Denis Kelly. *Time Unguarded: The Ironside Diaries, 1937–1940*. New York: David McKay, 1962.

Maurois, André. *Tragedy in France*. Trans. Denver Lindley. New York: Harper, 1940.

Medlicott, W. N. *The Economic Blockade*. Vol. 1. London: HMSO, 1952.

Milward, Alan S. *War, Economy, and Society, 1939–1945*. Los Angeles: University of California Press, 1977.

Murray, Williamson. "Munich, 1938: The Military Confrontation." *Journal of Strategic Studies*, 2 (December 1979), 282–302.

Peden, G. C. *British Rearmament and the Treasury*. Edinburgh: Scottish Academic Press, 1979.

Postan, M. M. *British War Production*. London: HMSO, 1952.

Reynaud, Paul. *In the Thick of the Fight, 1930–1945*. Trans. James D. Lambert. New York: Simon and Schuster, 1955.

Rowe, Vivian. *The Great Wall of France*. London: Putnam, 1959.

Shay, Robert P. *British Rearmament in the Thirties*. Princeton: Princeton University Press, 1977.

Sheppard, E. W. "Two Generals, One Doctrine." *Army Quarterly*, 41 (October 1940), 105–18.

Shirer, William L. *The Collapse of the Third Republic: An Inquiry into the Fall of France in 1940*. New York: Simon and Schuster, 1969.

Slessor, John. *The Central Blue*. New York: Praeger, 1957.

Spears, Edward. *Assignment to Catastrophe*. 2 vols. London: Heinemann, 1954.

Spengler, Joseph J. *France Faces Depopulation*. Durham: Duke University Press, 1938.

Stolfi, R. H. S. "Equipment for Victory in France in 1940." *History*, 52 (February 1970), 1–20.

Taylor, Telford. *Munich: The Price of Peace*. Garden City: Doubleday, 1979.

U.S. Strategic Bombing Survey. Overall Economic Effects Division. *The Effects of Strategic Bombing on the German War Economy*. Washington, D.C.: GPO, 31 October 1945.

Waites, Neville, ed. *Troubled Neighbors: Franco-British Relations in the Twentieth Century*. London: Weidenfeld and Nicolson, 1971.

Watt, Donald Cameron. *Too Serious a Business: European Armed Forces and the Approach to the Second World War*. London: Temple Smith, 1975.

Webster, Charles, and Noble Frankland. *The Strategic Air Offensive against Germany, 1939–1945*. 4 vols. London: HMSO, 1961.

Weygand, Maxime. "How France Is Defended." *International Affairs*, 18 (July-August 1939), 459–77.

Williams, John. *The Ides of May: The Defeat of France, May-June 1940*. New York: Knopf, 1968.

Wolfers, Arnold. *Britain and France between Two Wars*. New York: Harcourt, Brace, 1940.

Young, Robert J. *In Command of France: French Foreign Policy and Military Planning, 1933–1940*. Cambridge: Harvard University Press, 1978.

———. "La Guerre de Longue Durée." In *General Staffs and Diplomacy before the Second World War*, ed. Adrian Preston. London: Croom Helm, 1978.

———. "Preparations for Defeat: French War Doctrine in the Inter-War Period." *Journal of European Studies*, 2 (June 1972), 155–72.

————. "The Strategic Dream: French Air Doctrine in the Inter-War Period, 1919–1939." *Journal of Contemporary History,* 9 (October 1974), 57–76.

German Decision Making, 1939–1940

Addington, Larry H. *The Blitzkrieg Era and the German General Staff, 1865–1941.* New Brunswick: Rutgers University Press, 1971.

Alexandroff, Alan, and Richard Rosecrance. "Deterrence in 1939." *World Politics,* 29 (April 1977), 404–24.

Benoist-Méchin, J. *Sixty Days That Shook the West.* London: Jonathan Cape, 1963.

Blumentritt, Guenther. *Von Rundstedt: The Soldier and the Man.* Trans. Cuthbert Reavely. London: Odhams, 1959.

Carroll, Berenice A. *Design for Total War.* The Hague: Mouton, 1968.

Cooper, Matthew. *The German Army, 1933–1945.* New York: Stein and Day, 1978.

Deighton, Len. *Blitzkrieg.* New York: Knopf, 1980.

Ellis, L. F. *The War in France and Flanders, 1939–1940.* London: HMSO, 1953.

Fest, Joachim. *Hitler.* Trans. Richard and Clara Winston. New York: Harcourt Brace Jovanovich, 1974.

Goutard, A. *The Battle of France, 1940.* Trans. A. R. P. Burgess. London: Frederick Muller, 1958.

Hassell, Ulrich von. *The Von Hassell Diaries.* Garden City: Doubleday, 1947.

Hauner, Milan. "Did Hitler Want a World Dominion?" *Journal of Contemporary History,* 13:1 (1978), 15–32.

Hofmann, Rudolf. "The Battle for Moscow." In *Decisive Battles of World War II: The German View,* trans. Edward Fitzgerald, ed. Hans-Adolf Jacobsen and J. Rohwer. New York: Putnam, 1965.

Irving, David. *Hitler's War.* 2 vols. New York: Viking, 1977.

Jacobsen, Hans-Adolf. "Dunkirk 1940." In *Decisive Battles of World War II: The German View,* trans. Edward Fitzgerald, ed. Hans-Adolf Jacobsen and J. Rohwer. New York: Putnam, 1965.

————, ed. *Dokumente zur Vorgeschichte des Westfeldzuges, 1939–1940.* Göttingen: Musterschmidt, 1956.

Kennedy, Robert M. *The German Campaign in Poland.* Washington, D.C.: U.S. Army, 1956.

Klein, Burton H. *Germany's Economic Preparations for War.* Cambridge: Harvard University Press, 1959.

Leach, Barry K. *The German General Staff.* New York: Ballantine, 1973.

————. *German Strategy against Russia, 1939–1941.* Oxford: Clarendon Press, 1973.

Louis, William Roger, ed. *The Origins of the Second World War: A. J. P. Taylor and His Critics.* New York: John Wiley, 1972.

Lukacs, John. *The Last European War.* Garden City: Doubleday, Anchor Press, 1976.

Macksey, Kenneth. *Guderian: Creator of the Blitzkrieg.* New York: Stein and Day, 1975.

Marshall, S. L. A. *Blitzkrieg: Its History, Strategy, Economics, and the Challenge to America.* New York: William Morrow, 1940.

Mason, T. W. "Some Origins of the Second World War." *Past and Present,* 29 (December 1964), 67–87.

Memoirs of Field Marshal Keitl. Trans. David Irving. London: William Kimber, 1965.

Milward, Alan S. *The German Economy at War.* London: Athlone, 1965.

Nazi Conspiracy and Aggression. 10 vols. Washington, D.C.: GPO, 1948.

Nuremberg Military Tribunals. High Command Case. *Exhibits and Documents at Trials of War Criminals.* Bk. 15. Law School Library, Harvard University, Cambridge.

[281]

————. High Command Case. *Official Transcript at Trials of War Criminals*. Law School Library, Harvard University, Cambridge.

The Private War Journals of Generaloberst Franz Halder, Chief of the General Staff of the Supreme Command of the German Army (OKH), 14 August 1939 to 24 September 1942. 8 vols. Trans. Arnold Lissance. Nuremberg: Office of the Chief of Counsel for War Crimes of the American Military Government, 1948.

Schramm, Percy Ernst. *Hitler: The Man and the Military Leader*. Chicago: Quadrangle, 1971.

Seaton, Albert. *The Russo-German War*. New York: Praeger, 1970.

Seeckt, Hans von. *Thoughts of a Soldier*. Trans. Gilbert Waterhouse. London: Ernest Benn, 1930.

Strawson, John. *Hitler as Military Commander*. London: Batsford, 1971.

Taylor, A. J. P. *The Origins of the Second World War*. Greenwich: Fawcett, 1961.

Taylor, Telford. *The March of Conquest: The German Victories in Western Europe, 1940*. New York: Simon and Schuster, 1958.

————. *Sword and Swastika: Generals and Nazis in the Third Reich*. New York: Simon and Schuster, 1952.

Trial of the Major War Criminals before the International Military Tribunal. 42 vols. Nuremberg: Allied Control Authority for Germany, 1948.

Trials of War Criminals before the Nuremberg Military Tribunals. 15 vols. Washington, D.C.: GPO, 1951.

Warlimont, Walter. *Inside Hitler's Headquarters, 1939–45*. Trans. R. H. Barry. London: Weidenfeld and Nicolson, 1964.

Wheeler-Bennett, John W. *The Nemesis of Power: The German Army in Politics*. New York: St. Martin's, 1954.

Middle East Cases

Allon, Yigal. *The Making of Israel's Army*. London: Sphere, 1971.

Amiel, Saadia. "Deterrence by Conventional Forces." *Survival*, 20 (March-April 1978), 58–62.

Amos, John W. *Arab-Israeli Military/Political Relations: Arab Perceptions and the Politics of Escalation*. New York: Pergamon, 1979.

Badri, Hassan el, Taha el Magdoub, and Mohammed Dia el Din Zohdy. *The Ramadan War, 1973*. Dunn Loring, Va.: T. N. Dupuy, 1978.

Bar-Siman-Tov, Yaacov. *The Israeli-Egyptian War of Attrition, 1969–1970*. New York: Columbia University Press, 1980.

Ben-Horin, Yoav, and Barry R. Posen. *Israel's Strategic Doctrine*. R-2845-NA. Santa Monica: Rand, September 1981.

Ben-Moshe, Tuvia. "Liddell Hart and the Israel Defence Forces—A Reappraisal." *Journal of Contemporary History*, 16 (April 1981), 369–91.

Brecher, Michael, with Benjamin Geist. *Decisions in Crisis*. Los Angeles: University of California Press, 1980.

————. *Decisions in Israel's Foreign Policy*. New Haven: Yale University Press, 1975.

————. *The Foreign Policy System of Israel: Setting, Images, Process*. New Haven: Yale University Press, 1972.

Churchill, Randolph S., and Winston S. Churchill. *The Six Day War*. London: Heinemann, 1971.

Dayan, Moshe. *Diary of the Sinai Campaign*. New York: Schocken, 1967.

————. *Story of My Life*. London: Sphere, 1976.

Dupuy, Trevor N. *Elusive Victory: The Arab-Israeli Wars, 1947–1974*. New York: Harper and Row, 1978.

Eban, Abba. *Abba Eban: An Autobiography*. New York: Random House, 1977.

Evron, Yair. *The Role of Arms Control in the Middle East*. Adlephi Paper 138. London: International Institute for Strategic Studies, 1977.

Flapan, Simha. "The Theory of Interceptive War." Review of *Masach Shel Chol [Curtain of Sand]*, by Yigal Allon. *New Outlook: Middle East Monthly*, 3 (April 1960), 42–53.

Gelb, Leslie H. "Why Did the Mideast Erupt Again? The Experts Offer Some Theories." *New York Times*, 9 October 1973, p. 17.

Golan, Galia. *Yom Kippur and After: The Soviet Union and the Middle East Crisis*. Cambridge: Cambridge University Press, 1977.

Handel, Michael I. *Israel's Political-Military Doctrine*. Occasional Paper 30. Cambridge: Harvard University, Center for International Affairs, 1973.

———. "The Yom Kippur War and the Inevitability of Surprise." *International Studies Quarterly*, 21 (September 1977), 461–502.

Hareven, Alouph. "Disturbed Hierarchy: Israeli Intelligence in 1954 and 1973." *Jerusalem Quarterly*, 9 (fall 1978), 3–19.

Haselkorn, Avigdor. *Israeli Intelligence Performance in the Yom Kippur War*. Hudson Institute Discussion Paper 2033. Croton, N.Y.: Hudson Institute, 17 July 1974.

Heikal, Mohamed. *The Road to Ramadan*. New York: Ballantine, 1976.

———. *The Sphinx and the Commissar*. New York: Harper and Row, 1978.

Horowitz, Dan. *Israel's Concept of Defensible Borders*. Jerusalem Paper 16. Jerusalem: Hebrew University, 1975.

Insight Team of the London *Sunday Times*. *The Yom Kippur War*. Garden City: Doubleday, 1974.

"Israel's Combat Arms." *Armed Forces Journal International*, 111 (October 1973), 64–71.

Kimche, David, and Dan Bawly. *The Six-Day War: Prologue and Aftermath*. New York: Stein and Day, 1968.

Meir, Golda. *My Life*. New York: Putnam, 1975.

October 1973 War. Proceedings of an international symposium held on 27–31 October 1975. Cairo: Ministry of War, 3 October 1976.

Partial Reports of the Agranat Commission. Jerusalem: Government Press Office, 2 April 1974 and 30 January 1975.

Peres, Shimon. *David's Sling*. London: Weidenfeld and Nicolson, 1970.

Perlmutter, Amos. "The Covenant of War." *Harper's*, 248 (February 1974), 51–61.

———. "Israel's Fourth War, October 1973: Political and Military Misperceptions." *Orbis*, 19 (summer 1975), 434–60.

Prittie, Terence. *Eshkol: The Man and the Nation*. New York: Pitman, 1969.

Quandt, William B. *Decade of Decisions*. Los Angeles: University of California Press, 1977.

Rabin, Yitzhak. *The Rabin Memoirs*. Boston: Little, Brown, 1979.

Rosen, Steven J. *Military Geography and the Military Balance in the Arab-Israel Conflict*. Jerusalem Paper 21. Jerusalem: Hebrew University, 1977.

Rosen, Steven J., and Martin Indyk. "The Temptation to Pre-empt in a Fifth Arab-Israeli War." *Orbis*, 20 (summer 1976), 265–85.

Sadat, Anwar el-. *Anwar el-Sadat: In Search of Identity*. New York: Harper and Row, 1978.

Safran, Nadav. *From War to War*. New York: Pegasus, 1969.

———. *Israel: The Embattled Ally*. Cambridge: Harvard University Press, Belknap Press, 1978.

Schiff, Zeev. *A History of the Israeli Army (1870–1974)*. Trans. Raphael Rothstein. San Francisco: Straight Arrow, 1974.

Shapiro, Sraya. "Begin's Ismailiya Trip Almost Caused a War." *Jerusalem Post*, 28 September 1978, p. 3.

Shazly, Lt. Gen. Saad el. *The Crossing of the Suez*. San Francisco: American Mideast Research, 1980.

Sheehan, Edward R. F. "Sadat's War." *New York Times Magazine*, 18 November 1973, pp. 35, 112–30.

Shlaim, Avi. "Failures in National Intelligence Estimates: The Case of the Yom Kippur War." *World Politics*, 28 (April 1976), 348–80.

Shlaim, Avi, and Raymond Tanter. "Decision Process, Choice, and Consequences: Israel's Deep-Penetration Bombing in Egypt, 1970." *World Politics*, 30 (July 1978), 483–516.

Slater, Robert. *Rabin of Israel*. London: Robson, 1977.

Stein, Janice G., and Raymond Tanter. *Rational Decision-Making*. Columbus: Ohio State University Press, 1980.

Tal, Israel. "Israel's Doctrine of National Security: Background and Dynamics." *Jerusalem Quarterly*, 4 (summer 1977), 44–57.

Teveth, Shabtai. *Moshe Dayan: The Soldier, the Man, the Legend*. Trans. Leah Zinder and David Zinder. Boston: Houghton Mifflin, 1973.

———. *The Tanks of Tamuz*. New York: Viking, 1969.

Thomas, Hugh. *Suez*. New York: Harper and Row, 1967.

Wagner, Abraham R. *Crisis Decision-Making: Israel's Experience in 1967 and 1973*. New York: Praeger, 1974.

Weizman, Ezer. *On Eagles' Wings*. New York: Berkley, 1979.

Whetten, Lawrence L. *The Canal War: Four-Power Conflict in the Middle East*. Cambridge: M.I.T. Press, 1974.

Williams, Louis, ed. *Military Aspects of the Israeli-Arab Conflict*. Tel Aviv: University Publishing Projects, 1975.

Zamir, Dani. "Generals in Politics." *Jerusalem Quarterly*, 20 (summer 1981), 17–35.

The North Atlantic Treaty Organization and Precision-Guided Munitions

Aspin, Les. "A Surprise Attack on NATO: Refocusing the Debate." *Congressional Record*, 7 February 1977, pp. H911–14.

Atkeson, Col. Edward B. "Is the Soviet Army Obsolete?" *Army*, 24 (May 1974), 10–16.

"AUSA '79: Crash Programs to Counter Deployed Soviet Armour." *International Defense Review*, 13:1 (1980), 89–91.

Bétit, Eugene D. "Soviet Tactical Doctrine and Capabilities and NATO's Strategic Defense." *Strategic Review*, 4 (fall 1976), 95–107.

———. "Soviet Technological Preparations for Night Attack." *Military Review*, 55 (March 1975), 89–93.

Betts, Richard K. "Hedging against Surprise Attack." *Survival*, 23 (July-August 1981), 146–56.

———. "Surprise Attack: NATO's Political Vulnerability." *International Security*, 5 (spring 1981), 117–49.

Blaker, James, and Andrew Hamilton. *Assessing the NATO/Warsaw Pact Military Balance*. Washington, D.C.: Congressional Budget Office, December 1977.

Bonds, Ray, ed. *The U.S. War Machine*. New York: Crown, 1978.

———, ed. *The Soviet War Machine*. New York: Chartwell, 1976.

Bracken, Paul. "Urban Sprawl and NATO Defence." *Survival*, 18 (November-December 1976), 254–60.

Burt, Richard. *New Weapons Technologies: Debate and Directions*. Adelphi Paper 126. London: International Institute for Strategic Studies, summer 1976.

———. "Soviet Said to Add to Its Bloc Troops." *New York Times*, 8 June 1980, p. 4.

Canby, Steven L. *The Alliance and Europe*. Pt. 4, *Military Doctrine and Technology*. Adelphi Paper 109. London: International Institute for Strategic Studies, 1974–75.

———. "Mutual Force Reductions: A Military Perspective." *International Security*, 2 (winter 1978), 122–35.

———. *NATO Military Policy: Obtaining Conventional Comparability with the Warsaw Pact*. R-1088-ARPA. Santa Monica: Rand, June 1973.

———. "NATO: Reassessing the Conventional Wisdoms." *Survival*, 19 (July-August 1977), 164–68.

———. *Short (and Long) War Responses: Restructuring, Border Defense, and Reserve Mobilization for Armored Warfare*. Report Prepared for Office of the Assistant Secretary of Defense, Director of Special Studies. Washington, D.C.: Department of Defense, March 1978.

———. "Tactical Air Power in Armored Warfare." *Air University Review*, 30 (May-June 1979), 2–20.

Carnegie Panel on U.S. Security and the Future of Arms Control. *Challenges for U.S. National Security: Assessing the Balance: Defense Spending and Conventional Forces*. Preliminary Report, pt. 2. Washington, D.C.: Carnegie Endowment for International Peace, 1981.

Cliffe, Trevor. *Military Technology and the European Balance*. Adelphi Paper 89. London: International Institute for Strategic Studies, August 1972.

Close, Robert. *Europe without Defense?* New York: Pergamon, 1979.

———. "The Feasibility of a Surprise Attack against Western Europe." Typescript. Rome: NATO Defence College, 24 February 1975.

Cohen, Irvine. "Israel Rebuilds Her Army." *Army*, 25 (June 1975), 22–27.

Collins, John M. *U.S.-Soviet Military Balance*. New York: McGraw-Hill, 1980.

Despres, John, Lilita I. Dzirkals, and Barton Whaley. *Timely Lessons of History: The Manchurian Model for Soviet Strategy*. R-1825-NA. Santa Monica: Rand, July 1976.

Digby, James. *Precision Guided Weapons*. Adelphi Paper 118. London: International Institute for Strategic Studies, 1975.

Donnelly, Christopher N. "Modern Soviet Artillery." *NATO's Fifteen Nations*, 24 (June-July 1979), 48–54.

———. "Soviet Tactics for Overcoming NATO Anti-Tank Defenses." *International Defense Review*, 12:7 (1979), 1099–1106.

———. "Soviet Techniques for Combat in Built Up Areas." *International Defense Review*, 10:2 (1977), 238–42.

———. "Tactical Problems Facing the Soviet Army: Recent Debates in the Soviet Military Press." *International Defense Review*, 11:9 (1978), 1405–12.

Douglass, Joseph D. *The Soviet Theater Nuclear Offensive*. Washington, D.C.: GPO, 1976.

Dunn, Keith A. "Soviet Military Weaknesses and Vulnerabilities: A Critique of the Short War Advocates." Memorandum. Carlisle Barracks: U.S. Army War College, Strategic Studies Institute, 31 July 1978.

Dzirkals, Lilita I. *"Lightning War" in Manchuria: Soviet Military Analysis of the 1945 Far East Campaign*. P-5589. Santa Monica: Rand, January 1976.

Enthoven, Alain C. "U.S. Forces in Europe: How Many? Doing What?" *Foreign Affairs*, 53 (April 1975), 513–32.

Epstein, Joshua M. "On Conventional Deterrence in Europe: Questions of Soviet Confidence." *Orbis*, 26 (spring 1982), 71–86.

Erickson, John. "Soviet Breakthrough Operations: Resources and Restraints." *Journal of the Royal United Services Institute*, 121 (September 1976), 74–79.

———. "Soviet Ground Forces and the Conventional Mode of Operations." *Journal of the Royal United Services Institute*, 121 (June 1976), 45–49.

———. "Soviet Military Capabilities in Europe." *Journal of the Royal United Services Institute*, 120 (March 1975), 65–75.

Erickson, John, and E. J. Feuchtwanger, eds. *Soviet Military Power and Performance*. Hamden: Archon, 1979.

Fair, Col. Stanley D. "Precision Weaponry in the Defense of Europe." *NATO's Fifteen Nations*, 20 (August-September 1975), 17–26.

Fischer, Robert Lucas. *Defending the Central Front: The Balance of Forces*. Adelphi Paper 127. London: International Institute for Strategic Studies, 1976.

Foster, James L. *The Future of Conventional Arms Control*. P-5489. Santa Monica: Rand, August 1975.

Furlong, R. D. M. "Europeans Oppose Single-Type Standardization of NATO Anti-Tank Missiles." *International Defense Review*, 14:2 (1981), 141–42.

Goldhamer, Herbert. *Soviet Military Management at the Troop Level*. R-1513-PR. Santa Monica: Rand, May 1974.

Goodman, Hirsch. "The Tank Killers." *Jerusalem Post Magazine*, 23 February 1979, pp. 8–9.

Gouré, Daniel, and Gordon McCormick. "PGM: No Panacea." *Survival*, 22 (January-February 1980), 15–19.

Gouré, Leon, and Michael J. Deane. "The Soviet Strategic View." *Strategic Review*, 8:1 (winter 1980), 84–85.

Gray, Colin. "The Blitzkrieg: A Premature Burial?" *Military Review*, 56 (October 1976), 15–18.

Grechko, A. A. *The Armed Forces of the Soviet Union*. Trans. Yuri Sviridov. Moscow: Progress, 1977.

"GSFG Ground Force Reorganization." *International Defense Review*, 14:6 (1981), 701.

Hackett, John, et al. *The Third World War: A Future History*. London: Sidgwick and Jackson, 1978.

Herspring, Dale R., and Ivan Volgyes. "Political Reliability in the Eastern European Warsaw Pact Armies." *Armed Forces and Society*, 6 (winter 1980), 270–96.

Hillier, Pat. *Strengthening NATO: POMCUS and Other Approaches*. Washington, D.C.: Congressional Budget Office, February 1979.

Hillier, Pat, and Nora Slatkin. *U.S. Ground Forces: Design and Cost Alternatives for NATO and Non-NATO Contingencies*. Washington, D.C.: Congressional Budget Office, December 1980.

Hollingsworth, J. F. "Conventional War Fighting Capability and Potential of the U.S. Army in Central Europe." Memorandum. Unclassified version. N.p., October 1976.

Holst, Johan J., and Uwe Nerlich, eds. *Beyond Nuclear Deterrence*. New York: Crane, Russak, 1977.

Inman, Adm. Bobby. Speech delivered before the ninety-sixth annual convention of the American Newspaper Publishers Association, San Francisco, 27 April 1982.

Johnson, A. Ross, Robert W. Dean, and Alexander Alexiev. "The Armies of the Warsaw Pact Northern Tier." *Survival*, 23 (July-August 1981), 174–82.

Karber, Phillip A. "Anti-Tank Weapons and the Future of Armor." *Armed Forces Journal International*, 114 (November 1976), 20–23.

———. "The Soviet Anti-Tank Debate." *Survival*, 18 (May-June 1976), 105–11.

Kemp, Geoffrey, Robert L. Pfaltzgraff, and Uri Ra'anan, eds. *The Other Arms Race: New Technologies and Non-nuclear Conflict.* Lexington: D. C. Heath, 1975.

Kulikov, V. "Soviet Military Science Today." *Strategic Review*, 5 (winter 1977), 127–34.

Kyle, Deborah M., and Benjamin F. Schemmer. "Technology Won't Save Us If We Don't Field It." *Armed Forces Journal International*, 118 (August 1981), 26–28.

Lawrence, Richard D., and Jeffrey Record. *U.S. Force Structure in NATO: An Alternative.* Washington, D.C.: Brookings Institution, 1974.

Lind, William S. "Military Doctrine, Force Structure, and the Defense Decision-Making Process." *Air University Review*, 30 (May-June 1979), 21–27.

———. "Some Doctrinal Questions for the U.S. Army." *Military Review*, 57 (March 1977), 54–69.

Löser, Hans-Joachim. "Vorneverteidigung der Bundesrepublik Deutschland?" *Österreichische Militärische Zeitschrift*, 18 (March-April 1980), 116–23.

Luttwak, Edward N. "The American Style of Warfare and the Military Balance." *Survival*, 21 (March-April 1979), 57–60.

Mearsheimer, John J. "Precision-Guided Munitions and Conventional Deterrence." *Survival*, 21 (March-April 1979), 68–76.

———. "Rejoinder." *Survival*, 22 (January-February 1980), 20–22.

"The Merkava Mk 1." *International Defense Review*, 11:7 (1978), 1049–52.

Middleton, Drew. "Soviets Introducing New Tank in Europe." *New York Times*, 16 March 1980, p. 7.

The Military Balance, 1980–1981. London: International Institute for Strategic Studies, 1980.

Morse, John H. "Advanced Technology in Modern War." *Journal of the Royal United Services Institute*, 121 (June 1976), 8–16.

Nacht, Michael L. "Technology and Strategy." *National Defense*, 61 (November-December 1976), 199–201.

New Conventional Weapons and East-West Security. Pts. 1 and 2. Adelphi Papers 144 and 145. London: International Institute for Strategic Studies, spring 1978.

Ogorkiewicz, Richard M. "Trends in Tank Technology." *Armor*, 89 (July-August 1980), 8–14.

Perry, William J. *The FY 1981 Department of Defense Program for Research, Development, and Acquisition.* Washington, D.C.: GPO, 1 February 1980.

Polk, James H. "The North German Plain Attack Scenario: Threat or Illusion?" *Strategic Review*, 8 (summer 1980), 60–66.

Range and Lethality of U.S. and Soviet Anti-Armor Weapons. TRADOC Bulletin 1. Fort Monroe: U.S. Army, Training and Doctrine Command, 30 September 1975.

"Rearming without Tears." *Economist*, 268 (19 August 1978), 10–11.

Record, Jeffrey. "The October War: Burying the Blitzkrieg." *Military Review*, 56 (April 1976), 19–21.

———. "Outwitting 'Smart' Weapons." *Washington Review of Strategic and International Studies*, 1 (April 1978), 83–85.

Rose, John P. *The Evolution of U.S. Army Nuclear Doctrine, 1945–1980.* Boulder: Westview, 1980.

Schorr, Daniel. "The Red Threat and NATO Today." *Norfolk Virginian-Pilot*, 2 October 1978, p. 19.

Shishko, Robert. *The European Conventional Balance: A Primer.* P-6707. Santa Monica: Rand, 24 November 1981.

Sokolovskiy, V. D. *Soviet Military Strategy*. Ed. Harriet Fast Scott. 3rd ed. New York: Crane, Russak, 1968.

"Tank Breaker/IMAAWS Situation Still Confused." *International Defense Review*, 14:6 (1981), 703.

Turbiville, Graham H. "Invasion in Europe—A Scenario." *Army*, 26 (November 1976), 16–21.

U.S. Army. Concepts Analysis Agency. *Weapon Effectiveness Indices/Weighted Unit Values* [*WEI/WUV*]. Study Report CAA-SR-73-18. Bethesda, April 1974.

————. Training and Doctrine Command. *Division Restructuring Study*. Phase 1 Report, Executive Summary. Vol. 1. Fort Monroe, 1 March 1977.

U.S. Comptroller General. *Critical Considerations in the Acquisition of a New Main Battle Tank*. PSAD-76-113A. Washington, D.C.: General Accounting Office, 22 July 1976.

U.S. Congress. House. Armed Services Committee. *Hearings on Military Posture*. Pt. 3, bk. 2. 96th Cong., 1st sess. Washington, D.C.: GPO, 19 March 1979.

————. House. Armed Services Committee. *Hearings on Military Posture and H.R. 6495, Department of Defense Authorization for Appropriations for Fiscal Year 1981*. Pt. 2. 96th Cong., 2nd sess. Washington, D.C.: GPO, 1980.

————. House. Armed Services Committee. *Hearings on Military Posture and H.R. 10929*. Pt. 3, bk. 1. 95th Cong., 2nd sess. Washington, D.C.: GPO, 1 March 1978.

————. Senate. Armed Services Committee. *Hearings on Department of Defense Authorization for Appropriations for Fiscal Year 1981*. Pt. 5. 96th Cong., 2nd sess. Washington, D.C.: GPO, 1980.

————. Senate. Armed Services Committee. *NATO and the New Soviet Threat*, by Senators Sam Nunn and Dewey F. Bartlett. 95th Cong., 1st sess. Washington, D.C.: GPO, 24 January 1977.

————. Senate. Armed Services Committee. Subcommittee on Manpower and Personnel. *Hearing on NATO Posture and Initiatives*. 95th Cong., 1st sess. Washington, D.C.: GPO, 3 August 1977.

Vernon, Col. Graham D. *Soviet Options for War in Europe: Nuclear or Conventional?* National Security Affairs Monograph 79-1. Washington, D.C.: National Defense University, January 1979.

Vigor, Peter. "Doubts and Difficulties Confronting a Would-Be Soviet Attacker." *Journal of the Royal United Services Institute*, 125 (June 1980), 32–38.

Vigor, Peter, and Christopher Donnelly. "The Manchurian Campaign and Its Relevance to Modern Strategy." *Comparative Strategy*, 2:2 (1980), 159–78.

Viksne, Lt. Col. J. "The Yom Kippur War—In Retrospect." Pt. 2, "Technology." *Army Journal*, 324 (May 1976), 15–43.

Walker, Paul F. "Precision-Guided Weapons." *Scientific American*, 245 (August 1981), 37–45.

Whetten, Lawrence L., ed. *The Future of Soviet Military Power*. New York: Crane, Russak, 1976.

White Paper 1979: The Security of the Federal Republic of Germany and the Development of the Federal Armed Forces. Bonn: Federal Minister of Defence, 4 September 1979.

Wilson, George C. "Defense Getting the Upper Hand." *Astronautics and Aeronautics*, 18 (May 1980), 26–27.

Wilson, Peter A. "Battlefield Guided Weapons: The Big Equalizer." *U.S. Naval Institute Proceedings*, 101 (February 1975), 18–25.

Wohlstetter, Albert. "Threats and Promises of Peace: Europe and America in the New Era." *Orbis*, 17 (winter 1974), 1107–44.

Wolfe, Thomas W. *Soviet Power and Europe, 1945–1970*. Baltimore: Johns Hopkins University Press, 1970.

Other Crises

Appleman, Roy E. *South to the Naktong, North to the Yalu (June-November 1950)*. Washington, D.C.: U.S. Army, Office of the Chief of Military History, 1961.

Chanda, Nayan. "Cambodia: Fifteen Days That Shook Asia." *Far Eastern Economic Review*, 103 (19 January 1979), 10–13.

Chopra, Pran. *India's Second Liberation*. Cambridge: M.I.T. Press, 1974.

Collins, J. Lawton. *War in Peacetime*. Boston: Houghton Mifflin, 1969.

Deming, Angus. "Hanoi's Power Play." *Newsweek*, 63 (22 January 1979), 29–34.

Mankekar, D. R. *Pakistan Cut to Size*. New Delhi: Indian Book, 1972.

Palit, Maj. Gen. D. K. *The Lightning Campaign*. New Delhi: Thomson, 1972.

Index

A-10 aircraft, 200
Acheson, Dean, 15, 24
Adam, Gen. Ronald, 84
Air-ground balance, 156–161, 191, 198–200, 268n9. *See also* Close air support
Airplane crash, German (1940), 118, 121, 123, 133
Allies (World War II):
  number of divisions raised, 91–96
  staff talks, 82–84
  strategy on western front (1939–40), 43, 52, 82–96, 99, 125–126
  strategy on western front (1944–45), 42–43
Allon, Yigal, 145, 151, 254n107, 255n119, 258n191
America. *See* United States
Amiens, battle of, 31
Amit, Meir, 153–154
Antitank guided missiles. *See* Precision-Guided Munitions
Arab-Israeli wars:
  1948 war, 134
  1956 war, 134–143, 203, 209–210
  1967 war, 134, 143–155, 162–164, 203, 210–211
  war of attrition, 134, 156, 161, 163–164, 211
  1973 war, 134, 155–164, 190, 192, 195, 198–199, 201, 208–211, 271n42
  Lebanon invasion, 134
Ardennes Forest, 43–44, 119, 122, 125–127, 130, 172
Argov, Nehemia, 142
Armor Corps (Israeli), 143, 152
Armored Brigade (Israel's 190th), 190
Armored division equivalents (ADE), 168–169, 173, 182, 260n7

Armored personnel carriers (APC), 194–195
"Armored wedge," German, 126–130
Arras, battle of, 31
Artillery:
  and attrition strategy, 34, 71–72, 88–89
  and blitzkrieg, 39–40, 183–184, 192–195, 198–200
  and Israeli military, 152, 190–191
  NATO-Pact balance, 167–168
  and PGMs, 190–195, 198–200
  "smart," 190, 192
Assad, Hafez al-, 208
Attaque brusquée, 57–58, 72–73, 80
Attrition strategy:
  with clear-cut superiority in numbers, 59–60, 85, 98, 168–169, 209
  definition of, 29–30, 33–35
  and deterrence, 34–35, 58–60, 63–66, 68, 98, 206–208
  employing for limited objectives, 56–58
  reemergence of, 52–53
Attrition warfare. *See* Maneuver
Auftragstaktik, 41–42. *See also* Initiative
Aurora, Gen. J. S., 206

Badri, Gen. Hassan el, 155–156, 159
Balance of forces. *See* Force ratios
Barbarossa, Operation, 204
Bar-Lev, Chaim, 145, 149, 159–160
Bar-Lev Line, 156, 158–159
Belgian forces, 179–182
Ben-Gurion, David, 136–143, 145, 147, 150, 209, 249n1
Bismarck, Otto von, 62
Blitzkrieg strategy:
  with clear-cut superiority, 59–60, 209

Library of Congress Cataloging in Publication Data

Mearsheimer, John J.
    Conventional deterrence.

    Bibliography: p.
    Includes index.
    1. Deterrence (Strategy)—History—20th century. 2. Military history, Modern—20th
century. I. Title.
U162.M43   1983   355.4'305   83-5317
ISBN 0-8014-1569-1